MARITIME LOGISTICS: CONTEMPORARY ISSUES

MARITIME LOGISTICS: CONTEMPORARY ISSUES

EDITED BY

DONG-WOOK SONG

Heriot–Watt University, Edinburgh, UK

PHOTIS M. PANAYIDES

Cyprus University of Technology, Limassol, Cyprus

United Kingdom – North America – Japan
India – Malaysia – China

Emerald Group Publishing Limited
Howard House, Wagon Lane, Bingley BD16 1WA, UK

First edition 2012

Copyright © 2012 Emerald Group Publishing Limited

Reprints and permission service
Contact: booksandseries@emeraldinsight.com

British Library Cataloguing in Publication Data
A catalogue record for this book is available from the British Library

ISBN: 978-1-78052-340-8

INVESTOR IN PEOPLE

Contents

Part II Green and Sustainability Issues

List of Contributors

Bjørn E. Asbjørnslett	Department of Marine Technology, Norwegian University of Science and Technology; Norwegian Marine Technology Research Institute, Trondheim, Norway
John Dinwoodie	International Shipping, Logistics and Operations Group, School of Management, Plymouth University Business School, Plymouth, UK
Patric A. Drewes	Institute for Transport Planning and Logistics, Hamburg University of Technology, Hamburg, Germany
Philine Gaffron	Institute for Transport Planning and Logistics, Hamburg University of Technology, Hamburg, Germany
Alexandros M. Goulielmos	Department of Maritime Studies, University of Piraeus, Greece
Harriet Knowles	Maritime Sustainable Development Officer, Falmouth Harbour Commissioners, UK
Ioannis N. Lagoudis	Department of Shipping, Trade & Transport, University of the Aegean, Greece
Kee-Hung Lai	Department of Logistics and Maritime Studies, Hong Kong Polytechnic University, Hong Kong
Jasmine Siu Lee Lam	Division of Infrastructure Systems and Maritime Studies, School of Civil and Environmental Engineering, Nanyang Technological University, Singapore
Chae-Kwan Lim	Department of Distribution Management, Tongmyong University, Korea
Haakon Lindstad	Department of Marine Technology, Norwegian University of Science, Trondheim, Norway
Venus Y. H. Lun	Department of Logistics and Maritime Studies, Hong Kong Polytechnic University, Hong Kong

Hilde Meersman	Department of Transport and Regional Economics, University of Antwerp, Belgium
Hokey Min	College of Business Administration, Bowling Green State University, Bowling Green, United States
Daniel S. H. Moon	Specialisation of Shipping and Port Management, World Maritime University, Malmö, Sweden
Ada Suk Fung Ng	Institute of Transport and Logistics Studies, Business School, University of Sydney, Australia
Adolf K. Y. Ng	Department of Logistics and Maritime Studies, Hong Kong Polytechnic University, Hong Kong
Athanasios A. Pallis	Department of Shipping, Trade & Transport, University of the Aegean, Greece
Photis M. Panayides	Department of Commerce, Finance and Shipping, Cyprus University of Technology, Limassol, Cyprus
Nam-Kyu Park	School of Port Logistics, Tongmyong University, Korea
Thomas Pawlik	Centre of Maritime Studies, Bremen University of Applied Sciences, Bremen, Germany
Jan Tore Pedersen	Norwegian School of Business (BI), Norway
Dong-Wook Song	Logistics Research Centre, Heriot-Watt University, Edinburgh, UK
Sarah Tuck	International Shipping, Logistics and Operations Group, School of Management, Plymouth University Business School, Plymouth, UK
Eddy Van de Voorde	Department of Transport and Regional Economics, University of Antwerp, Belgium
Thierry Vanelslander	Department of Transport and Regional Economics, University of Antwerp, Belgium
Thomas K. Vitsounis	Department of Shipping, Trade & Transport, University of the Aegean, Greece

Chapter 1

Introduction

Dong-Wook Song and Photis M. Panayides

An academic discipline evolves as knowledge, experiences and insights are accumulated and tested over the period by scholars and scientists as well as industry professionals. Maritime logistics is certainly one of the newly generated disciplines, which is currently being developed from segmented or occasionally fragmented sector-based works on shipping and ports from the managerial, economic and operational perspectives of shipping, ports and logistics. Transportation in general is regarded as a main engine for logistics and supply chain management. Transportation by sea is well recognised as the main means for regional and international trade: so-called seaborne trade; it carries almost 90% of world freight cargoes. Recent developments in the business environment such as globalisation, off-shoring and outsourcing have, however, caused sea transport to be incorporated into a global logistics supply chains. In other words, shipping and ports are to be managed and operated from a logistics and supply chain perspective.

Both editors have been for over 50 years collectively researching and teaching the subjects of shipping, port and logistics management. Over those years, we have observed an evolution in discipline development with the convergence of two distinct fields of shipping and port operations and management. The convergence occurs with the use of another field of study: logistics and supply chain management. This change has created the necessity to launch a bridge linking the traditional sector-oriented approach with the more integrated one with other players along the global logistics and supply chains. The present work is an outcome of our efforts to bring all latest works in the field into a single volume discussing the contemporary issues in the maritime logistics field.

Topics and contributors were carefully scrutinised and selected to represent at least some 'key' aspects of what maritime logisticians are faced with and should think of as a way of looking ahead. The book is divided into two parts: 'management, operations and strategic issues' and 'green and sustainability issues'. The first part discusses container shipping and container port development, operational empty container repositioning, congestion and its implications to maritime logistics, port choice model for transhipment cargoes, security and risk management matters, IT

Maritime Logistics: Contemporary Issues
Copyright © 2012 by Emerald Group Publishing Limited
All rights of reproduction in any form reserved
ISBN: 978-1-78052-340-8

and value chains. On the other hand, the second part covers corporate social responsibility, green and environmental matters. It can be said that the book covers a fair share of the contemporary issues associated with maritime logistics management and operations. Each chapter deals with its unique areas but to some degree there is overlap with others. This does in fact reflect the fact that those overlapped or repeated topics or themes seem to carry the heavier weight in terms of importance and significance in the industry. You will surely find these topics interesting as the more or less same topics are discussed from a similar but different angle and viewpoint.

It is our hope that the present volume provides a platform with which stakeholders in the field of maritime logistics can further the ongoing discussion and debates so as to identify and harmonise the trajectory forward for the further evolution of maritime logistics. The editors would love to join those discussions and debates as well and hear from you on any area for improvement and inclusion in the future edition.

Enjoy reading it.

PART I
MANAGEMENT, OPERATIONS
AND STRATEGIC ISSUES

Chapter 2

Container Liner Shipping, Port Development and Competition

Adolf K. Y. Ng

Abstract

This chapter reviews and analyses the contemporary development of liner shipping, port development and competition. It begins with a comprehensive review on the latest developmental trends of liner shipping and business strategies, as well as their impacts on port development and competition. Then, it discusses the responses of ports, past, present and (likely) future, in addressing these new demands and challenges. A very important point from this analysis indicates that, in the past decade, port development and competition have gradually evolved from being individual, technical efficiency-oriented to become more regional, economic efficiency-oriented. At the same time, ports have also moved out of their rather passive positions and undertaken positive steps to avert the traditionally strong bargaining power of shipping lines. This illustrates that port development and competition is a continuous morphological process which can change dramatically within a rather short period of time. This chapter provides a new perspective on port development and competition and a decent platform for further research.

Keywords: Container liner shipping; port development; competition; regional governance

2.1. Introduction

Persistent increases in international trade, industrial outsourcing and global economic developments have significantly increased the demand for container liner

Maritime Logistics: Contemporary Issues

ISBN: 978-1-78052-340-8

shipping since the 1990s. With an average annual growth of more than 8% since the 1980s, it had continuously developed rapidly in the past decades (Peters, 2001). In the foreseeable future, maritime transportation will continue its important role in international trades with more than 80% of trans-regional cargoes still being carried by maritime transportation (Ng & Liu, 2010). Indeed, being part of the global transportation system, liner shipping generated substantial economic benefits for globalization and enabled regional specialization (Hanson, 2000). Quoting Nijkamp, Vleugel, Maggi, and Masser (1994), maritime transportation served as the 'blood circulation' of the global economy through linking marine corridors into complex shipping networks (especially freight) and made different regions around the world more proximate to each other (Hall & Jacobs, 2010). Towards the end of the twentieth century, a number of factors had re-shaped the liner shipping industry, including the growth of international trade, the emergence of new markets, global division of labours, regional specialization of production and the development of multimodal supply chains. These factors were triggered by direct presence in particular overseas locations or markets, complemented by the successful conclusion of the Uruguay Round of the General Agreement on Tariffs and Trade (GATT) (1986–1994) and the commencement of the World Trade Organization (WTO) in 1995.

However, it was unlikely to prosper without the support of a good transportation system, which was an important attribute in deciding the sophistication, productivity and thus the competitiveness of firms (Porter, 2000). A good transportation system was not only essential in offering better access between producers and consumers, but also a necessity to allow specialization and geographical concentration (Krugman, 1998). According to Dunning (2000), changes in the pattern of foreign direct investments were possible only if it could be accompanied by the minimization of distance-related costs so that firms could find incentives to explore overseas markets. The world had thus entered a new phase where consumers emphasized on higher flexibilities and varieties, with producers needing to employ customer-oriented business strategies so as to fit individual consumer demands and better quality. This implied that the produces and merchandizes needed to be delivered within a short, and appropriate, period of time, or the so-called just-in-time.

These factors were complemented by technological innovation, notably the container revolution (Brooks, 2000). Being the blood circulation of the global economy, it implied the transformation of the nature and structure of maritime transportation. According to Notteboom and Winkelmans (2001), to succeed in such an environment, producers and service suppliers should possess flexible business attitudes and strategies, with traders and customers expecting innovative transportation system for the smooth and low-cost delivery of commodities. Not surprisingly, this had led to higher expectation from transport service operators. Instead of only spreading fixed costs so as to achieve economies of scale, transport service operators, including shipping lines, also needed to put more emphasis on customer tastes, wider geographical coverage as well as more diversified and higher quality services. Based on this background, this chapter reviews and analyses the recent development of container liner shipping, port development and competition. The chapter focuses on the latest trends of shipping lines when developing their business strategies, as well as their effects on port development and competition. Then, it discusses the responses of ports, past, present and (likely) future, in addressing these new demands and challenges. The future aspects of port development and competition are discussed in Section 2.5.

2.2. Recent Development in Container Liner Shipping

The recent development that the liner shipping industry had experienced could be summarized by three major trends, namely scale economies, re-structuring and differentiation. Scale economies were characterized by the deployment of vessels with significantly larger dimensions and container-carrying capacity, or the so-called mega-sized container vessels, more frequent services and transhipment strategies. The significant increase in vessel size, in terms of both physical dimensions and container-carrying capacity, had been recognized since the 1980s (Chilcote, 1988), and this trend sustains nowadays. In 1989, the average container-carrying capacity of vessels of the top 20 shipping lines was 1,500 twenty-foot equivalent units (TEUs), which rose to 2,000 and 3,500 TEUs in 1994 and 1999, respectively. The average carrying capacity of the largest vessels of top 20 shipping lines was equally impressive, from 2,600 TEUs in 1989 to 4,000 and 5,000 TEUs in 1994 and 1999, respectively (Drewry, 1998). Also, due to globalization, global division of labours and the need to keep pace with the development of other economic sectors, shipping lines sought to increase the provision of liner services (Martin & Thomas, 2001). The total liner services provided by top 20 shipping lines had risen from little more than 400 in the 1980s to nearly 600 in the late 1990s (Slack, 2001). Some went even further and argued that the nature of the liner shipping market had shifted fundamentally from a demand-pull to supply-led phenomenon, of which containers followed vessels rather than the other way round (cf. Chilcote, 1988; Cullinane & Khanna, 2000).

Although capital concentration within the shipping industries existed before (Chrzanowski, 1975), containerization had accelerated its development. By the turn of the century, the deployment of mega-sized vessels had become a common practice among major shipping lines. Nearly all the top 20 shipping lines possessed vessels with container-carrying capacities of more than 8,000 TEUs, while Maersk Line deployed container vessels with carrying capacities of 15,000 TEUs, notably the Emma Maersk, in the mid-2000s. By the time when this chapter was written, Maersk had signed an agreement with Daewoo, the Korean shipbuilder, and ordered 10 'super-sized' vessels (with a further option to purchase another 20) with container-carrying capacity of 18,000 TEUs. The first round order is scheduled to be delivered in 2013 (Drewry, 2011). Such persistent increase in vessel size could be explained by several factors. First, anarchy of the open sea[1] implied the scarcity of artificial forces, thus enabling shipping lines to construct their networks largely in accordance to their own benefits. In other words, liner shipping was largely able to operate under free competition (cf. Chrzanowski, 1975; McCalla, 1999). Unlike other transport modes where governments, or public authorities, often imposed operating licences, they usually had little influence on the operation, structure and networks of maritime transportation, especially trans-continental routes. Of course, this was not helped by the popular use of flags of convenience (FOC).[2] Second, technological innovation required more dedicated, capital-intensive facilities for handling containers, and this led to the reduction of firms possessing the financial and technical strengths in offering quality service. As pointed out by Palmer (1999), containerization had occurred so rapidly that the liner shipping industry, as a whole, was not allowed a gradual response. With continuous growth in vessel size and service frequency, major shipping lines believed that they could survive only if scale economies were adopted as the strategic direction. Indeed, transport planners were often fascinated by the (perceived) close relationship between infrastructure and prosperity, between network characteristics and what went on at the transport nodes along the stated networks (Hanson, 2000).

Some scholars were concerned whether the continuous growth in vessel size was sustainable (Bekemans & Beckwith, 1996; Johnson & Garnett, 1971), citing the physical limitation of ports, implications of the oil crisis and environmental issues among major concerns. Moreover, the increasing size of container vessels was directly proportional to the financial cost of their construction, that is, high proportion of fixed costs, in addition to operational and maintenance costs. As per Table 2.1, in 2010, the new-built prices of vessels with carrying capacities of 1,500, 3,500 and 6,500 TEUs were US$24.0, 38.6 and 74.8 million, respectively, while larger and newer generation vessels would cost more than US$100 million. Given the global shortage of steel and rapidly accelerating Far East trade, the new-built prices of vessels would remain high in the foreseeable future, with each 18,000 TEUs vessel costing as much as US$190 million (Drewry, 2011).

However, development since the 1990s suggested that such concern was largely ignored. Given the high speculative nature of capital investments, liner shipping gradually became an 'expensive lottery', of which only those who took the risks of heavy investments had a chance of winning, leaving players who were unable (or unwilling) to participate to fade out. Speculation had completely altered the liner shipping industry's

---

1. According to the Convention on the Law of the Sea by the United Nations (UN), a 12-mi zone stretching from coasts are declared 'territorial seas' with national sovereignty, while all other maritime surfaces are declared as anarchic, where vessels of any states enjoy the right of 'innocent passages'.
2. Under the Geneva Convention on High Seas, each country or region should fix the conditions for granting its nationality to vessels for the registration of vessels in its territory. A vessel registered to a country or region will be governed and protected by the laws of that particular country/region and has the right of flying its national or regional flag. Thus, FOC becomes a popular way among ship owners and operators to escape from high taxes and regulatory measures by registering their vessels at somewhere with fewer restrictions. For further details, see Alderton (1973) and Stubbs et al. (1984).

Table 2.1: Estimated prices of newly built container vessels, 2006–2010.

TEU	1,500	2,500	3,500	5,500	6,500	8,000	10,000	12,000
Dwt	22,000	35,000	40,000 –45,000	65,000 –70,000	75,000	105,000	120,000	140,000
Type	GD	GS	GS	GS	GS	GS	GS	GS
2006	33.4	45.8	54.4	85.0	94.9	119.0	134.5	144.5
2007	34.0	44.9	58.0	85.0	97.6	117.1	136.4	154.6
2008	38.6	55.9	63.3	93.7	104.6	128.7	138.8	146.4
2009	26.8	40.5	45.4	79.0	86.4	100.5	107.5	113.5
2010	24.0	35.0	38.6	68.6	74.8	86.1	100.0	106.1

Notes: GD — Geared; GS — Gearless. All currencies are expressed in US million dollars; TEU — Twenty-Tool Equivalent Unit, Dwt — Dead weight Tonnage. *Source*: Drewry (2011).

landscape where, despite its high costs, containerization occurred at a surprisingly rapid rate. This was not really due to high confidence or optimism, but more out of fear of not joining the revolution. As noted by Campell (1993), no major shipping lines had the 'gut' to leave themselves out. Here the dilemma was that, investments must preserve the delicate balance of providing adequate capacity to meet customer demands, while simultaneously without creating significant overcapacity. The adoption of scale economies in such a capital-intensive industry could substantially lower the market contestability which lowered the flexibility of market entry and exit (Notteboom, 2002). During this process, substantial sunk costs[3] were accumulated and counterbalanced the advantages of scale economies, and often the best way forward was to get on with it and got as much out of the sunk costs as possible. In other words, after investments had been made, substantial obstacles would exist, of which it would prevent investors from abandoning the project, even if it was clear afterwards that forecasted demands were overtly optimistic and profits would be minimal, if not zero or negative.

Such defects on major shipping lines had been felt during the global economic downturn in 2008–2009, of which mega-sized vessels struggled to gather enough cargoes to fill up their slots, thus fulfilling their economic potential. During this period, the world's container-carrying capacity fell by 15% (Slack, 2010), with decision-makers scratching their heads to find alternative ways to reduce (or delay) operational losses, including re-routing, withdrawal of liner services from certain markets, laying up vessels, to name but a few. This clearly showed that massive capital investments could exert substantial financial and operational pressure on shipping lines when the global economy was going against their strategic direction. Such setbacks, however, seemed to achieve little in deterring major shipping lines from their initial plans, of which they continued to order the construction of new mega-sized vessels. As per Table 2.2, the number of mega-sized vessels with more

---

3. Sunk cost had two main characteristics, namely few opportunity costs and long paybacks. Transport infrastructure projects often involved considerable sunk costs due to the substantial amount of capital investments.

Table 2.2: The order book of container vessels, 2011–2015.

Ship size in TEU	Scheduled delivery year					Total	Percentage (%) of current fleet
	2011	2012	2013	2014	2015		
<500	4	0	0	0	0	4	1.0
500–999	26	3	0	0	0	29	3.5
1,000–1,499	36	24	3	4	0	67	9.6
1,500–1,999	14	3	6	2	0	25	4.3
2,000–2,499	6	1	0	0	0	7	2.3
2,500–2,999	11	9	8	0	0	28	7.0
3,000–3,999	12	11	18	0	0	41	12.2
4,000–4,999	34	52	17	2	0	105	17.9
5,000–5,999	12	4	2	0	0	18	5.9
6,000–6,999	8	13	3	0	0	24	12.2
7,000–7,999	11	12	0	0	0	23	52.3
8,000–8,999	19	23	31	14	0	87	45.3
9,000–9,999	4	0	8	1	0	13	22.4
10,000+	40	59	38	15	3	155	203.9
Total	237	214	134	38	3	626	12.5

Notes: Last updated in April 2011. *Source*: Drewry (2011).

than 10,000 TEUs of carrying capacity in order would be more than 200% of the existing fleet, with this figure likely to continue to rise.

New orders of mega-sized vessels, and their eventual deployment, were significant problems for major shipping lines even before the 2008–2009 global economic downturn, and a 'ticking bomb' existed which intensified the overcapacity problem (Slack, 2010). Also, these mega-sized vessels created other significant problems, for example, high insurance premiums, difficulties in serving peripheral regions, more complicated stevedoring and long idle time in ports, etc. (Chilcote, 1988; Slack, 2003; Stubbs, Tyson, & Dalvi, 1984). Demands from peripheral regions would mostly unable to fill up the slots provided by these mega-sized vessels. From the shipping line perspective, these regions would usually be 'given up' and mega-sized vessels should concentrate on major routes between the major economic powerhouses where there were usually more demands to fill up their slots. However, even these powerhouses did not always possess adequate demands throughout the year.[4] After nearly four decades, such unfavourable situation of liner shipping, characterized by highly capital-intensive but relatively low revenues (cf. Brooks, 2000; Chrzanowski,

---

4. These included North America, North Europe and East Asia, occupying 90% and 33% of global trade and TEU throughputs, respectively (Drewry, 2005). However, seasonal variations existed within these regions which often affected the load factors of container vessels. Typical examples included the Christmas period in December and the Chinese New Year in January or February (Wang & Ng, 2011).

1975),[5] had still not been satisfactorily addressed, with competition between shipping lines being intensified. Most of the time, vessels must achieve high load factors and be in operation more frequently (Liu, 1995), and this posed serious problems to ports. In 2000, Cullinane and Khanna analysed the impacts of port productivity on the voyage costs of mega-sized vessels. They found that, if port productivity doubled the current rate,[6] the unit costs of trans-Atlantic, trans-Pacific and Asia–Europe liner routes would be reduced by about 20%, 13% and 10%, respectively (Cullinane & Khanna, 2000). To operate more frequently, they argued that vessels should minimize idle time, hence demanding much higher port efficiency, notably stevedoring time and custom procedures, as well as reducing port calls (de Souza Junior, Beresford, & Petit, 2003; Slack, 1998). Their result was supported by Ng (2009a), whose work on the competitiveness of short sea shipping in Europe also came to a similar conclusion. The impacts on ports will be further discussed later in this chapter.

On the other hand, with intensified competition between shipping lines, re-structured networks should widen geographical coverage so that demands for liner shipping could sustain increasing supplies. Slack (2003) argued that geographical market presence was vital to maintain the competitive positions of shipping lines. Understanding such necessity, major shipping lines established the 'trunk-and-feeder' system, where a few ports within the region would be chosen and trans-continental vessels would load and unload their containers there, while smaller, intra-regional vessels would take containers to final destinations (Figure 2.1).

As per Figure 2.1, a few chosen ports would become 'distribution hubs' where containers would agglomerate and distribute to various (usually proximate) destinations within its surrounding region. Under such arrangement, a shipping line could serve the peripheral regions which initially did not economically justify direct links by large vessels — the so-called transhipment strategies. This implied that only a few ports could benefit and the current business of other ports would likely to be taken away with containers being agglomerated geographically to a few hubs, especially since mega-sized vessels implied wider access channels and deeper draughts (Table 2.3). According to Drewry (2011), although vessels with a carrying capacity of 18,000 TEUs would not necessarily lead to fewer direct port calls, only an extremely limited number of ports would have sufficient operational efficiency to turn vessels around fast enough, while most ports, including some major ones, would not have sufficient productivity to make the vessel operation viable.[7] Under such system, focus would likely centre on the major economic powerhouses, and shipping lines sought to provide services to the region by selecting particular ports as their distribution hubs. The result was the creation of a regional 'port hierarchy' where feeder ports would be connected by smaller-sized vessels to a few chosen distribution hubs. Such

---

5. For example, throughout the late 1980s and the whole of 1990s, profits of only US$0.40 per year were realized by a sample of 11 global major liners (Slack et al., 1996).
6. The 'current year' of Cullinane and Khanna's work was 2000.
7. Drewry exemplified North American ports, like Los Angeles, being those which were unlikely to handle the latest generation of vessels without significant increase in their productivities.

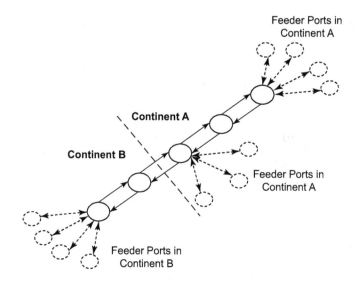

Figure 2.1: A diagram illustrating the trunk-and-feeder system in container liner shipping

Table 2.3: The average dimensions of different generations of container vessels.

Generation	Capacity in TEU	LOA (m)	Beam (m)	Draught (m)
First (1968)	1,100	(NA)	(NA)	(NA)
Second (1970–1980)	2,000–3,000	213	27.4	10.8
Panamax (1980–1987)	3,000–4,500	294	32.0	12.2
Post-Panamax (1988–1995)	4,000–5,000	280–305	41.1	12.7
Fifth (1996–2005)	6,400–7,500	300–347	42.9	14.0
Sixth (2006–2007)	8,000–9,000	330–380	47	14.5
Seventh (2007–2013)	12,500–15,000	380–400	58	15.0
Near future (2013–2014)	18,000	400	58	16.0

Source: OSC (2002) and Drewry (2011).

a hierarchy could be found in various major economic regions, with China being a notable example (Wang & Ng, 2011).

   Reinforcing the scale of operation, liner shipping had also undertaken a rationalization process of horizontal integration which included acquisitions, mergers and the establishment of strategic shipping alliances. This was exemplified by the takeover of APL by NOL, the merging between P&O and Nedlloyd (P&O Nedlloyd itself was acquired by Maersk Line in 2006), the formation of Global, New World and CKYH Alliances, respectively. The advantages for rationalization included the protection of market shares, cost reduction through slot re-arrangements, better market perception through efficient information exchange, opportunities to enter new markets and wider geographical coverage, stronger bargaining position against ports, to name but a few. The objectives were to increase control in the decision-making process, combination of financial power to expand and the sharing of financial risks (cf. Heaver, 2002; Kumar, 2000). The restructuring process was similar to the global market trend of liberalization and technological advances where horizontal integration in other industries had also increased by the turn of the century (Dunning, 2000). It was a rather proactive approach in accumulating industrial capital and expanding market presence. The formation of strategic alliances allowed shipping lines to construct larger vessels, as individual firms were only required to operate certain routes of which they excelled within the corporate umbrella (World Bank, 2000). This process had become so rapid that only a few major shipping lines remained uncommitted to any alliances (MSC being a notable exception). Shipping lines seemed to believe that they had discovered the benefits of combining collaboration and competition in their strategies.

At the same time, to enhance efficiency and smoothness of the transportation process as discussed earlier, many shipping lines had undertaken differentiation, notably vertical integration, of which they diversified their operation and service into various components along the multimodal supply chain system. Since the turn of the century, many shipping lines, especially the top 20, had participated in the operation of port terminals (like COSCO in Hong Kong, Maersk in Rotterdam and Hanjin in Osaka) and other (usually inland) transportation modes, for example, the European Rail Shuttle (ERS) operated by Maersk (ERS B.V. being a fully owned subsidiary under the AP Moller–Maersk Group) which connected the port of Rotterdam (of which Maersk operated a dedicated terminal) with various inland destinations in Europe which included Germany, the Benelux countries, Italy and Central European states; the operation of inland terminals (like APL, CMA-CGM and Maersk in the city of Dadri in India). Moreover, some major shipping lines had even established logistical branches, or fully owned logistics subsidiaries, with the aim to provide the so-called total logistical solutions to their customers, notably shippers, with APL Logistics, NYK Logistics and OOCL Logistics being illustrative examples. These solutions usually saved shippers from the need to search multiple service suppliers along the (initially fragmented) multimodal supply chain, thus providing significant added values to their cargoes through savings in monetary costs, time and coordination problems.

The stated strategies had the potential to cause cost savings through facilitating the use of standardized containers, minimizing the chance of purchasing and operating duplicated facilities, avoiding queuing time for containers to be loaded/unloaded, coherence and coordination between different transport modes and logistical stakeholders, thus reducing uncertainty. However, whether such potential could be fulfilled was dependent on the ability of shipping lines in overcoming various obstacles, including (i) whether additional savings could cover the extra costs triggered; (ii) possible reduction in flexibility due to higher switching costs; (iii) the possibility of longer and more complicated decision-making process; and (iv) the possible organizational complexity and different management cultures between different firms and transport modes. In a nutshell, these strategies could suffer trade-offs and exert substantial upward pressures to the overall operational costs of shipping lines (Bergantino & Veenstra, 2002). For instance, Notteboom and Winkelmans (2001) argued that strategic alliances were often unstable and, hitherto, whether such a system could sustain as a long-term solution in stabilizing competition between shipping lines was yet to be confirmed. To increase stability, many alliances imposed strict contracts and agreements among themselves (cf. Ng, 2009b). In this sense, a vicious cycle was established, where a strong bind could cause potential problems and costs among shipping lines, given that the decision-making process had become more complicated, with the P&O Nedlloyd unwillingness to use the container terminal operated by NYK (both Grand Alliance member at the time) in the port of Amsterdam (cf. Ng, 2009b) in the early and mid-2000s being an illustrative example. These underlying problems, together with the fact that dramatic rise in freight rates to shippers was not always possible (Panayides & Cullinane, 2002), implied that shipping lines always needed to think of ways to minimize costs. The degree of success of the stated strategies depended on the balance between savings and additional costs generated by their own business strategies (Taaffe, Gauthier, & O'Kelly, 1996). Shipping lines needed to identify and implement the optimal solution under certain constraints within the maritime logistical system.

2.3. Implications on Ports: Changing Roles, Functions and Development

As shipping line strategies could be backfired by the existence of rising logistics costs, they regarded ports as critical components in deciding their success. As witnessed in the past decades, many ports were pressurized by shipping lines to improve so as to minimize the 'generalized' costs of the overall multimodal supply chain. These included monetary costs, time, efficiency and service quality (Huybrechts et al., 2002; van Klink & van den Berg, 1998). The negative implications of container liner shipping on ports had been discussed as early as the 1970s, with Gilman (1980) arguing that ports often found it difficult to handle mega-sized vessels, as the latter could not be laid idle for too long (cf. Chilcote, 1988; Notteboom, 2002; Panayides & Cullinane, 2002). As the development of substantially greater speed mega-sized vessels was deemed economically impractical in the foreseeable future,[8] the service frequency and turnaround time of mega-sized vessels had to increase and decrease, respectively, while port calls needed to be reduced.

Also, contemporary development in liner shipping had considerably enhanced their bargaining power against ports. With improved transportation networks through technological innovation, vessels increasingly became 'footloose' in port choice decision, and the traditional perception that ports possessed 'natural hinterlands', and thus little need to worry about the lack of users, had become obsolete. McCalla (1999) claimed that ports gradually became the 'servants' of their

---

8. The estimated maximum speeds of the newly ordered 18,000 TEU container vessel and Emma Maersk are 23 and 25 knots, respectively, while the optimal cruising speed of the former is 19 knots (Drewry, 2011).

customers, while Hayuth and Hilling (1992) proposed the concept of 'common hinterlands' to be competed by ports, as different regions moved towards more borderless trades. Also, when conducting their business, until recently, most ports negotiated with shipping lines independently, leaving the latter to possess better information and able to play 'threatening games' to different ports. Actually, shipping lines also did not have many choices but to pressurize ports, as the economic potential of their mega-sized vessels could not materialize if containers were not handled efficiently, especially in face of global crisis and economic recessions, like the 9/11 terrorist attack and the 2008–2009 global economic downturn, respectively (Ng & Liu, 2010). As a result, similar to shipping lines, inter-port competition had intensified and ports, as described by Slack (1993), had become 'pawns' in global transportation and supply chain systems.

With changing demands, the traditional philosophy in port operation and management, like the assumption of natural hinterlands and as a base to control its hinterlands during the colonial period (World Bank, 2000), became obsolete. Intensified inter-port competition became especially explicit in regions where the emergence of single market and regional integration had started to exert pressure to public authorities to avert protective measures, with the Hamburg–Le Havre Range (HLR) in North Europe and the Pearl River Delta (PRD) in southern China being illustrative examples. Not to be left out, many ports continuously improved and constructed (capital-intensive) infra- and superstructures so as to retain and attract existing and new customers, respectively (Meersman & van de Voorde, 1998). It did not take long for the labour-intensive landscape of ports being replaced by fully mechanized landscapes with container cranes and ancillary vehicles (Martin & Thomas, 2001), while many were forced to re-locate from city cores to peripheral areas due the abundance of cheap lands for large warehouses and the storage of containers and mechanized equipment. Ports perceived that only through such improvements they could realistically reduce vessel's idle time and thus their competitiveness. Hence, while shipping lines invested heavily to accommodate global economic development and technological improvements, the commitments from ports were even more (Slack, 1998). Ports needed to be specifically designed and substantially more innovative so as to add values to their customers. As Heaver (1993) and Slack, Comtois, and Sletmo (1996) pointed out, these specifically designed, capital-intensive ports had led to a more competitive environment as ports needed to recover the financial burden imposed on them within a rather short period of time. This was not helped by the rather fragile economic situation in the past few years which had, unsurprisingly, made private equity cash providers for port investments nowadays far more questioning than before (Pawlik, Stemmler, Baird, & Helch, 2011). All these transformed port operation to become more complex with particular dedicated functions (Robinson, 2002).

However, even after such commitments, there was no guarantee that vessels would come and use their facilities and services. The loyalty of shipping lines could not be taken for granted due to their frequent network re-structuring and strategic alliance commitments (Notteboom, 2002). In this respect, Pawlik et al. (2011) argued that ports often constructed facilities far ahead of existing (and near future) demands fearing that they might be 'lagged off' if they did not do so, while Psaraftis (1998) and van Ham (1998) highlighted the risks of ports being trapped into vicious circles of creating wasteful overcapacity based on unrealistic speculation. McCalla (1999) put it even further claiming that the major challenge of contemporary ports was to find ways to turn local 'pain' to 'gain' based on pure perception of the demands of port services in the (often unforeseeable) medium and long term future. Similar to shipping lines, port decision-makers faced the dilemma that heavy investments were required to remain competitive but with no guaranteed demands. Here the study by Dion, Slack, and Comtois (2002) offered an illustrative example. Throughout the years, the Canadian government had established a vast network of ports and provided substantial infrastructural support. Nevertheless, only several of them were profitable with the vast majority of traffic concentrated within around 10% of the public ports. Port operation had also become a highly speculative lottery and investments in facilities (usually durable and dedicated) would bear significant risks (Hayuth & Hilling, 1992). The pressure from intensified inter-port competition did affect not only small ports, but also large and established ports. The large ports which sought to become distribution hubs within the trunk-and-feeder system were highly vulnerable to the ever-changing economic climate, as well as the fortunes and strategic direction of shipping lines.

To enhance their competitive position, port managers were forced to alter their traditional focus from whether their ports could handle containers effectively. As long as customers were offered alternatives, rather than measuring physical outputs, port performance within such an environment also needed to be assessed through evaluating whether they possessed the ability to attract customers and to fight off competitors. The situation was made more complex, with making realistic forecasts more and more difficult due to common hinterlands, transhipment and 'hub hopping', of which the number of competing ports was growing so rapidly that mega-sized vessels could usually shift port calls with minimal costs (Huybrechts et al., 2002; World Bank, 2007). This complemented the view of Bennathan and Walters (1979) who argued that if inter-port competition existed within a region, then the demands of their users (shipping lines) would be highly elastic. A good example involved the dealings between Maersk and port of New York/New Jersey in 1999. Facing the threat of dumping the port as the transhipment hub along the US East Coast by its big customer, US$570 million was spent on improving port facilities (World Bank, 2000). Similar danger was also prominent in North Europe, where there were considerable established ports which could offer transhipment services within a rather small region. Along the HLR, with about 130 seaports possessing container-handling capacity (ESPO, 2011), the total throughput of ports was about 100 million TEUs in 2008. Likewise, similar strategies were also used as a bargaining tool by shipping lines in the PRD, of which nearly 20 ports with container-handling capacity could be found within an area of only 23,000 km^2. Such strategies reduced port's monopoly power which made it more difficult to cover costs, let alone making profits.

Hence, it seemed that finding solutions to obtain some longer term commitments from shipping lines, or reducing their elasticity, in using port services was necessary to maintain the competitive position of ports. To tackle the stated challenges, ports needed to strengthen their own power against shipping lines and other ports, notably by transforming port management and operation towards more business-like approach. Port management had to be more responsive to customer requirements because new developments in the global economy and shipping ensured that the physical layouts of ports were no longer in line with user requirements (Juhel, 2001). This partly explained the increasing private sector participation and privatization in port operation around the world, of which an abundance of research works had underlined this evolution (cf. Baird, 2002; Heaver, 2002; Ng & Pallis, 2010; Wang, Ng, & Olivier, 2004; World Bank, 2000). For example, container terminal operation in most ports along the HLR was recently undertaken by the private sector, notably the multinational terminal operators like HPH, PSA and DPW, operating under the 'tool', 'landlord' or 'fully privatized' port models (cf. World Bank, 2000, 2007) under various concession agreements, for example, Build-Operate-Transfer (BOT), Build-Own-Operate-Transfer (BOOT), Build-Own-Operate (BOO), etc.[9]

Also, ports had transformed from traditionally simple sea–land interfaces to more complex distribution nodes along the multimodal supply chains emphasizing the coherent flow of cargoes. Inevitably, this would require the synchronization and close cooperation between ports and other different stakeholders along the supply chain, notably shipping lines, transport service providers and freight forwarders, leading to the establishment of 'maritime logistics hub', and this concept was thoroughly discussed by Nam and Song (2011). Nowadays, ports are particularly crucial due to their roles in the coordination of materials and information flows, cost minimization and the provision of reliable services so as to facilitate global logistics and supply chain management. Demanding customers push service providers hard to provide speedy, just-in-time services at competitive prices. Activities, including smooth communication, the adoption of information technologies, effective inter-organizational relationship, facilitation of multimodal integration, value-added services and efficient operation of supply chains, needed to be well supported by such maritime logistics hubs (cf. Panayides, 2002). The transformation of ports to become maritime logistics hubs would not only involve basic physical facilities and functions, but also involve those which could facilitate and accelerate integration between different transport modes, both land and maritime, and logistics stakeholders. In short, a maritime logistics hub would play an intermediary role of connecting the whole logistical process. Indeed, ports could serve as ideal locations of which different stakeholders involving in the transportation and logistical process could meet and interact. Ports needed to ensure that the supply chain could be optimized in the best possible way so as to reach the lowest possible overall cost.

As mentioned before, recent development in liner shipping, especially the rise of the establishment of trunk-and-feeder systems, as well as the need for wider

---

9. For detailed discussion on changing port management, see Ng (2011a, b). For detailed explanation on concession agreements, see Theys, Notteboom, Pallis, and de Langen (2010).

geographical coverage of shipping networks, had led to the growing prominence of transhipment, supplemented by the increasing global trade which greatly favoured developments of trans-continental routes (Ng, 2006; Palmer, 1999; Stubbs et al., 1984). Rather than shifting between different transport modes (like vessel and road vehicle), transhipment implied shifting from large, trans-continental vessels to smaller ones for short sea purpose. Although transhipment could be dated back to the 1960s when containers were initially introduced (de Langen, 1998), its development did not fully takeoff until the mid-1990s (World Bank, 2000). In the early 1980s, transhipment occupied only 12% of global container throughputs, compared to less than 15% in 1990, but since then accelerated to more than 20% by the turn of the century (Damas, 2001). Since then, as per Table 2.4, transhipment had become an important strategy within liner shipping, including the emerging markets, say, East Asia and Latin America. Indeed, some traditional hubs are nowadays

Table 2.4: Container transhipment traffic of selected regions around the world, 2006–2010.

Region	2006	2007	2008	2009	2010
(By TEU)					
Western Europe	24,768,415	28,715,651	29,736,033	25,935,401	28,139,013
Eastern Europe	825,403	1,283,781	1,297,936	544,569	602,841
Far East	33,539,720	39,788,081	42,748,155	45,135,636	52,875,280
Southeast Asia	30,586,030	35,369,575	38,116,787	34,607,323	38,453,883
Middle East	11,071,775	10,874,786	13,420,669	12,621,858	13,916,866
South Asia	2,538,027	2,816,020	3,063,402	2,906,221	3,401,300
North America	2,717,500	2,771,211	2,623,723	2,250,083	2,541,122
Latin America	9,281,959	11,067,565	11,587,411	10,566,591	11,947,918
Oceania	431,158	469,503	578,311	584,393	631,693
Africa	4,501,599	4,869,086	6,538,639	6,826,964	7,821,186
World Total	120,261,587	138,025,258	149,711,066	141,979,041	160,331,101
(By percentage of regional throughput)					
Western Europe	30.5	31.7	32.7	33.1	32.5
Eastern Europe	15.1	17.8	16.1	10.6	8.8
Far East	21.2	22.0	22.0	25.3	25.1
Southeast Asia	51.1	52.4	53.5	52.1	51.4
Middle East	45.1	39.6	41.3	40.6	40.9
South Asia	22.1	20.8	20.6	20.7	20.5
North America	5.8	5.8	5.7	5.6	5.6
Latin America	29.3	31.4	31.3	31.6	31.0
Oceania	5.5	5.4	6.2	6.6	6.7
Africa	28.8	27.7	31.4	32.6	33.6

Source: Drewry (2011).

nearly completely relying on transhipment traffic so as to sustain its continuous container throughput growth, with Hong Kong being a notable example.[10]

With increasing vessel size, higher service frequency and wider geographical coverage, complemented with the need to call fewer ports, it was not surprising that transhipment was largely adopted only in the past two decades. The implication was that many ports needed to keep their traditional function serving respective hinterlands while, at the same time, added the transit function and enabled them to facilitate the establishment of efficient maritime logistics and multimodal supply chains. Although increase in transhipment implied extra business granted to the port, at least in theory, such generosity could be withdrawn by shipping lines at any time they deemed relevant. Especially any innovations in the reduction of transhipment inefficiencies, notably extra costs generated from the transfer of containers from one vessel to another, were important to the competitive positions of shipping lines themselves (Taaffe et al., 1996). Especially in more developed regions where ports were geographically proximate to each other, the increase of transhipment further intensified inter-port competition (Fleming & Hayuth, 1994) and diminished the monopolistic nature of port's hinterlands as cargo flows became more geographically concentrated (de Lombaerde & Verbeke, 1989; Heaver, 2002).

The increase in transhipment also highlighted that ports were clearly the victims as demands on transhipment were mainly driven by network re-structuring of shipping lines, although ports usually had few opportunities to participate in this process (OSC, 2004). An illustrative example was Antwerp, of which limitations on water depth and locks along River Scheldt partly explained why the port focused more on trans-Atlantic liner routes rather than Far East–European ones (where the vessels serving the latter routes were usually larger in size). Furthermore, as shipping lines needed ensure that their benefits would not be extracted due to price discrimination from ports, as stated before, they had undertaken mergers, acquisitions and strategic alliances to counterbalance the former monopoly power of ports. Hence, the traditional practice of price discrimination between transhipment and direct shipment traffic (of which the former usually enjoyed a much lower charge), which had been commonly imposed by port in the 1970s (Bennathan & Walters, 1979), had become obsolete. This further weakened ports' ability in covering their capital and operational costs. As noted by Fleming and Hayuth (1994), in a deregulated environment, an increase in transhipment implied the rising prominence of 'intermediacy', rather than 'centrality', in deciding port competitiveness.[11] Although the rise of transhipment hubs could possibly trigger overall port demands (Notteboom, 2002; Ha, 2003; and Baird, 2004), still the use of transhipment strategy

---

10. Between 2004 and 2009, the direct shipment cargoes via the port of Hong Kong experienced an average negative growth of 0.5%, while the port had experienced an average of 4.5% growth for transhipment cargoes within the same period (Census and Statistics Department of the HKSAR Government, 2011).

11. According to Fleming and Hayuth (1994), centrality was generated from locally generated demands while intermediacy was generated from port en route which usually involves long-distance in-transit and transhipment.

was likely to further intensify inter-port competition as vessels became even more footloose. Such concern could be found in the British Isles where the British (Felixstowe, Southampton, Thamesport and Tilbury) share of within the North European transhipment market had risen from 11% in 1990 to 20% in 1999 and dropped to 8% in 2003 (OSC, 2004). The increase in transhipment and the need for effective strategic investments prompted ports to evaluate their competitive position frequently, which acted as the platform in establishing their strategic direction. Such understanding involved both exogenous and endogenous factors, including the foreseeable trend within the maritime industries, customer satisfaction to their services, their future development prospects and relations with their potential competitors. Moreover, ports should develop strategies which could enhance bargaining power against their users. Hence, Palmer (1999) was right by claiming that a revolution had taken place within the maritime industries.

2.4. A New Trend Emerging: Coopetition and Regional Port Governance

As mentioned in the previous section, one of the great challenges that ports need to tackle is to reduce the flexibility of shipping lines and minimize destructive competition. Since the turn of the century, one could witness another wave of port development had started to take root with the increasingly popularity of cooperation between ports while competing at the same time — the so-called coopetition (cf. Song, 2003, 2004). To enhance competitive advantages, rather than just employing competitive strategies, ports started to adopt coopetition as a new option to strengthen their competitive position by formulating a set of objectives and choices from a variety of co-operative arrangements. Such a strategy was formalized through the choice of various objectives and co-operative arrangements, thus leading to a coherent and consistent strategic option (cf. Aaker, 1984). This strategic direction was encouraged by global economic development and various economic turmoil which took place between 1997 and 2009, of which service suppliers within particular regions, including ports, started recognizing the advantages to collaborate with proximate partners so as to deter challenges from other regions or customers, or the so-called regional governance. As noted by Yang (2010), such a development trend was largely a response to counterbalance the challenges triggered by intensified global competition.

Here an interesting phenomenon could be found. Especially in the past half a decade, collaboration and integration between ports within similar regions had gradually shifted from 'bottom-up' to becoming more 'top-down', where inter-port collaboration had emerged from merely the regionalization of port terminal operators (Airriess, 2001) to more comprehensive multi-level governance which involved national, regional and local authorities, as well as cooperation between public and private sectors. This could be found in various regions around the world. For instance, the corporatization of (previously public) port authorities, of which the newly established corporation (usually with the public sector still owning part or all of the shares) would carry out both public and private responsibilities (which facilitated port's strategic development, negotiation and collaboration with other ports and private firms), had taken place among major ports around the world, say, Busan, Rotterdam, Piraeus, to name but a few (Ng & Pallis, 2010). On the other hand, in Scandinavia, the Danish and Swedish ports of Copenhagen and Malmo, respectively, collaborated and were managed by a joint venture — *Copenhagen Malmo Port* — jointly owned by the Danish government and the city governments of Copenhagen and Malmo (Figure 2.2). On the other hand, in The Netherlands, plans had been proposed by the Council for Transport and Water Management of the Dutch government to merge the ports of Amsterdam and Rotterdam so as to deter destructive competition and resource wastage, forming the so-called Gateway Holland (NRC, 2010). In East Asia, according to the National 12th Five Years Plan (FYP) of the Chinese government, as well as policy release document published by the National and Development and Reform Commission, entitled: *The Outline of the Plan for the Reform and Development of PRD (2008–2020)* (Article 2, Chapter 11), the ports located within PRD, including Hong Kong, Shenzhen, Guangzhou, should collaborate and establish the 'Pan-PRD Port Region', of which different ports were expected to play different roles, complemented with each other, and realized common development. This strategic direction was complemented by the *Framework Agreement on HK/Guangdong Co-operation* (2010), signed between the HKSAR and Guangdong provincial governments, of which different ports located within PRD were expected to integrate so as to establish a system with the functions of different ports complementary to each other (Chapter 9, Article 4).

The latest development in regional port governance required us to review carefully so as to effectively establish a co-value network among ports in the future. Nevertheless, a number of challenges on this development direction have, hitherto, remained unresolved, and thus the transformation process is still rather blurred. A number of important questions include (i) what exactly co-value networks should be, and the necessary conditions for it to perform and remain competitive? (ii) How should we measure its degree of efficiency and competitiveness? (iii) Will such development direction independent of physical cargo throughputs? (iv) What should be the roles of the different stakeholders, and the priorities, when all the ports involved sought to develop themselves as the leader within the region? With diversified interests between different levels, what is the definition of 'win-win'

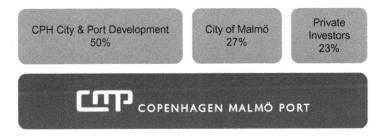

Figure 2.2: The ownership structure of Copenhagen Malmo Port
Source: Copenhagen Malmo Port (2011).

situation, and how to achieve it? (v) How can multi-level governance contribute to effective regional governance? (vi) Given the increased complexity of regional port governance, what should/would be the way forward and opportunities for traditional, but gradually declining, ports (like Hong Kong)? Should they concentrate on the 'softer' aspects of shipping and seek to become the 'Shipping Manhattan' which can play the role as broker in facilitating effective regional port governance, given their usually more mature and efficient bureaucratic, commercial and legal systems? Further research on these questions is not only desirable but also an urgent necessity. The need for the effective implementation of regional port governance encourages us to define a completely new operational and logistics system which diversified our traditional understanding on port management and governance emphasizing on individual ports.

2.5. Concluding Remarks

Global economic development and technological innovation, notably containerization, had fundamentally transformed the nature of liner shipping. Major shipping lines undertook a number of business strategies in tackling the new environment. These included scale economies, re-structuring and differentiation, which involved massive capital investments on the construction of new, mega-sized vessels, shipping network re-structuring, merger, acquisitions, the establishment of strategic shipping alliances, as well as the participation of other transport and logistics-related business. Such strategies had posed significant impacts on ports. Shipping line had pressurized ports to continuously improve their efficiency, although the increasing footloose nature of port selection intensified inter-port competition. Being critical nodal points and distribution centres along multimodal supply chains, ports gradually transformed themselves into maritime logistics hubs and possessed the ability to handle increasing transhipment traffic, as well as facilitated the operation and efficiency of supply chains. To deal with the new situation, ports had invested heavily in dedicated, capital-intensive facilities, thus changing their management philosophy. More recently, the intensified inter-port competition had resulted in increasingly coopetition between proximate ports, as well as regional port governance, which was especially noticeable in East Asia and Europe.

It was very clear that port development and competition had evolved from being individual, technical efficiency-oriented to become more regional, economic efficiency-oriented. This view was confirmed by a recent review study on the evolution and research trends of port research, which indicated that, in the past two decades, much more attention had been given to port's relation with other transport modes and its surrounding regions (cf. Ng, 2011b). Also, the latest development suggested that ports had gradually moved out of their rather passive positions within the game, and, instead, undertook positive steps to avert the existing strong bargaining position of shipping lines. Perhaps more importantly, the above discussions illustrated that the process and structure of port development and competition, respectively, was a continuous morphological process which could change dramatically within a short period of time. Indeed, there are numerous rising issues which are very like to pose significant implications on future port development and competitive structures. These include climate changes, the expected increasingly navigable channels along the Arctic due to melting ice, as well as the possible re-establishment of the Eurasian Land bridge connecting East Asia and Europe. These new issues imply that port development, and inter-port competition, will become more multi-faceted and complex. Hence, when undertaking further research, a number of new aspects, notably environmental sustainability (including vulnerability and adaptation of ports, their infrastructures, and climate changes), as well as competition between shipping routes and even transport modes for trans-continental traffic, should be given more attention by researchers. We are very likely to witness a completely new paradigm in port development and competition as we enter the second decade of the 21st century. Ports, especially major ones, cannot remain isolated from global issues anymore.

To conclude, this chapter comprehensively reviews the recent development of liner shipping, as well as the implications of their business strategies on the past, present and the (likely) future port development and competition. The author genuinely believes that this chapter provides a decent platform for further research in the future of shipping and port development.

Acknowledgements

This study is supported by the Hong Kong Research Grant Council (RGC) under the project title *Performance and Competitiveness of Seaports in Transformation* (project code A-SA32). Usual disclaimers apply.

References

Aaker, D. (1984). *Developing business strategies*. New York: John Wiley & Sons.

Airriess, C. A. (2001). The regionalization of Hutchison Port holdings in Mainland China. *Journal of Transport Geography, 9*, 267–278.

Alderton, P. M. (1973). *Sea transport: Operation and economics*. London: Thomas Reed.

Baird, A. J. (2002). Privatisation trends at the world's top 100 container ports. *Maritime Policy and Management, 29*(3), 271–284.

Baird, A. J. (2004, May). Transhipment: Hub port selection. *Cargo Systems*, pp. 44–47.

Bekemans, L., & Beckwith, S. (1996). *Ports for Europe: Europe's maritime future in a changing environment*. Brussels: European Interuniversity Press.

Bennathan, E., & Walters, A. A. (1979). *Port pricing and investment policy for developing countries*. Oxford: Oxford University Press.

Bergantino, A. S., & Veenstra, A. W. (2002). Networks in liner shipping — Interconnection and coordination. *International Journal of Maritime Economics, 4*(3), 210–229.

Brooks, M. R. (2000). *Sea change in liner shipping: Regulation and managerial decision-making in a global industry*. Oxford: Pergamon.

Campell, S. (1993). Increasing trade, declining port cities: Port containerisation and the regional diffusion of economic benefits. In H. Noponen, J. Graham & A. R. Markusen (Eds.), *Trading industries, trading regions* (pp. 212–227). New York: Guilford.

Census and Statistics Department of the HKSAR Government. Available at www.censtatd. gov.hk. Retrieved on August 2011.

Chilcote, P. W. (1988). The containerisation story: Meeting the competition in trade. In M. J. Hershman (Ed.), *Urban ports and harbour management* (pp. 125–146). London: Taylor and Francis.

Chrzanowski, I. H. (1975). *Concentration and centralisation of capital in shipping*. Westmead: Saxon House.

Copenhagen Malmo Port. Available at http://www.cmport.com. Retrieved on August 2011.

Cullinane, K., & Khanna, M. (2000). Economies of scale in large container ships. *Journal of Transport Economics and Policy*, *33*(2), 185–208.

Damas, P. (2001, June). Tranship or direct – a real choice. American Shippers, pp. 56–60.

de Langen, P. W. (1998). The future of small and medium sized ports. In G. Sciutto & C. A. Brebbia (Eds.), *Maritime engineering and ports* (pp. 263–279). Southampton: WIT.

de Lombaerde, P., & Verbeke, A. (1989). Assessing international seaport competition: A tool for strategic decision-making. *International Journal of Transport Economics*, *XVI*(2), 176–192.

de Souza, Jr., G. A. S., Beresford, A., & Petit, S. J. (2003). Liner shipping companies and terminal operators: Internationalisation or globalisation? *Maritime Economics and Logistics*, *5*(4), 393–412.

Dion, S., Slack, B., & Comtois, C. (2002). Port and airport divestiture in Canada: A comparative analysis. *Journal of Transport Geography*, *10*(3), 187–193.

Drewry (1998). *World container terminals: Global growth and private profits*. London: Drewry Shipping Consultants.

Drewry (2005). *The Drewry container market quarterly (March 2005)*. London: Drewry Shipping Consultants.

Drewry (2011, August). Unpublished materials provided to author.

Dunning, J. H. (2000). Globalisation and the new geography of foreign direct investment. In N. Woods (Ed.), *The political economy of globalisation* (pp. 20–53). London: Macmillan.

ESPO. Available at http://www.espo.be. Retrieved on August 2011.

Fleming, D. K., & Hayuth, Y. (1994). Spatial characteristics of transportation hubs: Centrality and intermediacy. *Journal of Transport Geography*, *2*(1), 3–18.

Gilman, S. (1980). A critique for the super-port idea. *Maritime Policy and Management*, *7*(2), 1.

Ha, M. S. (2003). A comparison of service quality at major container ports: Implications for Korean ports. *Journal of Transport Geography*, *11*(1), 131–137.

Hall, P. V., & Jacobs, W. (2010). Shifting proximities: The maritime ports sector in an era of global supply chains. *Regional Studies*, *44*(9), 1103–1116.

Hanson, S. (2000). Transportation: hooked on speed, eyeing sustainability. In E. Sheppard & T. J. Barnes (Eds.), *A companion to economic geography* (pp. 468–483). Oxford: Blackwell.

Hayuth, Y., & Hilling, D. (1992). Technological change and seaport development. In B. Hoyle & D. Pinder (Eds.), *European port cities in transition* (pp. 4–58). London: Belhaven.

Heaver, T. D. (1993). Shipping and the market for port services. In G. Blauwens, G. de Brabander & E. van de Voorde (Eds.), *De dynamiek van een haven* (pp. 227–248). Kapellen: Uitgeverij Pelckmans.

Heaver, T. D. (2002). The evolving roles of shipping lines in international logistics. *International Journal of Maritime Economics*, *4*(3), 210–230.

Huybrechts, M., Meersman, H., van de Voorde, E., van Hooydonk, E., Verbeke, A., & Winkelmans, W. (2002). *Port competitiveness: An economic and legal analysis of the factors determining the competitiveness of seaports*. Antwerp: de Boeck.

Johnson, K. M., & Garnett, H. C. (1971). *The economics of containerisation*. London: George Allen & Unwin.

Juhel, M. H. (2001). Globalisation, privatisation and restructuring of ports. *International Journal of Maritime Economics*, *3*, 139–174.

Krugman, P. (1998). What's new about the new economic geography? *Oxford Review of Economic Policy*, *14*(2), 7–17.

Kumar, S. (2000). An evaluation of liner strategies in the context of contemporary supply chain management practices. *Journal of Transport Management*, *12*(2), 55–64.

Liu, Z. (1995). Ownership and productive efficiency: The experience of British ports. In J. McConville & J. Sheldrake (Eds.), *Transport in transition* (pp. 163–182). Aldershot: Avebury.

Martin, J., & Thomas, B. J. (2001). The container terminal community. *Maritime Policy and Management*, *28*(3), 279–292.

McCalla, R. J. (1999). Global change, local pain: Intermodal seaport terminals and their service areas. *Journal of Transport Geography*, *7*(4), 247–254.

Meersman, H., & van de Voorde, E. (1998). Coping with port competition in Europe: A state of the art. In G. Sciutto & C. A. Brebbia (Eds.), *Marine engineering and ports* (pp. 281–290). Southampton: WIT.

Nam, H. S., & Song, D. W. (2011). Defining maritime logistics hub and its implication for container port. *Maritime Policy and Management*, *38*(3), 269–292.

Ng, K. Y. A. (2006). Assessing the attractiveness of ports in the North European container transhipment market: An agenda for future research in port competition. *Maritime Economics and Logistics*, *8*(3), 234–250.

Ng, A. K. Y. (2009a). Competitiveness of short sea shipping and the role of port: The case of North Europe. *Maritime Policy and Management*, *36*(4), 337–352.

Ng, A. K. Y. (2009b). *Port competition: The case of North Europe*. Saarbrucken: VDM Verlag.

Ng, A. K. Y. (2011a). Global ports and logistics facilitation. In J. J. Liu (Ed.), *Supply chain and transport logistics* (pp. 398–415). London: Routledge.

Ng, A.K.Y. (2011b). The evolution and research trends of port geography. *The Professional Geographer* (in press).

Ng, A. K. Y., & Liu, J. J. (2010). The port and maritime industries in the post-2008 world: Challenges and opportunities. *Research in Transportation Economics*, *27*(1), 1–3.

Ng, A. K. Y., & Pallis, A. A. (2010). Port governance reforms in diversified institutional frameworks: Generic solutions, implementation asymmetries. *Environment and Planning A*, *42*(9), 2147–2167.

Nijkamp, P., Vleugel, J. M., Maggi, R., & Masser, I. (1994). *Missing transport networks in Europe*. Aldershot: Avebury.

Notteboom, T. E. (2002). Consolidation and contestability in the European container handling industry. *Maritime Policy and Management*, *29*(3), 257–269.

Notteboom, T. E., & Winkelmans, W. (2001). Reassessing public sector involvement in European seaports. *International Journal of Maritime Economics*, *3*(2), 242–259.

NRC (2010). Merger of Amsterdam, Rotterdam ports proposed. Available at http://vorige.nrc.nl/article2533975.ecevorige.nrc.nl/article2533975.ece. Retrieved on 28 April.

OSC (2002). *Containerisation in North Europe to 2015*. Surrey: Ocean Shipping Consultants.

OSC (2004). *Felixstowe south reconfiguration: The need for deepwater container capacity*. Surrey: Ocean Shipping Consultants.

Palmer, S. (1999). Current port trends in an historical perspective. *Journal for Maritime Research*, *1*(1), 99–111.

Panayides, P. M. (2002). Economic organization of intermodal transport. *Transport Reviews*, *22*(4), 401–414.

Panayides, P. M., & Cullinane, K. (2002). Competitive advantage in liner shipping: A review and research agenda. *International Journal of Maritime Economics*, *4*, 189–209.

Pawlik, T., Stemmler, L., Baird, A. J., & Helch, M. (2011). The value of container terminal investment to ocean carrier strategy. *Maritime Economics and Logistics*, *13*(3), 319–341.

Peters, H. J. F. (2001). Developments in global seatrade and container shipping markets: Their effects on the port industry and private sector involvement. *International Journal of Maritime Economics*, *3*, 3–26.

Porter, M. E. (2000). Locations, clusters and company strategy. In G. Clark, M. P. Feldman & M. S. Gertler (Eds.), *The Oxford handbook of economic geography* (pp. 253–274). Oxford: Oxford University Press.

Psaraftis, H. N. (1998). Strategies for Mediterranean port development. In G. Sciutto & C. A. Brebbia (Eds.), *Maritime Engineering and Ports* (pp. 255–262). Southampton: WIT.

Robinson, R. (2002). Ports as elements in value-driven chain systems: The new paradigm. *Maritime Policy and Management*, *29*(3), 241–255.

Slack, B. (1993). Pawns in the game: Ports in a global transportation system. *Growth and Change*, *24*(4), 579–588.

Slack, B. (1998). Intermodal transportation. In B. Hoyle & R. Knowles (Eds), *Modern Transport Geography* (2nd ed., pp. 263–290). New York: John Wiley & Sons.

Slack, B. (2001, March 27). Globalisation and container shipping. Presentation delivered to the Department of Geography, The University of Hong Kong, Hong Kong.

Slack, B. (2003). The global imperatives of container shipping. In D. Pinder & B. Slack (Eds.), *Shipping and ports in the twenty-first century* (pp. 25–39). London: Routledge.

Slack, B. (2010). Battening down the hatches: How should the maritime industries weather the financial tsunami? *Research in Transportation Economics*, *27*(1), 4–9.

Slack, B., Comtois, C., & Sletmo, G. (1996). Shipping lines as agents of change in the port industry. *Maritime Policy and Management*, *23*(3), 289–300.

Song, D. W. (2003). Port co-opetition in concept and practice. *Maritime Policy and Management*, *30*(1), 29–44.

Song, D. W. (2004). The motivation for port co-opetition: Strategic implications to Korea. *Journal of Shipping and Logistics*, *43*(1), 141–156.

Stubbs, P. C., Tyson, W. J., & Dalvi, M. Q. (1984). *Transport economics* (2nd ed.). London: George Allen & Unwin.

Taaffe, E. J., Gauthier, H. L., & O'Kelly, M. E. (1996). *Geography of transportation* (2nd ed.). New Jersey: Prentice Hall.

Theys, C., Notteboom, T. E., Pallis, A. A., & De Langen, P. W. (2010). The economics behind the awarding of terminals in seaports: Towards a research agenda. *Research in Transportation Economics*, Elsevier, *27*(1), 37–50.

van Klink, H. A., & van den Berg, G. C. (1998). Gateways and intermodalism. *Journal of Transport Geography*, *6*(1), 1–9.

van Ham, J. C. (1998). Changing public port management in the Hamburg-Le Havre range. In G. Sciutto & C. A. Brebbia (Eds.), *Maritime engineering and ports* (pp. 13–21). Southampton: WIT.

Wang, J. J., & Ng, A. K. Y. (2011). The geographical connectedness of Chinese seaports with foreland markets: a new trend? *Tijdschrift voor Economische en Sociale Geografie, 102*(2), 188–204.

Wang, J. J., Ng, A. K. Y., & Olivier, D. (2004). Port governance in China: A review of policies in an era of internationalising port management practices. *Transport Policy, 11*(3), 237–250.

World Bank (2000). *World Bank port reform toolkit*. Washington, DC: The World Bank Group.

World Bank (2007). *World Bank port reform toolkit* (2nd ed.). Washington, DC: The World Bank Group.

Yang, C. (2010). The greater Pearl River Delta cross-border mega-city region and the Hong Kong-Zhuhai-Macau bridge. In C. Mo & Y. H. Kim (Eds.), *The emerging cross-border mega-city region and sustainable transportation* (pp. 82–123). Seoul: KMI.

Chapter 3

Container Flows and Empty Container Repositioning

Ada Suk Fung Ng

Abstract

This chapter explains the impact containerisation has on the various partners of the global supply chain and the challenges companies encounter and the solutions they use in dealing with empty container repositioning.

The phenomenon of imbalanced container flows and its impact on shipping lines, shippers, container haulage companies, port development and the economy are presented. Special attention is given to explain the many solutions companies use to reduce the impact of empty container repositioning, hence tracing out the past research that led to these solutions and pointing to potentially new research directions in the future.

Because of the widespread use of containerisation and the imbalanced container flows that results from globalisation, empty container repositioning will be an ongoing issue for the maritime logistics industry. Many solutions are being used, but there is room for improvement and more research is needed.

Empty container repositioning is an important issue but has not been deemed as such in the literature. This chapter explains the reasons it is important and that its impact is not limited to shipping lines only but affects the whole supply chain.

Keywords: Container flows; empty container repositioning; supply chain collaboration; containerisation

Maritime Logistics: Contemporary Issues
Copyright © 2012 by Emerald Group Publishing Limited
All rights of reproduction in any form reserved
ISBN: 978-1-78052-340-8

3.1. Introduction

The uniformity in size of shipping containers and the ease of their handling have contributed to their success. Their widespread use has led to a safer, more productive, efficient and cost-effective transportation process. They have become an essential part of the international trade. About 15% of the world's seaborne trade is currently containerised. According to the United Nations, container shipping has been growing at an annual rate of around 10% for the last two decades, despite a sharp fall of 9% in 2009 because of the global financial crisis. The total number of containers around the world increased from 16 million twenty-foot equivalent units (TEUs) in 2001 to 27.1 million TEUs in 2009.

Amidst this tremendous growth, container shipping has been suffering from a persistent container flow imbalance. Globalisation has encouraged countries to specialise economically, which has resulted in an imbalance of trade flows among them. The rapidly increasing global trade volume among the major trading regions has caused cargo to move in one direction over time—from the point of production to the point of consumption. The relocation of empty containers from the surplus to the deficit regions has become a challenging and costly operation not only for the shipping lines, as commonly believed, but also for the whole maritime logistics industry.

In the rest of the chapter, we begin with a description of the ways containerisation facilitates trades and the effects it has on the globalisation process. Then we describe the imbalance of container flows as a result of the imbalance of trade flows. After a detailed account on a typical container flow is presented, we explain the impact the imbalance of container flow has on the shipping lines and on the various supply chain partners. We then describe the strategies companies are using and some of the solutions suggested in the literature to deal with the challenge. The last section concludes the chapter.

3.2. Containerisation and Globalisation

Containerisation is considered one of the greatest inventions in the twentieth century. The first shipping container, Ideal X, was invented by Malcolm Mclean in 1956. He was a trucker in the United States with more than 20 years of experience in transporting cargo from inland to ports. He observed that most of the shipments his company handled were sent by a single shipper to a single consignee. The transportation process would be more efficient if the whole 'truck' could be moved to the ship instead of loading and unloading individual packages separately. He bought Pan Atlantic Tanker Company, which later changed its name to Sea-Land Shipping, to continue to experiment with his revolutionary idea. In 1956, he took two old World War II tankers and inserted sockets on the spar deck such that legs of the Ideal X could be locked into these sockets to stabilise the containers during the voyage. In the following years, work was done on standardising the size of the containers. The modern ISO shipping containers are metal boxes with 8 ft wide and either 20 or 40 ft long. The height of the ISO shipping containers is not standardised, however. The most commonly used container is 8 ft 6 in. height, whereas it is 9 ft 6 in. height for high cube.

Before containerisation, cargo was packed in barrels, sacks or wooden crates, with different sizes and shapes. Individual packages were stowed by hand for loading and unloading when moving from land transport to ship and vice versa. It was a labour-intensive and cumbersome process. Inside the port, individual packages were stowed by dock workers from the reception area to the place of rest awaiting loading onto the vessel. These individual packages were then stowed to appropriate holds in the vessel by hand or by simple machinery. As a result, ship could easily spend more time being idle in ports than carrying cargo sailing in waters. This is costly because a ship generates revenue only when it is moving cargo from one place to another in the water. In addition, since cargo was packed in small individual packages and was stowed by hand, the risk of accidents, losses and theft is high.

After containerisation, rather than loading and unloading individual packages again and again in the shipping process, individual packages are loaded and unloaded only once in the entire trip. When transferring from one transport mode to another, the whole container is transferred. It streamlines the process of loading and unloading between land and ship inside the port. This improves greatly the efficiency and reduces the cost of the transportation process. In 1956, loading loose cargo onto a medium-sized ship costed US$ 5.83 per ton, whereas it costed less than US$ 0.16 per ton by using Ideal X.

As a result, containerisation facilitates industrial globalisation and helps reshape the topology of manufacturing supply chains. A manufacturer can reduce its labour cost by relocating its manufacturing plant to countries with lower labour cost. It also provides manufacturers flexibility in choosing where to source raw materials, as it becomes cheaper and more efficient to bring raw materials from overseas. In addition, manufacturers no longer need be close geographically to customers in order to compete for market share. The reduction in transportation cost resulted from containerisation makes selling internationally possible and competitive. Finished goods can be sent and sold profitably to locations with higher selling price without the friction of high transportation cost.

3.3. Imbalance Flows of Containers

Countries have become more specialised economically as a result of globalisation. Because international transportation is cheap and efficient, companies set up their manufacturing plants in countries where labour cost is low and the overall business environment is more favourable for manufacturing in order to reduce their total production cost. As a result, some countries, particularly developing countries in Asia, such as China and Thailand, become the world's manufacturing hinterlands. Their imports are mainly raw materials, which are usually transported as bulk cargo. Meanwhile, they export manufactured products that are containerised. In the other direction are some developed countries, such as the United States and Australia, which are strong consumption markets for manufactured products that are transported as containerised cargo. As more manufacturing plants are moved to developing countries, the volume of export containerised cargo is often lower than import containerised cargo in developed countries. This creates an imbalance of container flows.

Table 3.1 shows cargo flows in the world's three main East–West container trade routes, which link the major industrial hinterlands in South and Southeast Asia with North America and Western Europe. In the trans-Pacific route, there were 13.4 and 11.5 million TEUs flowing eastward in 2008 and 2009, respectively, whereas there were only half of the volume, 6.9 million TEUs, flowing westward. In the United States, 10 million TEUs were imported and 6.6 million TEUs were exported in 1999. In 2009, the import figure was 14.6 million TEUs while the export figure remained at 10.4 million TEUs. This is shown in Table 3.2. We can also see that the imbalance

Table 3.1: Estimated cargo flows on major East–West container trade routes, 2008–2009 (millions of TEUs).

	Trans-Pacific		Europe–Asia-Europe		USA–Europe-USA	
	Far East–North America	North America–Far East	Asia–Europe	Europe–Asia	USA–Europe	Europe–USA
2008	13.4	6.9	13.5	5.2	3.3	3.3
2009	11.5	6.9	11.5	5.5	2.5	2.8

Source: Adapted from Review of Maritime Transport 2010 (Table 1.5), United Nations Publication, UNCTAD/RMT/2010, Sales No. E.10.II.D.4, ISBN 978-92-1-112810-9.

Table 3.2: U.S. international maritime container volumes (millions of TEUs).

Year	Export	Import	Imbalance (import–export)
1999	6.6	10	3.4
2000	6.9	11.1	4.2
2001	6.8	11.3	4.5
2002	6.8	12.9	6.1
2003	7.4	13.9	6.5
2004	8	15.8	7.8
2005	8.7	17.4	9
2006	9	18.6	9.6
2007	10.5	18.5	8
2008	11.3	17	5.7
2009	10.4	14.6	4.2

Source: Adapted from Transportation Statistics Annual Report 2009 (Table 2.4.6), U.S. Department of Transportation, Research and Innovative Technology Administration, Bureau of Transportation Statistics, Washington, DC, 2009.

Table 3.3: Containerised trade in Australia (TEUs) for 2009–2010.

| | 2009–2010 | | | | | |
| | Imports | | | Export | | |
	Full	**Empty**	**Total**	**Full**	**Empty**	**Total**
Melbourne Port Corporation	1,034,742	98,314	1,133,056	766,626	336,951	1,103,577
Sydney Ports Corporation	951,027	25,188	976,215	442,567	508,725	951,292
Port of Brisbane Pty Ltd	405,215	57,914	463,129	258,327	197,542	455,869
Fremantle Ports	263,815	24,648	288,463	178,888	90,092	268,980
Port Adelaide (Flinders)	89,782	47,616	137,398	118,549	18,554	137,103
Other	143,777	60,531	204,308	148,722	60,973	209,745
Total	2,888,358	314,211	3,202,569	1,913,729	1,212,837	3,126,566

Source: Adapted from Trade Statistics 2010, Ports Australia. Adapted with permission.

between import and export increased as the total trade increased. A similar trend appeared in the Asia–Europe route; there were 13.5 and 11.5 million TEUs moving from Asia to Europe, compared with only 5.2 and 5.5 million TEUs moving from Europe to Asia, in 2008 and 2009, respectively.

The North–South trades link Europe, Asia and North America with countries in the southern hemisphere. Compared with the East–West routes, the North–South routes have a smaller container volume. Australia is one of the countries suffering from a surplus of empty containers in the North–South routes. Table 3.3 shows the container movement in and out of Australia during the 2009–2010 period. There was an imbalance of cargo flows with 2.9 million TEUs of full containers imported and only 1.9 million TEUs of full containers exported. During the same period, there were 1.2 million TEUs of empty containers exported, which accounted for 38.8% of the total export.

3.4. Container Flow

A typical container flow involves ports, container depots, importers and exporters. Container flows through landmasses and oceans, as shown in Figure 3.1. After a vessel carrying imported containers arrives at the port of destination, laden containers are picked up by importers and are unloaded at the importers' premises. Then they are returned to a pre-defined location, which is either a depot of the shipping line or an empty container park. This has to be done within the free unloading period; otherwise, demurrage charge is incurred. Before an empty

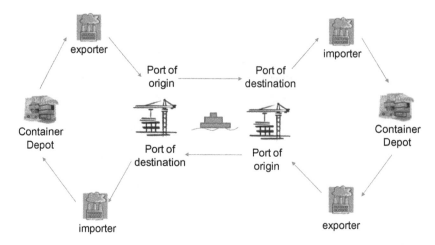

Figure 3.1: Basic container flow

container can be used to fulfil the demand from exporters, it is usually surveyed at a depot of the shipping line to ensure the quality of the container is fit for serving exporters. This is extremely important for food grade containers. If repair work is needed, it will be done before the container is used to fulfil the exporter's demand. However, in countries with high labour cost, such as Australia and the United States, containers that require a high level of repair work are sent to the empty container park waiting for global repositioning. These containers are repaired in an export-oriented country where labour cost is lower.

After being surveyed and repaired, empty containers are sent to exporters' premises, where the containers are stuffed. Finally, they are sent to the terminal (port of origin) for export. Ideally, if every imported container could be filled by an exporter and used for export, there would not be any empty container repositioning issue. However, because of the imbalance of trade, shipping lines have to relocate empty containers from the surplus areas to the deficit areas. It is estimated that around US$ 15 billion was spent in empty container repositioning in 2002. It accounted for around 27% of the total spending in container management (Song et al., 2005). An effective empty container repositioning strategy can save a large amount of operational cost. Therefore, the maritime logistics industry cannot afford to ignore the empty container repositioning issue.

3.5. Impacts to Shipping Lines and Supply Chain Partners

Currently, there are two major groups that own marine (ISO) containers: shipping lines and leasing companies. In general, shipping lines and container leasing companies have different perspectives on empty container management. While the former are handling containers as transportation equipment, the latter consider containers as their core assets. Container leasing companies typically focus on the depreciation of empty containers and try to amortise the investment and generate sustainable profits during the lease period. Because the lessees, usually shipping lines, are responsible for the full management of empty containers, including their repositioning and repair, leasing companies tend to ignore the issue of empty container repositioning because they can still make a profit even when their containers become empty within the lease period.

Moreover, to avoid off-hire in the high empty container surplus areas, they take into account of the issue of empty container repositioning in the leasing arrangements. When a shipping line off-hires empty containers at a surplus area, which has a high number of idle empty containers, additional surcharge is imposed. Even so, only a fixed number of off-hires of empty containers in these areas are accepted. Obviously, shipping lines are seriously affected by the imbalance of trade. The effects are also passed onto other partners in the supply chain, such as shippers and container haulage companies.

3.5.1. *Impacts to Shipping Lines*

With the tremendous growth of international trade and globalisation, empty container management is no longer an issue shipping lines can afford to ignore due to the increasing number of idle empty containers. It is estimated that around US$ 15 billion was spent in empty container repositioning in 2002. It accounted for around 27% of the total spending in container management (Song et al., 2005). This directly impacts profitability and the competitive advantages of shipping lines. It is viewed as one of the most complicated problems for shipping lines in achieving cost minimisation and profit maximisation.

3.5.1.1. Inventory cost in the surplus areas Because of the imbalance of trade, containers are accumulated in the surplus areas where the demand is less than the supply of imported full containers. Before these excess empty containers are repositioned to the deficit areas to fulfil demand, they are usually stored in an empty container park before repositioning. This imposes a high inventory cost to shipping lines in the surplus areas.

3.5.1.2. Operational costs Even though empty container repositioning is usually piggybacked on the regular liner services, fuel and handling cost is still incurred and added to the cost of operating these liner services. In some areas such as Southeast Asia, empty containers are highly deficit in the peak season and dedicated vessels are used to transport empty containers from the regional hub to the area. In this case, the empty container repositioning cost includes vessel chartering cost, fuel cost and container handling cost and no revenue can be generated in the voyage.

3.5.1.3. Utilisation of equipment and vessel space For shipping lines, its container fleet is considered as transportation equipment with a lifespan that ranges between 10 and 15 years, depending on the level of usage and preventative maintenance such as rust treatment. A container cannot generate revenue when it is idle or is repositioned. Because of the imbalance of trade, a large number of containers are idle or are repositioned. Because of the lower utilisation of containers, a shipping line has to invest in more new containers, resulting in a larger container fleet size that requires additional working capital.

3.5.1.4. Customer satisfaction   The longer empty containers become idle in the surplus areas, the more unfulfilled customers' requests are in the deficit areas. Without an efficient and effective empty container repositioning strategy at the global scale, shipping lines would suffer from the severe problem of lost sales in the deficit areas, which would result in a lower level of customer satisfaction. To alleviate this problem, shipping lines reposition excess empty container inventory overseas by regular services. With a limited vessel fleet size, it is crucial to allocate vessel slots to transport both laden and empty containers. While shipping lines generate revenue by transporting laden containers, they earn nothing when vessel slots are used for empty containers. Although empty container repositioning does not generate revenue, shipping lines need to move empty containers to fulfil customer demand in the deficit areas. If any shipping line employs effective strategies in allocating empty containers to fulfil requests from customers, it is able to gain competitive advantages in terms of cost-effectiveness and improve its customer satisfaction.

3.5.2. Impacts to Shippers

The negative impact of inefficient handling of empty repositioning is not limited to the shipping lines. It flows through to the shippers in the supply chain. From Table 3.1 we can see that there is an imbalance in the trans-Pacific route. The number of containers that flow from Asia to the United States is higher than that of the back haul. In order to offset losses in the back haul and the repositioning cost, shipping lines normally impose a higher freight rate in the head haul. We can see from Table 3.4 that the head haul rate is 50–80% higher than the back haul rate.

In the deficit areas, it is clear that the challenge is the insufficient supply of empty containers. The problem becomes more serious when demand is higher during the peak season. If shipping lines cannot reallocate empty containers at the regional and global scales effectively, they will not have sufficient empty containers to fulfil requests from customers. This not only hurts the profitability of the shipping lines, but also creates an adverse effect in the demand forecast, a process illustrated in Figure 3.2. If exporters experience unfulfilled demand or delayed services because of insufficient availability of empty containers, their confidence in container availability will decrease. They will try to secure empty containers for export in various ways. One way is to book the empty container when the expected date of pick-up is still uncertain. Alternatively, shippers may double book with multiple shipping lines, resulting in last minute cancellations. In both cases, it becomes more difficult for shipping lines to forecast the demand of empty containers. As a result, the uncertainty in the availability of empty container is worsened.

Table 3.4: Freight rates per TEU (in dollars).

	Trans-Pacific		Europe–Asia		Transatlantic	
	Asia–US	US–Asia	Europe–Asia	Asia–Europe	US–Europe	Europe–US
2008						
1st Quarter	1757	845	1064	2030	1261	1637
2nd Quarter	1844	987	1104	1937	1381	1610
3rd Quarter	1934	1170	1141	1837	1644	1600
4th Quarter	1890	1196	1109	1619	1731	1600
2009						
1st Quarter	1670	913	853	1023	1481	1325
2nd Quarter	1383	802	742	897	1431	1168
3rd Quarter	1232	817	787	1061	1424	1133
4th Quarter	1322	883	920	1422	1527	1250

Source: Adapted from Review of Maritime Transport 2010 (Table 4.5), United Nations Publication, UNCTAD/RMT/2010, Sales No. E.10.II.D.4, ISBN 978-92-1-112810-9.

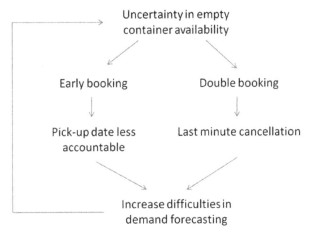

Figure 3.2: Container booking adverse cycle

3.5.3. *Impacts to Container Haulage Companies*

Most exporters and importers do not have their own cranes to lift containers in their yard. Therefore, when a full container is delivered to an importer for cargo unloading, not only the laden container but also the trailer remains in the premise of the importer. The trailer is returned to the haulage company only after the importer has finished unloading and returned the empty container to the depot of the shipping line. Similarly, when an exporter requests an empty container, the haulage company moves the empty container from the depot of the shipping line to the premise of the exporter. Both the empty container and the trailer stay in the premise of the exporter for cargo loading. The trailer can only be used after the loading process is finished and the full container is sent to the terminal for export. Because of this, the trailer–mover ratio of a container haulage company is usually higher than 1. If exporters are uncertain of the availability of empty containers, they will order empty containers earlier. As a result, the period of time they hold the empty container and the trailer becomes longer. The longer the shippers keep the container and in turn the trailer, the higher is the ratio. As a result, the utilisation rate of trailer is lower and extra cost is needed for investing in more trailers.

3.5.4.   *Impacts to Port Development*

As the container trade grows, the number of empty container increases accordingly in the surplus areas. Take the case of Sydney Ports as an example of capacity constraint in the surplus areas. Sydney Ports is faced with an increasing number of empty containers, which diminishes its capacity and efficiency in its container parks. In the 2009–2010 financial year, container throughput at Sydney Ports exceeded 1.9 million TEUs. The average inventory level in the empty container parks, which had a total maximum capacity of 60,000 TEUs, was estimated to be 41,312 TEUs, or 2.17% of the port throughput. It is estimated that the port throughput will rise to 3.2 million TEUs in 2021. In order to maintain the same level of efficiency, it is estimated that a total capacity of 92,700 TEUs, a 54% increase, is needed at the empty container parks. Empty containers are usually stored in empty container parks located in the port area. This creates pressure to port development as space is scarce in the port area. It is a serious issue for depot operators and port operators who are faced with limited storage capacity and facility.

In addition, the dispatching of empty containers to the terminal for global relocation sometimes adds pressure to the already congested landside traffic in the port area. Typically, after a vessel finds itself with empty slots that are not filled by laden containers, empty containers are then dispatched to the terminal at the last moment to fill the empty slots on the vessel. Therefore, unlike the flow of regular cargo that is relatively stable, the flow of empty containers can appear erratic and spike whenever a dispatch happens just before the vessel departs.

3.5.5.   *Impacts to the Whole Supply Chain and Economy of the Region*

Given the current imbalanced flow of cargo in the world market, the issue of empty container repositioning can be considered as a significant challenge not only to the shipping industry, but also to all the parties in the global supply chain. Although it is reasonable to think that shipping lines can cover these costs, they typically recover the storage cost and the other costs of repositioning of empty containers by charging more for full containers in a number of export routes. If shipping lines can reallocate empty containers globally at lower costs, those surcharges that shipping lines usually impose on full containers in a number of export routes should decrease. This means that if shipping lines can reposition empty containers cost effectively, shipping lines may be able to offer cheaper ocean transport for their customers. It ultimately creates advantages for both exporters in the deficit areas and importers in the surplus areas. The former could enjoy the lower costs to ship containerised cargo while the latter could obtain cheaper imported cargo. Consequently, it is possible for all parties in the global supply chain to improve their competitiveness, particularly in terms of cost-effectiveness.

Empty containers are one of the most essential equipment used in containerised cargo trade. While we can concentrate on the efficiency and effectiveness of the forward cargo flow, we cannot set aside the reverse logistics of this essential equipment. The reverse flow of empty containers actually facilitates the forward flow of cargo. Without effective and efficient management of this reverse flow of essential equipment, there will not be an efficient and effective forward flow of cargo. The adverse effect would eventually affect the performance of the entire supply chain and jeopardise international trade.

3.6.   Current Practices and Suggested Solutions

Shipping lines can mitigate the impact of imbalanced container flows by taking internal and external actions. Internal actions include container management at both the strategic and the operational levels. The aim is to take empty container repositioning into consideration starting from the strategic level, such as liner network design and vessel fleet planning and management, and extend to the operational level. External actions include collaboration with other supply chain partners, development of innovative technology in foldable containers, and investigation of new markets that can utilise empty containers in the back haul journey.

3.6.1.   Internal Mitigating Strategies

As mentioned before, shipping lines spend around 27% of the total container management cost in empty container repositioning. They are the ones who are impacted directly and deeply. Therefore, they benefit the most by considering actions at all planning levels that would mitigate the effect of imbalanced container flows.

3.6.1.1.   Strategic planning   Effective and efficient container management should start at the strategic planning level of a shipping line. At this level, a shipping line defines its business direction and makes decisions on resource management. This includes liner network design and vessel fleet size planning. In liner network design, shipping lines decide on the ports to be called according to the estimated future demand of laden containers at each potential port. In fleet size planning, shipping lines plan ahead for the fleet size of container vessels and the number of vessels they need in each fleet within a longer planning horizon, as a result of the long lead time in building container vessels. Service network design and fleet size planning in air and road transport are well studied in the literature. However, similar studies in ocean transport, liner shipping in particular, are scarce. The work of Dantzig and Fulkerson (1954) is considered as the first in the literature to study ship network routing issues. However, their work focuses on tankers routing. Cho and Perakis (1996) develop a linear programming model to determine the optimal fleet size and liner network design. Fagerholt (1999) formulates the fleet size planning issue as a multi-trip vehicle routing problem and solves with a three-stage algorithm. Xie, Wang, and Chen (2000) provide a dynamic model for the optimal fleet planning issue. Hsu and Hsieh (2007) study the fleet planning and scheduling problem in a hub-and-spoke network. Similarly, Bendall and Stent (2001) investigate the optimal fleet planning problem with an application in a short sea shipping hub-and-spoke network. Christiansen, Fagerholt, and Ronen (2004) provide a detailed review on ship routing and scheduling. However, empty container repositioning is not considered in these studies.

Research that considers empty container management at the strategic level appears in the literature only recently. Song et al. (2005) assign global trade into a pipe network by considering transhipment and direct shipment. It formulates empty container movements as the difference between the total number of import containers and export containers. Similarly, Shintani, Imai, Nishimura, and Stratos (2007) determine the voyage itinerary, ship size and calling frequency by considering both laden and empty container movements. However, reducing the need of empty container repositioning is not an objective of their research, as mentioned by Song et al. (2005). More research needs to be done on how to reduce the number of empty containers in repositioning. In practice, the issue of empty container repositioning is seldom taken into consideration explicitly at this planning level. Shipping lines tend to concentrate on making profits and increasing their market share. In fact, they reduce their risk from unused equipment, particularly empty containers, during the low demand period by leasing a proportion of those from leasing companies.

3.6.1.2. Operational planning   Planning at the operational level focuses on the day-to-day operational activities. For container movement by sea transportation, most key issues regarding vessel fleet, shipping routes, port callings and container fleet capacities have already been set at the strategic level. Therefore, the critical decision to make at this level is related to the use of vessel capacities at each port and the efficiency and effectiveness of the inland container dispatching process.

Landside container dispatching   Empty container repositioning at the regional scale involves empty container allocations between the surplus and the deficit regions that are connected by land transport. Empty containers are moved over land by rail and sometimes by trucks at a regional level to meet customer demand. Shipping lines have to manage the inland movement of both laden and empty containers in a cost-effective and time-efficient manner such that laden imported containers are delivered to importers on time and empty containers are dispatched efficiently to fulfil the demand from exporters.

Optimal flow management reduces the number of unnecessary flow of containers, especially empty containers, in a region. As a result, it is more cost-effective and efficient. Crainic, Gendreau, and Dejax (1993) provide dynamic and stochastic models for the land container dispatching operation including landside empty container repositioning among depots. Crainic, Gendreau, Soriano, and Toulouse (1993) look at the location/allocation problem by using a tabu search heuristic to find the optimal locations of depots. Customers are allocated to these depots. The model is modified and used in different applications in Gendron and Crainic (1997), Gendron, Potvin, and Soriano (2003) and Cheung and Chen (1998). Besides, Choong, Cole, and Kutanoglu (2002) study the optimal planning horizon in the landside container dispatching problem.

The other group of researchers focuses on the truck routing issue when dispatching laden and empty containers at the local level. Zhang, Yun, and Kopfer (2010) model the issue as an extension of the travelling salesman problem with time window consideration. Caris and Janssens (2009) model it as a full truckload pick-up and delivery problem with time window consideration. Other studies are Zhang, Yun, and Moon (2009), Coslovich, Pesenti, and Ukovich (2006), Imai, Nishimura and Current (2007) and Namboothiri and Erera (2008). Instead of providing a mathematical model to improve the efficiency of the container dispatching operations, Cheung, Shi, Powell, and Simao (2008) provide an attribute-decision model to investigate system performance under various cross-border regulatory policies.

However, none of these studies, except Cheung et al. (2008), considers the complication of equipment usage in the container dispatching process. Basically, there are four different types of transportation trips with different equipment requirements, as shown in Figure 3.3. When an import laden container arrives, a prime mover with a trailer is dispatched to the terminal to pick up the container and deliver the container to the importer. Since importers and exporters often do not have their own cranes, the container together with the trailer will be left with the importer for the unloading of cargo. After the cargo is unloaded, a prime mover is dispatched to pick up the empty container and haul it back to the depot for surveying and maintenance. When an exporter requires an empty container, a prime mover with a trailer is dispatched to pick up an empty container from the depot and deliver to the premise of the exporter. Again, the empty container and the trailer will stay with the exporter. When the loading process is finished, a prime mover is dispatched to collect the laden container and move it to the terminal for export. As we see, the equipment requirements for different trips complicate the dispatching process. Therefore, this should be considered in container truck routing and scheduling.

Global empty container repositioning Because of the imbalance of international trade mentioned before, even the best landside dispatching management cannot prevent the accumulation of empty containers in the surplus areas and unfulfilled demand in the deficit areas. Therefore, empty containers are repositioned globally from the surplus areas to the deficit areas. Often, this level of repositioning is done by

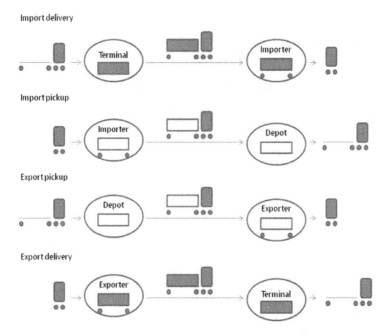

Figure 3.3: Different type container dispatching trips

using the empty slots of the vessels that serve the regular liner service. Another way of moving empty containers from import-oriented regions to export-oriented regions is to charter dedicated vessels. These vessels are not deployed in the regular liner services; no laden container with a specific destination is loaded on board. The relocation costs in this case are higher. This method is used only in deficit regions where extremely high demand cannot be met by repositioning through regular service alone. For example, this happens in Asia during peak seasons. Container management at this level aims to organise movement of empty containers between regions such that empty container storage and repositioning costs are minimised and the demand at the global level is fulfilled.

Studies in global empty container repositioning are generally quite recent. Li, Leung, Wu, and Liu (2007) take into consideration the inventory of multiple ports to decide on the amount of empty containers to be transported from the surplus areas to the deficit areas. Wong, Lau, and Mak (2010) study the empty container repositioning problem by using dedicated shuttle services, with only single container type considered. Song (2007) focuses on empty container shuttle services. Random customer demand and finite reposition capacity are considered in order to obtain an optimal stationary policy. Compared with studies in dedicated services, there are more articles on empty container repositioning by using regular liner services. Lam, Lee, and Tang (2007) study the empty container allocation problem among seaports. Their study concentrates on a two-port and two-voyage liner system which can be extended to the multiple-ports and multiple-voyages system. Moon, Ngoc, and

Hur (2010) model the empty container repositioning issue with leasing and purchasing considerations, with only one shipping route considered. On the other hand, Song and Dong (2008) examine the issue by considering a cyclic liner network. Feng and Chang (2010) study the issue by using revenue management modelling approach. Feng and Chang (2008) provide case studies in the intra-Asia liner shipping of Taiwan Liner Shipping Company. Most recently, Song and Dong (2011) compare two repositioning policies for global empty container repositioning by using daily services. They show that a policy that coordinates all the ports in a shipping route is more efficient and cost-effective than a policy that balances container flows between port pairs. Finally, Shen and Khoong (1995) provide a decision support framework for container distribution planning.

3.6.1.3. Other commonly used repositioning policies In addition to the empty container repositioning policies mentioned above, shipping lines often charter short-term leases from container leasing companies during the peak season to fulfil the demand from exporters. Shipping lines are usually allowed to choose the location to return the empty containers from a list of off-hiring locations. Shipping lines can minimise their repositioning cost while the leasing company is protected from having to relocate the container. Shipping lines can also consider purchasing new containers, if the purchasing cost is lower than the relocation cost. Alternatively, shipping lines might scrap a container in a surplus area, when it is close to its end of life to remove the need for relocating it to a deficit area. Substitution policies are also commonly used in the industry to improve the availability of empty containers. Shipping lines may provide an exporter another type of container that can also serve the particular requirement of that exporter. The substitutes are usually premium grade for which the exporter normally needs to pay an extra charge. For example, a shipping line can provide the exporter a reefer, where temperature can be controlled, to substitute for a food grade dry container for carrying food products.

3.6.2. *External Mitigating Strategies*

It is important to tackle the issue of empty container repositioning by using internal mitigating strategies. However, external mitigating strategies can be used to complement the internal mitigating strategies mentioned in the Section 3.6.1.

3.6.2.1. Collaborations between supply chain partners As mentioned in the Section 3.5, the impact of imbalanced container flow is not limited to shipping lines only, but passes onto other partners in the supply chain. In the end, the performance of the whole supply chain is affected. As a result, supply chain partners should collaborate to solve the problem together. Container flow visibility plays an important role in supply chain collaboration. In practice, various parties in the supply chain have their own tracking system. RFID tags are used in ocean terminal to track the movement of containers inside the terminal. Trucking and container haulage companies have GPS systems attached to their movers and trucks to identify their locations and the containers they are carrying. Shipping lines know whether a container is in a depot or in an empty container park. However, because of the concern that the release of the data may be misused by other parties and may not be advantageous, companies usually keep the information proprietary. This greatly reduces container flow visibility.

One of the difficulties in container management is the uncertainty in demand forecast. Even when shippers book the container in advance, often the day of pick-up is unpredictable. Currently, shipping lines set up contracts with big shippers, such as big retail chains or freight forwarding companies. Shippers let shipping lines know their estimated number of empty containers needed, and the shipping lines guarantee a certain number of empty containers are available to the shippers. This helps the shipping lines in their demand forecast, which leads to a slimmer inventory needed in the surplus areas and allows more empty containers to be sent to the deficit areas to fulfil the demand. It also provides the shipper security in getting empty containers. However, this kind of arrangement accounts for only a small proportion of business of a shipping line.

Recently, a few one-stop-shopping business platforms are proposed in the industry. These platforms would offer to a certain extent container flow visibility in different systems. They would provide shippers information about the location of containers and empty container availability of each shipping line. When container availability is transparent to shippers, double booking is no longer needed to secure empty containers for export. This would reduce the uncertainty in the demand forecast of and the inventory level needed for empty containers for the shipping lines. It would reduce the high trailer–mover ratio of container haulage companies.

Empty containers must be surveyed before they can be used by an exporter. This is often done in the depot of the shipping lines. After cargo unloading at the premises of the importers, empty containers are hauled to the shipping lines' depot before they can be used by exporters. This creates unnecessary empty runs in the empty container dispatching process. If container surveying is done at the premises of the shippers instead, the closest exporter may be identified and containers that pass the quality test can be dispatched directly from the importer to the exporter. This would improve the efficiency of the inland container dispatching process.

3.6.2.2. Foldable containers   If containers can be folded during repositioning, more empty containers can be carried by regular liner services. This can save a significant amount of repositioning costs. Foldable containers can also save the storage space for empty containers in the empty container parks at the surplus areas. With these advantages, foldable containers are very attractive to shipping lines that are burdened with repositioning. In fact, it is not a new concept in the industry, as engineers have been racing to provide new designs of foldable containers in the past few decades.

The main issue of foldable containers occurs in the folding and unfolding process. These additional steps require extra time and manpower in handling the containers, which increases the cost in the repositioning process. In addition, special equipment is needed during the folding and unfolding process. Even though foldable containers have been available in the market for a few decades, the technology is yet to be standardised, with different designs of foldable containers requiring different kinds of equipment. Given that terminals or container depots may not have the right equipment for the folding and unfolding of the containers, shipping lines are hesitant to adopt the technology.

Another issue of foldable containers is its durability. To be able to be folded, the sides of the container are usually joined by hinges and joints. As a result, the container is not able to withstand the rough handling in the transportation process. Also it is not as stable when it is being stacked up. As a result, it incurs a high maintenance cost for the shipping lines. Because of the complexity of the design, the purchasing cost is usually higher.

3.6.2.3. New market investigation   Instead of passively trying to reduce the repositioning costs, shipping lines can also actively look for new opportunities in the back haul market. Products that are transported as bulk shipment are one of the markets shipping lines should focus on. In some container surplus areas, such as Australia and the United States, there are quite a large amount of exporting cargo that are transported as bulk shipment. One of the characteristics of bulk shipping is that it is the shippers who bear the cost of repositioning the empty bulk vessels back to the origin or to the origin of the next shipment. With the rising chartering cost of bulk vessels, the shippers of bulk shipping are looking for a more cost-effective way to ship their cargo. If container shipping lines provide a concession freight rate in those back haul routes to these bulk cargo shippers to offset the extra handling cost needed for containerised shipping, they may be able to attract these shippers to ship their bulk cargo in containers. This can cover at least the repositioning cost needed for transporting empty containers on the back haul routes.

The soybean industry in the United States is one example. The U.S. soybean export council has done a study in transporting soybean as containerised cargo (USSEC, 2011). As there are more containerised cargo flowing from Asia to the United States, shipping lines have to reposition empty containers back to Asia. Any cargo flowing from the United States to Asia will reduce the repositioning cost of the shipping lines. Therefore, shipping lines usually do not mind offering a lower freight rate on the back haul routes. Given the rising freight rate of bulk shipping to Asia and the much longer turnaround time of bulk shipping than containerised shipping, the U.S. soybean export council has identified that transporting soybean as containerised cargo would create a win-win situation for both the soybean industry and the shipping lines.

Recycling and reverse logistics offer another new market. They have grown in importance in the logistics and the manufacturing industry as the global community becomes more aware of its environmental impact. One of the phenomena that results from globalisation is that most of the export-oriented countries are strong in manufacturing. They import raw materials by bulk shipping and produce manufactured products that are exported as containerised cargo. These products are usually consumed in strong consumption markets such as the United States and Australia, which are also import-oriented countries. Often, these countries have strict regulations in reusing and recycling end-of-life products, especially electronic products. Meanwhile, it is expensive to recycle these products in these countries as labour cost is high. Since export-oriented countries have low labour costs and they often have a strong manufacturing industry, reusable materials from the recycling process can be directly used for manufacturing. When these end-of-life products are transported to the export-oriented countries, it creates a win-win situation for the manufacturing and the recycling industry as well as the shipping lines.

3.7. Conclusion

Since the invention of containers in the 1950s, containerisation as a means of transporting cargo has become dominant in the maritime logistics industry. The imbalanced flow of international trade that results from globalisation has brought with it the phenomenon of imbalanced container flow. If left alone, empty containers would accumulate in the consumption markets while insufficient supply of them in the manufacturing countries would affect the efficiency of export. We saw how serious the issue has become in the major trading routes, the three East–West container routes in particular. By understanding the process of container flow, we learned that shipping lines are not the only ones affected by the empty container repositioning problem, but rather the problem impacts all the partners in the supply chain. To the shipping lines, the need to reposition empty containers globally adds to the inventory and operational cost, raises their working capital due to a larger investment in containers and creates a delicate balance between cost minimisation and satisfaction of customers' demand of empty containers. To the shippers, uncertainty of the availability of empty containers has led some to adopt booking policies that make forecasting the demand of empty containers even more difficult. We saw also how empty containers are taken into consideration in port planning and development.

Companies reduce the impact of empty container repositioning by improving on its liner network design and vessel fleet size planning at the strategic level and on its landside container dispatching and global empty container repositioning at the operational level. They also use solutions that involve other parties, including collaboration with other supply chain partners, deployment of innovative technology such as foldable containers, and investigation of new markets for empty containers. Since so much is at stake and there is room to improve on the current practices, research on empty container repositioning is bound to grow in the years to come.

References

Bendall, H. B., & Stent, A. F. (2001). A scheduling model for a high speed container ship service: A hub and spoke short-sea application. *International Journal Maritime Economist*, *3*(3), 262–277.

Caris, A., & Janssens, G. K. (2009). A local search heuristic for the pre- and end-haulage of intermodal container terminals. *Computers and Operations Research*, *36*(10), 2763–2772.

Cheung, R. K., & Chen, C. (1998). A two-stage stochastic network model and solution methods for the dynamic empty container allocation problem. *Transportation Science*, *32*(2), 142–162.

Cheung, R. K., Shi, N., Powell, W. B., & Simao, H. P. (2008). An attribute-decision model for cross-border drayage problem. *Transportation Research Part E, 44*(2), 217–234.

Cho, S. C., & Perakis, A. N. (1996). Optimal liner fleet routing strategies. *Maritime Policy and Management, 23*(3), 249–259.

Choong, S. T., Cole, M. H., & Kutanoglu, E. (2002). Empty Container management for intermodal transportation networks. *Transportation Research Part E, 38*(6), 423–438.

Christiansen, M., Fagerholt, K., & Ronen, D. (2004). Ship routing and scheduling: Status and perspectives. *Transportation Science, 38*(1), 1–18.

Coslovich, L., Pesenti, R., & Ukovich, W. (2006). Minimizing fleet operating costs for a container transportation company. *European Journal of Operational Research, 171*(3), 776–786.

Crainic, T. G., Gendreau, M., & Dejax, P. (1993). Dynamic and stochastic-models for the allocation of empty containers. *Operations Research, 41*(1), 102–126.

Crainic, T. G., Gendreau, M., Soriano, P., & Toulouse, M. (1993). A tabu search procedure for multicommodity location/allocation with balancing requirements. *Annals of Operations Research, 41*(4), 359–383.

Dantzig, G. B., & Fulkerson, D. R. (1954). Minimizing the number of tankers to meet a fixed schedule. *Naval Research Logistics Quarterly, 1*(3), 217–222.

Fagerholt, K. (1999). Optimal fleet design in a ship routing problem. *International Transactions in Operational Research, 6*(5), 453–464.

Feng, C. M., & Chang, C. H. (2008). Empty container reposition planning for intra-Asia liner shipping. *Maritime Policy and Management, 35*(5), 469–489.

Feng, C. M., & Chang, C. H. (2010). Optimal slot allocation with empty container reposition problem for Asia ocean carriers. *International Journal of Shipping and Transport Logistics, 2*(1), 22–43.

Gendron, B., & Crainic, T. G. (1997). A parallel branch-and-bound algorithm for multicommodity location with balancing requirements. *Computers and Operations Research, 24*(9), 829–847.

Gendron, B., Potvin, J. Y., & Soriano, P. (2003). A tabu search with slope scaling for the multicommodity capacitated location problem with balancing requirements. *Annals of Operations Research, 122*(1), 193–217.

Hsu, C. I., & Hsieh, Y. P. (2007). Routing, ship size, and sailing frequency decision-making for a maritime hub-and-spoke container network. *Mathematical and Computer Modelling, 45*(7), 899–916.

Imai, A., Nishimura, E., & Current, J. (2007). A Lagrangian relaxation-based heuristic for the vehicle routing with full container load. *European Journal of Operational Research, 176*(1), 87–105.

Lam, S. W., Lee, L. H., & Tang, L. C. (2007). An approximate dynamic programming approach for the empty container allocation problem. *Transportation Research Part C, 15*(4), 265–277.

Li, J. A., Leung, S. C. H., Wu, Y., & Liu, K. (2007). Allocation of empty containers between multi-ports. *European Journal of Operations Research, 182*(1), 400–412.

Moon, I. K., Ngoc, A. D. D., & Hur, Y. S. (2010). Positioning empty containers among multiple ports with leasing and purchasing considerations. *OR Spectrum, 32*(3), 765–786.

Namboothiri, R., & Erera, A. L. (2008). Planning local container drayage operations given a port access appointment system. *Transportation Research Part E, 44*(2), 185–202.

Shen, W. S., & Khoong, C. M. (1995). A DSS for empty container distribution planning. *Decision Support System, 15*(1), 75–82.

Shintani, K., Imai, A., Nishimura, E., & Stratos, P. (2007). The container shipping network design problem with empty container repositioning. *Transportation Research Part E, 43*(1), 39–59.

Song, D. P. (2007). Characterizing optimal empty container reposition policy in periodic-review shuttle service systems. *Journal of the Operational Research Society, 58*(1), 122–133.

Song, D. P., & Dong, J. X. (2008). Empty container management in cyclic shipping routes. *Maritime Economics and Logistics, 10*(4), 335–361.

Song, D. P., & Dong, J. X. (2011). Flow balancing-based empty container repositioning in typical shipping service routes. *Maritime Economics and Logistics, 13*(1), 61–77.

Song, D. P., Zhang, J., Carter, J., Field, T., Marshall, J., Polak, J., et al. (2005). On cost-efficiency of the global container shipping network. *Maritime Policy and Management, 32*(1), 15–30.

USSEC (2011, August 16). Containerized shipping: Opportunities for soy product. US Soybean Export Council. Retrieved from http://www.ussec.org/resources/USSEC_container.pdf

Wong, E. Y. C., Lau, H. Y. K., & Mak, K. L. (2010). Immunity-based evolutionary algorithm for optimal global container repositioning in liner shipping. *OR Spectrum, 32*(3), 739–763.

Xie, X., Wang, T., & Chen, D. (2000). A dynamic model and algorithm for fleet planning. *Maritime Policy and Management, 27*(1), 53–63.

Zhang, R., Yun, W. Y., & Kopfer, H. (2010). Heuristic-based truck scheduling for inland container transportation. *OR Spectrum, 32*(3), 787–808.

Zhang, R. Y., Yun, W. Y., & Moon, I. (2009). A reactive Tabu search algorithm for the multi-depot container truck transportation problem. *Transportation Research Part E, 45*(6), 904–914.

Chapter 4

Port Congestion and Implications to Maritime Logistics

Hilde Meersman, Eddy Van de Voorde and Thierry Vanelslander

Abstract

Ports are widely recognised as crucial nodes in international trade and transport. However, for various reasons, capacity does not always match demand: sometimes there is overcapacity, whereas in other cases, demand exceeds capacity and there is a shortage of the latter. This chapter therefore looks at where port congestion occurs, both globally and in the port-calling chain; it analyses actual responses by various chain actors, and it sheds some light on potential future evolution and reaction patterns.

Congestion, in general, can feature various forms of appearance: it can be more or less hidden, featuring congestion costs, or it can be visually present, featuring queues which are building up. The chapter discerns eight zones in the port-calling chain where congestion may emerge. As a result of a wide literature search, supplemented with a survey, it can first of all be observed that quite some congestion seems to occur, globally spread, and hitting larger as well as smaller ports. Most of the congestion is generated at the terminals, hinterland connection points and hinterland transport itself.

In terms of reaction patterns, one would assume that pricing throughout the system is adapted in such way that demand equals capacity. In practice, prices are hardly making any effort to make marginal revenue equal marginal cost. The reason is mainly that the power balance is quite strongly in favour of shipping companies, who impose on port and port operators the need to expand capacity at low fees. Port operators, in turn, apply various kinds of technical and procedural adaptations. The same is true for hinterland operators.

Looking towards the future, it seems that with the increase in world trade, the risk of port congestion will be even more outspoken, be it in some parts of

Maritime Logistics: Contemporary Issues
ISBN: 978-1-78052-340-8

the world more than in others. It is also very much likely that most problems will occur landside, as this is the part of the chain where solutions are least easy: who is going to take the initiative, how will co-ordination take place and where will the funding come from? Most actors seem to be aware of this trend, and seek for solutions like dedicated terminals and vertical integration or co-operation.

With the above observations, the chapter sheds some light on where the future needs and trends in the abatement of capacity will lie. It is therefore useful from a scientific point of view as well as with an eye on policy-making and operational port management.

Keywords: Port congestion; maritime access; berths; terminal; hinterland connection

4.1. Introduction

Ports more than ever before are important nodes in logistics chains. On the one hand, they are important as their core activity, loading and unloading of goods, is key to international trade and transport of goods. On the other hand, they are also important as their activity represents a relatively large share in the total chain cost. For these reasons, port activity is increasingly required to fit perfectly into the logistics chains of which seaports are an integral part. In practice, this is by far not always the case. One of the important phenomena preventing a match between ports and their logistics chains is congestion.

It speaks for itself that congestion will have a detrimental impact on the generalised cost and on the overall transport or throughput performance. After all, to a shipping company, congestion implies time loss and thus a higher generalised cost. However, congestion is also problematic for the other port actors. Vessels whose arrival at berth is delayed through congestion may be difficult to fit into the loading and unloading schedule of the terminal operator. This will have implications for capacity management and result in higher costs. The same holds for other actors, including in the fields of storage and hinterland transportation. Moreover, a knock-on effect may be felt elsewhere in the maritime transport chain: delays can have an impact on operations in other ports of call. Therefore, it is important that we should acquire adequate insight into how port congestion arises, the associated costs, and how it can be avoided or eliminated most effectively.

This chapter discusses the issue of port congestion in detail. More specifically, its purpose is to define the congestion issue in transport economics, with special focus on seaport activity (including types of congestion, the corresponding money and time loss (at locks, berth, etc.)). Next, the results are presented of a literature review of global port congestion reporting and a survey on congestion conditions in some European and American ports. Observations are made as to how congestion developed lately and what its causes are. Furthermore, a typology is made of reactions patterns by different actors. Finally, a number of future scenarios are dressed.

4.2.   A conceptual Framework

Congestion implies that one transport user, i.e. a ship, impedes another. Consequently, a cost is imposed upon a third party. The busier traffic gets, the greater the imposed cost. Jansson and Shneerson (1982, p. 52) define this situation as follows: 'Congestion costs exist if the other short-run costs of port operations, per unit of throughput, are an increasing function of the actual capacity utilization. When actual demand exceeds capacity, extreme congestion costs arise, which we call queuing costs. When a port is said to be congested, it is commonly meant that ships are queuing, waiting to obtain a berth'.

Congestion costs are made up of time loss, additional fuel consumption, greater inconvenience and possibly even accidents. However, time loss is the most substantial contributing factor. An additional transport user imposes a time loss on others. The other losses are often proportional to those time losses.[1] In fact, congestion costs are a negative effect of a high capacity utilisation.

This means that it is necessary to calculate accurately how great a time loss an additional user imposes on third parties. This time loss may be caused in two ways: by slowing down the traffic flows or by generating a queue. In the former case, the congestion costs are calculated on the basis of speed–volume relationships, while in the latter one, it relies on queuing theory.

A seaport typically has a great number of internal bottlenecks, each of which can result in a queue: pilot service, towing service, locks, loading and unloading quays, bunkering, etc. In practice, it is sheer impossible to observe every bottleneck separately in order to conduct counts, let alone impose the appropriate congestion levies (Blauwens, De Baere, & Van de Voorde, 2010).[2,3]

---

1. In the case where a ship is delayed, one usually assumes additional fuel consumption to be proportional to the time loss. Fuel consumption is then regarded as a component of the time cost.

2. Jansson and Shneerson (1982, p. 52) opt for a restricted interpretation of congestion: 'We prefer to restrict the term congestion costs to effects that show up as increases in the cargo handling costs and/or the service time of ships (which, in turn, will influence the queuing time of ships'. They go on to explain that 'if empirical observations showed that the short-run total variable costs (excluding queuing time costs) increase progressively with rises in port throughput, this would be an indication that congestion costs exist. Conversely, if total variable costs increase proportionally to throughput, the inference would be that congestion costs do not exist' (Jansson & Shneerson, 1982, p. 52).

3. Moreover, it is important to guarantee that any congestion charge imposed is actually related to a specific congested unit. The charge shall be imposed on vessels if the problem is the number of berths, available quays, the use of locks, or a canal or river. If, however, the berths are causing capacity problems, then the charge should be imposed on the tonnages put through those berths, not on the vessel. The extent of substitution between various activities in the port operation and the extent to which use of congested particular facilities can be economised can be revealed only by detailed examination (Bennathan & Walters, 1979, p. 80). This has consequences for, among other things, the so-called dwell time. Owners of cargo, or their agents, who would previously leave their freight at the port terminal, as a relatively cheap storage option up to the point of sale or processing, will undoubtedly adapt their behaviour in response to a charge.

In practice, seaport activity is a very complex affair, not in the least because so too is the port calling process. After all, it involves ships of varying sizes and is therefore not homogeneous in terms of required assistance and handling needs. There are various possibilities for substitution: between cargo, between ship and cargo, between ship and port, between terminals within a port, and between berths within a terminal. The heterogeneity of vessels and cargo has efficiency implications for cargo handling. Cargo-handling performances are influenced strongly by various external factors, irrespective of volume of traffic.[4] It is the mismatch of this cargo-handling activity with other activities in the logistics chain which causes port congestion.

The consequence of this complexity is that congestion in a maritime and seaport context can be observed at different levels. A ship that is heading from open sea to a seaport may experience congestion consecutively in the following places or corridors, depending on the location and structure of the port:

- *Maritime access route*: In the case of capacity restrictions, e.g. because of tide dependence, congestion may occur on the river or canal between open sea and the port. Ships often adapt their speed in open sea to the expected slot.[5]
- *Locks*: For vessels whose docking destination lies behind a system of locks, congestion may arise if the number of vessels wishing to use a lock is greater than the lock capacity. In practice, however, vessels do not queue outside the lock, but rather adapt their speed out on the river or canal in order to approach the lock in accordance with the expected slot.
- *Berths*: A ship may be confronted with congestion at berths, i.e. the specific berth may be occupied because another ship is not ready to depart yet. In such situations, the waiting ship may be moored temporarily at another berth.
- *Loading and unloading*: Once all berths at a terminal are occupied, a shortage may arise in loading and unloading equipment (e.g. gantry cranes, straddle carriers). In practice, the response to such a situation would be to start loading or unloading the ship rather quickly, but using less equipment than is customary.
- *Storage*: Storage areas, through bad configuration but also through unexpected moves to be made, may impose waiting time upon cargo and vessel. The choice of automated versus manual handling is to be well considered.
- *Customs inspection*: The organisation and procedures of customs checks can cause congestion at the point where cargo enters or leaves the country. Enhanced security checks in the frame of international anti-terrorism measures may further worsen the fluent flow of cargo through the port.
- *Hinterland loading and unloading*: The use and operability of specific hinterland modes can feature disruptions or delays, impacting also on the maritime side

---

4. In the past, port authorities and even terminal operators used to collect little or no data on such aspects. This in part explains why very few ports imposed a congestion charge.
5. In the case of an Antwerp-bound ship on the river Scheldt, the vessel may choose to pull up to an anchoring buoy at the estuary into the North Sea.

of the port-handling process. In case of truck use, gate systems are often a bottleneck impeding normal terminal operations.

- *Hinterland connections*: Excessive capacity utilisation of hinterland infrastructure, often in combination with non-port-bound traffic where ports are located in crowded city environments, may cause delays in evacuating cargo from or delivering cargo at seaports, therefore holding up terminal processes. On Antwerp motorways, for instance, it was surveyed that in 2006 only 18% of all traffic was commodity related, and of that portion, only 23% had the port as an origin or destination. Moreover, the peaks in port-bound traffic seem to coincide with commuter rush hour peaks (Port of Antwerp, 2007).

4.3. Literature Review and Survey Results on Current State of Congestion

From a social welfare point of view, estimates should be made of all the elements of social marginal costs, including external congestion and scarcity costs. This requires first of all the identification and localisation of bottlenecks which result or may result in congestion in the port. Once the bottlenecks are identified, estimates of the increase in journey time of other traffic and a measure of the unreliability for other traffic caused by an increase in port traffic are needed.

For the identification of port competition all over the world, and its main causes, we relied upon existing, mostly business-oriented, literature covering the period 2009–2011. It is complemented with the results of a survey on congestion conditions in Europe and the United States, dating back to 2006.[6] The latter concerns a survey held among various actors in and/or related to seaports and a review of existing literature on the matter, especially with regard to quantification of existing congestion problems in the two continents' seaports.[7]

For the results of the 2011 literature review, we refer to Appendix B, whereas the survey results are summarized in Appendix A. Appendix B contains an overview of the ports mentioned featuring some form of congestion, the timing at which congestion was observed, and the nature of the causes of congestion. Appendix A features very brief characterisations of issues on traffic quality measurement,

---

6. Research was carried out in the frame of the service contract by the European Commission No. TREN/05/MD/S07.53585 entitled 'Analysis of the contribution of transport policies to the productivity and competitiveness of the European economy and comparison with the United States—COMPETE'.

7. The survey combined a paper questionnaire sent out, supplemented by a telephone survey to complete or clarify respondents' answers. In some cases, telephone answers were the only source of reaction as completing the written questionnaire often turned out to be a demanding exercise. Out of the total 32 contact persons that formally confirmed over the telephone to transfer their answers to the researchers, 26 effectively sent in their paper questionnaire and/or answered by phone. This number should be sufficient to draw significant conclusions. The validity of the answers is strengthened by the representativeness of the answers: respondents cover various businesses, from port authorities over cargo-handling companies and shipping companies to rail and inland navigation operators.

the current state of congestion of delays, the future expectation of the delay situation and policy plans envisaged to fight congestion for the port sector.

From Appendix B, it appears that congestion mainly originates from the terminals and the hinterland connections. This conclusion seems largely in line with the results from the earlier survey, as reported in Appendix A. Only in the identified case of Saint-Petersburg, where ice formation on maritime access ways occurs, the cause lies in the wet part of the port chain. In quite some of the cases, congestion originates from lack of berthing capacity. Impacts however in most of the cases spread out over various sections of the chain, and even on to other ports, where ships, for instance, miss their slots due to late arrival.

A strong indication of high congestion probability on the terminals side, especially at container terminals, is given by the terminal capacity utilisation figures in Table 4.1. It is found that especially terminals at the large North-European ports are operating very close to their capacity limits. Of course, one can go through the theoretical capacity border, but that usually implies a sharp rise in cost. Leach (2010) states that by 2015 container terminal utilisation levels can amount up to 80%, and in fast-growing regions (Far East + Middle East) up to 95%.

Other indicators of congestion can be, for instance, the utilisation of the road network in the neighbourhood of ports, and inland navigation lock capacity utilization. Fairplay refers to a number of other sections in the chain where congestion can occur. A first example is the Panama Canal, where congestion due to too big vessels is observed. Furthermore, it is identified that repair yards and scrapping facilities are becoming new sources of maritime congestion.

When comparing the results on expected developments of port congestion with the actual state of congestion from the current literature search, it turns out that whereas most actors and most ports in 2006 expected an improvement of the congestion situation, the number of cases of congestion at current actually is very long, as can be seen from Appendix B. In some of the cases where interviewed actors were pessimistic in 2006, like for Rotterdam, this pessimism actually turned into reality. Although congestion turns out to be a global phenomenon, it seems that the Middle and Far East seem to be worst hit.

Table 4.1: Terminal capacity utilisation in North European deep seaports—2004.

Port	Capacity utilisation (%)
Le Havre	89.6
Antwerp	92.9
Rotterdam	92.5
Bremerhaven	95.5
Hamburg	93.2
Southampton	99.3
Felixstowe	77.1
Others	41.9
Total average	86.6

Source: Drewry Shipping Consultants.

When looking at the causes of congestion, Appendix B shows that the weather very often is the cause of delays, either directly or indirectly. Directs impacts come through, for instance, floodings, winter conditions, shallow water due to drought, etc. Indirectly, the weather impacts on the speed at which certain crops develop, with concentrations of volumes of, for example, sugar, grain, etc. to be handled by ports, leading to congestion again. The latter in principle should be easier to plan, as the occurrence is not sudden. It turns out however that not all operators are planning in the same, efficient way. Lack of truck capacity in hinterland transport seems an additional big source of congestion. Furthermore, also equipment and labour shortages are causing congestion. All of these of course can be indirectly related to peaks in traffic, and linked, for instance, to weather conditions. But very often, they are just due to inability to find a sufficient number of skilled workers, to a strike or to a lack of capital to invest in additional equipment.

Interesting to note also is that no commodity seems to be free from congestion. Appendix B shows that next to containers, also dry and liquid bulk seem to be severely hit. For some commodity types, the weather is a much bigger cause of congestion than for other commodity types.

It is also interesting to see to what extent actual measurement of congestion exists. From Appendix A, it turns out that, in general, congestion is not well measured, and in the cases where a measurement is done, the latter is very fragmented. On the other hand, a general feeling and consensus is there on the existence of congestion, mainly at terminals and in hinterland connections.

When comparing port ranges, the picture is quite mixed. In terms of measurement, the United Kingdom seems to have the more structural data collection, which is more or less absent in Baltic ports and Mediterranean ports. In all port ranges, congestion on the maritime side turns out to be nearly non-existent, while nearly all ports report problems at terminals, gates and/or the hinterland. As to the future prospects, it can be observed that in all ranges especially the hub ports where no immediate initiatives are deployed expect a worsening.

4.4. Actor Reaction Patterns to Port Congestion

From Appendix B, the different reaction patters from different actors can be observed, involving different time ranges. They can be summarized into a typology as follows.

Time loss due to congestion during port calls overall generates enormous costs, cf. the high vessel operating costs coupled with high investment costs. Every effective measure to cut or avoid congestion therefore reduces cost and increases efficiency. On the other hand, the mere existence of congestion means that a port is a valuable and scarce good. Therefore, the solution to the congestion problem would seem straightforward: port authorities should increase port dues and consequently benefit from the scarcity of capacity. The benefits of a congestion charge are quite clear. First and foremost, they generate higher income. The charges are a source of funding for expanding port infrastructure and services, which will enhance the port's degree of self-sufficiency and make it less dependent on public subsidising. Moreover, a congestion charge will encourage the efficient utilisation of available port facilities.

There are, however, also some downsides to take into consideration. There is, for instance, the administrative complexity of imposing a charge: demand — and thus congestion — may fluctuate seasonally, and may moreover contain a random component, such as the weather. Relatively strong shipping companies may pass on the congestion charges to third parties, possibly with a mark-up, which would have an indirect negative effect on demand for port services.

In practice, most port authorities seem not to operate in this manner. Port charges are deliberately kept low, even in congested ports. The reason is that port authorities are usually convinced that higher charges will cause not only loss of traffic, but also higher prices for imported goods. Port authorities will usually not adopt charges, even in situations when congestion is putting substantial pressure on the cost level. To a considerable degree, this economic cost is passed on to goods handlers or so-called terminal operating companies (TOCs). The latter are expected by port authorities and, even more so, by shipping companies to load and unload more quickly, resulting in a higher cost per unit of output. A number of actions through which they try to achieve this are mentioned in Table 4.2. If this higher cost is passed on through higher rates for the customer, i.e. the owner of the freight, then this will equally generate downward pressure on the competitive position of the port in question.

Shippers, next to shifting port, may also engage in cargo redistribution, transportation demand planning, virtual warehousing and solving communication problems to government (Blanchard, 2007).

It is clear that, in the economic power struggle, the port authorities occupy a relatively weak position vis-à-vis the shipping companies, as is apparent from the fact that the latter often impose congestion surcharges on the owner of the cargo.[8] Bennathan and Walters (1979, p. 84) assert the following in this context: 'The shipowner would rather suffer the average normal delay than pay for the additional cost of immediate service. A balance between the incremental cost of providing more capacity and the consequential reduction in the cost of ship delays is the criterion for defining normal capacity'. Appendix B shows that congestion surcharges do indeed get applied more and more often. The balance between normal delay and the additional price of service may have changed, but the principle about defining normal capacity is still fully valid (Stopford, 2002).

A pattern emerges in the observed competitive struggle between shipping companies and port authorities in recent decades. In the scheduling of operations and in pricing, the shipping companies took as their starting point a normal level of congestion. Abnormal congestion, i.e. any congestion on top of whatever was assumed to be the normal level, was passed on by those shipping companies as a congestion surcharge. The long-term strategy of the port authorities, on the other hand, was aimed at continuously increasing capacity, often with financial support from the public authorities. This way, normal congestion was kept very low, or even reduced to zero, but at the cost of substantial overcapacity. Extra capacity is also indirectly

---

8. The manner in which shipping companies can pass on the costs associated with congestion obviously depends on the demand elasticity of shipping services.

Table 4.2: Terminal optimization measures.

Type of measure	Example
Multi-pick lifting	Twin (two 20-in. containers) and tandem (two 40-in. containers) lifting are concepts that are rapidly being introduced at many terminals worldwide, since about 2005.
Truck appointment systems	Common procedure at most Asian terminals, U.S. and European ports have since 2005 started applying truck appointment procedures, in an attempt to reduce hinterland delay and increase terminal velocity. A similar initiative was the synchronised time slot use for trans-loading cargo from ocean vessels to barges.
Extending gate opening hours	In Europe, for most terminals, it is quite common for the waterside to be operating around the clock. On landside, however, there are often limited terminal opening hours. In 2004, Antwerp stevedore Hessenatie has taken the initiative to have longer gate opening hours but got insufficient co-operation from other chain partners. In the same year, South California ports have developed a similar plan, initially meeting labour shortage obstacles however.
Electronic document transmission	Many ports worldwide have introduced various electronic document transfer systems. Customs as well as payment documents can be transferred through this kind of system. Australia was a primer by introducing such a system in 2000.
High-speed gates	At West Basin Container Terminal, Los Angeles, automated gate systems, using, for instance, optical character recognition, have allowed in 2009 reducing the number of data entry clerks required to process up to 5100 transactions per day from 18 to 9, resulting in over $1million in saving/year, through higher speed as well as accuracy.
Automated yard marshalling	ECT Rotterdam used to have fully automated terminal operations since its start, although the low flexibility was often detrimental to productivity. DP World Antwerp is testing a semi-automated system, where waterside activities would still be performed manually, whereas terminal and hinterland (un-)loading would be automated.

Source: Own composition.

generated by port authorities through allowing for yard extensions and improved space utilisation, through concession conditions, for instance (Thongrung, 2011).

Almost all shipping companies are constantly implementing measures to try and reduce operational cost. They often do so in response to exogenous influences, such as higher bunkering rates and/or growing port congestion. During 2010, a number of shipping companies or alliances decided to apply slow steaming and to deploy an additional ship on

Table 4.3: MSC Europe–Far East loop restructuring, May 2011.

Service	Vessels deployed	Ports of call
Lion	From 10,000 to 14,000 TEU average vessels	Felixstowe added to Le Havre, Antwerp, Bremerhaven and Hamburg
Silk	11 vessels of 13,500 TEU average	Antwerp, Felixstowe, Hamburg, Bremerhaven, Rotterdam and Antwerp

Source: DynaLiners.

certain loops. The envisaged goals were smoother port operations with less congestion, more port calls and reduced fuel consumption through lower speeds. At the same time, transit time obviously increases. Beginning of 2011, DynaLiners observes that shippers start calling for a share of the gains made by shipping companies.

A permanent analysis of the operational decisions taken by shipping companies and/or alliances can yield information with regard to possible congestion problems in various ports and at various terminals. By way of illustration, we consider Mediterranean Shipping Company (MSC), which reorganised its loops between Europe and the Far East beginning of 2011. The purpose was to enhance efficiency and reduce cost. Avoiding congestion was one of the means of achieving these goals. For ports, there is the additional struggle to be either the first or the last port of call in the range. In the MSC case, Antwerp occupies an important role, particularly in the Silk route, being the first and last European port of call in the loop (Table 4.3).

Under permanent threat of potential reshuffling of port calls, port, terminal and hinterland operators are taking measures to relieve congestion on the port access ways, often still at own initiative and without co-ordination along the logistics chain. Table 4.4 summarizes the most important types of measures occurring, with examples. It should be noted that also a number of actions from Table 4.2 should improve hinterland congestion. Each of the measures can, on their own or in combination, deliver an important contribution to the diminishing or avoiding of congestion.

Finally, it can also be observed that in most cases, neither port authorities nor operators are fully prepared for tackling the congestion problem. Co-ordination and co-operation among actors is in most cases insufficient.

4.5. Future Evolution

It is clear that the port and maritime sector evolve very quickly and are facing a number of challenges; each of those developments will have consequences in terms of capacity utilisation and will therefore possibly relate to port congestion.

The world economy continues to be the driving force behind the maritime sector (Meersman, Van de Voorde, & Vanelslander, 2010). The world economy is, however, subject to enormous change, cf. the enormous growth in international trade, the international redistribution of labour and capital, and the integration and globalisation of markets. The strong growth of the BRIC's and other Asian countries will continue to generate huge volumes of maritime trade with considerable

Table 4.4: Operational measures in the hinterland.

Type of measure	Example
Hinterland traffic diversion	End of 2007, China Shipping has diverted a large part of its traffic to the Port of Ipswich in order to avoid strong congestion at other UK ports.
Congestion pricing	Tolling attempts have been existing for quite some time in some European countries (for instance, France), or were recently introduced (for instance, Germany in 2005, Poland in 2011). Time and place flexibility is however to be introduced. The Port of New York/New Jersey has taken such initiative in 2005 for diverting rush hour traffic in the wider port zone. By crossing overnight, truckers in 2011 pay per axle costs of $3.50, compared to $6 at peak times, and $5 during afternoon and evening off-peak times. Cars pay $4 each during all off-peak hours, $1 less than during peak hours. In the meantime, various ports and regions are considering introducing road pricing. Examples in Europe are Antwerp and Rotterdam.
Off-dock container yards	Hanjin Shipping has started operating off-dock container yards in 1994, and now operates six of them, in co-operation with local partners each time. In Felixstowe and Southampton, Kuehne + Nagel has established a rail service for moving cargo as quickly as possible off the docks to inland yards.
Fast rail shuttles	European Rail Shuttle since 1994 connects four of Europe's most important seaports to 20 inland terminals, often located in Eastern Europe. Shuttles run several times a week.
Expanded rail connections	The Betuwe line connecting the Port of Rotterdam to the German Ruhr area and the Iron Rhine connecting the Port of Antwerp to the German Ruhr area are examples of rail projects aiming at faster bridging the distance between large seaports and important hinterland load centres.

Source: Own composition.

imbalances, especially in the container trade. According to UNESCAP (2007), 1264 new container berths will be required to meet the anticipated world demand in 2015, the majority of which will be needed in East Asia and the Pacific. This will clearly require large investments in port infrastructure. To improve their competitive position, port authorities and port operators will try to avoid congestion by providing as much as possible available capacity to the shipowners.

Shipowners are large and strategically significant customers of seaports and they have increased their market power considerably. Moreover, in recent times we have witnessed scale increases in the shipping sector, first and foremost through horizontal co-operation and/or mergers and acquisitions. An example of the latter is the takeover in 2005 of P&O Nedlloyd by Maersk. A recent example of co-operation is the slot exchange agreement between Maersk and Evergreen on the Asia–Europe trade. In the second instance, shipowners have been showing greater interest in terminal operations and hinterland transportation, a consequence of the growing tendency to think in terms of complex logistics chains, whereby each link must contribute to a continuous optimisation of the chain as a whole. This development has tipped the market balance in favour of shipowners, as they now control some powerful logistics chains (Heaver, Meersman, & Van de Voorde, 2001).

The future of the ship-owning sector may be summarised in three core notions: rationalisation, mergers and company scale increases. Especially in the container business, ship owners are continuing to invest heavily in additional capacity in the hope of deploying it at a lower operational cost per slot.[9] Moreover, they regard a mixed fleet as a way of spreading risk (Det Norske Veritas, 2007). Additional cost control may be achieved through mergers and acquisitions and ensuing capacity reductions. Pressurised by the strategic and financial considerations of the holdings that control the shipping companies, capacity will be further kept in check through strategic alliances, new partnerships and the rerouting of vessels. This will give rise to shifts in terms of direct port calls, which could, in turn, impact on existing congestion or indeed create new congestion (Peters, 2001; Song & Panayides, 2002).

Landside, the following rule will apply: the economic benefits that shipowners seek through substantial ship scale increases and ensuing cost reduction must not be wasted through potential bottlenecks and the loss of time and money that they entail, neither on the quay, nor in the terminals, nor indeed during hinterland transportation. As regards capacity, there is clear evidence of heavy growth, associated with a concentration movement among terminal operators.[10] As far as the shipping companies are concerned, a further concentration of terminal operators represents an evident danger: less mutual competition, lower productivity growth, longer turnaround times for vessels and, above all, higher handling rates.[11] One may readily assume that shipowners will not continue to undergo this development passively. As their relative market power is under threat, they may be expected to make greater efforts to acquire so-called dedicated terminals, be it under a joint venture with locally active terminal operators or otherwise.[12]

Even in larger ports, certain shipping companies can occupy a relatively dominant position. MSC, for example, carried out a total of 4,500,000 movements in 2009 at its

---

9. Overcapacity is not necessarily perceived negatively by shipowners, as they assume it will be partly absorbed by the problem of port congestion. This expectation is then coupled with the notion of longer haul cargoes, which would change the tonne/mile ratio.

10. This concentration movement, coupled with the market entry of new players, such as PSA, HPH and DP World, has also created a buffer against possible vertical integration on the initiative of shipowners.

11. The latter is due primarily to the fact that shipowners are no longer confronted with different, vehemently competing terminal operators, but rather with larger players who are active in different locations and are therefore able to negotiate package deals covering various ports and longer periods of time.

12. As far as port authorities are concerned, this need not be a negative evolution, as it would make shipowners a lot less footloose, in the sense that a longer term relationship may develop that will reduce their urge to relocating (Heaver et al., 2001). In the short term, the use of 'dedicated terminals' may lead to lower capacity utilisation rates for terminals.

Home Terminal at Delwaide Dock in Antwerp, amounting to 3.9 million TEU. This means that MSC accounted for almost 48% of overall container traffic in the port of Antwerp in that year.

Yet strikingly, MSC was also interested in acquiring a terminal at Tweede Maasvlakte in Rotterdam. However, it failed. Shipping companies such as COSCO, K Line and Yang Ming, who are also involved in a terminal at Deurganck Dock in Antwerp, have set up a joint venture with the Rotterdam-based cargo handler ECT (a subsidiary of HPH) with a 49% stake in the Rotterdam Euromax Terminal.

These kinds of developments show that if a shipping company or an alliance acquires a significant stake in a particular port, this does not necessarily result in diversion of traffic. The main concern of companies is simply to be present in the principal traffic-generating ports. At the same time, such a strategy allows shipping companies to gain degrees of freedom, among other things, with a view to avoiding congestion in ports and at terminals.

With regard to ports, there have been some significant structural changes. The characteristic make-up of the traditional stevedoring business has evolved towards more complex TOCs, often because the need for capital has given rise to mergers, takeovers and externally funded expansion projects. External capital has in some cases been provided by shipping companies. Port authorities, for their part, initially looked on rather passively as this trend unfolded.

As a result of scale increases, takeovers and mergers, especially among shipowners, an increasingly small number of customers are accounting for a growing share in turnover achieved by terminal operators. Often, this implies a concentration of throughput, i.e. higher peaks in demand for handling capacity (Fusillo, 2003). As shipping companies invariably expect there to be sufficient capacity, at increasingly high productivity, terminal operators are forced to invest in more and bigger cranes.

Some terminal operators therefore seek cooperation with shipping companies. A recent example of such a development is Antwerp International Terminal, a joint venture created in 2005 involving the shipping companies K Line, Yang Ming and Hanjin on the one hand and terminal operator PSA Antwerp on the other hand. Also in Antwerp, PSA, together with MSC, operates the MSC Home Terminal.

In Singapore, PSA has in 2008 set up a dedicated container terminal for Pacific International Lines. This type of strategy was not at all found before 2002, when the company used to take a common user approach. After being confronted with significant competition from the Malaysian concern Tanjung Pelepas, a choice was made for intensive cooperation with shipowners, in the hope of achieving greater integration. One example of this new policy is the joint venture with COSCO. This was followed towards the end of 2005 by a joint venture with MSC for the purpose of operating three berths at the Pasir Panjang Terminal.

The sums involved in investments in vessels and port terminals are enormous. The traditional companies, often being family businesses (such as the former Antwerp-based stevedore Noord Natie), are no longer able to raise the required capital for the extensive scale of operations that feature at container terminals nowadays, where profit margins per unit are rather low moreover, and thus inevitably become takeover targets.

Initially, the purchasers, such as HPH and PSA, belonged to the sector itself (Wiegmans, Ubbels, Rietveld, & Nijkamp, 2001). Subsequently, however, capital was increasingly found beyond the traditional maritime and port industry. Apparently, port infrastructure is seen to offer a strategic value added, with an almost guaranteed return. Moreover, it is expected to become increasingly difficult to build additional port infrastructure. It will, in other words, become a scarce good.

The relationship between port competition and shipping companies always boils down to the same one key concept: available capacity. Capacity seems to be a crucial factor in the analysis of port competition, and turns out to play at various levels.

In port competition, and, in particular, competition in container traffic, available capacity is not only an important factor in attracting new flows, but surely also for keeping freight transport. Shipping companies choose ports without congestion and bottlenecks. They think ahead, choose open space, with growth potential. This means that freight transfer from sea to port and vice versa needs to be performed in an efficient way, but the way hinterland transport enrolls (mode choice) is an important factor (Aronietis, Van de Voorde, & Vanelslander, 2010; Huybrechts et al., 2002).

From certain fast-growing ports like Rotterdam, Antwerp and Hamburg, new port and hinterland projects need to be seen primarily as addition of available capacity that needs to enable future port growth. In a number of European ports, container traffic grew by about 11% between 2000 and 2010. This implied that all elements in the maritime logistics chains need to prepare for continuous growth figures. If one does not take this into account, congestion will show up, or existing congestion will move on to an unacceptable high. Maritime flows risk getting moved to other ports.

4.6. Conclusion

Congestion implies loss of time and money, and therefore undermines the competitive position of ports and maritime logistics chains. Consequently, maximum efforts must be made to avoid such maritime congestion. To this end, insight is required into present and future developments in maritime transport and port throughput, as well as into the strategic behaviour of the various market players involved.

With respect to that behaviour, it is clear that shipping companies opt for ports with sufficient available capacity. This avoids the risk that the huge amount of capital, which is embedded in their vessels, get used sub-optimally. Available capacity implies not only berths, but also efficient terminal operations and good hinterland connections. It is up to all actors involved in terminal and hinterland operations to safeguard the provision of sufficient free capacity.

The most likely future scenarios, which therefore deserve to be studied in depth, are more or less known. However, some uncertainty remains as regards the timeframe in which the expected developments will unfold. The speed at which the various market players within the maritime logistics chain will take specific initiatives shall depend on a battery of exogenous and endogenous variables. As is the case with pricing in the maritime sector, and with successfully covering oneself against price fluctuations and other risks, timing is what ultimately determines who will emerge as the winner.

Further quantification of decisions taken by various chain actors is needed. This should help understand why they take certain decisions, but also where congestion occurs, sometimes in a hidden way. This will reflect in higher operator costs, implying action to be taken.

References

Aronietis, R., Van de Voorde, E., Vanelslander, T. (2010). Port competitiveness determinants of selected European ports in the containerized cargo market. Paper presented at IAME 2010.

Bennathan, E., & Walters, A. (1979). *Port pricing and investment policy for developing countries*. United Kingdom: Oxford University Press.

Blanchard, D. (2007). Five strategies to avoid port congestion. *Industry Week*. October 1.

Blauwens, G., De Baere, P., & Van de Voorde, E. (2010). *Transport Economics* (4th ed.). Belgium: De Boeck Ltd.

Det Norske Veritas. (2007). Port congestion and loading speed. Retrieved from http://www.dnv.com/industry/maritime/shiptypes/orecarrier/portcongestionandloadingspeed.asp

Fusillo, M. (2003). Excess capacity and entry deterrence: The case of ocean liner shipping markets. *Maritime Economics and Logistics, 5*, 100–115.

Heaver, T., Meersman, H., & Van de Voorde, E. (2001). Co-operation and competition in international container transport: Strategies for ports. *Maritime Policy and Management, 28*(3), 293–306.

Huybrechts, M., Meersman, H., Van de Voorde, E., Van Hooydonk, E., Verbeke, A., & Winkelmans, W. (Eds). (2002). *Port Competitiveness. An economic and legal analysis of the factors determining the competitiveness of seaports*. Belgium: De Boeck Ltd.

Jansson, J., & Shneerson, D. (1982). *Port Economics*. United States of America: MIT Press.

Leach, P. (2010). Port congestion could resume in some sectors. *Journal of Commerce Online*. Retrieved from www.joc.com

Meersman, H., Van de Voorde, E., & Vanelslander, T. (2010). *Future challenges for the port and shipping sector*. United Kingdom: Informa.

Peters, H. J. F. (2001). Developments in global seatrade and container shipping markets: Their effects on the port industry and private sector involvement. *International Journal of Maritime Economics, 3*, 3–26.

Port of Antwerp (2007). *Analyse hinterlandverkeer Haven van Antwerpen*. Antwerpen.

Song, D.-W., & Panayides, P. M. (2002). A conceptual application of cooperative game theory to liner shipping strategic alliances. *Maritime Policy and Management, 29*(3), 285–301.

Stopford, M. (2002). *Maritime economics*. United Kingdom: Routledge.

Thongrung, W. (2011). Shippers irked by port congestion. *The Nation*, May 28.

UNESCAP (2007). *Container traffic forecast—Regional shipping and port development—2007 update*. Thailand: UNESCAP.

Wiegmans, B. W., Ubbels, B., Rietveld, P., & Nijkamp, P. (2001). Investments in container terminals, public private partnerships in Europe. *International Journal of Maritime Economics, 4*, 1–20.

Appendixes

Appendix A: Survey Country Reviews on Congestion

Table 4.A.1: Synthesis of survey country reviews on congestion.

Port	Measurement and data used	Current state of congestion	Expected development of congestion	Policy plans
Miami	No structural measurement	Problem landside: gate, location close to city	Increasing	Major port redevelopment, new gate system
Antwerp	Time registration for every vessel	Sometimes congestion, especially at terminals	Situation will improve: new quays, better rail, inland navigation and trucking system	Barge Traffic Services, new rail system, trucking assignment
Gdynia	No structural measurement	No congestion, at least not on maritime side	Worsening if no measures	Better hinterland connections
London	Every vessel is registered by the Port Authority	No structural congestion on maritime side	Probable worsening in hinterland	No structural plans
Rotterdam	No vessel registration	Only congestion on hinterland side	Pessimistic	No new infrastructure plans
Humber	Time measurement for every vessel	No congestion	No immediate worsening	No plans needed at this stage
Hamburg	No measurement	Congestion occurs, but not quantified	No worsening	No plans available
Long Beach	Some measurement, not structural	Road and rail increasingly congested, terminals equally congested	As traffic increases, problems may worsen	No immediate plans
Felixstowe	Shipping companies do measurements	No congestion	No worsening expected	No plans
Barcelona	Measurement of time that goods spend in port	Some inland congestion	No worsening expected	Discussion groups, no plans yet
Kotka	Data are collected for ships and at terminal	No real congestion	No worsening expected	No plans

Table 4.A.1: (*Continued*)

Port	Measurement and data used	Current state of congestion	Expected development of congestion	Policy plans
Rostock	No structural measurement	Congestion at gates and at terminal	Road situation may get worse	Regular check-ups with road authorities
Portuguese ports	No measurements by ports	No congestion	No worsening	No plans
Aarhus	Measurement by port and terminals	Minor congestion at terminals	Worsening through overflow from other ports	Terminal extension
Corck	Statistical ex-post measurement	Constant inland congestion	Sharp rise	Downstream extensions
Rauma	No structural measurement	No recurring congestion	No worsening	No action plans
Genova	No measurement by port authority	Minor congestion in hinterland	No clear view	Planned reinforcing of rail
Marseille	For ships: no structural measurement; for hinterland: structural measurement	Only congestion for tankers	Other commodity types may be affected too	Terminal extensions plans
Zeebruges	Only ships followed by port; terminal situation assessed by terminal operators	Mainly congestion in hinterland	No immediate worsening	Port authority has entrance improvement plans and lobbies for better roads
Tacoma	Measurement for ships	Strong hinterland congestion	Problems may rise without action	Freight Action Plan, involving all actors

Appendix B: Literature Search on Global Port Congestion

Table 4.B.1: Synthesis of literature search on global port congestion.

Port	Date	Type of congestion and/or reaction
Nava Sheva (India)	Since early 2010	Yard congestion and rail delays
	July 2010	Maersk levies surcharge
	July 2010	APL levies surcharge
	July 2010	OOCL, NYK and HMM levy surcharge
	June 2010	Maersk Line and CMA-CGM divert traffic to Mundra and Pipavav
	July 2010	COSCO levies surcharge
Australia	July 2010	Delays to sugar exports
	April 2010	Congestion at coal terminals
	End 2007	10–14 days waiting offshore for bulk vessels
Port Botany, Sydney (Australia)	February 2011	Port congestion surcharge introduced
	December 2010	Months of delays for vessels, aggravated by successful grain + coffee crops; in March 2011, penalties were installed by Sydney Ports Corporation.
	August 2009	Sydney Ports Corporation gives up plans for voluntary behaviour change by road operators, and introduces PierPass system.
	June 2009	New performance and penalty system introduced.
Colombo (Sri Lanka)	Halfway 2010	Terminal congestion through lack of equipment, especially for transhipment from Bangladesh, India and Pakistan; SLPA to build freight village
Chittagong (Bangladesh)	Halfway 2010	Terminal congestion through lack of equipment
Brazil	September 2010	Delay mainly for sugar vessels caused by heavy rains
	End 2007	6–8 days waiting offshore for bulk vessels
Newcastle (Australia)	October 2010	Congestion for coal export
Jebel Ali (UAE)	September 2008	Several days of delay

Table 4.B.1: (*Continued*)

Port	Date	Type of congestion and/or reaction
Bangkok	June 2011	Congestion due to port closure, due to union problems
Suez	April 2011	Terminal congestion due to political unrest, with lack of labour and fuel
Bremerhaven	July 2010	Increasing vehicle exports + staff shortages lead to congestion for ro/ro services
Kolkata	October 2009	Port traffic slowed. Surcharges imposed by NYK and MISC.
Dar-es-Salaam	January 2011	Tanzania Revenue Authority urged better pre-arrival declaration processing.
	First half 2009	Port congestion. New inland container depot to be built as from January 2011.
Itajai	November 2008	Congestion due to flooding with consequential shallow depths
Los Angeles/ Long Beach	September 2008	Congestion risk due to potential truck capacity lack due to clean truck program
Barcelona	May 2008	Construction of 9th cruise terminal to alleviate cruise congestion
Singapore	April 2008	Imminent cruise congestion
East-Malaysia	April 2008	Congestion due to lack of terminals
Otay Mesa	April 2011	Road corridor project to alleviate road congestion
Chennai	January 2011, since mid-November 2010	Hampered road connectivity. As of February 2011, port congestion charge introduced.
Seattle	December 2010	Congestion relief measures decided
Buenos Aires	October 2010	Congestion due to lack of barge capacity on Rio de la Plata due to shallow water, and to increased scanning in view of drug control.
Rotterdam	July 2010	Congestion due to increasing volumes, labour shortage during summer, unability of shipping companies to keep schedules, empty container pick-ups and overflow from Le Havre where strikes occur; Feeder lines threaten with surcharge
Miami	April 2009	Lacking tunnel leads to hinterland congestion
Saint-Petersburg	May 2011	Ice formation caused congestion for vessels during winter again
	May 2010	Congestion impacts through heavy winter

Table 4.B.1: (*Continued*)

Port	Date	Type of congestion and/or reaction
China	August 2010	10% of dry bulk fleet absorbed in congestion
	June 2010	Congestion at Chinese petrol discharging terminals
Durban (South-Africa)	July 2010	Congestion due to labour dispute
Singapore	October 2009	Cruise terminals impose high docking as ships in congestion need to berth
Lagos	March 2009	Congestion with impact on jobs
Melbourne	August 2010	Two road projects launched to alleviate congestion around the port
Papua New Guinea	April 2010	Efforts taken by government
Manila (The Philippines)	January 2011	South Harbor and Manila International Container Terminal
Johor Port (Malaysia)	April 2011	
Jeddah (Saudi-Arabia)	April 2009	Port mismanagement of concession contracts

Source: Journal of Commerce Online, World Cargo News Online, Lloyd's List, TanzaniaInvest, Global Van Lines.

Chapter 5

Port Choice Model of Transhipment Cargo Using System Dynamics

Nam-Kyu Park, Daniel S. H. Moon and Chae-Kwan Lim

Abstract

The aim of this chapter is to identify factors that have been affecting the increase of transhipment (T/S) cargoes of the port of Busan and to explore how these factors can be utilised more effectively to attract and increase T/S cargoes through the development of a port choice model using the technique of system dynamics (SD). To clarify the reason why T/S cargoes have increased in the port of Busan, several steps have been taken as follows.

The first step was to design a quantitative model to explain the development of T/S cargoes during the last decade. The second step was to define dependent and independent variables for multiple regressions after testing variable significance. For this, data collection and the accuracy of validation have been achieved by using the direct interview procedure involving experienced experts from both Korean and foreign shipping companies. After validating the model with the collected data, the final step was to find variables that confidently explain the model.

It is found that two variables are clearly identified as core factors that describe well the development of T/S cargoes in the port of Busan: 'Mohring effect' and total cost. Further, it is strongly recommended, through this empirical study, that an incentive scheme be changed to the way in which more feeder vessels rather than mother vessels can reduce their direct costs to call at the port of Busan.

Based on regression analysis, it is also found that the sensitivity model for transhipment cargo is useful for dynamic forecasting in changing the cost factor and Mohring factor with time-series technique.

Keywords: Northeast Asia; transhipment port; port choice (or selection) model; incentive scheme; simulation; system dynamics (SD)

Maritime Logistics: Contemporary Issues
Copyright © 2012 by Emerald Group Publishing Limited
All rights of reproduction in any form reserved
ISBN: 978-1-78052-340-8

5.1.   Introduction

Attracting more transhipment (T/S) cargoes to regional hub ports has become a hot issue, particularly in Northeast Asia where there are a number of major ports such as Busan, Shanghai, Ningbo, Kaosiung and Yokohama. This is directly related to overcoming the problem of under-utilisation of container terminal facilities, together with the indirect contribution of port to the regional and national economies.

The ports of Busan, Shanghai, Ningbo, Kaosiung and Yokohama are competitors in terms of transhipment attraction. In the context of competition, Busan Port Authority (BPA) has implemented the volume incentive policy to encourage shipping lines to bring more T/S cargoes into the port of Busan, by applying different individual schemes in terms of the exemption of port dues, discounting terminal rental fees or cargo handling charges.

This chapter suggests the 'port choice model' in order to indentify impacting factors to the increase in T/S cargoes and to check the sensitivity of the model by using the technique of multiple regression analysis. Steps for achieving the research objectives are as follows.

The first step was to design a quantitative model for explaining the real phenomena about the share of T/S cargoes, followed by defining dependent and independent variables for multiple regressions after testing variable significance. At this stage, data collection and the accuracy validation have been achieved by using the direct interviews procedure involving experienced people from both Korean and foreign shipping companies. As the distribution of T/S cargoes in Northeast Asia has a unique pattern depending on the characteristics of each country, the T/S cargoes from China, Japan or Southeast Asian countries are to be considered independently. The third step was to validate the model using the collected data to identify which variables explain the model quite well. Lastly, the port choice sensitivity model was developed to make a proper estimation of T/S cargoes according to the ever-changing independent variables.

As shown in Figure 5.1, the analytical scope of this study is restricted to North Chinese ports (Shanghai, Ningbo, Qingdao, Tianjin and Dalian) and the port of Busan.

5.2.   Literature review

Ohashi, Kim, Oum, and Yuc (2005) studied the choice problem of air cargo transhipment in Northeast Asia. Based on a unique data set of 760 air cargo transhipment routings to/from the Northeast Asian region in 2000, they applied an aggregate form of a multinomial logit model to identify the critical factors influencing air cargo transhipment route choice decisions. The analysis focused on the trade-off between monetary cost and time cost while considering other relevant variables for the choice of transhipment airport. The estimation method considered the presence of unobserved attributes, and corrected for resulting endogeneity via a two-stage least-squares estimation using instrumental variables. The empirical results

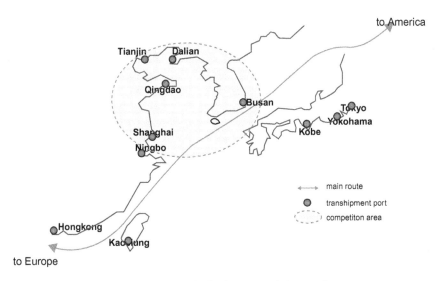

Figure 5.1: Analytical scope of the study

showed that the choice of the air cargo transhipment hub was more sensitive to time cost than the monetary costs such as landing fees and line-haul price.

Veldman and Bückmann (2003) analysed earlier container port competition in Northwest Europe. They estimated demand functions for both the continental and the overseas hinterland of the West European major container ports and assessed the demand function for a port expansion project for the port of Rotterdam.

Veldman, Bückmann, and Saitua (2005) estimated demand functions for a project to improve the accessibility of the port of Antwerp by deepening the Scheldt River and thereby reducing waiting times for the tide and increasing the ability to accommodate bigger ships. In their publications, the parameters of a logit model were estimated with regression analysis and the demand function could be derived from systematically changing cost and assessing the resulting market shares.

Again Veldman and Vroomen (2007) carried out their study to search for significant factors for understanding the competitiveness of transhipment ports and the elasticity of port choice in the market of the Mediterranean. Statistical tests were applied using a 10-year time series of aggregate transhipment flows between 15 transhipment ports and 9 feeder regions. Tests of logit models with regression analysis showed that variables such as feeder costs, mainline port access costs and Mohring effects were statistically significant.

Also Lirn, Thanopoulou, and Beresford (2003 and 2004) and Ng (2006) have analysed the decision factors for transhipment port and have identified that the cost of a shipping company, route accessibility, and time are important decision factors. Meanwhile, the domestic researches on deciding a transhipment port are as follows: a study of inducement strategies of transhipment cargo (Bae, 1999; Jung & Kwak, 2002; Park & Kim, 2003), a study of transhipment port decision based on ISM and AHP technique from the viewpoint of a global container shipping company

(Baek, 2005) and a study of selection attribution for transhipment port from the viewpoint of a shipping company at home and abroad (Park & Sung, 2008).

However, these previous studies mainly focused on the inducement strategies for transhipment cargo or suggested the selection attribution for transhipment port as well as the method to select key attributes. They have shown that, according to the questionnaire respondents (such as a shipping company, cargo owner, importer, exporter and forwarder), their study results were different from each other in terms of port choice factor, lacking consistency and validity. Moreover, these preceding studies had a limitation in the sense that they were trying to find decision factors only by way of questionnaire surveys, not performing an analysis based on actual data.

With 10-year actual data, this chapter has performed a quantitative analysis to identify decision factors for T/S port choice, by using logit regression model and the regression model of Veldman and Vroomen (2007) that lead to useful findings for futuristic port planning.

5.3. Analysis of Transhipment

5.3.1. Calling Pattern in Northeast Asia

As illustrated in Figure 5.2, many shipping companies have recently changed their calling patterns from traditional route to China-oriented one. Before 2000, shipping companies showed typical calling pattern that included Singapore, Hong Kong, Kaohsiung, Busan, Yokohama, Tokyo and Seattle sequentially. With this pattern, shipping companies were forced to select a transhipment port in Busan or one of Japanese ports in Northeast Asia region.

The calling pattern of 2007, however, has changed due to China effect. According to Drewry report (Drewry, 2006), in case of US-bound ships, the frequency of calling at Chinese ports such as Hong Kong, Shanghai and Yantian has increased in comparison with 2000 (Figures 5.3, 5.4 and 5.5). Furthermore, due to the increase in Chinese trade volume, the direct service TP5 (ETE) from Shanghai and Ningbo to Los Angeles was initiated by Maersk Line with 28 days for one round trip (Figure 3.3).

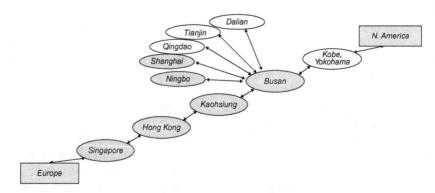

Figure 5.2: Traditional route to North America and transhipment ports

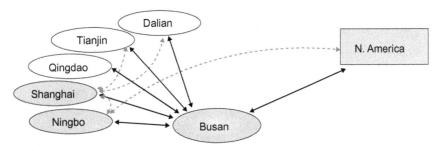

Figure 5.3: Current route to North America and transhipment ports

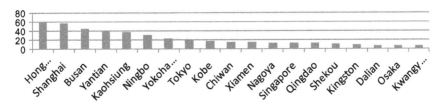

Figure 5.4: Calling frequency for US-bound ships
Source: Drewry (2006), compiled by authors.

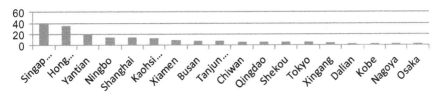

Figure 5.5: Calling frequency for Europe
Source: Drewry(2006), compiled by authors.

5.3.2. The Scope of Research

According to the change of ship calling pattern, recent port competition picture for more T/S cargoes in Northeast Asia has been drawn mainly due to the rapid development of Chinese ports. For example, in terms of transhipment volume including coastal cargoes, the port of Shanghai has been increasing faster than that of the port of Busan during the last 10 years. Judging from the number of ships' calling and the handling volume of container cargoes, as shown in Figure 5.6, two ports apparently have been competing with each other to attract more T/S cargoes.

To improve the accuracy and applicability of port choice model that can explain the transhipment flow in Northern China, it is necessary to make the scope of analysis. This study deals with transhipment cargoes to/from the Northern Chinese ports that were passing through the port of Shanghai and/or the port of Busan.

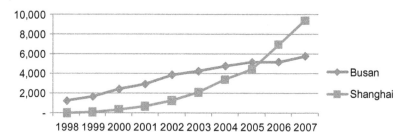

Figure 5.6: Transhipment trend in Busan and Shanghai
Source: SIPG internal report, and PORT-MIS, 2008.

5.4.   Port Choice Model of Transhipment Cargo

5.4.1.   *Factors for Selecting a Transhipment Port*

Prior to suggesting the port choice model, the factors are to be selected from experts who are responsible for designing the shipping line's route. The 15 items to be surveyed were collected from the published papers. According to published papers regarding the competitiveness of a port, the port that has an advantage in facility flexibility, and the efficiency of port labour is favoured by shipping companies (Haezendock, Coeck, & Verbeke, 2000). Notteboom and Fleming asserted that the port location, container volume to be handled and high ratio of transhipment are critical factors to the port's competiveness (Notteboom, 1997; Fleming, 1989). McCalla and Starr added hinterland transportation as a competing factor on top of Notteboom's assertion (McCalla, 1994; Starr, 1994). UNCTAD claimed that the competitive edge of a port consists of port location, hinterland transportation, the efficiency of port service, port cost, the social stability of port and the technology of ICT. Slack (1985) asserted that the main factors of being selected by shipping company are the frequency of ship calling, transportation fee of hinterland, port congestion, the networks for linking other mode, the convenience of customs clearance, the capability of facility, port cost, scale and safety.

The collected items from the research result of several papers were questioned for measuring the importance degree with five scores from senior managers of major container shipping lines.

Items that are related to T/S port selection by shipping lines were derived from the previous researches as shown Table 5.1.

A questionnaire survey has been performed by direct interviews with a responsible person in a shipping company, or the on-site visit with the explanation of the purpose in front of a group of responsible personnel in shipping companies. The questionnaires were sent to 30 container shipping lines including both Korean and foreign companies. The response rate was 90% of planned responses. The analysis of the questionnaire revealed that the most important factor for port selection by shipping lines was 'cargo handling capacity', that is, handling moves per ship per hour, followed by 'terminal handling charge' as the second important factor. The sequence of priority was listed in Table 5.1. Among these factors, 'container handling capability', 'berth facility', 'feeder frequency', 'feeder network', 'free time' and 'overtime storage fee' are a service factor that can be represented as a proxy variable.

As shown in Figure 5.7, these 15 port selection factors can be grouped into five types of attributes: cost, service, cargo volume, deviation cost and incentive.

Table 5.1: Score of transhipment port selection factors.

Item	Response	Mean	SD
Cargo handling capability	27	4.294	0.686
THC(terminal handling charge)	27	4.176	0.809
Berth facility	27	4.059	0.748
Feeder frequency	26	4.000	0.632
Main route location	26	4.000	0.632
CY facility	27	3.941	0.748
Feeder network	27	3.941	0.966
Cargo volume	25	3.933	0.961
Free time	27	3.706	0.985
Port dues	27	3.471	1.007
Overtime storage fee	27	3.412	0.87
Incentive	27	3.294	0.92
CIQ service	27	3.294	0.985
Providing berthing priority	26	2.938	0.929
Bunker supply, ship repair Service	27	2.824	1.074

Notes: Mean scores computed on five-point scale; 1 = strongly disagree, 5 = strongly agree.

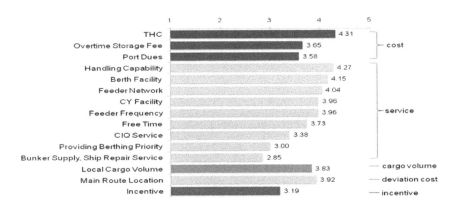

Figure 5.7: Transhipment decision factors

5.4.2.   Model Specification

The probability that a shipping company in region (r) selects transhipment port (p) can be expressed as:

$$P_P^r = \frac{e^{U_p^r}}{\sum_{p=1}^{p=P} e^{U_p^r}}, \quad (P = 1, 2, \ldots, P) \tag{5.1}$$

where U is the 'utility' attached to transhipment port (p) by a shipping line in region (r) and p is the index of the transhipment port in a total of P ports.

Considering Veldman's model (2007) and the factors to be surveyed, the utility function is modified as:

$$U_P^r = \alpha_1 CT_{pr} + \alpha_2 CI_{pr} + \alpha_3 CD_{pr} + \alpha_4 L_{pr} + \alpha_5 M_{pr} \tag{5.2}$$

where CT_{pr} is the sum of feerdering cost (CF_{pr}) and mother ship access cost (CM_{pr}). The feeder transport cost CF is incurred between transhipment port and feeder port (p,r) in r region; CM is the mainline access cost to transhipment port; CI is the incentive between transhipment port and competition port ($p,p'r$); CD_{pr} is deviation cost between transhipment hub port and feeder port. L_{pr} represents the attraction of a port given its volume of local cargoes. M_{pr} represents the total handling throughput of a port including local and transhipment cargo. This is a part of Mohring effects (Mohring, 1972) and expressed as a function of the level of port throughput. As feeder calling frequency increases, waiting time of cargo decreases. This makes cargo demand to increase and triggers the frequency of ship calling to increase in turn. This effect can be used as a substantial variable of port service. The Greek symbols α_1, α_2, α_3, α_4 and α_5 are the coefficients of the utility function.

By taking for each region (r) the ratio of the market share of transhipment port (p) and of an arbitrarily chosen basic port (p^*), it follows from Eq. (5.1):

$$\left(\frac{P_P^r}{P_{P^*}^r} \right) = \frac{e^{U_p^r}}{e^{U_{p^*}^r}} = e^{U_p^r - U_{p^*}^r} \tag{5.3}$$

By combining Eqs. (5.2) and (5.3) and taking their logarithms lead to:

$$\ln \left(\frac{P_P^r}{P_{P^*}^r} \right) = \alpha_1 (CT_{pr} - CT_{p^*r}) + \alpha_2 (CI_p - CI_{p^*}) + \alpha_3 (CD_p - CD_{p^*})$$
$$+ \alpha_4 (L_p - L_{p^*}) + \alpha_5 \left(M_p - M_p^* \right) \tag{5.4}$$

5.4.3.   Variable Description

5.4.3.1.   Dependent variable $\ln (P_P^r / P_{P^*}^r)$ is the share of transhipment in the port of Busan among total transhipment in the region.

5.4.3.2. Independent variables Selecting independent variables is dependent on research outputs on the topic. Researchers insist that deciding transhipment port is affected by cost, location, service factors like productivity and incentive system.

$CT_{pr} - CT_{pr'}$ is the total cost difference between the port of Busan and the port of Shanghai for moving containers from origin to destination in Northeast Asia region. This cost consists of operation cost, running cost and logistics cost.

$CI_{pr} - CI_{p'}$ is the incentive difference between the port of Busan and the port of Shanghai, where THC of deep sea volume is discounted with some percentage or where compensation for the growth of transhipment compared with a previous year throughput is paid to shipping company.

$CD_{pr} - CD_{p'}$ means the difference of deviation cost from main line route to the port of Busan or the port of Shanghai. In Northeast Asia, traditionally, main trunk route for United States has been established via Singapore, Hong Kong, Kaosiung, Busan and Yokohama to Los Angeles (Figure 5.2).

$L_p - L_{p'}$ can be obtained by the ratio of local cargo in Busan and the region. This is a proxy variable representing attraction effect.

$M_{pr} - M_{p'}$ can be acquired by the ratio of total handling cargo of Busan and the region. This is a proxy variable representing Mohring effect.

5.5. Data Gathering for Input Variable

5.5.1. Value of Dependent Variable Trade direction is one of the important factors to consider regarding the scope of research. Two trade directions of USA-bound and Europe-bound can be taken into consideration. Another issue that has attracted the attention is a regional scope that can be drawn from the relationship between the feeder service network and major ports in Northeast Asia. In this chapter, four Chinese ports such as Dalian, Tianjin, Qingdao and Shanghai are considered in relation to a port choice model.

For the quantitative model in 5.4.2, ports in Northeast Asia and cargoes to/from North America will be examined together. In Eq. (5.4), while the denominator is defined as transhipment containers in the Northern Chinese ports, the numerator is T/S containers in Busan for the last 10 years (see Table 5.2).

5.5.2. Value of Independent Variable In the ship operation, different types of cost are occurred on the supply chain. Ship cost is composed of voyage cost and running cost. Ship voyage cost again consists of fuelling cost and port dues. Prior to the

Table 5.2: Dependent variable and its value for 10 years, unit: 1000 TEU.

Year	Regional volume (Northern China, Busan and Shanghai)	Regional T/S volume (Northern China, Busan and Shanghai)	TS ratio (Busan to regional)
1998	12,328	981	0.436
1999	16,141	1,779	0.361
2000	19,955	2,549	0.337
2001	22,645	3,261	0.311
2002	28,360	4,404	0.303
2003	33,855	4,854	0.285
2004	41,699	5,904	0.261
2005	49,478	6,458	0.266
2006	57,257	7,364	0.239
2007	65,036	8,162	0.236

Table 5.3: Mother ship's specification for quantitative model.

Gross tonnage	51,836 GT
Net tonnage	22,101 NT
Deadweight tonnage	61,153 DWT
Draft	13.6 m
TEU capacity	4,400 TEU
Unloading containers	600 TEU (120 TEU, 240 FEU)
Loading containers	600 TEU (120 TEU, 240 FEU)
Total handling containers (assumed full containers)	720 BOX
Ratio of local and transhipment	63%:37%
Berthing time	24 h
Handling times	12 h
Bunker C consumption	27 ton per day
Bunker A consumption	2–3 ton per day

calculation of ship cost, dimensions of mother ship and feeder ship are to be defined for estimating costs.

5.5.2.1. Mother ship dimension for cost estimation   In this chapter, as indicated in Table 5.3, mother ship's dimension is assumed to be 51,836 GT, 22,101 NT, 61,153 DWT, 4,400 TEU capacity, and navigation speed is 22 knots, draft is 13.6 m, the handling moves being 360 unloading containers (120 TEU and 240 FEU) and 360 loading containers (120 TEU and 240 FEU), total 720 boxes with full condition, berthing time is 24 h and handling time is 12 h, the ratio of local cargo and transhipment is 62.6%:37% and bunker C consumption rate is 27 ton per day and bunker A consumption rate is 2.5 ton per day.

5.5.2.2. *Feeder ship dimension for cost estimation* Feeder ship's dimension is assumed to be 6,764 GT, 3,958 NT, 9,981 DWT, 576 TEU capacity, and navigation speed is 13.5 knots, draft is 7.9 m, total 300 boxes of handling containers that consist of 150 unloading moves (75 TEU and 75 FEU) and 150 loading moves (75 TEU and 75 FEU), berthing time is 8 h and handling time is 5 h, the ratio of local cargo and transhipment is 63%:37% and bunker C consumption rate is 19 ton per day and bunker A consumption rate is 2 ton per day (Table 5.4).

5.5.2.3. *Ship voyage cost* Variable cost includes expenses related to a specific voyage. Port cost and logistics cost, such as THC, lashing, shuttling, tally cost and cargo wharfage, and fuel consumption cost are grouped into voyage cost category.

5.5.2.4. *Port dues* When a mother ship calls at a port, it has to pay for various kinds of fees to port authority, terminal operator, pilot, tug company, and so on for services provided (Table 5.5).

5.5.2.5. *Fuel cost for transportation* Fuel consumption cost for transportation is calculated by distance from origin to destination and daily bunker consumption. In calculating fuel consumption of mother vessel, the distance difference of two cases is considered from Hong Kong to Shanghai and from Hong Kong to Busan. Tracking historic data for the last 10 years, RIM data are used for bunker C and A prices (Table 5.6).

5.5.2.6. *Port logistics cost* Within the scope of port logistics cost, THC, lashing cost, shuttle cost, wharfage, and tally cost are included in the category. Even though port

Table 5.4: Feeder ship's specification for quantitative model.

Gross tonnage	6,764 GT
Net tonnage	3,958 NT
Deadweight tonnage	9,981 DWT
Draft	7.9 m
TEU capacity	576 TEU
Unloading containers	225 TEU (75 TEU, 75 FEU)
Loading containers	225 TEU (75 TEU, 75 FEU)
Total handling containers (assumed full containers)	300 BOX
Ratio of local and transhipment	63%:37%.
Berthing time	8 h
Handling times	5 h
Bunker C consumption	19 ton per day
Bunker A consumption	2 ton per day

Table 5.5: Port dues.

Year	Port dues in Busan ($)	Port dues in Shanghai ($)	Difference ($)
1998	16,531	23,278	− 6,747
1999	16,714	20,398	− 3,684
2000	16,714	21,598	− 4,884
2001	16,714	21,358	− 4,644
2002	16,903	22,600	− 5,697
2003	16,903	24,200	− 7,297
2004	16,935	30,920	− 13,985
2005	17,203	37,672	− 20,469
2006	17,257	32,184	− 14,927
2007	17,336	30,280	− 12,944

Table 5.6: Fuel cost for transportation.

Year	Fuel cost in Busan ($)	Fuel cost in Shanghai ($)	Difference ($)
1998	31,136	31,339	− 203
1999	45,910	46,206	− 296
2000	71,529	72,253	− 724
2001	62,045	62,673	− 628
2002	66,720	67,406	− 686
2003	77,384	78,179	− 795
2004	87,932	88,815	− 883
2005	123,496	124,743	− 1,247
2006	149,574	151,092	− 1,518
2007	173,509	175,291	− 1,782

authority used to announce THC tariff, most of terminal operators have privately contracted with a shipping company on the practicable tariff according to promised volume. In Shanghai port, a shipping company pays THC that includes lashing fee, storage charge in CY and shuttle fee in the same terminal. In comparison, the port of Busan charges the elements of port disbursements separately to shipping companies. For this reason, it is not fair to list the difference of individual cost one by one (Table 5.7).

5.5.2.7. Ship running cost Running cost is calculated with capital and operating expenses according to the period of voyage. The purchase price of the ship consists of the key part of capital cost, whether it is a new shipbuilding or a second-hand ship.

Deposit, repayment of loan principal and interest are the part of capital cost. Within the overall ship cost, it is operation cost category where ship owners have the

Table 5.7: Port logistics cost.

Year	Logistics cost of transhipment cargo in Busan ($)	Logistics cost of transhipment cargo in Shanghai ($)	Difference ($)
1998	44,736	14,590	30,146
1999	45,665	14,590	31,074
2000	47,184	14,590	32,593
2001	48,721	14,590	34,130
2002	50,308	15,658	34,650
2003	51,533	17,009	34,524
2004	52,196	17,009	35,187
2005	52,617	20,643	31,974
2006	52,325	20,643	31,682
2007	50,012	20,643	29,369

Table 5.8: Ship voyage cost.

Year	Ship voyage cost in Busan ($)	Ship voyage cost in Shanghai ($)	Difference ($)
1998	88,507	62,098	26,409
1999	96,348	67,698	28,650
2000	108,843	79,366	29,477
2001	102,018	70,862	31,156
2002	100,477	69,217	31,260
2003	115,511	85,128	30,383
2004	130,144	102,102	28,042
2005	144,784	122,989	21,796
2006	148,512	124,653	23,859
2007	151,932	129,611	22,322

greatest influence over the choices made out. The difficulty that owners face is that suppliers of services to ships operate within their markets. The core operating cost elements are manning costs, insurance costs, repair cost, the cost of stores and supplies, and management and administration (Drewry, Ship Operating Cost, 2008).

As these costs have been so changeable depending on market situation, it is not easy task to track them for the past 10 years data. Drewry suggested that the time charter rate be used as a proxy value for calculating the ship running costs. Table 5.8 shows that there are differences between Busan and Shanghai in terms of running cost for feedering. From the viewpoint of major shipping lines, by calling in the port of Busan rather than Shanghai, they could have contributed to reducing the feeder's running costs (Table 5.9).

Table 5.9: Running cost.

Year	Mother ship running cost to Busan or Shanghai ($)	Feeder running cost between Dalian and Busan ($)	Feeder running cost between Dalian and Shanghai ($)	Difference ($)
1998	56,228	13,195	16,240	− 3,045
1999	62,100	10,855	13,360	− 2,505
2000	64,868	11,830	14,560	− 2,730
2001	52,178	11,635	14,320	− 2,685
2002	38,948	11,635	14,320	− 2,685
2003	63,923	12,935	15,920	− 2,985
2004	85,253	18,395	22,640	− 4,245
2005	81,972	23,881	29,392	− 5,511
2006	71,051	19,422	23,904	− 4,482
2007	63,923	17,875	22,000	− 4,125

Table 5.10: Total cost of transhipment via Busan and Shanghai.

Year	Total cost of T/S cargo to Busan ($)	Total cost of T/S cargo to Shanghai ($)	Difference ($)
1998	88,507	62,098	25,988
1999	96,348	67,698	28,229
2000	108,843	79,366	29,056
2001	102,018	70,862	30,735
2002	100,477	69,217	30,840
2003	115,511	85,128	29,962
2004	130,144	102,102	27,621
2005	144,784	122,989	21,375
2006	148,512	124,653	23,439
2007	151,932	129,611	21,901

5.5.2.8. Ship total cost including mother and feeder ship   Ship total costs including fuel cost, running cost and port charges from origin to destination are summed up for the comparison between Busan and Shanghai (Table 5.10).

5.5.2.9. Data for measuring port attraction   Mohring effect is defined as the ratio of captive cargo of Busan port to total captive cargo in the region. Busan's captive container throughput is obtained from PORT-MIS and the regional data are from OSC report (OSC, Container Port Strategy, 2007) (Table 5.11).

5.5.2.10. Deviation cost   Due to the recent change of routing pattern, defining deviation is complex and variable. The mainline deviation distance is measured as the

Table 5.11: Mohring effect of Busan port.

Year	Regional local volume (Northern China, Busan and Shanghai)	Local cargo in Busan (1,000 TEU)	Mohring effect
1998	11,347	4,539	0.400
1999	14,362	4,678	0.326
2000	17,406	5,035	0.289
2001	19,384	5,011	0.259
2002	23,956	5,522	0.231
2003	29,001	6,035	0.208
2004	35,795	6,495	0.181
2005	43,020	6,579	0.153
2006	49,893	6,803	0.136
2007	56,874	7,444	0.131

Table 5.12: Deviation cost of Busan and Shanghai.

Year	Mother ship transportation cost from Hong Kong to Busan ($)	Mother ship transportation cost from Hong Kong to Shanghai ($)	Difference ($)
1998	28,437	28,773	− 336
1999	41,935	42,427	− 492
2000	65,593	66,354	− 761
2001	56,897	57,557	− 660
2002	61,173	61,891	− 718
2003	70,950	71,783	− 833
2004	80,643	81,572	− 929
2005	113,252	114,563	− 1311
2006	137,177	138,763	− 1586
2007	159,087	160,953	− 1866

Source: Port MIS and OSC report (2006).

extra distance needed to call at a transhipment port compared to the distance of the shortest navigation course between the Hong Kong, Shanghai, Yokohama and Hong Kong, Busan, Yokohama. The remaining distance to North America is not considered because of the same distance to United States (Table 5.12).

5.6. The Result of Model Test

The multiple regression model is tested with 10 years data. One observation per year has been made ending up with 10 data. The reason why just 10 data were selected is

Table 5.13: Variable definition of model.

Variable		Definition	Unit
Dependent variable y		Ratio of transhipment of Busan with region transhipment	Ratio
Independent variable	X1	Ratio of local container of Busan with region local container	Ratio
	X2	Difference of incentive payment of transhipment	US $
	X3	Difference of mother vessel deviation cost of transhipment	US $
	X4	Total transhipment cost of mother ship and feeder	US $
	X5	Ratio of total handling container of Busan with region total handling container	Ratio

mainly because of the attribute of dependent variable and independent variables. If we increase the number of observations by quarterly or monthly, the result of analysis shows the anomaly, that is, the significant probability of most of independent variables is under 5% (Table 5.13).

5.6.1. Step-1 Model Test

The regression model has been tested in two steps. In the beginning, five variables are selected as an independent variable similar to Veldman's model (Veldman, 2008). The result shows that X1 (Mohring effect) and X4 (total cost) are accepted, and X2 (deviation cost) and X3 (incentive payment) are rejected with 5% significance level. As the adjusted R square is 0.986, the model indicates the high explanation of phenomena.

R	R Square	Adjusted R square	Standard error	Durbin–Watson
0.998	0.996	0.996	0.00386	0.449

As the result of ANOVA, the regression model has effective meaning because a significant probability level is less than 5%.

	Sum of square	Degree of freedom	Mean square	F	Significant probability
Model	0.137	5	0.127	1,827.373	0.000*
Residual	0.001	34	0.000		
Sum	0.137	39			

*$p<0.01$.

The coefficient of regression model is as follows:

Variable	Non-standard coefficient		t	Significant probability	Multi-collinearity	
	B	S.E.			Tolerance	Variance inflation factor (VIF)
A	0.1750000	0.0190	8.9940	0.000		
X1	0.0200000	0.0970	0.2020	0.841	0.0060	175.917
X2	− 0.00000214	0.0000	− 1.6820	0.102	0.3590	2.7830
X3	0.00000412	0.0000	0.7040	0.486	0.0510	19.6870
X4	− 0.0000043	0.0000	− 11.4980	0.000*	0.1970	5.0730
X5	0.7830000	0.1180	606440	0.000*	0.0040	247.471

*$p < 0.01$.

5.6.2. Step-2 Model Test

According to step-1 test, the model to be tested is modified with the deletion of three variables that show weak significant probability. The independent variables to be selected are X4 (Total Cost) and X5 (Mohring effect). The result of test is that adjusted R square is 0.995. According to ANOVA, significance probability is 0 that implies an effectiveness of the model. Furthermore, the fact that correlation indicator, variance inflation factor (VIF), is less than 10, meaning that any dependence does not exist in between independent variables. The coefficient of model is $Y = 0.179291199–0.000004782589 \cdot X4 + 0.810489669 \cdot X5$. This expression will be used for sensitivity analysis.

R	R Square	Adjusted R square	Standard error	Durbin–Watson
0.998	0.996	0.996	0.00386	0.512

	Sum of square	Degree of freedom	Mean square	F	Significant probability
Model	0.137	2	0.068	4584.348	0.000*
Residual	0.001	37	0.000		
Sum	0.137	39			

*$p < 0.01$.

Variable	Non-standard coefficient		t	Significant probability	Multi-collinearity	
	B	S.E			Tolerance	Variance inflation factor (VIF)
A	0.17000000	0.0050	36.597	0.000*		
X4	− 0.000004503	0.0000	− 21.695	0.000*	0.629	1.590
X5	0.82200000	0.0090	87.179	0.000*	0.629	1.590

*$p < 0.01$.

5.6.3. Step-3 Model Test

According to step-2 test, the model is to be expanded to identify which one has stronger impact to attract T/S cargo between mother ship cost and feeder ship cost. Keeping X5 the same, X4 independent variable (total Cost), needs to be divided into X6 and X7. X6 describes the total cost difference due to mother ship operation from Hong Kong to Busan, while X7 represents the total cost due to feeder ship operation from Dalian to Busan. The result of test is that adjusted R square is 0.999. According to ANOVA, significance probability is 0 that shows an effectiveness of the model. Furthermore, the fact that correlation indicator, VIF, is less than 10, meaning that any dependence does not exist in between independent variables. The coefficient of model is $Y = 0.94 - 0.9 \cdot X5 - 0.00000231 \cdot X6 - 0.00001104$. This implies that the impact of feeder ships is stronger than that of mother ships in terms of attracting T/S cargoes.

R	R Square	Adjusted R square	Standard error	Durbin–Watson
0.999	0.999	0.999	0.00229	0.691

	Sum of square	Degree of freedom	Mean square	F	Significant probability
Model		3	0.046	8689.812	0.000*
Residual	0.000	36	0.000		
Sum	0.137	39			

*$p < 0.01$.

Variable	Non-standard coefficient		t	Significant probability	Multi-collinearity	
	B	S.E.			Tolerance	Variance inflation factor (VIF)
A	0.0940000	0.0100	9.7760	0.000		
X5	0.9000000	0.0110	81.880	0.000*	0.163	6.135
X6	− 0.00000231	0.0000	− 7.9150	0.000*	0.263	3.806
X7	− 0.00001104	0.0000	− 13.8540	0.000*	0.088	11.415

*$p<0.01$.

5.6.4. Port Choice Model for Sensitive Analysis Using System Dynamics Tool

The model that helps estimating the T/S cargoes in Busan can be retransformed to system dynamics (SD) model. The SD model is a useful tool for presenting social phenomena. The model is made up of total cost and Mohring sub-system. One of the characteristics of SD model is time sensitivity. This chapter has been working with the past 10-year data for the cost-related values and the amount of container that were handled in the Northeast Asia. In making port choice model using Powersim tool, the main level is defined as the transhipment ratio of the port of Busan. The level variable is linked to inflow variable and outflow variable. Inflow variable consists of two sub-modules of 'Mohring Effect' and 'Difference of Total Cost' that are linked to T/S inflow module.

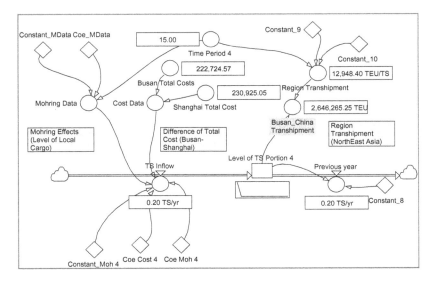

Figure 5.8: SD model for estimation of transhipment

Table 5.14: Forecast of T/S volume by adjusted THC in Busan (mainly from northern Chinese ports).

Year	− 20%	− 15%	− 10%	0	10%	15%	20%
2009	144,215	108,533	71,364	0	− 69,877	− 104,073	− 139,755
2010	151,060	113,684	74,751	0	− 73,193	− 109,013	− 146,388
2011	155,433	116,976	76,915	0	− 75,312	− 112,169	− 150,626
2012	156,971	118,133	77,676	0	− 76,058	− 113,279	− 152,117
2013	155,311	116,884	76,855	0	− 75,253	− 112,081	− 150,508

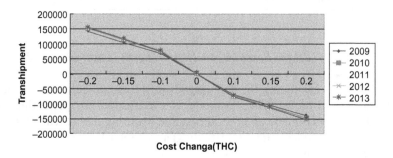

Figure 5.9: Demand curve of transhipment

Figure 5.8 describes that a demand curve can be drawn in the SD model. For example, as shown in Table 5.14, if the THC is discounted 10%, transhipment will be increased to 71,364 TEU in Northeast Asia in 2009 (Figure 5.9).

5.7. Conclusion

The purpose of this chapter was to develop a port choice model to estimate the transhipment cargoes in the future. For this, it was required to identify port selection (or choice) factors for transhipment cargoes. To this end, this study has adopted the logit model suggested by Ohashi (2005) and Veldman (2007) that has been commonly used as a port selection model. In addition, by taking into consideration of the port selection factors that come from the previous studies, this chapter has identified five factors based on data from the last 10 years: namely cargo volume at a local port, incentive amount, deviation expenses of a mother ship, total expenses of a mother ship and feeders, and total cargo volume as a service substitution.

For empirical applications, the following assumption was made: the mother ship of 65,000 GT departs from Hong Kong via Busan or Shanghai to the US West Coast, and the feeder, a 6,700 GT containership, sails from Dalian to Shanghai or from Dalian to Busan.

The data used in the model are based on the latest 10-year data available from 1998 to 2007 and have been collected from related organizations during on-site visits. The collected data have been used for the above-mentioned port selection model to calculate the difference of values between the two ports of Shanghai and Busan. In the first test, the two variables among the five—'the difference of T/S cargo expenses between Busan and Shanghai in both a mother ship and a feeder' and 'the rate of Busan Port's total cargo volume against the regional total cargo volume' —are statistically significant being at the 0.01 level. Therefore, the second test has been made for these two variables that are statistically significant, and as a result these two are again also statistically significant with the same level. This implies that 'the cost reduction of a mother ship and a feeder ship' and 'total cargo increase at the local port' are the most important factors for the increase in transhipment cargo volume in ports. After separating the mother ship's expenses from feeder's expenses, the third test has been conducted. The result has indicated that these two factors are statistically significant being at the 0.01 level, and that the feeder's expenses carry more significance than the expenses of mother ships. This means that more incentives should be given to the feeders that are suffering financial difficulty.

In this study, a port choice model to estimate the T/S cargoes was developed using the PowerSim tool. It was found that the port choice of shipping lines has been influenced by two factors: the Mohring effect and the ship's operating costs. In particular, the model can be used to anticipate the future volume by adjusting independent variables like 'the transhipment cargo expenses difference' or 'the rate of Busan Port's total cargo volume against the regional total cargo volume'.

This study has several academic implications. First, inspite of the importance of the issue of port choice factors regarding T/S cargoes, there have not been many analytical studies based upon recent data. This chapter therefore contributes to enrich the contemporary literature on how the research issue can be addressed effectively by using the technique of SD. Further, as this study employs the PowerSim tool for the SD model, it facilitates the understanding of how this technique can be applied to address the research issue in the T/S port selection context. This study also offers insights into and practical applications of the management of container terminals and port authorities. As this study reveals the factors that are the most important in terms of attracting more T/S cargoes into a specific port, management can use these findings to focus on their marketing strategies in those areas with higher priority so as to achieve more effective, efficient and thus more attractive outcomes.

However, it has a limitation of confining the scope in northern Chinese ports. Since this may make the model somewhat less reliable if applied to a broader region, it could be tackled in a further study.

References

Bae, B. T. (1999). The devices to increase transshipment cargoes of the port of Pusan. *Journal of Korea Port Economic Association*, *15*, 179–208.

Baek, I. (2005). Transshipment Port Selection ISM and AHP. *The Journal of Shipping and Logistics*, *54*(June), 43–64.

Drewry (2006). *Annual Container Market Review and Forecast 2006/2007.*

Drewry. (2008). *Ship Operating Costs Annual Review and Forecast 2008/09.*

Fleming, D. K. (1989). West-coast container port competition. *Maritime Policy and Management, 16*(2), 93–107.

Haezendock, E., Coeck, C., & Verbeke, A. (2000). The competitive position of seaports: Introduction of the value added concept. *Maritime Economics and Logistics, 2*(2), 107–118.

Jung, T. W., & Kwak, K. S. (2002). Strategies to attract transshipment container cargos from/ to China by Korea ports. *Journal of Transportation Research Society of Korea, 20*(2), 7–16.

Lirn, T. C., Thanopoulou, H. A., & Beresford, A. K. C. (2003). Transshipment port selection and decision-making behavior: Analysing the Taiwanese case. *International Journal of Logistics: Research and Application, 6*(4), 229–244.

Lirn, T. C., Thanopoulou, H. A., & Beresford, A. K. C. (2004). An application of AHP on transshipment port selection: A global perspective. *Maritime Economics and Logistics, 6*(1), 70–91.

McCalla, R. (1994). Canadian container: How have they fared? How will they do? *Maritime Policy and Management, 21*(3), 207–217.

Mohring, H. (1972). Optimization and scale economies in urban bus transportation. *American Economic Review*, 591–604.

Ng, K. Y. A. (2006). Assessing the attractiveness of ports in the North European container transshipment market: An agenda for future research in port competition. *Maritime Economics and Logistics, 8*, 234–250.

Notteboom, T. E. (1997). Concentration and load centre development in the European container port system. *Journal of Transport Geography, 5*(2), 99–115.

Ocean Shipping Consultants. (2007). *Container Port Strategy*, Emerging issues.

Ocean Shipping Consultants. (2007). *Marketing of Container Terminals, 2004.*

Ohashi, H., Kim, T. S., Oum, T. H., & Yuc, C. Y. (2005). Choice of air cargo transshipment airport: An application to air cargo traffic to/from Northeast Asia. *Journal of Air Transport Management, 11*, 149–159.

Park, B. I., & Sung, S. K. (2008). The decision criteria on the transshipment container ports. *Journal of Korea Port Economic Association, 24*(1), 41–60.

Park, Y. T., & Kim, Y. M. (2003). A study on the strategies to attract transshipment container cargoes in Korea. *Journal of Logistics Association, 13*(1), 95–121.

Slack, B. (1985). Containerisation, inter-port competition and port selection. *Maritime Policy and Management, 12*(4), 293–304.

Starr, J. (1994). The mid-Atlantic load centre: Baltimore or Hampton Road? *Maritime Policy and Management, 21*(3), 219–227.

Veldman, S., & Bückmann, E. (2003). A Model on container port competition, an application for the West European container hub-ports. *Maritime Economics and Logistics, 5*(2), 3–22.

Veldman, S., Bückmann, E., & Saitua, R. (2005). River depth and container port market shares: The impact of deepening the Scheldt river on the west European container hub-port market shares. *Maritime Economics and Logistics, 7*(4), 336–355.

Veldman, S., & Vroomen, B. (2007). A model of container port competition: an application for the transshipment market of the Mediterranean. *IAME Conference Athens 2007*, 1–17.

Chapter 6

Maritime Logistics and Supply Chain Security

Hokey Min

Abstract

Despite a hangover from the worldwide economic crisis, international trade rebounded nicely with a record-level growth in late 2010. A sharp rise in international trade has sparked the international traffic growth. A majority of this traffic growth originated from maritime logistics which could move cargoes in large volume and at cheaper freight costs. Due to its cost-efficiency and easy access, maritime logistics typically accounts for more than half of the worldwide freight volume. However, maritime logistics poses a greater supply chain risk, since ocean carriers used for maritime logistics are more vulnerable to unpredictable weather conditions, piracy attacks, terrorist hijacking, and cargo damages on the open sea than any other modes of transportation. Also, given the vast areas that maritime logistics covers, it is more difficult to protect maritime logistics activities from potential hazards and threats.

To better protect maritime logistics activities from potential security lapses, this chapter introduces and develops a variety of systematic security measures and tools that were successfully used by best-in-class companies and government entities across the world. Also, this chapter proposes a total maritime security management model as a way to formulate maritime risk mitigation strategies. To elaborate, this chapter sheds light on the roots of maritime security measures and tools, the ways that those measures and tools are best utilized, the roles of advanced information technology in maritime security from the global supply chain perspectives, the visualization and identification of potential maritime and its related supply chain risks, and policy guidelines that will help enhance maritime security.

Keywords: Maritime logistics; supply chain risk management; security measures; global supply chains; information technology; international trade

Maritime Logistics: Contemporary Issues
Copyright © 2012 by Emerald Group Publishing Limited
All rights of reproduction in any form reserved
ISBN: 978-1-78052-340-8

6.1. Introduction

Despite the recent decline in international trade volume resulting from the worldwide economic crisis, international trade has almost doubled the average annual growth rate of world Gross Domestic Product (GDP) since 1950 (WTO, 2009). As cross-border trade increases, international traffic will continue to grow. As a matter of fact, total freight handled worldwide in January 2008 rose by 6% compared to January 2007, with international freight up strongly by 8% (Airport Council International, 2009). In particular, the Far Eastern Asia region (e.g., Japan, Korea, and China) sustained a relatively high traffic growth, which could be attributed to their dominant roles in international trade and free trade movements across the world. A majority of this traffic growth originated from maritime transportation which could haul cargoes in large volume and at cheaper freight costs. Thanks to its cost-efficiency and easy accessibility, maritime transportation accounts for 57% of the worldwide freight volume (Gee, 2002). However, maritime transportation poses a greater transit risk, since ocean carriers used for maritime transportation are more vulnerable to unpredictable weather conditions, piracy attacks, terrorist hijacking, and cargo damages on the open sea than the other modes of transportation. Especially, big cargo ships which often carry millions of dollars of cargoes but are run by a small number of crews can be vulnerable to potential hazards, natural disasters, and piracies.

To protect these cargo ships from potential security lapses and subsequently reduce maritime insurance costs, systematic security measures and tools should be developed. Such security measures include government initiatives, similar to the Customs Trade Partnership Against Terrorism (C-TPAT) that was introduced by the U.S. government. Also, the example of systematic security tools may include ubiquitous information technology such as wireless technology linked to radio frequency identification (RFID) and electronic data interchange (EDI). In an effort to develop effective and efficient security measures and tools, we propose a total maritime security management (TMSM) model from four different aspects of maritime security: (1) physical, (2) personnel, (3) procedural, and (4) information technology.

To elaborate, physical security refers to security measures that prevent or deter pirates or terrorists or thieves from accessing a ship, port facilities, maritime resources, or information stored on physical media. The physical security may also refer to specific guidance on how to design physical structures to resist various hostile acts (Task Committee, 1999). Some of the physical security measures include security locks, fencing, walls, fireproof safes, water sprinklers, surveillance cameras, close-circuit television (CCTV) monitors, smoke detectors, heat sensors, and intrusion detectors. In addition, to enhance physical security, all ships, port terminals, and ship yards may be constructed of materials that resist unlawful entry and protect against outside intrusion. Another physical security measure includes the assessment of vulnerability of the existing buildings and infrastructure with appropriate follow-up (Sweet, 2006). Personnel security involves security measures that handle investigations and background checks to ensure that personnel (e.g., crews, sailors, and stevedore gangs) in positions of trust can be allowed access to restricted information. These measures include employee screening, periodic background checks, and application verifications. Procedural security deals with the identification, development, establishment, and enforcement of security policies about the procedures that regulate the usage of a maritime system and infrastructure (Weldemariam & Villafiorita, 2008). Procedural security measures include an examination of the integrity of documentation, shipping manifests, and cargo discrepancy checks. Information technology security aims to control access to sensitive electronic information so that only those with a legitimate need to access it can do so. Its objectives are ensuring confidentiality, integrity, and availability of data (Feinman, Goldman, Wong, & Cooper 1999).

Confidentiality requires appropriate classification of the information so that access to the information can be limited only to those in need of that information. Maintaining confidentiality requires having sound policies that are enforced strictly. These policies may include password protection, authentication and authorization for every information request which would allow only the authorized users to access to the information. Integrity involves ensuring that the information being shared is valid and reliable. This could involve information in a database such as the inventory level for a specific product or the shipment status of a product. In today's maritime transportation environments, shippers, carriers, and port authorities may require access to propriety information using wireless devices such as Personal Digital Assistants (PDAs). Since information flows over the airwaves, one could protect the information in transit using an encryption such as The Public Key Cryptography (PKI) tools (RSA, 2007). Also, various antihacking measures would help information integrity. Availability means that the supply chain partners are able to get the information they need when they need it. This requires a high level of assurance that the information system will be up and running so that all authorized users can access to information such as advanced shipping notice and shipment status. In order to guarantee a high level of availability, information systems must be backed up remotely. The tools available for this purpose are hot and warm sites.

In the following sections, we will elaborate on the roots of maritime security measures and tools, the ways that those measures and tools are best utilized, the roles of advanced information technology in maritime security from the global supply chain perspectives, the visualization and identification of potential maritime and its related supply chain risks, and policy guidelines that will be helpful for enhancing maritime security.

6.2. Evolution and Trends of the Maritime Security Measures and Tools in the United States

Over 80% of world merchandise trade was carried by sea. In 2007, the volume of global maritime transportation reached 8.02 billion tons — a 4.8% increase from the previous year. Indeed, during the past three decades, the annual average growth rate of global maritime transportation is estimated to be 3.1% (UNCTAD Secretariat, 2008). Due to its scale, complexity, and role in the global supply chain, maritime transportation can be a prime subject of terrorism, sabotage, and piracy. Despite serious threats of various security breaches, maritime transportation as compared to air transportation has received little attention from government authorities and parties involved in maritime transportation. For example, in the United States, only about 2% of cargo containers entering the U.S. territories are physically inspected by the customs officials (Frittelli, 2003). Considering the vulnerabilities of maritime transportation, there is an urgent need for systematic security measures. Such measures can be built upon a total maritime security management (TMSM) model that can identify the weakest link of the maritime transportation channel and then enhance supply chain resilience. Generally speaking, total maritime security management (TMSM) is referred to as the best management practice of developing and implementing enterprise-wide risk prevention and reduction plans to enhance maritime security. TMSM includes an evaluation of international shipping routes/channels and international maritime policies and procedures in terms of preparedness for disruptive events such as terrorism, political upheaval, labor strikes, natural disasters, severe weather, accidents, and pilferage. Its basic architecture of TMSM can be graphically displayed in Figure 6.1 (Ritter, Barrett, & Wilson, 2007).

To achieve its objectives, the TMSM focuses on five security measures (Ritter et al., 2007):

(1) Tracking and monitoring cargoes throughout the entire maritime transit;
(2) Coordinating the security practices with supply chain partners;
(3) Verifying the credentials of all personnel involved in the movement and storage of goods throughout maritime transportation;
(4) Increase the ability to rapidly, efficiently, and effectively reroute freight in transit when disruptions occur;
(5) Engaging, delegating, and training personnel at all levels to follow established security protocols.

Especially, the TMSM should be designed to incorporate continuity and standardization of maritime security plans, company-specific policies and procedures, and maritime security regulations such as the International Convention for the Safety of Life at Sea (SOLAS) and International Ship and Port Facility Security Code (ISPS). The ISPS is aimed at enhancing maritime security on board ships and at ship–port interface areas (Min, 2011). It contains detailed maritime security measures — related

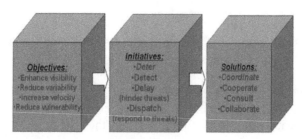

Figure 6.1: Graphical architecture of the TMSM model
Source: Adapted and modified from Ritter et al. (2007).

requirements for government, port authorities, and shipping companies in a mandatory section (Part A) together with a series of guidelines about how to meet these requirements in a second, nonmandatory section (Part B). These requirements include approval of ship and port facility security plans; issuance of International Ship Security Certificates (ISSC) after verification; carrying out and approval of Port Facility Security Assessment; determination of port facilities which need to designate a Port Facility Security Officer; and an exercise of control and compliance measures such as port state control procedures (Branch, 2007). In addition, the ISPS code was designed to establish a framework for international cooperation among governments, their agencies, the shipping industry, and port authorities to detect security threats and take preventive measures against security incidents affecting maritime transportation by exchanging security-related information among them (Bragdon, 2008). Other related regulatory disciplines that complement the ISPS code are Contracting Government aka Flag States (e.g., U.S. Maritime Transportation Act of 2002) and Port State Control (e.g., Panama Maritime Authority).

6.3. Best Practices for Supply Chain and Maritime Security Management

Due to increased complexity and uncertainty involved in international trade, global supply chains have become more vulnerable to security breaches than ever before. These security breaches may range from terrorism to computer hacking and natural disasters. To take a more active stance to these potential security breaches, a growing number of multinational firms (MNFs) and government organizations have developed and implemented various supply chain security management systems and policies. Typically, a supply chain security management system comprises six security measures: (1) facility management, (2) cargo management, (3) human resource management, (4) information and communication management, (5) business network and company management, and (6) crisis management as shown in Figure 6.2 (Mooney, 2007).

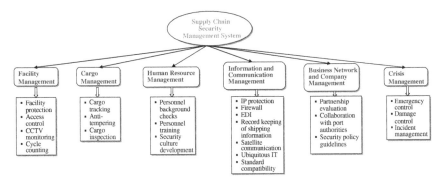

Figure 6.2: The components of the supply chain security management system
Source: Adapted and modified from Mooney, T. (2007).

If unguided, however, many of those systems and policies will fail to achieve their intended objectives. In an effort to provide such guidance, both ISO (International Organization for Standardization) and GAO (Government Accountability Office) promoted various supply chain security standards and initiatives such as ISO28000:2007 and ISO31000:2009. Other notable supply chain security initiatives include C-TPAT, Authorized Economic Operator as part of the World Customs Organization SAFE framework of standards, the Container Security Initiative led by U.S. Department of Homeland Security, International Ship and Port Facility Security (ISPS) Code initiated by the International Maritime Organization (IMO), the Free and Secure Trade (FAST) regulated by NAFTA countries, Basic Alliance for Security Commerce (BASC) initiated by Latin American companies, Operation Safe Commerce supported by the U.S. Department of Transportation, and the Secure Freight Initiative launched by the U.S. Department of Homeland Security and Energy.

To elaborate, the ISO guidance for supply chain security aims to establish adequate levels of security within those parts (e.g., maritime transportation, customs process, and port operations) of an international supply chain which multinational organizations control and monitor. Especially, ISO 28000:2007, *specification for security management systems for the supply chain,* offers a framework for effective physical security management through a supply chain security system that identifies security threats, assesses risk, establishes objectives for implementing controls, and continuously improves the physical security of the organization (JBW Group International, 2009). Also, as integral part of ISO 28000 series, specific ISO 28001:2007 security guidelines, *best practices for implementing supply chain security, assessments, and plans — requirements and guidance,* include (ISO, 2007):

- Definition of the supply chain boundary that is covered by the security plan;
- Identification of the vulnerable supply chain areas and the assessment of risk involved in those areas including the development of security threat scenarios;
- Security measures needed for potential threats and risks;
- The method of training security personnel to meet their assigned security-related duties;

These guidelines also suggest the security processes graphically displayed in Figure 6.3.

ISO 28001 guidelines also have extended checklists to evaluate the supply chain security performances of the international organization with respect to a number of security categories. Those checklists include (ISO, 2007):

(1) Management of Supply Chain Security
- Does the organization have a management system that addresses supply chain security?
- Does the organization have a person designated as responsible for supply chain security?

(2) Security Plan
- Does the organization have (a) current security plan(s)?

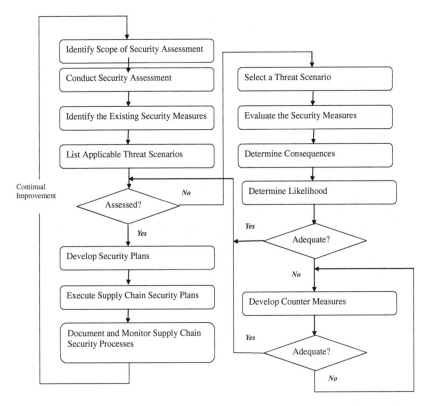

Figure 6.3: Supply chain security processes suggested by ISO 28000/28001
Source: ISO (2007), *Security Management Systems for the Supply Chain*, Unpublished White Paper, Geneva, Switzerland: ISO Copyright Office.

- Does the plan address the organization's security expectations of upstream and downstream business partners?
- Does the organization have a crisis management, business continuity, and security recovery plan?

(3) Asset Security
- Does the organization have in place measures that addresses
  - the physical security of buildings,
  - monitoring and controlling of exterior and interior perimeters,
  - application of access controls that prohibit unauthorized access to facilities, conveyances, loading docks and cargo areas, and managerial control over the issuance of identification (employee, visitor, vendor, etc.) and other access devices?
- Are there operational security technologies which significantly enhance asset protection? For example, intrusion detection, or recorded CCTV/Digital Video Systems (DVS) cameras that cover areas of importance to the supply chain

activity, with the recordings maintained for a long enough period of time to be of use in an incident investigation.

- Are there protocols in place to contact internal security personnel or external law enforcement in case of security breach?
- Are procedures in place to restrict, detect, and report unauthorized access to all cargo and conveyance storage areas?
- Are persons delivering or receiving cargo identified before cargo is received or released?

(4) Personnel Security

- Does the organization have procedures to evaluate the integrity of employees prior to employment and periodically relative to their security duties?
- Does the organization conduct specific job appropriate training to assist employees in performing their security duties for example: maintaining cargo integrity, recognizing potential internal threats to security and protecting access controls?
- Does the organization make employees aware of the procedures the company has in place to report suspicious incidents?
- Does the access control system incorporate immediate removal of a terminated employee's company-issued identification and access sensitive areas and information systems?

(5) Information Security

- Are procedures employed to ensure that all information used for cargo processing, both electronic and manual, is legible, timely, accurate, and protected against alteration, loss, or introduction of erroneous data?
- Does an organization shipping or receiving cargo reconcile the cargo with the appropriate shipping documentation?
- Does the organization ensure that cargo information received from business partners is reported accurately and in a timely manner?
- Is relevant data protected through use of storage systems not contingent on the operation of the primary data handling system (is there a data backup process in place)?
- Do all users have a unique identifier (user ID) for their personal and sole use, to ensure that their activities can be traced to them?
- Is an effective password management system employed to authenticate users and are users required to change their passwords at least annually?
- Is there protection against unauthorized access to and misuse of information?

(6) Goods and Conveyance Security

- Are procedures in place to restrict, detect, and report unauthorized access to all shipping, loading dock areas, and closed cargo transport unit storage?
- Are qualified persons designated to supervise cargo operations?
- Are procedures in place for notifying appropriate law enforcement in cases where anomalies or illegal activities are detected or suspected by the organization?
- Are procedures in place to ensure the integrity of the goods/cargo when the goods/cargo are delivered to another organization (transportation provider, consolidation center, intermodal facility, etc.) in the supply chain?

- Are processes in place to track changes in threat levels along transport routes?
- Are there security rules, procedures, or guidance provided to conveyance operators (for example, the avoidance of dangerous routes)?

If answers to the above checklists are mostly "yes," the organization is considered to be supply chain resilient. Otherwise, the organization is considered to be ill-prepared for potential security breaches. With respect to the level of supply chain security preparedness, the organization can be classified into the following four categories:

(1) "Precompliant" Organization
- Places disaster recovery plans on the back burner.
- Plays catch-up when its supply chain is disrupted by the unforeseen events (e.g., Land Rover is not prepared for the sudden supplier bankruptcy that cut off the supply of chassis frames in 2001).
(2) "Compliant" Organization (Cook, 2008)
- Views supply chain resiliency or security merely as a cost of doing business.
- Complies with C-TPAT and thinks that imposed measures are enough.
(3) "Secure" Organization
- Is proactive about working with suppliers and customers to head off supply chain disruptions.
(4) "Resilient" Organization (Waters, 2007)
- Views risk management as part of its business strategy and an opportunity to boost competitiveness.
- Builds some measures of redundancy into its supply chains and can detect and respond to potential disasters.

As illustrations of supply chain "resilient" organizations, we would introduce several multinational firms and government organizations that conduct the best supply chain security practices.

(1) Cisco's Supply Chain Security Management Practices

Teaming with supply chain partners across the globe, Cisco recently launched the supply chain risk management (SCRM) program that streamlines risk mitigation efforts and improves supply chain resiliency. The SCRM consists of four key elements (Harrington & O'Connor, 2009):

(a) Business Continuity Planning (BCP) Program develops recovery plans, document recovery times, and drive resiliency standards with Cisco's supply chain partners such as suppliers, manufacturing partners, and logistics service providers.
(b) Crisis Management monitors and responds to supply chain disruptions globally on a 24/7 basis.

(c) Product Resiliency addresses vulnerabilities in product design decisions, translate long-term risk mitigation strategies into short-term priorities, and reduce the cost of risk mitigation strategies and programs.
(d) Supply Chain Resiliency identifies supply chain areas with recovery times outside Cisco's established tolerance and develops corresponding resiliency plans.

Within the SCRM program, Cisco utilized National Center for Crisis and Continuity Coordination (NC4) alert risk profiles based on specific locations and geographies. Depending on the level of potential risks and threats, Cisco's supply chain partners such as suppliers are categorized as three different color codes: (1) "Green" requiring no action; (2) "Yellow" needing monitoring; and (3) "Red" needing mitigation. Similarly, Cisco developed color-coded "resiliency index" at the product, site, regional, geography, and business unit to prioritize risk mitigation efforts.

(2) Dow Chemical's Supply Chain Security Management Practices

Though less than 1% of Dow Chemical product shipments involve the transportation of highly hazardous materials, Dow Chemical frequently uses multimodal transportation and clear customs to serve customers in 175 countries. To ensure the safe and secure shipments of its products, Dow Chemical developed the supply chain security system that included the Most Effective Technology (MET) such as RFID and Loss Prevention Principles (LPP) which go beyond government requirements and industry practices. The core of Dow Chemical's supply chain security system is RFID which allows it to achieve the following benefits (Allemang, 2006):

- 50% improvement in response time to identify and resolve in-transit problems.
- 20% reduction in excess product/safety stock inventory.
- 20% container fleet reduction.
- Up to 90% improvement in reliability of delivery time windows.
- Elimination/early detection of product theft.
- Elimination of historical 10%–15% human error rate associated with manual work processes to capture and enter data.
- Leveraging the RFID, Dow Chemical's supply chain "disaster-proofing" strategy focuses on four elements: (1) safe and secure shipping container design; (2) supply chain visibility; (3) greater collaboration with both public and private supply chain partners; (4) more resilient supply chain redesign (Reese, 2007). The examples of specific "disaster-proofing" strategies include incremental upgrade of container design; use of the "next-generation" railcars equipped with head and side impact limiters, electronically controlled pneumatic brakes, and crumple zones and impact-resistant coatings; a mix of tract-and-trace technology based on both RFID and global positioning systems (GPS); a 24-hour emergency call center to facilitate immediate emergency responses; the redesign of supply chains in such a way that the number of shipments and container-miles for highly hazardous materials is minimized.

(3) SAIC's Supply Chain Security Management Practices

In the wake of supply chain disruptions caused by Hurricane Katrina, SAIC (Science Application International Corporation) developed its own supply chain security system that helps it protect itself from potential disasters and security breaches. Since SAIC's business heavily depends on government contracts — 88% of its revenue comes from the U.S. government, SAIC is required to perform its business activities regardless of adverse conditions such as disasters and security lapses. To sustain its operations continuously in the unexpected disruptive events, SAIC takes the following security measures:

- A Basic Ordering Agreement (BOA) for the purchase of emergency supplies and services at fixed price for a predetermined period of time (usually three to five years) (Koskovich & Luke, 2010);
- The use of cell phones and satellite communication systems in case of communication breakdowns;
- Risk mapping that color-coded the level of risk at the vulnerable supply chain area (e.g., Gulf coast in the United States).
- The customized web-enabled status report that offers real-time supply chain visibility throughout the order cycle time;
- A development of the Cyber Supply Chain Assurance Model that combines cyber security with the supply chain risk analysis to protect critical information and communication infrastructure (Boyson & Rossman, 2009);
- The use of the Operation Safe Commerce (OSC) initiatives that identify vulnerabilities at each step of the supply chain and prevent the introduction of the unmanifested material into the global supply chain by using biometric access control, supply chain event management, RFID e-seal, GPS tracking, smart card technology, remote monitoring of firewalls in a 24/7 network operations center, and CCTV monitoring at terminals, ports, and warehouses.
- The development of the Integrated Container Inspection System (ICIS) that improves the early detection of potential security risk associated with U.S. bound cargoes (SAIC, 2011).

(4) Port of the Singapore's Maritime Security Management Practices

The port of Singapore is located at one of the major crossroad of the world and regarded as one of the largest container ports in the world which often plays a role as the major logistics hub. Due to its strategic location and heavy traffic with 200 different shipping lines, disruptions at the port of Singapore will have a lasting impact on the entire global trade and supply chain. To better prepare for potential disruptions, the port of Singapore developed and implemented a maritime security system that was built on the Secure Trade Partnership (STP) program in May of 2007. In an effort to increase the awareness of importance of maritime security and prevent supply chain disruptions, the STP program spells out a set of security guidelines that are meant to help various supply chain partners identify and focus on the security gaps and then undertake necessary measures to plug those gaps (Singapore Customs, 2007).

Other important security measures taken by the port of Singapore include (1) the establishment of maritime security task forces comprise Republic of Singapore Navy, Police Coast Guard, Maritime and Port Authority, and Immigration & Checkpoint Authority; (2) the use of protocols set by the so-called SOLAS convention, the International Ship and Port Facility Security (ISPS) code, and UN Convention against Illicit Traffic in Narcotic Drugs and Psychotropic Substances; (3) the formalized cooperation with neighboring nations that encompasses the sharing of law enforcement resources, the acceleration of request-response process, the pursuit and entry into territorial sea and archipelagic waters, and the boarding and detention of suspect vessels from the flag or coastal state; (4) multilateral efforts to safeguard key chokepoints and sea lines of communication; and (5) risk-profiling of cargoes based on information about the nature, transportation mode, origin, and destination of cargoes.

(5) YCH Group's Security Awareness through ISO 28000: 2007 Certification

YCH Group Pte, Ltd., headquartered in Singapore provides end-to-end logistics and supply chain management solutions to Fortune 500 multinational clients such as Canon, Dell, Moet-Hennessy, and Motorola in Asia Pacific including Singapore, Malaysia, Thailand, Indonesia, China, Taiwan, Hong Kong, Philippines, and Australia. It offers integrated logistics services, such as warehousing and inventory management, transportation and distribution management, and freight management services. It also provides supply chain management services through a suite of supply chain solutions for raw materials management, consumer goods distribution, and service and returns management. Due to its cross-border supply chain operations, it heavily involves in maritime logistics covering the areas more vulnerable to various supply chain risks. To enhance its supply chain security, it became the first logistics company in the world which received ISO 28000: 2007 certification. Their security measures comprise two major steps: (1) site assessment and (2) independent audit. The purpose of site assessment is to identify any security gaps requiring adjustments to bring it into line with ISO 28000: 2007 standards by thoroughly reviewing documents and maritime logistics procedures. Given that supply chains security is every employee's business, the YCH Group often conducted interviews with senior management of all departments that had an interface with supply chain security. Following on site assessment, the YCH Group performed independent audits based on the Lloyd Register Quality Assurance to take proactive stance for security management. These audits go beyond physical security measures taken by the security personnel and go through the Plan-Do-Check-Act cycle. The YCH Group's ISO 28000: 2007 certification brought following benefits:

- Enhance image and credibility
- Better monitoring of freight flows throughout the supply chain
- Better protection from smuggling, piracies, and terrorist attacks

- Faster recovery from unforeseen disasters
- Better alignment to customs processes
- Reduced risk of project cost overruns

6.4. Recent Advances in Ubiquitous Information Technology for Supply Chain and Maritime Security

On a daily basis, IBM imports more than 5.5 million pounds of hardware valued at $68 million via 2500 customs declarations. In fact, IBM's global supply chain comprises 30 individual supply chains across 61 countries with 19,000 employees. To manage this stretched global supply chain, IBM often coordinates its assets, delivery operations, and information flows through integrating the global supply chain. Effective global supply chain planning brought IBM a total of $12 billion savings in business expenditures during 2002 and 2003 (Richardson, 2005). As evidenced by the IBM example, global supply chain planning is essential for the firm's business success. The effectiveness of global supply chain planning often rests on the utilization of information technology that enables supply chain partners (e.g., shippers, carriers, and port authorities) to share crucial order and shipment status information among them. In particular, during maritime transit which represents important part of the global supply chain operations, real-time sharing of the shipment status information can enhance supply chain visibility and thus improve supply chain security. Since vessels are in constant move during the maritime transit, the availability of ubiquitous information will allow the carriers, shippers, and port authorities to update the shipment status information on a real-time basis and exploit such information in a timely manner. Thus, ubiquitous information technology which can provide information on "anything, anytime, and anywhere," will be useful for effective maritime transportation planning which is the core of global supply chain planning. Given the importance of ubiquitous information technology to global supply chain planning, it is worth investigating which ubiquitous information technology is available for maritime transportation planning and how such technology has been evolving. One emerging technology that can facilitate ubiquitous information sharing includes RFID technology. Thus, our discussions about ubiquitous information technology will center on the evolution of RFID for maritime transportation planning.

In general, ubiquitous information technology necessitates the addressable objects/devices (e.g., unique identification) and wireless connectivity. Since RFID is often characterized as a tagged object with a unique ID number and wireless Bluetooth communication devices, RFID can be an important stepping stone for embracing the ubiquitous information technology. The increasing popularity of RFID in the logistics sector is attributed to its ability to tract assets (including moving assets) and to transmit real-time information about those assets throughout the supply chain. In particular, maritime transportation can reap significant benefits from RFID applications that automate the tracking of high-value transportation equipment, unit load devices, and reusable shipping containers, while ensuring that right products are shipped to right customers. RFID carries data in transponders (i.e., tags) attached permanently to an asset to read data stored on a microchip using radio waves as shown in Figure 6.4. The examples of this asset include a container, a case, a bin, a pallet, a package, and an individual product item as illustrated in Figure 6.5. This asset can also be a living animal and a human. Depending on the reading mechanism, the RFID tag can take several different forms: (1) *active* tags carry their own power source and broadcast their own signals to communicate with readers; (2) *passive* tags will be activated to broadcast data once they are within the electromagnetic field of the reader's antenna; and (3) *semi-passive* tags contain a tiny battery for logging the data received from the connected sensors (Moeeni, 2006; Carr, Zhang, Klopping, & Min, 2010). The further

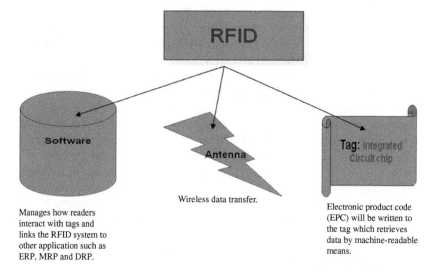

Figure 6.4: The Key components of RFID

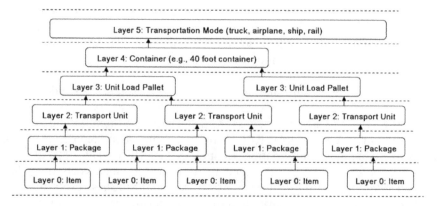

Figure 6.5: The layers of RFID assets

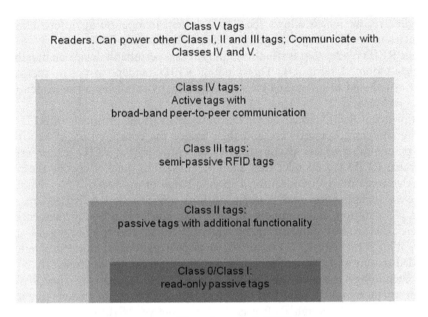

Figure 6.6: Five classes of RFID tags

details about the different classes of RFID tags with respect to their evolution and sophistication can be found in Figure 6.6.

Despite the enormous benefit potentials of RFID for maritime security, the efficiency of RFID can be restricted without resolving some hardware, software, and standard issues. For example, passive RFID tags have read ranges of only approximately 20 feet. Also, traditional bulky batteries that are used to power radio signals for active RFID tags can limit the RFID's life span and its use to track large assets. Furthermore, RFID tags are susceptible to skimming (being read surreptitiously) without installing safeguard devices and tools such as encryption technology and tag protectors (O'Connor, 2007). As such, the use of most advanced technologies for RFID hardware can significantly enhance its efficiency in ensuring maritime security. Some illustrations of the recent advances in RFID technology include:

- Thin-film lithium and lithium-ion batteries that can be used to power temperature, humidity, shock, and other types of sensors linked to RFID tags, making it easier, more durable, and cheaper to track various of types, shapes, and sizes of assets during maritime transit;
- A radio-isotope powered alpha voltaic battery that can prolong the RFID life span because it can run for years without replacement or recharging. It also poses less environmental and health risks because it is not made of chemical substances;
- A "*PlusID*" or a *PAD* (personal authentication device) tag protector equipped with an integrated fingerprint reader that uses a biometric lock to prevent suspected individuals from getting access to the RFID system and cloning the data onto another device;

- An "agile" reader which allows the RFID system to operate at different radio frequencies in a wide variety of geographical locations (see Table 6.1);
- A mobile RFID reader that is usually employed as a peripheral device on handheld or vehicle-mounted terminals. This kind of RFID readers works in the same manner as tethered or integrated bar code scanners by capturing a single identifier as an object moves;
- A multiprotocol RFID reader/writer that retargets various protocols of RFID by changing configuration software and then reduce the consumption of electronic power by one-third or less as compared to the conventional RFID reader/writer;
- A wearable RFID tag encoder that enables workers to quickly encode the right EPCs (electronic product codes) for a specific batch of products;
- A Wireless Identification and Sensing Platform (WISP) that is battery-free for sensing, computation, and communication. WISP, which requires low maintenance, is powered and read by standards-compliant UHF-RFID reader at a range of up to 10 feet. With WISP, the RFID technology can be expanded to handle ubiquitous, embedded sensing tasks (Buettner, Greenstein, Sample, Smith, & Wetherall, 2008);
- RuBee technology is a two-way, active wireless protocol that uses Long Wave (LW) magnetic signals to send and receive short (128 byte) data packets in a local regional network. Although RuBee is similar to active RFID in that it actually transmits a data signal, it works in the low frequency (below 450 kHz and typically at 132 kHz) band and primarily uses the magnetic field, whereas active RFID typically works in the VHF, UHF or SHF bands and with the electric field (Pierce & Sanders, 2007). Unlike RFID, RuBee is not blocked by people, animal, or water and subsequently its readability is much better than RFID in harsh environments. It also is the only wireless device that does not pose eavesdropping or tempest risk. Thus, RuBee is considered the more secure alternative to RFID.

As illustrated above, RFID has a great potential for becoming an integral part of maritime security management. Indeed, the recent survey conducted by eyetransport (2006) indicated that an increasing percentage of practitioners recognized

Table 6.1: The level of radio frequency and its read distance.

Type/Frequency	Maximum read distance	Typical applications
Low (LF): 125 kHz	Less than 1.5 feet	Security access, electronic payment, animal identification, inventory control
High (HF): 13.57 MHz	Less than 3 feet	Tote tracking, access control, asset management, smart shelving
Ultra-High (UHF): 860928 MHz	6–10 feet	Case and pallet tracking, railroad car monitoring, toll collection
Microwave: 2.45 or 5.8 GHz	6–10 feet	Customs solutions

Source: Slightly modified from. Tompkins Associates (2004).

the importance of RFID to security management including maritime security (see Figure 6.7).

More specifically, RFID can be incorporated into the TMSM model as a catalyst for implementing the concept of "smart" containers and green lanes because it can bring numerous security benefits (see Table 6.2).

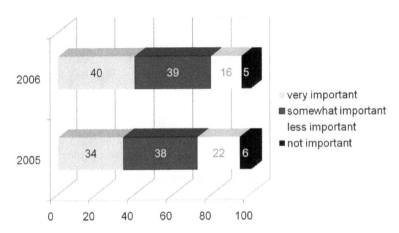

Figure 6.7: Reasons for deploying RFID for security management
Source: 3rd RFID conference for transport and logistics providers (2006).

Table 6.2: RFID for smart containers and green lanes.

Category	Customs requirements	Security benefits
Smart containers	• The container should remain sealed and tamper-free during transit. • The detailed information about the container should be available whenever requested by the U.S. Customs Office.	• Regarded as a low-risk container according to C-TPAT • Exempted from full customs inspections

Green lanes	• During the loading process, full compliances with C-TPAT are required.
	  ○ The port of origin (export) should be registered based on the CSI rule.
	  ○ Shipments should be made via C-TPAT certified carriers should be made.
		• Simplified customs procedures through Green Lane.
		• Improved lead time due to faster transit time.

Source: www.globalsecurity.org/security/systems/smart_containers.htm (2006).

6.5. Development of a Supply Chain Map that Shows the Shipping Routes/Channels Vulnerable to Maritime Security Breaches and Lapses

A supply chain is as strong as its weakest link. Unforeseen disruptions at the weakest link can cut off the flow of goods and information across the entire supply chain and adversely affect the supply chain efficiency. To obviate these disruptions, supply chain planers (e.g., Korean shippers, government agencies, and port authorities) should identify the weakest link of the supply chain vulnerable to security breaches by drawing a supply chain map. In general, a supply chain map refers to a graphical form of a communication device that helps supply chain planners visualize key information regarding distribution channel dynamics, strategic business environments, communication flows, physical product flows, relationships among supply chain partners, and geographical representations of logistics infrastructure and supply chain members (end-customers, service providers, and intermediaries) to identify overlapped supply chains, redesign or modify existing supply chains, and improve supply chain management procedures (Gardner & Cooper, 2003). Put simply, a supply chain map helps supply chain planners determine what risk and vulnerability they face at each stage of the supply chain. Once the supply chain map is presented, they can develop appropriate risk prevention measures that help them beef up identified weaknesses and reduce the sources of risk and variability. As shown in Figure 6.8, a supply chain map is the central piece of the supply chain risk model development that can pinpoint the various sources of risks including the maritime security risk.

To elaborate, such risk prevention measures may include strategic decisions as to which areas of ports and supply chain links to protect first, which shipping routes ocean carriers to take, which combinations of communication tools and information

Figure 6.8: The supply chain risk modeling procedure

technology to combine and which security measures to employ to prevent security failures. Depending on the types of risk and vulnerability, the supply chain map may differ. Thus, prior to developing the supply chain map, we need to classify the sources of risks into various types and categories. Following the framework suggested by Rao and Goldsby (2009) and Simchi-Levi, Kaminski, and Simchi-Levi (2008), the sources of global supply chain risks can be classified into external and internal drivers of risks. External drivers of risks that originate outside the company are often uncontrollable, whereas internal drivers of risks that originate inside the company are mostly controllable. These risks can be subdivided into financial, strategic, operational, and hazard risks. The further details of these risks are summarized in Table 6.3.

To illustrate how the supply chain map can be drawn, let us consider a global supply chain involving maritime logistics that transports and stores internationally traded goods from the point of origin (e.g., Incheon, Busan, and Kwangyang) and the point of destination (e.g., Long Beach). The development of the supply chain map starts with the presentation of risk maps. The risk maps can be drawn based on the questions that examine whether you and your supply chain partners are at the potential supply chain risks. These questions include:

(1) Does your supply chain deal with the free flow of goods across international borders?

Table 6.3: The various sources of global supply chain risks.

Types	Subcategories	Examples
External drivers of risks	Financial risks	Inflation, interest rates, tax rates, foreign exchange rates, and credit rating
	Strategic risks	Extent of competition in the market, changes in customer bases/supplier bases, changes in industry trends, customer demand, and mergers/acquisitions
	Operational risks	Human resource recruitment and retention, government regulations, cultural shifts, composition of the board of directors
	Hazard risks	(Marine) Piracies, weathers, climates, natural disasters, environmental impacts
Internal drivers of risks	Financial risks	Liquidity, cash flows
	Strategic risks	Functional integration, research and development (R&D), technology transfers, loss of the intellectual capital/property
	Operational risks	Accounting errors, information security breaches, labor- management conflicts, sabotages
	Hazard risks	Power failures, (computer) system downtime, pilferages/thefts

(2) Does your distribution channel or shipping lanes include logistics infrastructures such as bridges, tunnels, subways, airports, seaports, terminals, and warehouses?

(3) Does your communication channel relay on public telecommunication networks?

(4) Does your supply chain include refineries, chemical plants, nuclear or conventional power plants, oil pipelines, or agricultural farms?

(5) Does your distribution channel or shipping lanes pass through earthquake epicenters, cyclone/hurricane paths, and/or tornado alleys?

(6) Does your company deal with hostile labor unions and/or migrating/temporary workforce?

(7) Does one or more of your supply chain partners reside in the country where its local government is unstable?

Once the risk maps are developed, the extent of risk at each "pain point" should be measured. Herein, a "pain point" is referred to as the unsafe area where either a probability of physical or social or financial harm/detriment/loss is high or the severity of such harm/detriment/loss is great. Graphically, paint points represent all the unsafe areas shaded either yellow or red in Figure 6.9.

Using the U.S. Military Standard (2006), the probability of risk occurrence and its severity can be further classified as illustrated in Table 6.4. Table 6.5 defines the severity of risk.

After the supply chain map with paint points was displayed as shown Figure 6.10, a supply chain risk scorecard that shows the extent of supply chain risk at each stage of the supply chain with different color codes should be developed. For instance, Figure 6.11 demonstrates a supply chain risk scorecard for the washing machine example involving the transportation of imported parts of the washing machine from Korea to the United States.

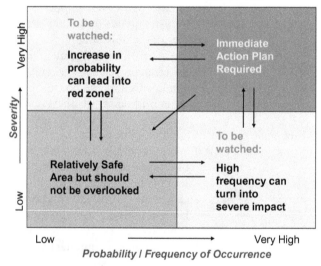

Figure. 6.9: A paint point map showing the extent of risk

Table 6.4: Risk matrix classifying the severity and likelihood of risk.

Severity	Likelihood					
	Impossible (0%)	Improbable (<10%)	Remote (10%–25%)	Occasional (25%–50%)	Probable (50%–75%)	Frequent (>75%)
Catastrophic						
Critical						
Marginal						
Negligible						

Source: Adapted and Slightly Modified from U.S. Military MIL-STD-882D (2006).

Table 6.5: The severity of risk categories.

Descriptive category	Injury to personnel	Equipment or product losses	Down-time
Catastrophic	Death	More than 1 million	Longer than 4 months
Critical	Severe injury	$250,000–$1 million	2 weeks to 4 months
Marginal	Minor injury	$1000–$250,000	1 day to 2 weeks
Negligible	None	Less than $1000	Less than a day

Source: Adapted and Slightly Modified from US. Military MIL-STD-882D (2006).

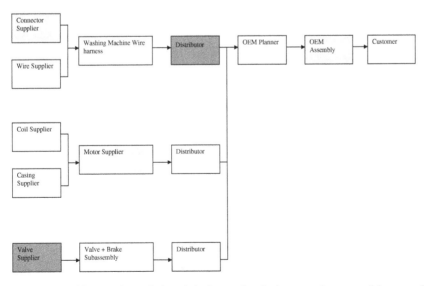

Figure 6.10: An illustration of the global supply chain map for a washing machine with pain points

	Physical security				Personnel security			Procedural security				IT security			
Category weighting	35%				15%			20%				30%			
	Access control	Facility protection	Surveillance	Risk assessment	Background check	Training	Application verification	Cargo checks	Documentation	Policy development	Standard compliance	Data protection	EDI communication	Confidentiality	Integrity
Sub-category weighting	30%	40%	5%	25%	25%	10%	30%	40%	45%	5%	10%	30%	25%	40%	5%
Supply															
Distribution															
OEM planning															
OEM assembly															

Level of risk:
Very High Risk
High Risk
Medium Risk
Low Risk
Very Low Risk

Figure 6.11: The illustrative supply chain risk scorecard

6.6.   Summary and Conclusions

Due to the heavy reliance of world economy on global trade, a continuous success of world economy rests on its ability to facilitate global trade by efficiently and effectively managing global supply chains. However, the global supply chain is often fraught with various environmental, political, financial, and managerial risks. The failure to handle these risks can disrupt the global supply chain and subsequently undermine the world economic prosperity for a long time to come. To aid the government authorities and private corporations across the world in predicting and mitigating these risks, we propose "holistic" security measures. The heart and soul of these security measures is the total maritime security management (TMSM) model that introduces the concept of total systems approach involving every supply chain partner at every step of maritime logistics within the global supply chain and helps to forge strategic alliances among supply chain partners in identifying and mitigating risks. Since the formation of strong strategic alliances necessitates communication links among the supply chain partners involved in maritime logistics, we stress the role of advanced information technology in maritime logistics. Such IT includes RFID, its variants (e.g.,

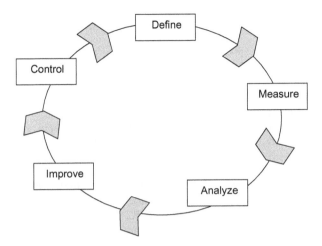

Figure 6.12: The Six Sigma DMAIC cycle for IT security management

RuBee), GPS, and EDI. Considering challenges of adopting and utilizing advanced IT for maritime logistics, we propose some practical guidelines specified below:

- Take the Advanced Trade Data Initiatives (ATDI) to share data among supply chain partners and to quality for Tier-3 Certification in C-TPAT;
- Launch the customs enterprise system (e.g., Automated Commercial Environments) to spot anomalies, integrate biometric information about personnel handling goods in transit, and develop risk profiles by mapping potential supply chain risks;
- Adopt the Transportation Worker Identification Credential (TWIC) that can control the unescorted access of all personnel to secure maritime IT infrastructure and equipment using the worker's tamper-resistant biometric fingerprints;
- Develop, document, communicate, and update IT security standards on a regular basis. These standards include: Standards for Digital Government (Internet) Applications, Data Content Standards (e.g., ISO/IEC 15963), ANSI, and EDIFACT;
- Apply the Six Sigma's DMAIC Cycle for IT security management as shown in Figure 6.12.

Acknowledgments

The author thanks the Korea Ocean Research & Development Institute (KORDI) for partly funding this research project and the President of KORDI, Dr. Jeung-Keuck Kang; Director General of the Maritime & Ocean Research Institute (MOERI), Dr. Yong-Kon Lim; and the KORDI Researcher, Dr. Jong-Won Park for their continuous support and encouragement throughout this research project.

References

Airport Council International (2009). *Annual traffic data.* Unpublished Report. Airport Council International, Geneva, Switzerland.

Allemang, A. (2006). Supply chain security and the business benefits. Presented at the Manufacturing Institute: Innovators in Supply Chain Security: Better Security Drives Business Value Forum, Washington, DC, August.

Boyson, S., & Rossman, H. (2009). Developing a cyber supply chain assurance model. Presented at the R.H. Smith School of Business, University of Maryland, April 2, 2009. Retrieved from http://csrc.nist.gov/groups/SMA/ispab/documents/minutes/2009-04/ispab_sboyson-hrossman_april2009.pdf. Accessed on May 8, 2010.

Bragdon, C. R. (2008). *Transportation security.* Burlington, MA: Butterworth-Heinemann.

Branch, A. (2007). *Elements of shipping* (8th ed.). London, Great Britain: Routledge.

Buettner, M., Greenstein, B., Sample, A., Smith, J. R., & Wetherall, D. (2008). Revisiting smart dust with RFID sensing networks. *Proceedings of the 7th ACM workshop on hot topics in RFID,* Retrieved from http://ww2.seattle/intel-research.net/~jrsmith/2008-hotnets-wisp.pdf

Carr, A., Zhang, M., Klopping, I., & Min, H. (2010). RFID technology: Implications for healthcare organizations. *American Journal of Business, 25*(2), 1–16.

Cook, T. A. (2008). *Managing global supply chains: Compliance, security, and dealing with terrorism.* New York, NY: Auerbach Publications.

Eyefortransport. (2006). *RFID in transportation and logistics: An analysis of RFID eyefortransport's recent survey.* Presented at the 3rd RFID Opportunities for Transport & Logistics Providers Conference, Scottsdale, AZ.

Feinman, T., Goldman, D., Wong, R., & Cooper, N. (1999). *Security basics: White Paper.* Unpublished Paper, Resource Protection Services, PricewaterhouseCoopers, London.

Frittelli, J. F. (2003). *Maritime security: Overview of issues.* CRS Report to Congress, The Library of Congress, Washington, DC.

Gardner, J. T., & Cooper, M. C. (2003). Strategic supply chain mapping approaches. *Journal of Business Logistics, 24*(2), 37–64.

Gee, A. (2002). Cargo shipping. *Worldmapper.* Retrieved from http://www.worldmapper.org/display.php?selected=40. Accessed on September 11, 2011.

Harrington, K., & O'Connor, J. (2009). How Cisco succeeds at global risk management. *Supply Chain Management Review, 13*(5), 10–17.

ISO (2007). *Security management systems for the supply chain — best practices for implementing supply chain security, assessments and plans — requirements and guidance.* Unpublished White Paper. ISO Copyright Office, Geneva, Switzerland.

JBW Group International (2009). *Supply chain security and ISO 28000.* Unpublished White Paper. JBW Group International, Minneapolis, MN.

Koskovich, M., & Luke, L. (2010). SAIC awarded basic ordering agreement (BOA) to Support naval surface warfare center (NSWC) Crane Division. Newswire, April 12. Retrieved from http://www.prnewswire.com/news-releases/saic-awarded-basic-ordering-agreement-to-support-naval-surface-warfare-center-nswc-crane-division-100519969.html. Accessed on September 30, 2010.

Min, H. (2011). Modern maritime piracy in supply chain risk management. *International Journal of Logistics Systems and Management, 10*(1), 122–138.

Moeeni, F. (2006). From light frequency identification (LFID) to radio frequency identification (RFID) in the supply chain. *Decision Line, 37*(3), 8–13.

Mooney, T. (2007). Securing competitive advantage. *Supply Chain Asia* (September/October), 11–15.

O'Connor, M. C. (2007). Keeping RFID tags from prying eyes. *RFID Journal, 4*(2), 50–51.

Pierce, J., & Sanders, R. (2007). The application of RuBee visibility systems in the orthopedic value chain. *BONEZon* (summer), 76–79.

Rao, S., & Goldsby, T. J. (2009). Supply chain risks: A review and typology. *The International Journal of Logistics Management, 20*(1), 97–123.

Reese, A. K. (2007). Disaster-proofing the supply chain: Using supply chain solutions to prepare for the next. *Supply and Demand Chain Executive*, (April/May).

Richardson, H. L. (2005). Shape up your supply chain. *Logistics Today, 46*(1), 26–29.

Ritter, L., Barrett, J. M., & Wilson, R. (2007). *Securing global transportation networks: A total security management approach.* New York, NY: McGraw-Hill.

RSA (2007). Retrieved from http://www.rsa.com. Accessed on November 14, 2007.

SAIC (2011). *SAIC corporate fact sheet.* MacLean, VA: SAIC. Retrieved from http://www.saic.com/news/pdf/corporatefactsheet.pdf

Simchi-Levi, D., Kaminski, P., & Simchi-Levi, E. (2008). *Designing and managing the supply chain: Concepts, strategies, and case studies.* New York, NY: McGraw-Hill.

Singapore Customs (2007). Singapore's supply chain security program. *World Customs Journal, 1*(2), 71–73.

Sweet, K. M. (2006). *Transportation and cargo security: Threats and solutions.* Upper Saddle River, NJ: Pearson Education, Inc.

Task Committee (1999). *Structural design for physical security.* Reston, VA: American Society of Civil Engineers (ASCE) Publications.

UNCTAD Secretariat (2008). *Review of maritime transport 2008.* Geneva, Switzerland: United Nations Conference on Trade and Development.

Waters, D. (2007). *Supply chain risk management: Vulnerability and resilience in logistics.* London: Kogan Page.

Weldemariam, K., & Villafiorita, A. (2008). Formal procedural security modeling and analysis. *Proceedings of risks and security of internet and systems, 2008. CRiSIS '08. Third International Conference*, October 28–20, pp. 249–254.

WTO (2009). *International trade and tariff data.* Unpublished Reports. World Trade Organization, Geneva, Switzerland.

Chapter 7

Risk Management in Maritime Logistics and Supply Chains

Jasmine Siu Lee Lam

Abstract

This study aims to critically review and analyse the classification of supply chain risks and disruptions and thereby suggest a suitable method for classifying maritime risks. It aims to discuss the propagation effects of port disruption on the supply chain and mitigation strategies.

In addition to secondary research, six semi-structured interviews were conducted with the management personnel of two terminal operators, two shipping lines and two insurance companies.

When a port disruption happens, the most immediate impact is the adverse effects on terminal operations. It also leads to a domino effect on other parties in the supply chain including shippers and consignees, shipping companies, inter-modal transport providers and other ports. Proper risk management needs to be embraced by the supply chain members. However, there is very little or no such collaboration between the supply chain members in practice.

This article proposes a more integrative approach in assessing various kinds of risks, and more research in this area to be done for Asia.

Risk management has been the concern for many stakeholders ranging from industry practitioners to the people who are affected by the maritime business throughout the world. The maritime industry should look into risk management in the maritime logistics and supply chain context instead of dealing with risk in isolation.

There is a serious lack of research for analysing supply chain disruptions with ports as a focal point. The paper contributes by filling the research gap.

Keywords: Risk management; maritime; supply chain; port

Maritime Logistics: Contemporary Issues
ISBN: 978-1-78052-340-8

7.1. Introduction

Under fierce competition in global market, companies have shifted their competition from among the companies to competing on supply chain management in seeking ways to maximize overall profitability (Craighead, Blackhurst, Rungtusanatham, & Handfield, 2007). Efficient supply chain management is essential as organizations strive to provide their products and services to customers in the global market in a faster and cost-efficient manner. Globalization has increased logistical risks and vulnerability in the supply chain (Juttner, 2005). Generally, supply chain is facing an increase in the probability and severity of disruption (Blackhursta, Craigheadb, Elkinsc, & Handfieldd, 2005; Knemeyer, Zinn, & Eroglu, 2009). As the world economy becomes more interconnected, a disruption at any stage of a supply chain leads to a domino effect on the rest of the parties and the impact can span several continents. Ports and shipping as vital trade facilitators and components of supply chains are among the most important causes for uncertainty (Sanchez-Rodrigues, Potter, & Naim, 2010). This prompts us to investigate this under-researched area. The paper contributes to the emerging field of supply chain risk management (SCRM) and specifically investigates the topic in connection to maritime logistics and supply chains. This study aims to critically review and analyse the classification of supply chain risks and disruptions exists in the literature and thereby suggest a suitable method for classifying maritime risks. It also aims to discuss the propagation effects of port disruption on the supply chain and mitigation strategies, with evidence from historical events and interviews with industry professionals. Recommendations for research and practice will then be given.

   After introduction, the reminder of this paper is organized as follows. An overview of supply chain and maritime risks literature will be given in the next section. The third section analyses the classification of supply chain risks and disruptions. Research methodology is then explained. After which, empirical results are discussed in two sections. The fifth section focuses on the impact of port disruption on supply chains. It is followed by a discussion on mitigation strategies adopted by the case companies and the author's recommendation. The last section draws the conclusion.

7.2. An Overview of Supply Chain and Maritime Risks Literature

The study of risk and risk management has a long history. Topics about individual risks such as organizational risk and financial risk have been researched and understood to a large extent. SCRM is a growing research area. The recent years have seen a substantial surge in SCRM studies, in both academia and industry (Rao & Goldsby, 2009; Seshadri & Subrahmanyam, 2005). However, a holistic view of risk management in the context of a supply chain is not prevailing. SCRM is still in its infancy (Khan, Burnes, & Christopher, 2007) with many areas still unexplored, and thus, plenty of research opportunities exist.

   Also, not many studies have been undertaken to address maritime supply chains which is an area of growing importance (Lam, 2011). Risks in maritime supply chains are an even more under-researched area (Asbjørnslett & Gisnaas, 2007). Ports and shipping, as compared to other transportation contexts, have more interfaces with other stages and members in the supply chains which represent potential weak points. The related risk issues have only been investigated in a limited scale. These areas include financial risk in shipping (Akatsuka & Leggate, 2001; Alizadeh & Nomikos, 2009; Dinwoodie & Morris, 2003), market risk in shipping (Kavussanos, Juell-Skielse, & Forrest, 2003; Scarsi, 2007), piracy and security concerns (Barnes & Oloruntoba, 2005; Hong & Ng, 2010; Raymond, 2006), risks to the environment (Giziakis & Bardi-Giziaki, 2002; LeClair, Pelot, & Xu, 2010), risks to humans involved (Bloor, Thomas, & Lane, 2000), information risk (Roumboutsos, Nikitakos, & Gritzalis, 2005), and smuggling risk (Tsai, 2005). An important research gap exists in risk management in maritime logistics and supply chains. A comprehensive risk management regime needs to be investigated and created.

7.3. Classification of Supply Chain Risks and Disruptions

It is essential to have a structured approach for identifying and quantifying risks in risk management (Frosdick, 1997). Identifying risks is the first step in developing a risk management process (Manuj & Mentzer, 2008). Hence, to examine this subject, the study firstly investigates risk classification.

Looking at a wide coverage of risks, Chopra and Sodhi (2004) classified supply chain risks into nine categories, namely, disruptions, delays, systems, forecast inaccuracies, intellectual property breaches, procurement failures, system break-down, inventory problems and capacity issues. Being one of the risks, disruption in this case is the disruption of material flows. The paper clearly eliminated the need to include delays in disruption risks, but the definition of disruption is not precise. Events such as deviation of shipping routes can easily fit into the disruption definition. More details should be elaborated to facilitate precise classification of events. The other way of risk classification was proposed by Spekman and Davis (2004) who grouped supply chain risks into 6 areas: physical movement of goods, information flow, money flow, security of the firm's internal information system, relationships between supply chain partners and corporate social responsibility, as well as the effect on a firm's reputation. Supply chain risks can also be grouped according to risk sources, consisting of environmental factors, industry factors, organizational factors, problem-specific factors, and decision-maker related factors. Sub-divisions under each risk sources were further made (Rao & Goldsby, 2009). Such classification is systematic and easily traceable. But disruption is not specifically identified as a kind of supply chain risk since it may happen due to various sources, though it would be more often under environmental factors since other risk sources pose mostly uncertainty rather than disruption.

In terms of broad classification, Mitroff and Alpaslan (2003) divided crisis into natural disasters, normal accidents and abnormal accidents. Normal accidents happen due to system overload problems, while abnormal accidents refer to intentional evil actions to cause damage. Sheffi and Rice (2005) classified disruptions into random events, accidents and intentional disruptions while Stecke and Kumar (2009) sorted disruptions into man-made catastrophes (i.e. non-terrorist intentional acts, terrorist acts and accidents) and natural calamities. These papers stressed on whether the risks are natural or otherwise. Christopher and Peck (2004) divided risks into process, control, demand, supply and environmental. This grouping is useful for a company to look into the risk it exposes and to identify the vulnerability towards risks. Kleindorfer and Saad (2005) broadly categorised supply chain risks into two kinds: supply and demand risks, and disruption risks. Disruption risks consist of operational risks which involve equipment malfunctions, unforeseen discontinuities in supply, human-centred issues, the risks from natural hazards, terrorism and political instability. Risks were categorized differently by Craighead et al. (2007) under the following 3 types: disruption, financial and operational risks. Disruption and operational risks are separately identified.

It is observed that so far there is no common approach in classifying supply chain risks in the literature. But one consensus on disruption is that it is a risk leading to disturbance in normal daily activities. Wagner and Bode (2006) illustrated disruption as an unintended, untoward situation that contributes to risks in supply chain and it is an exceptional and irregular situation compared to daily business. The study explained disruption as a sudden unexpected occurrence that deviates from the business norms. In our paper, the definition of disruption is an event that causes a sudden interruption on material flow in a supply chain, leading to a halt in movement of cargoes (Wilson, 2007), and jeopardizes the firms with operational and financial risks (Craighead et al., 2007). In addition, beside the direct impact on a particular supply chain node, it causes indirect impact on the rest of supply chain network. The merge of the two papers' definition explains the basis of disruption as well as the type of risks that firms are exposed to, thereby covering the objectives of this research.

To provide a detailed analysis on supply chain risks and disruptions, further classification of such events is required. Risks in the supply chain context can be divided into external and internal, where external risks refer to those driven by events upstream and/or downstream in the supply chain, while internal risks are driven by events within the company control (Kiser & Cantrell, 2006). Byrne (2007) grouped disruptions into three kinds, namely, uncontrollable, somewhat controllable and controllable. Uncontrollable events are natural disasters and geopolitical instability, somewhat controllable events are currency fluctuation and customer preference shifts, and controllable events are logistics capacity etc. The term 'somewhat controllable' is a grey area that is hard to distinguish from the other two groups. The grouping of the above two studies focuses on the degree of control that an organization has over disruptions. It would be more useful for devising mitigation strategies. But such categorization does not highlight the significance of disruption impact on maritime logistics and supply chains.

Disruptions can also be divided into direct and indirect disruptions. Classification of events can depend on cause or impact. To our knowledge, Gurning and Cahoon (2009)'s work is the only publication so far on classifying maritime disruptions which analysed maritime disruptive events and divided disturbances to normal activities into delays, deviations, disruptions and disasters. They proposed that disruption events can be grouped into direct and indirect factors due to different propagation effects (Blackhurst, Wu, & O'Grady, 2004; Zsidisin, Ellram, Carter, & Cavinato, 2004) and the multi-level of disruption factors (Peck, 2006). However, a combination of cause and impact would lead to complications in risk classification. The cause of one disruption event can be linked from one factor to another. By using causation of events for categorization, uncertainties and unreliability arise as personal judgment is involved. For example, a port strike is started due to political reason. Port strike has a direct impact on port, but the causation of strike is an indirect impact of politics. If causation of disruption is referred to, this strike will be under indirect event. On the other hand, if impact of disruption is considered, this event will be a direct event.

Categorization according to the impact of disruption on maritime logistics is proposed in the current and future studies, as the loss incurred by the parties can be factually justified. Furthermore, it is more systematic and comparable to have a quantitative loss value attached to each event. The scope of the impact will be defined by the research question concerned. It can be a firm, a node or a link in the supply chain, any segments of the supply chain, or the whole chain. For instance, if we consider port as a node in the supply chain as the research focus, earthquake causing port damage and shutdown is a direct disruption. In another case, if an earthquake hits the roads connecting the port causing disruptions in port operation, this earthquake is classified as an indirect disruption to the port since the earthquake hits the roads and the damaged roads in turn affects the port. Under this illustration, direct impact would have a higher severity to the port as compared to indirect impact since direct impact includes port damage and shutdown as well as business interruptions, while indirect impact contains business interruptions only. Such categorization gives a comprehensive coverage of supply chain disruptions. The highlights in Figure 7.1 show the path of classifying disruptive events.

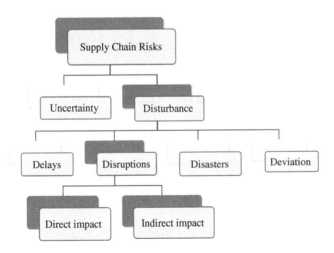

Figure 7.1: Categorization of supply chain disruptions
Source: Author.

As suggested by Gaudenzi and Borghesi (2006), risk evaluation is inherently subjective, because each analyst has his or her own concept of risk constitution. While the literature has tried to develop a typology, there is no uniform method of classifying supply chain risks. Individual judgment will lead to different outcomes. Perhaps the most important is not to have a consensus of the various methods, but rather choosing the most suitable method of risk classification according to the situation and point of interest, and also adopting the identified method consistently throughout the analysis.

7.4. Methodology

This study is accomplished by performing both primary research and secondary research. A thorough literature review has been conducted to understand the state of the prior studies related to the topic of interest. Also, various sources such as trade journals, market reports, databases and the Internet were consulted for collecting data and information. Six semi-structured interviews were carried out in the first half of 2011 to gain more insights from the industry. The interviews were targeted at the management personnel of two terminal operators, two shipping lines and two insurance companies. The three types of organizations are key market players in the maritime industry. Both terminal operators and shipping lines are crucial trade facilitators and provide maritime transport services directly. One part of the study focuses on port disruption so terminal operators were chosen. Shipping lines were chosen as the ability to be able to load/discharge cargo on time is deemed as very important for shipping lines and it is essential to have another perspective regarding disruptions on ports. Insurance companies are professional organizations in managing risks by underwriting insurance policies, thus being able to provide relevant information and opinion on the research topic. Though the interviews were carried out in Singapore, the organizations involved are all international entities serving a wide coverage of the global market. The organizations are among the world's largest in their respective industry sector. The interview setting was not limited to local specificity. The interviewees have given information and opinion on the impact of port disruption on supply chains and mitigation strategies. This study utilizes qualitative approach involving compilation, summary, comparison, classification and analysis of the data, information and opinion. In general, qualitative research is most appropriate in the early stages of research on a topic. It is ideal for exploring a study area (Zikmund, 2003) thus suits this paper's research purpose.

7.5. Impact of Port Disruption on Supply Chains: Empirical Evidence and Discussion

Turning to port as our focus, it is a crucial node in the supply chain. It is an interface for inter-modal transportation, specifically whereby goods are transferred between the sea and the shore. As 90% of world trade volume is transported by sea, maritime transport faces a great amount of supply chain risks should a disruption occur that extends its impacts to ports. In addition, the onset of fourth generation ports has transformed ports from a logistics centre to a link of the supply chain (Zhang, Zhen, & Gao, 2009). It would be a huge strain to the rest of supply chain if there is a disruption on ports (Christopher & Peck, 2004). Despite the importance of ports in supply chains, after a comprehensive literature search, it is observed that there is a serious lack of research for analysing supply chain disruptions with ports as a focal point. This section serves to fill the gap that exists in the literature by discussing the propagation effects of port disruption on the supply chain, with evidence from historical events and interviews.

Figure 7.2 illustrates the potential impacts of port disruption on various parties in the supply chain and were verified by the interviewees. The major parties including shippers and consignees, shipping companies, terminal operators and inter-modal transport providers are considered. When a port disruption happens, the most immediate impact is the adverse effects on terminal operations. Terminal operators suffer from higher costs including operations and labour costs. Reduction in throughput and revenue may incur an even higher loss. As confirmed by both shipping lines that were interviewed, safety is the most important concern in their operations and a key determinant whether they continue to call at a port. Carriers would bypass intended ports-of-call that are disrupted and a chain of effects such as lower schedule reliability, higher fuel costs, longer transit time may occur. Figure 7.2 has also included the losses due to physical damage of port infrastructure, facilities, equipment and cargoes when there are disastrous events. As an example, the 9.0 magnitude earthquake that happened on 11 March 2011 in Japan, which followed by a Tsunami with 10 m high, had subsequently led to damages to

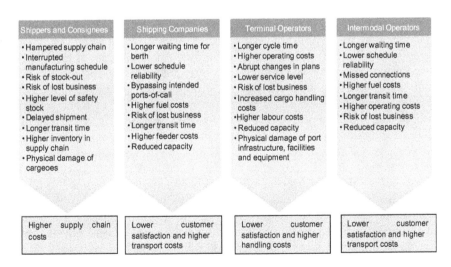

Figure 7.2: Potential impacts of port disruption on various parties in the supply chain
Source: Adapted from Stenvert and Ocean Shipping Consultants Limited (2007).

Fukushima Daiichi nuclear plant to have fire and explosion (BBC, 2011a, 2011b). This disaster has crippled many supply chains including the two largest car manufacturers Toyota and Nissan halted production (The Daily News Global, 2011). Fifteen ports were affected and closed. For those which have reopened, there is limited access to those ports till the time of writing this article. Sendai was most severely hit and had to shut down for more than 1 month (Reuters, 2011). Shortly after the disaster, Maersk Line stopped calling at the ports of Sendai, Onahama and Hachinohe as these ports were damaged by the disaster while Hapad-Lloyd stopped calling at the ports of Tokyo, Yokohama and Nagoya due to radiation concern (Bloomberg, 2011a). While the top 5 tanker lines still continue to call at Japan, some other tanker companies divert to other ports in Japan (Bloomberg, 2011b). The recovery process for all affected ports will be extensive. Cargoes at the ports were also damaged which affected shippers and consignees. Exporters were unable to ship their cargoes via the damaged ports which are nearer to their plants. Importers suffered from the delay in cargo shipment. These effects translate to hampered supply chains and higher supply chain costs. Inter-modal operators were also inevitably affected and the impacts included longer waiting time, longer transit time and missed connections among others.

As a whole, business interruptions and risk of lost business are common effects of port disruption on the various parties in the supply chain. Overall costs would increase and customer satisfaction would be lowered. The vulnerability of one part of the maritime supply chain in the presence of any risks and disruptions will have domino effects on other parties and the chain.

Furthermore, a disruption occurring in a port would affect other ports in both positive and negative ways. Should shipping companies decide to shift their port of call to nearby ports, those ports will gain from such disruption. For example, in 1995, the earthquake at Kobe completely destroyed Port of Kobe. For local containers, other Japanese ports, namely Port of Osaka, Port of Nagoya and Port of Yokohama, gained from Kobe's loss. However, this was mainly short-term losses as most of the diverted traffic has returned to Kobe after it has recovered. As for transhipment, Port of Busan in Korea and Port of Kaohsiung in Taiwan had benefited from Kobe's loss which is permanent. There is traffic that did not go back to Port of Kobe after the port has been restored (Chang, 2000). This shows that besides physical damage and financial loss during the crisis period, disruptions can have long-term negative impact on an organization's future performance (Tang, 2006). Disruptions may stain customer relationship and the impact is difficult to recover (Sheffi & Rice, 2005). Hence, ports and terminal operators should identify and minimize the possible future losses if such disruption occurs and not just look at the immediate losses. As for other ports which gain more business arising from such disruptions, there is a need for them to have sufficient capabilities to deal with the surge in cargo throughput. Otherwise, congestion may occur and other supply chains which do not deal with the disrupted port will be affected as well. The two terminal operators that were interviewed revealed that emergency preparation and risk mitigation are fundamental to terminal operations and their competitiveness.

7.6. Recommending More Integrative SCRM: Case Studies and Research Agenda

Facilitating seamless flow is a key principle in supply chain management. The supply chain should be as frictionless as possible. A firm has to work on a cooperative basis with its business partners in its supply chain in order to gain synergy leading to common success. The same applies to risk management. As discussed in the previous section, disruption occurred at one part of the maritime supply chain will spread across to other parts of the chain. What can be suggested from the issues brought up is that a holistic approach needs to be taken for risk management in maritime logistics. The maritime transportation industry is a fairly complicated one, consisting of different entities and players. This ranges from shippers, distributors, freight forwarders, shipping lines, port/terminal operators to inland transport operators and finally ending up with consignees. The whole process is facilitated by these players performing different but inter-related functions. This complexity is also not helped by the highly global nature of the industry. Realising proper risk management needs to be embraced by the supply chain members and collaboration is the key ingredient to success.

Nevertheless, industry practice is far from integrative SCRM. In Waters' (2007) study, five levels of SCRM were identified: (1) no risk management at all, (2) individual companies work in isolation, (3) joint risk management with immediate trading partners, (4) integrated risk management along more of the supply chain, and (5) integration along the whole chain. He found that most companies tend to work on risk management in isolation and few or no companies work at levels 4 and 5. In terms of port disruption, Table 7.1 illustrates the mitigation strategies taken by the interviewed companies based on case studies. The terminal operators have emergency preparation plan which is a proactive method. Terminal operator A is also flexible in adjusting its operations process in order to minimize the disruptive level. The shipping lines are capable of adjusting their shipping service by way of re-routing and changing ship's speed. But these measures are considered operational and reactive in nature. The insurance companies offer related in-house expert advice to client port which is more proactive. However, all six interviewees unanimously indicated that there is very little or no collaboration between the supply chain members in terms of risk management in practice. Based on interview results and secondary research on the companies, the level of SCRM approach is rated not higher than 3 as shown in Table 7.1.

While it will not be possible to achieve level 5 of SCRM integration from the current status easily, a more open mindset to have higher level of collaboration is necessary. Maritime supply chain parties should explore mutual interest and take a gradual approach. Visibility is essential in supply chain management (Christopher & Peck, 2004). High visibility means that there is a clear flow of information in the supply chain. In terms of port disruption, this means that when a terminal operator foresees a disruption coming, the operator should inform other members in the supply chain so that they can prepare for the disruption. The operator can provide alternative solutions such as offering the ship to stop at another port in the same

Table 7.1: Summary of port disruption mitigation strategies and SCRM levels.

Interviewed companies	Port disruption mitigation strategies	Supply chain risk management approach using the scale from Waters (2007)
Terminal operator A	1. Emergency preparation plan 2. Flexible in productivity level and capacity by adjusting operations process	2
Terminal operator B	Emergency preparation plan	2
Shipping line C	1. Re-routing of shipping service 2. Adjust ship's speed 3. Getting information from agents in ports	3 (between liner and agents)
Shipping line D	1. Re-routing of shipping service 2. Adjust ship's speed	2
Insurance company E	Offer in-house expert advice to client port on loss control	3 (between insurance company and client port)
Insurance company F	Offer in-house expert advice to client port on risk transfer	3 (between insurance company and client port)

Source: Author.

region owned by the same operator. In this way, as a whole, the terminal operator will not lose the business and at the same time, the supply chain remains undisrupted or disruption is minimized. This can be a relatively simple SCRM to start with. Nevertheless, it is hard to maintain high visibility in a supply chain when shipping lines and terminal operators have conflicting commercial interests. One of the interviewees mentioned that their company shipping line C has agents in many ports and therefore, they are able to understand the current situation and convey any important information to the company on time. This is because agents are more trustworthy than terminal operators due to their obligations towards the shipping lines.

Supply chain collaboration may also impose risks. Thompson, Gamble, and Strickland (2006) proposed that as there are many risks involved in any type of alliance, joint venture, or merger and acquisition, due research should be done before venturing into any such inter-company collaboration. Examples of some risks involved in vertical collaboration include higher business risk due to increased capital investment, massive changes needed in individual business capabilities, and slower adoption of new technologies. Also, the fear of leaking strategic information is an obstacle to integrative approach.

Other than joining force in managing risks, this paper proposes a more integrative approach in assessing various kinds of risks. As suggested by Lessard and Lucea (2009), a piece-meal and myopic method tends to look at risk each by each. Cause and consequence of risk are often inter-related. Considering a single event in isolation does not produce a comprehensive picture and may even result in misleading conclusions. The integrative perspective presents many opportunities for future research. For example, quantification of propagation effects in supply chain disruption, overcoming barriers in collaboration, and best practices in SCRM that can be applicable to maritime logistics are some interesting topics to be explored.

The author would like to propose more research to be done for Asia. There is an increase in the number of East Asian ports in the top 10 ranking over the years. In 2006, there were 6 out of 10 ports from East Asia while two years later, 8 out of 10 ports were from East Asia. In 2010, all the top eight container ports were from East Asia (AAPA, 2010; Containerisation International, 2011). It is projected that annual throughput of East Asian ports will increase healthily in the future. Thus, the severity of disruption on ports will be higher in the future despite being disrupted for the same number of days. The high and growing cargo volume involved affects numerous supply chains. Moreover, many countries in Asia face more natural disasters when compared to America or Europe (UNESCAP, 2010). There is an increase in natural disasters over the past 30 years (EM-DAT, 2009). Hence, the likelihood of natural disasters would continue to rise. The higher likelihood will result in higher supply chain risks. In terms of man-made risks, with more and more Asian countries liberalized, their citizens will fight for human rights, which include better salary or treatment by having labour strikes. For example, during our interview with an interviewee, who is in the management level of terminal company A, he mentioned that Chinese workers are starting to demand for better pay. There has been yearly strikes held in the port of Cochin, India started from 2008 (JOC, 2011). Therefore, in the future, the likelihood for strikes in Asia is expected to rise. With these significant issues in Asia, there is a pressing need for comprehensive studies to prepare Asian ports and related stakeholders from risk exposure and disruptions.

Furthermore, supply chains are getting leaner (Stecke & Kumar, 2009). A disruption will have a more adverse impact on the supply chain. For instance, to practise just-in-time, companies will minimize the amount of inventory they have on hand. Therefore, any disruption at the port or maritime leg will cause the flow to stop and a company will have a shorter time tolerance due to the low level of inventory the company possesses. Stopping the flow of products may cause the company to suffer huge losses. In order to minimize the risk of huge losses, supply chain players will choose its fellow players more carefully. Therefore, maritime transport operators have to mitigate their disruptions well so as to be selected by the other players. Lean supply chains, just-in-time practice and their relationships with risk management in maritime logistics is also an interesting area for future research.

7.7. Conclusions

Risk management has been the concern for many stakeholders ranging from industry practitioners to the people who are affected by the maritime business throughout the world. With the emergence of the concept and practice in SCRM, the maritime industry should look into risk management in the maritime logistics and supply chain context instead of dealing with risk in isolation. This is a new area of much potential to be explored. As suggested in the previous section, more research is encouraged for investigating the subject in greater depths. While a more integrated approach is recommended for maritime risk management, the same token applies to conducting such research. Research collaboration among academic institutions, government agencies, maritime and insurance companies is definitely conducive for maritime logistics research which spans over a wide range of parties. A proactive approach in risk management will ensure that individual firms as well as the supply chain at large can be more prepared and less vulnerable leading to higher competitiveness overall.

Acknowledgements

The author would like to thank the editors for their valuable time and comments. Thanks also go to the interviewees for providing valuable information and opinion on the research topic.

References

Akatsuka, K., & Leggate, K. (2001). Perceptions of foreign exchange rate risk in the shipping industry. *Maritime Policy & Management, 28*(3), 235–249.

Alizadeh, A. H., & Nomikos, N. K. (2009). *Shipping Derivatives and Risk Management*. UK: Palgrave Macmillan.

American Association of Port Authorities. (2010). *World port ranking-2008*. Retrieved from http://aapa.files.cms-plus.com/Statistics/WORLD%20PORT%20RANKINGS%2020081. pdf. Accessed on November 1, 2010.

Asbjørnslett, B. E. & Gisnaas, H. (2007). *Coping with risk in maritime logistics*. Paper presented at the ESREL 2007, Stavanger, Norway, June 25–27, 2007.

Barnes, P., & Oloruntoba, R. (2005). Assurance of security in maritime supply chains: conceptual issues of vulnerability and crisis management. *Journal of International Management, 11*(4), 519–540.

BBC, N. (2011a). In graphics: Fukushima nuclear alert. Retrieved from http://www.bbc.co.uk/news/world-asia-pacific-12726591

BBC, N. (2011b). Japan earthquake: Tsunami hits north-east. Retrieved from http://www.bbc.co.uk/news/world-asia-pacific-12709598

Blackhurst, J., Craighead, C. W., Elkins, D., & Handfield, R. B. (2005). An empirically derived agenda of critical research issues for managing supply-chain disruptions. *International Journal of Production Research, 43*(19), 4067–4081.

Blackhurst, J., Wu, T., & O'Grady, P. (2004). Network-based approach to modeling uncertainty in a supply chain. *International Journal of Production Research, 42*(8), 1639–1658.

Bloomberg. (2011a). Maersk, Hapad-Lloyd cancel calls at Japanese ports due to earthquake. Retrieved from http://www.bloomberg.com/news/2011-03-25/maersk-hapag-lloyd-cancel-calls-at-japanese-ports-because-of-earthquake.html

Bloomberg. (2011b). Japan oil ports still open to world's five largest tanker lines. Retrieved from http://www.businessweek.com/news/2011-03-30/japan-oil-ports-still-open-to-world-s-five-largest-tanker-lines.html

Bloor, M., Thomas, M., & Lane, T. (2000). Health risks in the global shipping industry: an overview. *Health, Risk & Society*, *2*(3), 329–340.

Byrne, P. M. (2007). Impact and ubiquity: two reasons to proactively manage risk. *Logistics Management, April*, 24–25.

Chang, S. E. (2000). Disasters and transport systems: loss, recovery and competition at the Port of Kobe after the 1995 earthquake. *Journal of Transport Geography*, *8*(1), 53–65.

Chopra, S., & Sodhi, M. S. (2004). Managing risk to avoid supply-chain breakdown. *MIT Sloan Management Review*, *46*(1), 53–61.

Christopher, M., & Peck, H. (2004). Building the resilient supply chain. *International Journal of Logistics Management*, *15*(2), 1–14.

Containerisation International. (2011). Container Traffic 2010. Retrieved from http://www.ci-online.co.uk/. Accessed April 2, 2011.

Craighead, C. W., Blackhurst, J., Rungtusanatham, M. J., & Handfield, R. B. (2007). The severity of supply chain disruptions: Design characteristics and mitigation capabilities. *Decision Sciences*, *38*(1), 131–156.

Dinwoodie, J., & Morris, J. (2003). Tanker forward freight agreements: The future for freight futures? *Maritime Policy & Management*, *30*(1), 45–58.

EM-DAT. (2009). Natural Disasters Trends. Retrieved from http://www.emdat.be/natural-disasters-trends. Accessed on March 30, 2011.

Frosdick, M. (1997). The techniques of risk management are insufficient in themselves. *Disaster Prevention and Management*, *6*(3), 165–177.

Gaudenzi, B., & Borghesi, A. (2006). Managing risks in the supply chain using the AHP method. *International Journal of Logistics Management*, *17*(1), 114–136.

Giziakis, K., & Bardi-Giziaki, E. (2002). Assessing the risk of pollution from ship accidents. *Disaster Prevention and Management*, *11*(2), 109–114.

Gurning, S., & Cahoon, S. (2009). *Analysis of Random Disruptive Events in Shipping and Port Operations*. Proceedings of the International Forum on Shipping, Ports and Airports (IFSPA) at Hong Kong, May 24–27, 2009, pp. 99–111.

Hong, N., & Ng, A. K. Y. (2010). The international legal instruments in addressing piracy and maritime terrorism: A critical review. *Research in Transportation Economics*, *27*(1), 51–60.

JOC. (2011). Retrieved from http://www.joc.com/maritime/strike-cripples-indian-port. Accessed on March 30, 2011.

Juttner, U., Peck, H., & Christopher, M. (2003). Supply chain risk management — outlining an agenda for future research. *International Journal of Logistics: Research and Applications*, *6*(4), 197–210.

Kavussanos, M. G., Juell-Skielse, A., & Forrest, M. (2003). International comparison of market risks across shipping-related industries. *Maritime Policy & Management*, *30*(2), 107–122.

Khan, O., Burnes, B., & Christopher, M. (2007). Risk and supply chain management — creating a research agenda. *International Journal of Logistics Management*, *18*(2), 197–216.

Kiser, J., & Cantrell, G. (2006). 6 steps to managing risk. *Supply Chain Management Review*, *10*(3), 12–17.

Kleindorfer, P. R., & Saad, G. H. (2005). Managing disruption risks in supply chains. *Production and Operations Management, 14*(1), 53–68.

Knemeyer, A. M., Zinn, W., & Eroglu, C. (2009). Proactive planning for catastrophic events in supply chains. *Journal of Operations Management, 27*(2), 141–153.

Lam, J. S. L. (2011). Patterns of maritime supply chains: Slot capacity analysis. *Journal of Transport Geography, 19*(2), 366–374.

LeClair, J., Pelot, R., & Xu, F. (2010). *A spatial risk analysis framework for effective oil spill response planning.* Paper presented at the 33rd AMOP Technical Seminar on Environmental Contamination and Response.

Lessard, D., & Lucea, R. (2009). Embracing risk as a core competence: The case of CEMEX. *Journal of International Management, 15*(3), 296–305.

Manuj, I., & Mentzer, J. T. (2008). Global supply chain risk management. *Journal of Business Logistics, 29*(1), 133–156.

Mitroff, I. I., & Alpaslan, M. C. (2003). Preparing for evil. *Harvard Business Review, 81*, 109–115.

Peck, H. (2006). Reconciling supply chain vulnerability, risk and supply chain management. *International Journal of Logistics Research and Applications, 9*(2), 127–142.

Rao, S., & Goldsby, T. J. (2009). Supply chain risks: A review and typology. *The International Journal of Logistics Management, 20*(1), 97–123.

Raymond, C. Z. (2006). Maritime terrorism in Southeast Asia: A risk assessment. *Terrorism and Political Violence, 18*(2), 239–257.

Reuters. (2011). Retrieved from http://af.reuters.com/article/metalsNews/idA FL3E7EE0AL20110314. Accessed April 30, 2011.

Roumboutsos, A., Nikitakos, N., & Gritzalis, S. (2005). Information technology network security risk assessment and management framework for shipping companies. *Maritime Policy & Management, 32*(4), 421–432.

Sanchez-Rodrigues, V., Potter, A., & Naim, M. M. (2010). Evaluating the causes of uncertainty in logistics operations. *International Journal of Logistics Management, 21*(1), 45–64.

Scarsi, R. (2007). The bulk shipping business: Market cycles and shipowners' biases. *Maritime Policy & Management, 34*(6), 577–590.

Seshadri, S., & Subrahmanyam, M. (2005). Introduction to the special POM issue on risk management in operations. *Production and Operations Management, 14*(1), 1–4.

Sheffi, Y., & Rice, J. B. (2005). A Supply Chain View of the Resilient Enterprise. *MIT Sloan Management Review, 47*(1), 41–48.

Spekman, R. E., & Davis, E. W. (2004). Risky business: Expanding the discussion on risk and the extended enterprise. *International Journal of Physical Distribution and Logistics Management, 34*(5), 414–433.

Stecke, K. E., & Kumar, S. (2009). Sources of supply chain disruptions, factors that breed vulnerability, and mitigating strategies. *Journal of Marketing Channels, 16*(3), 193–226.

Stenvert, R. Ocean Shipping Consultants Limited. (2007). *Container Port Strategy: Emerging Issues.* Chertsey, England: Ocean Shipping Consultants Limited.

Tang, C. S. (2006). Robust strategies for mitigating supply chain disruptions. *International Journal of Logistics: Research and Applications, 9*(1), 33–45.

The Daily News Global. (2011). Retrieved from http://www.dnewsglobal.com/japan-earth-quake-toyota-nissan-halted-production/3408.html. Accessed on May 30, 2011.

Thompson, A. A., Gamble, J. E., & Strickland, A. J. (2006). *Strategy: Winning in the marketplace.* McGraw-Hill.

Tsai, M. C. (2005). Constructing a logistics tracking system for preventing smuggling risk of transit containers. *Transportation Research Part A: Policy and Practice, 40*(6), 526–536.

UNESCAP. (2010). *First Asia-Pacific Disaster Report Launched by ESCAP and ISDR in Icheon, Republic of Korea.* Retrieved from http://www.unescap.org/unis/press/2010/oct/g53.asp. Accessed on November 6, 2010.

Wagner, S. M., & Bode, C. (2006). An empirical investigation into supply chain vulnerability. *Journal of Purchasing and Supply Management, 12*(6), 301–312.

Waters, D. (2007). *Supply chain risk management: Vulnerability and resilience in logistics.* Philadelphia: Kogan Page Ltd.

Wilson, M. C. (2007). The impact of transportation disruptions on supply chain performance. *Transportation Research Part E: Logistics and Transportation Review, 43*(4), 295–320.

Zhang, J., Zhen, H., & Gao, J. (2009). Studies of the Concepts, Features and Development Strategy for the Fourth Generation Port based on Supply Chain Thoughts. *Proceedings of the International Forum of Shipping, Ports and Airports (IFSPA)*, Hong Kong, China, May 24–27, 2009.

Zikmund, W. G. (2003). *Business Research Methods* (7th ed.). Ohio: Thomson.

Zsidisin, G. A., Ellram, L. M., Carter, J. R., & Cavinato, J. L. (2004). An analysis of supply risk assessment techniques. *International Journal of Physical Distribution & Logistics Management, 34*(5), 397–413.

Chapter 8

Information Technology in Maritime Logistics Management: A Case-Based Approach from CoA to SLA

Bjørn E. Asbjørnslett, Haakon Lindstad and Jan Tore Pedersen

Abstract

A trend in modern supply chain management has been to substitute information for inventory. In this chapter, an approach to how information and communication technology can be used to achieve this in a maritime logistics context is outlined and described based upon a bulk shipping case.

The approach used is based on data-driven modeling and analysis, in which current logistics and commodity storage costs are benchmarked against a "best possible solution."

To make a new solution operative, a change should be made based upon an analytical decision-making approach, ICT infrastructure development, and inter-organizational development. Thus, the proper use of analytical and transactional information and communication technology in maritime logistics would enable logistics chain stakeholders to track stock levels and ultimately allocate vessels to move cargo when that is logistically most cost effective. Further, this could support a development in the contractual relationships between producer and shipping line changing from a Contract of Affreightment to a Service Level Agreement relationship.

There is room for enhanced use of information and communication technology to provide decision and operational support at strategic, tactical, and operational levels within maritime logistics. This chapter explains some of the driving forces for this, together with a tested approach and method for this, given into a specific, practical case.

Keywords: Maritime logistics; information technology; data-driven analysis; transactional analysis; inventory routing; service-level agreement

Maritime Logistics: Contemporary Issues
Copyright © 2012 by Emerald Group Publishing Limited
All rights of reproduction in any form reserved
ISBN: 978-1-78052-340-8

8.1.   Introduction

Information and communication technology (ICT) has become an important part of business and industrial processes and practice, particularly in relation to developments within logistics and supply chain management. A clear trend in modern supply chain management is to substitute information for inventory. Flows of information surrounding the flow of physical cargo and related processes are important both for tracking progress and controlling logistics chains. Furthermore, ICT applications act as enablers for improved management of employed resources, for example, in the utilization of vessels.

Shipping is an important transportation link in supply chains. From a shipping line viewpoint, it is important to serve many supply chains in order to properly utilize vessels and other resources. For the supply chain manager, reducing overall logistics costs includes potentially reducing transportation costs. A relevant question then comes how can the shipping line better serve the needs of one or more integrated supply chains while at the same time increasing, or at least maintaining, profitability?

From a systems perspective, we know that total inventory and transportation costs can only be minimized if the two activities are planned and coordinated in an integrated manner. Integration between the shipping operations and the inbound or outbound logistics of the supply chains has traditionally been through contracts that serve as a framework, but one in which the partners have done the planning as separate activities (i.e., using Contracts of Affreightment). Input to the shipping line has consisted of order nomination and fixed jobs to be executed within stringent time windows. Although this reduces risk and planning problems for the supply chain, it also potentially precludes the shipping line from fully utilizing its vessels.

Transport costs are a direct function of fleet utilization. For the shipping line, fleet utilization depends on the total cargo flow in terms of geography, timing, and volume. Cargo is provided through supply chain contracts and available spot cargo. Mixing cargo properly from these sources to ensure the best possible use of its fleet of ships gives rise to a complicated planning problem with a fairly large degree of uncertainty.

This chapter presents a case-based road map for the use of transactional and analytical ICT in maritime logistics chains, based upon a business case of changing a contractual regime between manufacturer (logistics services client—LSC) and shipping line (logistics services provider—LSP), namely, from a contract of affreightment (CoA) to a service-level agreement (SLA) contractual situation. Transport and shipping is a game of balancing costs and service, and the contractual format is a core part of that. Addressing ICT in such a contractual framework brings ICT closer to the core business operation of shipping and maritime logistics, and could act both as a change agent and an enabler in the further development of maritime logistics solutions for shipping lines.

The structure of the chapter is as follows: Section 8.2 presents an introduction to maritime logistics and the approach to information and communication. Section 8.3 develops the case used to explain the ICT-based approach to cost and service improvements in maritime logistics. Section 8.4 presents the reasoning behind data-driven modeling, followed by Section 8.5 that provides some thoughts on ICT architecture. Section 8.6 then presents operational focus areas and ICT solutions required for the case. Finally, Section 8.7 gives a summary of the presented approach of ICT as a change agent in maritime logistics, as well suggestions for further reading.

8.2. Maritime Logistics and ICT

In a logistics context, information and communication systems may be divided into two categories: (i) systems for managing companies and logistics chains and processes (transactional ICT) and (ii) systems to support decision-making (analytical ICT). The efficiency of transport and logistics operations and the quality of decisions made rely on effective and meaningful interaction between the stakeholders in supply chains and skilled personnel with different expertise within each of the companies involved.

It is important to note that the quality of the decisions made and the efficiency of supply chain management are fully dependent on the quality and timeliness of the data available in these systems. The implementation and use of such systems cannot therefore be taken lightly. They should not be seen as replacing the knowledge of the people involved, but instead as a means for skilled people to remove tedious, repetitive tasks and to continuously improve their knowledge about the processes of maritime transport and logistics operations.

One way to truly minimize the combined inventory and transportation costs is to plan the two activities holistically. However, when doing this, we need to include the cost of support activities in addition to dealing with the so-called primary activities of the transport chain. The development and/or acquisition of appropriate information and communication systems fall into the latter category.

When performed jointly by LSC and LSP, integrated planning may help to facilitate increased volumes and economies of scale, or give rise to new and more cost-effective logistics processes. Such results, however, are not easily obtained. Joint inventory and shipment planning is conceivably more difficult than planning either activity in isolation. In most cases, the management of the supply chain and the operator(s) of transport services do not belong to the same organization (company). When establishing long-term relationships, a number of processes need to be harmonized (Figure 8.1). An integral part of establishing long-term relationships is to also choose the standards for communication between the parties involved.

Shipping lines typically serve a number of supply chains; hence, they need to plan in cooperation with several supply chain managers at the same time. The use of modern supply chain management and decision support tools may impact the way shipping line plans and executes its operations. Competitive shipping lines will strive to utilize developments in supply chain management tools and techniques. Even so, to be competitive is not just about applying new technologies. Shapiro (2001) points out that it has been observed that the barriers to integrated supply chain management are organizational rather than technical. Eliminating individual inefficiencies and increasing utilization of resources (the fleet being one example)

Figure 8.1: Analysis business process model: long- and short-term logistics processes

provide limited improvement. There are indications that much larger improvements can be realized by truly integrated planning and execution. Once the company understands the form and functions of information and communication systems to support integrated operations, it can start to adapt its business processes and organization to exploit the new possibilities.

8.2.1. A General View of Shipping Companies

When dealing with the introduction of decision support tools and ICT, we need to understand how companies conduct their decision-making processes. As pointed out by Porter (1985), the key to this is effective linkages between the various activities in the value chain. Linkages lead to a competitive advantage in two ways: optimization and coordination.[1]

A simple model of a shipping company may be presented as a circle or wheel (Figure 8.2). The circle is divided into functional areas, each corresponding to a functional area of the company. All of the functional areas must be present and in balance for the circle to be complete. As the hub of the circle, the central axis contains the ICT infrastructure. In this model, ICT corresponds to the organization's central nervous system. A continuous process of planning, decision-making, and execution is illustrated by arrows indicating the rotation of the wheel. This supports management by objectives and the company operating as a network of collaborating internal and external agents. Intense and continuous communication between highly skilled personnel at various levels and functional areas is essential for the company to reach its goals. Thus, this view of the company downplays any internal hierarchical structure. Rather, it displays concentric circles spanning the different functional areas and levels, and indicates the communication process and mutual impact of decisions.

Although plans are being developed (and decision support tools being used in the process), communication between planning and execution, functional areas, and decision-making levels (strategic, tactical, and operational) is essential. Indeed, one should not distinguish sharply between planning and execution, but instead see

---

1. Optimization and coordination could be regarded as being supported by analytical and transaction ICT, respectively.

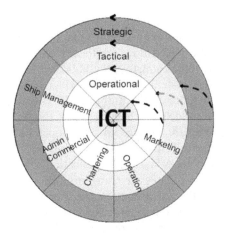

Figure 8.2: A network-centric view of the company, based on quality management, continuous improvement, and management by objectives

the planning process as a continuous cycle impacting on and carried out by all functional areas.

8.2.2. ICT Infrastructure

ICT should be understood here as the information technology infrastructure within a company, including hardware, software, and ICT personnel. ICT should provide a collectively accessible and encompassing set of technologies and information to "feed" the different planners, in addition to the computerized planning and decision support tools in use. The principal function of the tools is to overcome present cognitive limits by processing, aggregating, filtering, and analyzing large amounts of information. If this state of affairs can be reached, then the systems can be seen as communication tools facilitating coordination between various decision makers.

Transactional ICT is concerned with acquiring, processing, and communicating raw data about the company's supply chain and operation of resources. The compilation and dissemination of reports summarizing the resulting information is also included in this analysis. Shapiro points out that the widespread implementation of enterprise resource planning (ERP) systems offers the promise of homogeneous, transactional databases that will facilitate managerial decision-making. Many ERP systems do not support the management of multimodal supply chains (combining land and shipping operations). Therefore, a new breed of supply chain (or transport chain) management systems is becoming available.[2]

2. Such systems have been developed and demonstrated in EU-funded projects such as D2D, FREIGHTWISE, e-Freight, and PORTMOS.

By contrast, analytical ICT (decision support systems—DSS) evaluates supply chain planning problems by using descriptive or normative models. That is, their purpose is to invariably use the data available to feed models of the real world (Shapiro, 2001) to assist in making decisions about how the company should behave in the near or far future.

The status of analytical ICT systems for maritime logistics is that they are few and far between. Fagerholt (2001) cites other authors and finds evidence that very few applications of optimization models are being used in shipping, with this view also supported by Christiansen, Fagerholt, Nygreen, and Ronen (2007). It is interesting to compare shipping to the airline industry. Yu (1998) points out that operations research (optimization and simulation modeling and applications) have had a tremendous impact on the management of today's air transportation. Driven by demand from management to gain competitive advantage in the market, airlines have turned to advanced optimization techniques to develop mission-critical decision support systems for the management and control of airline operations. Today, running even the most modest airline would be inconceivable without advanced optimization-based decision support tools. In combination with new regimes imposed by environment and safety concerns, increasing competition from air and land transportation will challenge shipping companies to be more effective and efficient in the planning, as well as the tracking and tracing of their cargo and resource patterns.

8.3. From CoA to SLA, and the Use of ICT in the Transformation Process

The case described in this chapter, which is to visualize the use of ICT in bulk shipping, represents a situation with the inbound seaborne transport of a dry bulk commodity from a dry bulk storage/warehouse at a port of loading to a storage/warehouse at a port of discharge at or near the producer's production plant. A corresponding outbound seaborne transport chain of finished products may use the same vessel type as the inbound chain (Figure 8.3).

As a starting point, seaborne transportation is regulated by a CoA between the producer and the shipping line. This means that the size and frequency of shipments is managed by the producer. The producer notifies the shipping line in due time before a shipment is needed to replenish the dry bulk commodity stockpiles. The background for this case is a question of whether there is a potential to reduce logistics costs by managing transportation and storage under a new contractual arrangement, whereby the shipping line takes over the responsibility of maintaining the stock levels within certain bounds. In terms of direct transportation activities, this has the potential to increase fleet utilization, thereby reducing transportation costs.

8.3.1. Characteristics of the Finished Product Market

The finished product market and supply chain may be summed up in the following points:

- The production facilities are very capital intensive.
- Stable all-year production.

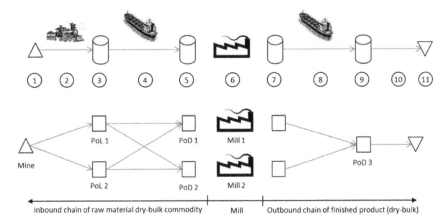

Figure 8.3: Outline of the dry bulk maritime logistics chain, with a combined shipping operation for the raw material commodity supply and the finished product distribution

- The demand is very seasonally dependent.
- The distribution system includes a large storage capacity.

From this, we can infer that there would potentially be heavy penalties related to an "out of stock" situation for raw materials. Since the production plants are capital intensive, any downtime due to a lack of raw material in the stock (stock-out) would be costly.

8.3.2.   The Basic Idea: From CoA to SLA

When using a CoA, dry bulk commodities are typically delivered free on board at the port of loading. The size and frequency of shipments is managed by the producer, who sends notifications to the shipping lines in due time before a shipment is needed.

Based on our description of the current state of affairs, we can tentatively conclude that the CoA transportation regime certainly seems to fulfill the producer's need for the stable delivery of a dry bulk commodity. What is more interesting though is whether the logistics cost for transportation and storage could be reduced? What if there was a shift in planning procedures and responsibility, such that the shipping line could nominate cargoes in light of both dry bulk commodity stock levels and their own prediction for fleet availability and other factors? This would maximize the potential for fleet utilization for the shipping line, thereby minimizing the sea transport cost. Thus, if the producer transfers responsibility for shipment planning to the shipping line, the shipping line will be free to plan the size and frequency of shipments on the basis of production plans and the level of dry bulk commodities at the two storage and production locations. However, it is clear that the producer will not be willing to accept an increase in "out of stock" situations for raw materials due to the heavy economic consequences. Hence, an important planning constraint is that a minimum level of raw materials must be maintained at both production plants.

Figure 8.4 illustrates the current situation in which a traditional CoA governs sea transportation. Typical for this picture is a segmented decision-making for each actor in the chain and the lack of a common understanding, which presents a situation with a high potential for suboptimization. The system is typically controlled by fairly strict orders, and we can safely assume that quite a bit of resources are used on planning and control for each involved actor.

Figure 8.5 illustrates the situation with an SLA. Although total integration is implemented here, there is less compartmentalization than when a CoA is in use. As seen from the producer's perspective, there is an increased degree of decentralized operational decision-making.

A typical SLA defines a minimum level of availability of material from key suppliers, and often determines what actions will be taken in the event of a serious disruption. As a result, the SLA requires careful consideration and attention, and must be carefully constructed. The SLA will be wide in scope, and cover key aspects of the service. Typically, it will fully embrace such issues as problem management, compensation, warranties and remedies, resolution of disputes, and legal compliance.

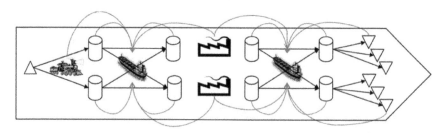

Figure 8.4: Contract of affreightment—information flow and compartmentalization

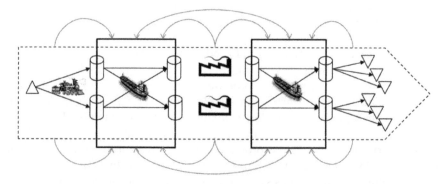

Figure 8.5: Service-level agreement—information flow and compartmentalization

It essentially frames the relationship, and determines the major responsibilities, both in times of normal operation and during emergency situations. When using an SLA, one cannot only focus on the cost of direct activities such as fleet utilization, as both direct and indirect costs must be taken into account. For example, the capabilities for controlling dry bulk commodity stock levels may require an investment in new ICT systems.

8.3.3.   *Mechanisms for Cost Reductions: Direct Activities*

The potential for cost reductions is closely tied to an increase in the planning scope and joint sharing of information. As a formulation of the problem relevant to direct costs, we suggest the following:

> Minimize the sum of transportation and stockholding costs subject to an agreed maximum probability of a stock-out situation and to constraints imposed by rules and regulations.

With this formulation at hand, we can go on to ask what mechanisms can be used to reduce the cost of direct activities. In principle, we have two overall mechanisms, namely, minimizing sea transport costs (thus maximizing fleet utilization) and minimizing stockholding costs. Nonetheless, from our formulation above, it is clear that we are talking of a multiple objective function in which it is the total sum of the two direct activities that is to be minimized.

8.3.3.1.   Minimizing the sea transport cost   The fleet utilization would be optimal if all vessels in the fleet were performing fully laden transport legs at all times.

From an operational perspective, the fleet is a fixed commodity. Improvements depend on acquiring profitable cargoes and scheduling the fleet in an optimal manner. Tactically, however, the fleet may be tailored to the expected business, for example, by acquiring or selling vessels, or by taking vessels in and out of charter. For this case, we assume that we have the option to adjust the fleet size used for dry bulk commodity transport (type and number of vessels).

Mechanisms for improving fleet utilization are described in Table 8.1.

As can be seen from Table 8.1, most of the detailed mechanisms are relevant for our case. Optimal routing selection may seem less relevant since there is not much choice in a single-source, single-destination scenario. Still, if the case was to include sea transport for other supply chains, then routing may become an issue. In other words, if we were to consider the combination of the dry bulk commodity transportation with other cargoes (spot or CoA cargoes), routing would become an important issue. Minimizing maintenance and crew costs is assumed to be an area of continuous effort regardless of the present case.

Table 8.1: Mechanisms to improve fleet utilization.

1	Reduce idle/waiting time.
2	Minimize ballast sailing/repositioning sailing.
3	Maximize cargo hold volume utilization for each leg (i.e., full loads).
4	Optimize routing selection.
5	Minimize time spent in all operational phases (terminal operations, docking, loading and discharging, technical off hire, etc.).
6	Consolidate other cargoes (spot, contract, or other SLAs).
7	Effective irregular operations/contingency management.
8	Minimize fleet maintenance time and cost, integrated scheduling of operations and maintenance.
9	Minimize crew costs (crew origin, crew scheduling).

8.3.3.2. Minimizing inventory cost   The next step in developing the case would be to describe the producer's current stockholding policy, planning procedures, tools, and organization. In lieu of specific information, we provide a list of reasons for holding stock, as well as an overview of some of the elements that would enter into estimating the cost of holding the stock. We have concentrated on those items that seem particularly relevant to the case. The various factors for keeping dry bulk commodity in stock are listed in Table 8.2, while the different categories of raw material stock cost are shown in Table 8.3.

Table 8.3 lists the categories of the raw material stock cost. Most of these cost factors are self-explanatory. In our case, the fixed cost of each replenishment action is the cost related to each shipment, which we want to minimize. This factor is already externalized into the shipment problem. We have found that the cost of insufficient short-term stock is high, perhaps to the point where it is completely unacceptable to run out of dry bulk commodities.

Table 8.2: Factors for holding a dry bulk commodity stockpile.

1	Cycle stock: shipments come in batches, so giving a constant demand and production-level storage at the production sites is required.
2	Nature of demand and time horizon: stable.
3	Supply issues: moderate.
4	Consequences of raw material stock-out: high. Expect producers to demand a very low probability of dry bulk commodity stock-out, and demand real-time information and insight to assure them of dry bulk commodity availability.
5	Raw material perishability: not an issue.
6	Stock status monitoring: if stock levels are not known precisely, one must necessarily have a higher stock to compensate for this uncertainty—quality assurance of technology.
7	Buffer/safety stock: low.
8	Anticipation stock: moderate.

Table 8.3: Categories of raw material stock cost.

1	Cost of material itself.
2	Fixed cost of each replenishment action.
3	Cost of having material in inventory, fixed, and variable part.
4	Cost of insufficient short-term stock (stock-out).
5	Cost of inventory control system.

8.3.4.   The Mechanisms and the View of the Shipping Company

As we can see from Tables 8.1–8.3, the mechanisms can be associated with different functional areas of the company. The overall result, however, depends on optimization and coordination across functional areas, supported by information and communication technologies. For example, to minimize ballast/repositioning sailing, the chartering/fleet operation functions must be performed well. Nevertheless, they can do little if there is not enough cargo available, which is the responsibility of the sales function. If the chartering/fleet operation is not performing well, there is less capacity to sell.

Reverting to our model of the company, an operational-level decision support tool may be able to support level-transcending[3] analysis if it conforms to the following requirements:[4]

1. It facilitates that effective decisions can be made in a timely manner. The quality of decisions is important since it directly affects the company's revenue, cost, performance, and customer satisfaction. If decisions are not made in a timely manner, the environment changes, and the opportunities and resources may no longer be available. During lengthy solution processes, the occurrence of new problems complicates the situation.
2. It should provide multiple alternatives so that the decision makers can make their choice based on their knowledge and many years of experience. It frees the decision makers from the tedious and time-consuming solution generation and validation process, and allows them to efficiently use their valuable time in evaluating the choices, framing problems, and in anticipating and preventing future problems.
3. It should incorporate decision makers' knowledge into the system. It should make proper use of decision maker's intuition and rules of thumb, which have proved to be effective. This will not only accelerate the generation of good solutions, but also enable effective handling of the many soft issues that are difficult to embody in the optimization model.

---

3. For instance, using an operational-level decision support system to conduct tactical analysis.
4. Based on *Operations Research in the Airline Industry* (Yu, 1998). The list conforms one-to-one with experiences gathered in developing and using TurboRouter, a fleet-scheduling and management system developed by the Norwegian Marine Technology Research Institute (MARINTEK).

4. It takes into account various scenarios and options. Often, complete solutions may not exist. Under this type of situation, the system should provide partial solutions that resolve the problem and leave less important problems for a later time.
5. It should facilitate interaction among decision makers. Interaction should be achieved through a "what-if" functionality. Before committing to a final decision, it should let all involved decision makers review their options and pass their feedback through the common interface for a collaborative and coordinated decision-making.
6. It should permit users to set parameters for limiting the scope of impact. It should embed the functionality for fixing or protecting partial and local solutions, which is very important for protecting certain markets.
7. It should have single instance of data, common GUI, in addition to a message-oriented, event-driven, and distributed components architecture. This guarantees data integrity, real-time update of data, the same look and feel to all system users, and easy integration with existing (and future) systems.

8.3.5.   Other Mechanisms: Cost of Indirect Activities

Our formulation of the problem to be solved was deliberately targeted toward direct costs. These are the simplest costs to establish and model; they relate mostly to physical processes such as vessel speeds, cargo transfer rates, etc. Establishing consequences for indirect activities must be external to any optimization or simulation model of the problem.

We have not yet dealt with the cost of the inventory control and information systems. This is an important factor that may change in the new regime since additional (ICT) elements must be added if the shipping line is to base shipments on information from the producer's inventory control system. This is an example of an important indirect activity cost related to the case. From the discussions about the undesirability of a dry bulk commodity stock-out, we infer that the producer would want similar real-time information from the shipping line's ongoing transport operations. If such (ICT) systems are not already in place, they must be implemented for the proposed solution to be accepted.

It is clear that the cost of implementing new systems must be small enough to ensure an acceptable return on investment in systems for joint planning and control of shipments and storage. In addition to our list of requirements for ICT/DSS tools, we add that information should be available in such a form that it can be easily but securely be shared with other stakeholders without any extra costs.

8.4.   Data-Driven Modeling and Analysis

Entering into a new SLA regime is a strategic decision for the involved shippers and carriers. To accomplish this, such a regime will have to be profitable for both parties.

For the shipping line, an SLA regime means added responsibility, most likely with demands for changes to the current business processes. For the producer, it means outsourcing some of their (core) operations (specifically the control of the dry bulk commodity raw material stock). To evaluate the potential for a change in contractual regime from CoA to SLA, an analysis needs to be carried out. The analysis should also bring attention to the potential and requirements for analytical and transactional ICT support, both for analysis and operations of the change in contractual regime.

Conceptually, the analysis is a two-step process:

- Estimate current logistics costs, including storage costs.
- Construct and estimate the cost of the best possible proposed solution.

If the proposed solution is better, and a given level of trust is put into the input data and validity of the models, the decision should be straightforward. Yet, if any of the factors are connected with uncertainty, work should commence to reduce uncertainty to the point where the proposed solution is deemed either too risky or too costly, or where the proposed solution looks economical, feasible, and within an acceptable risk level.

Unfortunately, the devil is in the details. Even if it is conceptually simple to compose an outline of the analysis process, it is not a simple task to carry out such an analysis to completion, communicate the results, and create new goals and processes. Even if the technical challenges will be much reduced by modern ICT architecture, the organizational problem still remains.

8.4.1. The Flow and Phases of the Analysis

An analysis of the ICT and organizational developments to support a change in the contractual relationship of the maritime logistics chain from CoA to SLA could follow a flowchart as shown in Figure 8.6.

Setting up a model of the physical/direct activities using a fleet-planning and scheduling tool requires that skilled modeling personnel be involved. Evaluating strategic elements and new ICT-related systems and processes must be carried out in parallel to the physical modeling.

Interestingly, although Shapiro sees a path of development from strategic modeling systems to tactical modeling systems,[5] experience gained from using a fleet-scheduling

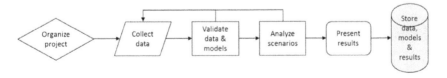

Figure 8.6: Major phases in the analysis

---

5. To quote (Shapiro, 2001, p. 447), "An operational system may be effectively applied to study potential or proposed changes in the company's operating environment."

tool for operational day-to-day decision-making indicates a possible growth model going from operational to tactical. Specifically, it should be possible to develop stage 3 "validate data and models," while simultaneously performing the "as-is" analysis. This is one stage in which a direct comparison between reality and the model is possible.

An analysis may require substantial resources. Given the current cost of personnel, it makes sense to first perform a short preliminary analysis to check the overall potential before committing more resources to a detailed analysis project. The main elements that should be addressed are:

- Cost of the shipping operation to estimate the total fixed and variable transportation costs.
- Storage costs, covering: costs of the material itself, costs of having material in inventory, and costs of the inventory control system.
- Cost of indirect activities.

Analytical ICT systems may be used in the analysis part, while transactional ICT systems may be used to support the operations under a new service-level agreement regime. Analytical ICT involves analytical models, and building the analytical model is often a task that cannot usually be done on a case-by-case basis. The chosen tool must be based on an available optimization model since the problem to be solved typically has difficult combinatorial aspects. These aspects (routing and assignment problems) put the problem into a class of problems considered to be intractable, meaning that in most cases heuristics and approximation algorithms must be used, rather than exact methods.

With a set of valid data and a valid model at hand, the next step is to construct a set of future scenarios. What is of particular interest in a case such as this is the interplay with the dry bulk commodity transport and other cargo options, that is, combining the dry bulk commodity transport with spot cargoes or potentially with traditional CoA cargoes, or on an even more advanced level, trying to combine two or more SLA arrangements.

If the work in the previous phase concluded with a viable alternative, it is time to perform a sensitivity analysis, including an evaluation of the risks involved. This is where valuable insight is gained for negotiating a new deal.

8.4.2.   Conclusion from the Analysis

Having performed the analysis, we should be left with important results:

- The direct result, the advice on whether to implement an SLA or not.
- A set of scenarios covering important aspects for the future and associated risk factors.
- Relationships between the scenarios and the company's financial bottom line.

If successful, an analysis should provide us with the most solid basis available for negotiating the contents of the new regime. Taken together, this provides us with an important part of a systematic basis for developing future business.

8.5. From Data-Driven Analysis to ICT Architecture

Having conducted the analysis, the question still remains as to whether it is really worth the effort to establish an SLA?

In his book "Modeling the Supply Chain," Jeremy F. Shapiro writes an in-depth summary of implementing data-driven analysis in industry. He draws up a new taxonomy of computer systems and shows how operations analysis and modeling are made increasingly feasible and profitable by modern ICT architecture. Although not specifically geared toward shipping, most of the topics covered and the advice given seem sound in a maritime logistics context as well. Shapiro claims that data-driven modeling is the answer. It is not only worth the effort; there will increasingly be no alternative. If the airline industry is an example, we may expect the same competitive pressures to be felt in shipping and maritime logistics. Perhaps of particular interest, Shapiro shows that data-driven modeling is most meaningful when we integrate the problems of decision-making, ICT infrastructure, and organization.

One of the main observations from the discussion this far was the necessary data spanned most of the company's functional areas. Gathering, filtering, and aggregating the necessary data for making decisions is costly in terms of time and man–hours required. Many attempts at alleviating this by, for example, using ERP systems are being made, although the progress has been limited. Most ERP systems support static business processes only. Most logistics operations, however, involve quite dynamic business processes.

How can we resolve this? Some tentative answers are emerging. Cloud and grid computing are identified as important technologies by a wide range of enterprises. Cloud and grid computing assume that most (ICT) services already exist or will be developed as components using service-oriented architectures (SOA). The focus is on how to seamlessly integrate known and unknown services alike in a dynamic fashion, thereby supporting the "virtual organization" paradigm. Cloud and grid computing are not yet mature as a part of maritime logistics. However, cloud and grid are the computing and data management infrastructure that shows promise in providing the framework for a global society in business, government, research, science, and entertainment. Both ERP and the cloud/grid approaches aim at integration, but only cloud and grid support integration and rapidly changing business processes.

8.6. Running the Operation: Processes and ICT

The gains of the new contractual regime come from increasing fleet utilization. From the tactical analysis, we have a very good idea about fleet suitability and the consolidation cargoes that are most relevant. At the operational level, we need to achieve the profits that have been planned at the tactical level, which means exploiting opportunities as they arise. It is a question of good scheduling based on up-to-date information of the dry bulk commodities stored at each production site and a prediction of consumption.

The producer will need information about planned and ongoing shipments. This will ensure the availability of material for the production process.

Predicting the future stock level of dry bulk commodities depends on estimates of both consumption and replenishment actions.

New solutions for exchanging information between SLA partners should be implemented using an SOA approach, which includes developing a web service application at both the producer and the shipping line. There are at least three important reasons for using web services. The approach is easily scalable, it distributes responsibilities in a very clean fashion, and the largest part of the necessary ICT infrastructure is already in place—the Internet.

Analytical ICT capabilities can be supported as follows: having established web service communication between shipper and carrier, we can form a prediction of future dry bulk commodity stock levels. Based on this, we can now provide the automatic generation of cargo candidates. The prediction of future stock level will indicate the earliest and latest time limits for the next unplanned dry bulk commodity cargoes, which will automatically translate into the earliest and latest pickup time for the next order. The desired planning horizon determines how many candidate cargoes to generate. The generated candidate cargo(s) can now be transferred back to the planning system. During the next iteration of assigning vessels to cargoes, the planning system will provide the optimum time to ship the next cargo, and it will provide this information subject to simultaneously considering all other available cargoes.

Figure 8.7 illustrates the web-service–oriented solution. A service residing on a web server at each site connects to the existing inventory and production planning and fleet management systems for the producer and shipping line, respectively. This means that a selected subset of data from each system can be transported using the Internet. A local web application or standard application will then merge the data from both partners, and at this stage the two sets of data can be used to provide a prediction of dry bulk commodity levels in the future. Note that the solution respects the boundaries of the "closed" systems used by the partners, and does not impact on those systems in any way. Furthermore, the solution is easily scalable.

If the new SLA type agreement is a success, we must expect growth. As a result, if the shipping lines expose parts of their fleet planning as a web service, very little is needed to hook up the next customer to the system. The producer could find it interesting to continue developing similar agreements for a larger part of inbound or outbound freight.

Building cross-functional and cross-company ICT in the form of web services such as we have outlined above is becoming an increasingly mature approach.[6]

---

6. Logit Sea is one example taken from shipping.

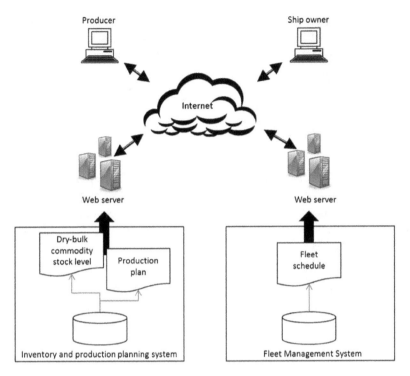

Figure 8.7: Web-service–oriented solution

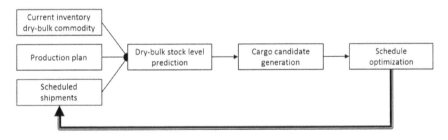

Figure 8.8: Improved fleet utilization information flow

What we have just shown is an example of what Shapiro mentions as maturing possibilities within transactional ICT. Another question is how to use the data to improve business?

The three leftmost information elements in Figure 8.8 provided via web services give us the possibility to predict dry bulk commodity stock levels as a function of time. Stock level prediction, cargo candidate generation, and schedule optimization are all examples of typical analytical ICT components, here listed in order of increasing complexity. Improving fleet utilization rests fairly and squarely on these components. Without some sort of automated help in generating better schedules, one would most likely have to resort to other measures (such as increasing staff), and much of the gains would be lost. Moreover, if more elements in the same supply chain or outside actors are included into the SLA, the complexity will increase to such an extent that one would be left with the traditional "divide and conquer" strategy, thus paving the way for a suboptimization that defies the goals of the SLA.

8.7. Summary and Further Reading

Shipping most often constitutes complicated planning problems with fairly large degrees of uncertainty. The traditional way of handling business complexity has been to erect hierarchical organizational structures, introducing compartmentalization and division into functional areas, though the price paid for this is often suboptimization.

People are increasingly coming to realize that more data and information pose as much of a problem as it is a solution (see, e.g., Sassi, 2006). Yet, competitive pressures require improved performance, which leads to increased integration, both internally within the company and externally in the form of integrated supply chains.

We have divided ICT into transactional and analytical ICT. The purpose of transactional ICT is to describe and track the activities of the company. The purpose of analytical ICT is to point out what should be done to ensure the best possible performance of the business, which almost invariably leads to optimization modeling or data-driven analysis. Modeling requires communication about the causal structure of the business. Not only is modeling technically challenging, it also challenges the company's segmented structure. Therefore, we have concluded that analytical ICT must be viewed not only as just a technical solution, but also as an important integrative and communicative device.

We addressed a business case in which the opportunity for changing contractual regime was addressed, as well as the ICT supporting such a change. Now we would like to draw attention to further reading material to help establish deeper insights into the issues addressed in this chapter. Combining vertical and horizontal collaboration for transport optimization (Mason, Lalwani, & Boughton, 2007), a generic view of developments in ICT within transportation is provided by Giannopoulos (2004), followed by analytical developments within maritime transportation by Christiansen et al. (2007), ship/port interface effectiveness by Alvarez, Longva, and Engebrethsen (2010), and, finally, an integrative ICT framework for multimodal transportation by Pedersen (2010).

Giannopoulos (2004) states that there are three principal areas of application of ICT in transport in general, as presented together with a reference to transactional versus analytical ICT in Table 8.4. Giannopoulos sets the ICT application areas into a development and market penetration process (Giannopoulos, 2004, pp. 315–318), predicting the industrial progress of ICT within the transport domain for the period ahead.

A comprehensive documentation of analytical ICT development in maritime transport and logistics is provided by Christiansen et al. (2007). Christiansen groups the developments within maritime transportation into strategic, tactical, and operational issues:

i. Strategic: ship design, fleet size and mix, network design, maritime transport system design, and contract evaluation;

Table 8.4: Three principal areas of application of information and communication technology (ICT) in transport (Giannopoulos, 2004) matched against Shapiro's (2001) division into transactional and analytical ICT systems in supply chain modeling.

Three principal areas of application	Maritime logistics oriented	Transactional ICT	Analytical ICT
Operation and management of networks	1. Ship communications and management information.	X	
	2. Interoperable maritime traffic management and navigation services (e.g., GPS, ECDIS, INMARSAT, AIS/LRIT).	X	
	3. Improved resource management at ports.	X	X
Information and guidance to the users of the transport system	"These applications have to do with the 'collection,' 'creation,' and 'supply' of accurate, timely ... 'real-time' data and information to the user (... various individuals or companies associated with the movement of goods or owners of the goods that are transported on the various networks)" (Giannopoulos, 2004, p. 311).	X	
Operation and management of freight transport systems	Freight resource management	X	X
	Terminal and port information and communication systems.	X	X
	Freight and vehicle tracking and tracing and "back-office" logistics.	X	

ii. Tactical: scheduling in industrial and tramp shipping, maritime logistics and inventory routing (the issue addressed in this chapter), fleet deployment, and ship management;

iii. Operational: operational scheduling, environmental routing, speed selection, ship loading, and booking of single orders.

An important contribution to the effectiveness of the ship/port interface is given by Alvarez et al. (2010), who present a methodology to assess vessel berthing and

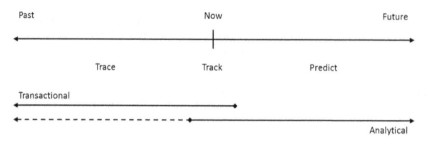

Figure 8.9: Time dimensions in transactional and analytical ICT: positioning transactional and analytical ICT systems into a predict, track, and trace timeline. Transactional ICT are status-keeping (track) and documenting system (trace), whereas analytical ICT are guiding (predict) based on status (track) and history (trace) (developed from Kelepouris, Theodorou, McFarlane, Thorne, & Harrison, 2006)

speed optimization policies that improve the ship/port interface effectiveness, with direct cost and emission impact through queuing principles and speed adjustment to avoid unnecessary bunker consumption and waiting for berth access.

Maritime logistics solutions are often multimodal solutions, and in multimodal transport and logistics systems, the management of interfaces is a challenging task. An example of an ICT architecture or framework for transport establishing a common multimodal platform of specifications for responsibilities, functionality, processes, and information flows in the transport sector is the Common Framework for information and communication systems in transport and logistics. The main objective of the Common Framework is to support efficient multimodal transport solutions, based on an approach to harmonize and coordinate as much as can be for all transport modes into one common framework architecture. The Common Framework also defines new standards for information exchange in transport and logistics (for all modes), and suggests the use of web services for information exchange purposes (Pedersen, 2010).

Finally, we would like to end this chapter with an illustration based on Kelepouris, Theodorou, McFarlane, Thorne, and Harrison (2006). Figure 8.9 shows the time dimension in transactional and analytical ICT, within a trace, track, and predict framework. Transactional ICT systems can be seen in this framework as status-keeping (tracking) and documenting (tracing) systems, while analytical systems are guiding (predicting) based on status (track) and history (trace) projections.

Acknowledgments

This chapter has drawn upon experiences gained from a set of research projects within maritime logistics at the Norwegian Marine Technology Research Institute in which senior researcher Arent Arntzen played a key role. The projects were financially supported by both the Norwegian Research Council and the Norwegian Shipowners' Association.

References

Alvarez, J. F., Longva, T., & Engebrethsen, E. S. (2010). A methodology to assess vessel berthing and speed optimization policies. *Maritime Economics and Logistics, 12*(4), 327–346.

Christiansen, M., Fagerholt, K., Ronen, D., & Nygreen, B. (2007). Maritime transportation. In C. Barnhart & G. Laporte (Eds.), *Handbook in operations research and management science* (Vol. 14, pp. 189–284). Amsterdam: Elsevier.

Fagerholt, K. (2001). Ship scheduling with soft time windows: An optimization based approach. *European Journal of Operational Research, 131*(3), 559–571.

Giannopoulos, G. A. (2004). The application of information and communication technologies in transport. *European Journal of Operational Research, 152*(2), 302–320.

Kelepouris, T., Theodorou, L, McFarlane, D., Thorne, A., & Harrison, M. (2006). *Track and trace requirements scoping.* AEROID-Cam-004, Auto-ID Lab, University of Cambridge, UK.

Mason, R., Lalwani, C., & Boughton, R. (2007). Combining vertical and horizontal collaboration for transport optimization. *Supply Chain Management: An International Journal, 12*(3), 187–199.

Pedersen, J.T. (2010). One common framework for information and communication systems in transport and logistics. Third ECITL conference, Bremen, 2010.

Porter, M. E. (1985). *Competitive advantage: Creating and sustaining superior performance.* New York: Free Press.

Sassi, S. B. (2006). The role of ICT in solving logistics complexity: An economic point of view. In Blecker, T. & Kersten, W. (Eds.), *Complexity management in supply chains.* Berlin: Eric Schmidt Verlag GmbH & Co.

Shapiro, J. F. (2001). *Modeling the supply chain.* Pacific Grove: Duxbury Thomson Learning.

Yu, G. (1998). *Operations research in the airline industry.* MA: Kluwer Academic Publishers.

Chapter 9

Port Value Chains and the Role of Interdependencies

Thomas K. Vitsounis and Athanasios A. Pallis

Abstract

The chapter analyses the ways actors in seaports are embedded in network configurations and develop Business to Business (B-2-B) relations. It also discusses the ways that the latter relations result in functional and relational values. The emphasis is on the presence of port value chains, wherein positioning and effective networking contribute to the total value proposition to the involved actors.

The chapter grounds on a literature review on B-2-B relations and the role of interdependencies developed between stakeholders within industrial markets. The empirical data discussed afterwards lead to the identification and analysis of the different types of interdependencies that might be found within port settings. In this context, the concept of *port value chains* is put forward. Interdependencies are attached to the various relationships developed between port stakeholders, in order to derive meaningful conclusions. The research is based and data provided through semi-structured interviews with major port stakeholders (e.g. port authorities, shipping lines, freight forwarders etc.) in a number of European seaports (Antwerp, Zeebrugge, Piraeus etc.).

The importance of co-creation of value via matching resources with upstream and downstream entities is established. The chapter also details how actors interdependence as a significant variable determining the level of co-creating value. The empirical analysis provides insights about the existence of three types of interdependencies in ports (namely, serial, pooled and reciprocal) that are found in a number of distinctive relationships developed between, terminal operators, freight forwarders, shipping lines and other key port actors.

Maritime Logistics: Contemporary Issues
Copyright © 2012 by Emerald Group Publishing Limited
All rights of reproduction in any form reserved
ISBN: 978-1-78052-340-8

In reference to future research, two fields are identified and are worth to be examined in terms of both academic and practical scope. These are the examination of relationship management and of the value generated in seaports respectively.

The present chapter is a first attempt to link port stakeholders' inter-dependencies with relationships generated throughout the process, and generate knowledge on what influences the value offered in seaports. Moreover, the innovative concept of port value chains is established.

Keywords: Port users; port value chains; interdependencies; port stakeholders relationships

9.1. Introduction

Major changes in trade systems have affected maritime-based freight transportation. The essential quest for ports integration in supply chains results in the functional and spatial expansion of port-related activities ('port regionalization': Ferrari, Parola, & Morchio, 2006; Notteboom & Rodrigue, 2005). International ports aim to attract large-scale companies, draw extra investments, exploit resources and attain efficiencies to be part of such integrated chains.

In this vein, understanding the emerging complex, diverse and of extended scope interactions, produced relations, and interdependencies between port service providers' and the users of these services are of particular importance. Among others, such understanding frames the ways and conditions within which port users extract — or, at least, perceive to extract – value when using a particular port.

This is not a framing of theoretical importance alone. In the context described, effectiveness ('*do the right thing*') is a vital performance component of increased importance that complements the more traditional target of the efficient use of the available factors of production (see Brooks & Pallis, 2008), with port users complaining even when efficiency ('*do the thing right*') — the traditional key issue in the fordist model of port development — is achieved (Farrell, 2009). Involved actors, in particular port authorities or port service providers, can outperform competitors via 'capture value' strategies that address unmet needs and exploit relevant opportunities (Magala, 2008). When any given port needs to serve its users both effectively and efficiently, knowing the type of interactions that develop in a particular port enables evaluations of the extent that such value is actually extracted.

The present study connects the concepts of *port actors' interdependence* and *value co-creation*. The review of recent studies establishes the importance of analysing the interactions that take place within a port, how port users are related, the resulting value offering within the port under examination, and how the latter offering is applied in network constellations. All these in the light of the formation of port value chains and the importance of co-creating value. This discussion suggests that the higher the level of interdependence between companies the higher the possibility of co-creating value. Hence, the paper discusses three types of interdependencies that may be found in port networks and illustrates the structures of their presence with the use of empirical findings from the port industry.

The findings presented are the outcome of semi-structured interviews with various port stakeholders (shipping lines, freight forwarders (FFs), shippers, port authorities and subcontractors) in four major Belgian and Greek ports (Antwerp, Zeebrugge, Piraeus and Thessaloniki). The conducted research is 'cargo-based', with containers being under examination. Actors' strategies in each trade are different, calling for attention to the unique set of actors and partners of ports usage develop in a particular trade (Hall, 2004). Containerized trade in particular implies organisational changes leading to a remarkable focus of port studies on this type of trade (Pallis, Vitsounis, & De Langen, 2010, 2011), and the present study contributes to this debate.

9.2. Studying Relationships in Ports

In recent times, port studies begun to focus on the under-researched relationships between port users and port services providers, as well as on the measurement of the value extracted by the users of a port. This debate established the need and creates the framework for further research of the particular issue.

Within a container port community perspective, Martin and Thomas (2001) describe the various organizational and institutional relationships, concluding that the competitive environment that exists between key port community members restricts the development of long-term co-operative relationships. Yet, they advocate that key members of the community have come closer together. Hence, the port system is influenced and framed by all the members of the relevant port community. Van Der Horst and de Langen (2008) seek arrangements to resolve the coordination problems in hinterland chains established by such community. The scholars underline coordination problems in container barging, railway and trucking hinterland chain, and identify mechanisms to address them, such as incentives for the creation of inter-firm alliances, changing scope of companies and creating collective actions.

Carbone and Martino (2003) study shippers' perspectives on port related satisfaction criteria. Decomposing the port product and the services supplied by each actor in the port community, they conclude that (a) the delivery of value is a major determinant of satisfaction and (b) shippers' relationships with other members of the supply chain, and the level of integration among the various actors, influence decisively the satisfaction of the involved parties. De Martino and Morvillo (2008) study the delivery of value advocating that 'port actors' integration' is a source of port competitive advantage. Based on a supply chain management paradigm, the scholars analyse ports endorsing a network perspective. The involved firms' capabilities to create inter-organisational relationships are a crucial factor for their strategic positioning.

In their study of port actors' relationships, Bichou and Bell (2007) acknowledge the presence of channels structures in global shipping and ports. With the use of structural equation modelling, they test the impact of power and conflict between channel members on the level of consolidation, mobility and channel performance.

Hall (2004) challenges the overlooking of the relations between individual firms in seaports as a means to understand commodity flows and underlines the need for a more actor-centred theoretical and empirical analysis. His analysis of automobile importers in United States demonstrates that the established relations between port actors leading to mutual specialization cause the concentration of high-volume imports in few ports. When actor-centred approaches are increasingly recommended for port analysis (also Olivier & Slack, 2006) the importance of the developed relations, and their implications for value generation cannot be ignored. With value being highly correlated with satisfaction,[1] and both of them influencing behavioural intentions, understanding the ways that the former is generated provides useful information for actors seeking to improve their own competitiveness.

9.3. Value Lies on Relations

The users of a port develop perceptions regarding the value that is generated and extracted by the use of this or any other port. For them this value (perceived value) mainly derives from three components. These are the two types of interactions that they develop with other port stakeholders and the port authority, which are the operational and commercial ones respectively, and the structural characteristics of the port (for detailed empirical evidence see Vitsounis, 2011). Operational interactions include the actual delivery of a service, that is, the loading of a container into a truck. Commercial interactions refer to all other interactions that are developed between the parties involved, such as communications, payment, agreements and so forth rather than physical transactions.

Port users and service providers develop relations that fall within a business-to-business (B-2-B) framework. In many cases these are long-term, close relations that involve complex patterns of interactions between and within each company and significant mutual adaptation by both parties (Hakansson & Johanson, 1992; Turnbull, Ford, & Cunningham, 1996). The involved parties put emphasis on the desired value, that is the perceived preference for, and evaluation of those service attributes, performances and consequences arising from use that facilitate (or block) achieving the user's goals and purposes in use situations (Woodruff, 1997).

Value in B-2-B markets places extra emphasis on relations developed between services providers and users. All actors perceive at least two different categories of value (Woodruff & Flint, 2003). The first one is functional value that lies in hierarchies centred on service availability and quality, delivery service quality, and pricing. The second one is relationship value that stems from the quality of the interactions going on between the user and the supplier of the service. Grönroos (1997) pointed that in a relational context, value for the customer is not embedded in a transactional exchange of a product for money. Instead customer-perceived value is

---

1. Still, the way that the three different constructs (value, satisfaction and behavioural intentions) are connected remains ambiguous (for an analysis: Graf and Maas, 2008).

also created and delivered over time as relationship develops. In that case, a poor episode value can be balanced by a positive perception of the relationship as a whole. Thus, it is important for the supplier to maintain a good relationship with the user, since this makes the latter more tolerant towards occasional inferior performance. For the user the vital issue is the entire relationship that is established with the provider, rather than any separate offering alone.

9.3.1. Port Network Orientation

In port settings each actor is part of a *network structure* that binds together actors, activities and resources in a certain pattern (see Hakansson & Johanson, 1992). Service suppliers expect that the demanded value by their immediate users to be influenced by the needs of the downstream users. Individual port, and related, entities are embedded in the broader chain, rather than independent units. These are a set of connected business relationships in which exchange in one relationship is contingent upon exchange in the other relationship and so on (cf. Tikkanen, Alajoutsijavri, & Tahtinen, 2000).

In this context, the relations between port actors are *not typical static dyadic* ones. Every supplier has an impact upon its customer's customer (for an analysis see Woodruff & Flint, 2003) as emerging complex inter-organisational relationships in the port network affect the dynamics of the value (perceived to be) offered in any specific setting. Developed relations involve a chain of intermediaries, with the 'end user', and its actual importance being difficult to be recognised by all the parts of the chain. What is important though to every participant in the chain is his own customer satisfaction. However, this customer is satisfied when he receives services that give him the opportunity to deliver the desired services to his own customer, and so on. Within this framework a complex set of interdependencies evolves gradually.

Relevant interactions include networks wherein a firm's activities and performance have an impact on its clients' performance and so forth. Empirical evidence produced in the context of the present study establishes that flows across a network are neither homogeneous nor actors confront them *sui generis*. Strategic choices of involved firms shape the networks formed, with these choices based on, or highly influenced by, the relations that develop with other actors; a situation calling for actor-centred studies that pay attention to these relations (Hall, 2004).

At the same time, supply chain interactions are a *fractal* of which port interactions stand as a part. Precisely as the broader chains, ports consist of multiple layers of involved entities, which pursue their own goals and strategies. In many instances, these entities might be unconcerned with the level of value that the port, and/or the chain offer as a whole. Yet, users (especially shippers) do not select a specific provider but make up decisions based on the whole port value chain, and the total of the firms involved in a mighty used port.

Based on that notion, port users need to be cautious of the value that the port and/or the port chain offer via the relationships that develop between actors who are active throughout the chain. The importance of the latter demands relationships that increase the chain's total value offering. A key question is how such relationships develop in a way that acts as promoter of value creation within the relevant network constellations.

9.3.2. Port Value Chains

A number of actors compete within any given port. An example is a container shipped from the departure point A to a destination B via a given port and the multiple companies that handle this container throughout this specific journey. Starting from the inland terminal, freight forwarders, shipping lines and terminal operators, a number of actors are involved, and several serial interdependencies (for more, see Section 9.4) developed. This means that the efficiency and effectiveness of the container's movement are subject to coordination and collaboration and rely on the efficient matching of the resources of the involved actors. Due to the presence of such interdependencies, port service providers are embedded in *port value chains* aiming to generate value for their users.

Port value chains refer to a system of functionally and spatially interacting regionalized units, rather than to individual terminals, warehouses, rail or trucks and so forth only. Port firms are in need of, and always use, services offered by other port stakeholders, and thus competition between the various port value chains to which various actors belong takes place. Subsequently, putting together a network of firms in order to build the set of capabilities necessary to deliver high value to the customer becomes a major strategic thrust. In these cases partner selection is a critical element in competitive strategy. A firm's procurement strategy may be the most important ingredient in its ability to deliver superior value to its customers (for a similar concept in a non-port context see Lewin & Johnston, 1997).

The competency of each actor is integrated with that of the other participants in the port value chain. It is often within, and because of, this integrated links where the most value is added within the chain (cf. Barber, 2008), whereas discrete sites wherein each actor pursues its goals independently do not lead to an improved productivity (Gunasekaran, Patel, & Tirtiroglu, 2001). Upstream suppliers in particular provide inputs to the focal firm which in turn adds value to them, and then pass these inputs downstream to the next actor and so on. The aim is to add more value to the core product via an immediate user-oriented activity (cf. Ravald & Grönroos, 1996) and ultimately via the overall port value chain oriented process. Evidence suggests that in these circumstances stronger relationships with partners lead to increased satisfaction and increases the performance of a firm (see also Hausman, 2001). Yet, not all inter-organisational relationships are strong ones, as in certain instances efforts to move towards a stronger relationship might be wasteful.

Advancing in essence Robinson's (2002) theoretical argument that ports and competition are embedded in supply chains, port actors interviewed in the context

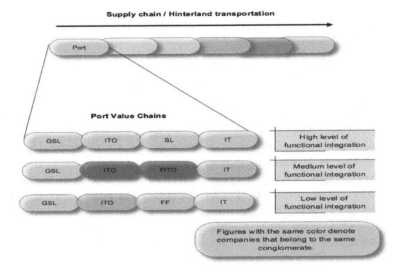

Figure 9.1: Port value chains. ITO: international terminal operator; GSL: global shipping line; SL: shipping line; FF: freight forwarder; IT: inland terminal

of the present research suggest that in a given port competition takes place between 'port value chains' (as illustrated in Figure 9.1) and not only between stand-alone firms. For this reason it is not sufficient anymore for a port stakeholder to deliver services of high value to its clients. This delivering has to be combined with services offered by other firms and add up, or at least sustain, this value. The end user ultimately evaluates the value offered by the whole port value chain. It is in the interest of individual firms to be embedded in port value chains that have the capability of producing and offering superior value to their users.

The existence of a supply chain presupposes the development of synergies among the players involved. This can lead to a competitive advantage (in line with De Martino and Morvillo (2008)). Port stakeholders take advantage of these synergies that are also present in port value chains and pursue the co-creation of value aiming to offer an augmented value to their customers.

9.4. Co-creating Value Via Inter-dependence Enhancement

Actors involved in a port value chain might pursue the co-creation of value in order to take advantage of the network dynamics. They can do so by configuring their activities in ways that enhance the various types of interdependencies and therefore facilitate value co-creation in network constellations.

Wilson (1995) identifies interdependence and power imbalance as two variables that determine the different relationships situations. Dependence is the product of the importance of a given input or output to a particular organization, and the extent that this is controlled by relatively few organizations. Power imbalance implies the ability of one partner to get the other partner to do something he would not normally do, whereas power inversely influencing dependence (Anderson and Weitz, 1989). Firms exploit interdependence when they realize the potential of cooperation and utilize each other's heterogeneous resources with the main aim being to co-produce value. The potential for value co-creation increases with the tolerance for interdependence and interaction over time (Forsström, 2004). Thus the members of port value chains have to willingly commit in interdependencies in order to produce and offer augmented value. Interdependencies are created due to mutual investments and tend to increase over time as the parties engage in different types of business activities (Forsstrom, 2005). The challenge for involved firms is to consider a partnership and realise the potential of co-creating value when being interdependent.

In the latter case, three types of interdependencies are identified within and between organizations: (a) serial or sequential, (b) pooled and (c) reciprocal interdependencies (in line with Thompson, 1967).

9.4.1.   Serial Inter-dependencies

2In serial interdependencies, the output of one port actor's activity is the input of another. The exploration of such interdependencies leads to the achievement of economies of integration. In Figure 9.2, the International Terminal Operator (ITO), the Global Shipping Line (GSL) and the Freight Forwarder (FF) are different companies carrying out the activities a, b and c, respectively. The outcome of the GSL's activity is the ITO's input, whereas the output of the latter is a third actor's input and so on. Beyond the apparent time dependencies, technological and/or administrative interdependencies between the involved firms might also exist (Hakansson & Persson, 2004). The coordination and adjustment of the activities a, b and c, across the port value chain, can reduce costs and increase services in relation to specific counterparts.

Time serial interdependencies are present throughout port value chains and involve all port actors. For example, a delay during the sea-going length of

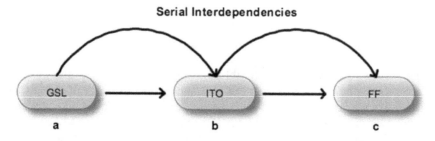

Figure 9.2: Serial interdependencies in ports

transportation has implications for the FF who receives a container delayed. In this case, even if a FF's operations are of top efficiency and effectiveness, the forwarder fails to deliver them to its customers due to the presence of inefficiencies in a previous part of the transportation length. As time interdependency prevails, port firms seek reliable partners that guarantee the delivery of a container on pre-defined time. The co-creation of value comes through the delivery of a container to the following actor on the predefined time and with no delays. That will give the opportunity to the following firms offer a better value to their clients and so on.

Notably, time buffers can be found in ports. For example, an FF might pick up a container some days after its initial unloading from the containership. If firms remain fragmented, do not exchange information and do not coordinate, these buffers are extremely difficult to be recognized and exploited. Therefore, another means for co-creating value is the establishment of proper mechanisms and relations that lead towards the exploitation of these buffers. Due to the fact that the proper mechanisms or initiatives are very difficult to be established, port users put extra emphasis on the productivity and the absence of delays.

Buffers do not apply to administrative and technological interdependencies. Administrative interdependencies exist between all port actors. The issue and exchange of bill of landings between the members of the chain is perhaps the most significant one. Vertical integration strategies target, *inter alia*, to address this issue. Shipping lines and terminal operators subsidiaries that offer freight forwarding services issue the 'throughput bill of landing'. In these cases the place of delivery of a container is different than the port (i.e. a hinterland point) and the responsibility of delivery at point lies in the respective firm. Shipping lines and terminal operators may also issue bill of landing for inland terminals operated by them. The same applies to private inland terminals that take the control of moving a container from the port to their inland terminal. Yet, vertical integration is a strategy addressing serial administrative and technical interdependencies between port actors. It is in the interest of those firms that do not endorse strategies of vertical integration, to devote resources in the search of alternative ways to address administrative interdependen-cies. Standardisation and increased connectivity and use of common information systems could be a possible avenue, with effective solutions increasing the value offered to each independent firm.

9.4.2. *Pooled Inter-dependencies*

Pooled interdependencies are present when two activities use the same resource, or two resources are used in one activity. When two activities are identical, the exploitation of pooled interdependencies leads to economies of scale. When the two activities are similar, they lead to economies of scope. Pooled interdependencies are presented in Figure 9.3 where GSL, ITO and FF carry out two activities. Activities, a.1, b.1 and c.1 are interdependent, consisting a port value chain. The terminal

Pooled Interdependencies

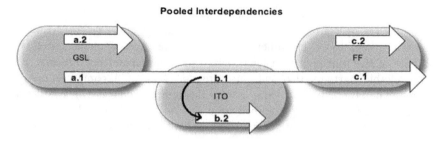

Figure 9.3: Pooled interdependencies in ports

Pooled Interdependencies

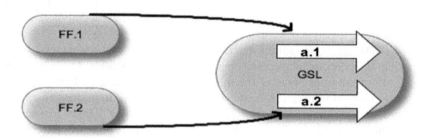

Figure 9.4: Pooled inter-organisational interdependencies in ports

operator, with a given productivity, delivers the b.1 activity (serving the ship a) as well as the b.2 activity (serving the ship b). Therefore the two activities are interdependent.

Figure 9.4 represents inter-organisational pooled interdependencies, wherein the shipping company seeks an amount of containers to fill the capacity of its ship, thus is dependent upon a number of shippers and/or FFs. In such cases, the challenge lies in combining different counterparts and the respective resources.

Both types of pooled interdependencies can be found in many instances. For port actors it is worth keeping a balance between them. In general, the services offered in port are segmented towards selected users. This leads to a great variation of activities carried out and resources needed devoted for servicing different firms. The challenge is to adjust services to users needs and, thus, deliver highly valued services. Yet, initiatives that increase the value offered to one user may be counterproductive as regards the value offered to another. An indicative example is a shipping line that is willing to participate into two different port value chains, that is by developing relationships with two different FFs. In an effort to offer addition value to an FF, the shipping line might adjust its services in a way that will reduce the value offered to the other. On the contrary, if an FF is seeking customised services, it will be confronted by the fact that the shipping line also serves a number of other actors and therefore cannot adjust its services to a great extent.

To recap, pooled interdependencies are present in port value chains but the mechanisms to address them are limited. Port firms do not commit themselves into close relationships that would increase their interdependence and thus co-creation of value remains limited.

9.4.3. *Reciprocal Inter-dependencies*

Reciprocal interdependency refers to a mutual exchange of inputs and outputs between two parties. A typical example exists when two related activities change at the same time, so that each one functions in relation to the other. Reciprocal interdependencies favour the emergence of economies of innovation and agility. Figure 9.5 represents the nature of reciprocal interdependencies, with the involved actors being the ITO and the FF carrying out the activities a.1 and b.1, respectively. To reach a situation wherein both activities are carried out independently (a.2 and b.2) both firms have to make changes in their operational patterns.

Value might also be co-created as a result of the reciprocal interdependencies and consequent collaboration between FFs and shipping lines. Typically, relationships between these actors are scarce. Servicing a major shipper though is of interest for both parties. Major shippers are in need of specialised services of increased value. In many instances, however, the size and the capabilities of standalone shipping lines or FFs are not sufficient to meet these needs. Therefore, FFs and shipping lines might do so via mutual commitment in collaboration and relationships that promote each other's advantages and, ultimately, offer to the shipper served an augmented value.

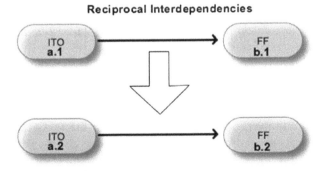

Figure 9.5: Reciprocal interdependencies in ports

This process implies changes and significant operational adjustments by both parties, whereas it increases the existing interdependence.

9.5. Co-creation of Value: The Role of Inter-dependencies

A *business relationship* is the process wherein two firms or other types of organizations *'form strong and extensive social, economic, service and technical ties over time, with the intent of lowering total costs and/or increasing value, thereby achieving mutual benefit'* (Anderson & Narus, 1991, p. 96). The various relationships that a firm maintains are among the most valuable resources that this firm possesses (Hakansson, 1987). Pure transactions stand at one end of the spectrum. At the other end stand the relations that develop through vertically integrated organisations. In the case of the least integrated settings, companies enjoy high levels of autonomy and pursue strategies aiming to achieve individual goals. In the most integrated ones collaborative relationships exist and the involved parties share mutual interests through *'purposive strategic relationships between independent firms who share compatible goals, strive for mutual benefit and acknowledge a high level of mutual interdependence'* (Mohr and Spekman, 1994, p. 135).

As such, the development of close relationships goes hand in hand with the rise of interdependencies between the involved actors. For ports, it remains questionable which type of interdependencies favour the co-creation of value in certain relationships developed between the various port stakeholders. The conducted empirical research in major European ports — as presented in the remaining of the present chapter — identified the presence of various interdependencies between port users and service providers depending on the different features of port constellations.

In particular, the conducted field research results in the categorization of port users on the grounds of the different strategies they deploy as regards the development of relationships with other port actors. The categorisation effectively generalises the differences observed, even with the same type of port stakeholders. FFs lay into two broad categories: (a) the traditional FF and (b) the integrated FF. Shipping lines might be categorized as (a) regional or feeder shipping lines, (b) non-integrated GSLs, (c) semi-integrated GSLs, and (d) integrated GSLs (for an analysis of the types of port stakeholders see Vitsounis, 2011).

Three parameters are found to influence remarkably the structure of port users' relationships: (a) the strategic patterns of the involved actors, (b) the market structures and (c) several case-specific factors. It is remarkable though that whenever two port stakeholders co-create value through the development of schemes developed between, pooled and/or reciprocal interdependencies do exist. At the same time, serial interdependencies are present throughout port value chains, yet they do not influence the co-creation of value practices. Table 9.1 and 9.2 present a number of alternative relationships developed between port stakeholders, with the emphasis being on co-creation of value schemes and the types of interdependencies found in each case.

Table 9.1: Freight forwarder relationships with key port actors.

	Shipping lines	**Inland terminals**	**Rail, trucking, barge**
'Small traditional' freight forwarder	No contractual agreements No co-creation of value	No contractual agreements No co-creation of value *Serial Interdependencies*	No contractual agreements No co-creation of value
'Major traditional' freight forwarder	Agreements on rates and capacity	Limited contractual agreements (following shippers wills)	No contractual agreements
	Limited co-creation of value efforts *Pooled and Serial Interdependencies*	No co-creation of value *Serial Interdependencies*	No co-creation of value
Integrated freight forwarder	Contractual agreements, efforts to limit the number of companies used	Investments and Contractual agreements	Contractual agreements
	Co-creation of value	Co-creation of value *Reciprocal, Pooled and Serial Interdependencies*	Co-creation of value

9.6. Conclusions

This study analysed the ways that port actors operate within network configurations that emerge within port value chains. The value offered to the users of these chains is not determined only by the capabilities of each actor but from upstream and downstream counterparts as well. In order to increase this value, the actors involved in a chain choose either to remain fragmented or to take advantage of the network dynamics through the establishment of close relationships with other port stakeholders. The latter focus on both the selection of the right partners and the development of meaningful relationships between them that work towards value co-creation and, consequently, to augmented value proposition. Out of the three types of interdependencies identified in ports, pooled and reciprocal are the ones that favour the development of close relationships and as such the emergence of value co-creation schemes. On the contrary, the presence of serial interdependencies is not sufficient to motivate port stakeholders to pursue the co-creation of value.

At the same time, imbalances of power between port actors increase further, particularly as port authorities regularly seek contracts with international terminals

Table 9.2: Shipping lines relationships with key port actors.

	Terminal operators (TO)	Freight forwarders (FF)	Inland terminals	Rail, truck, barge companies
Regional or feeder shipping lines	Close, contractual agreements towards value co-creation with TO of equivalent power	No contractual agreements	Limited if no relationships with inland terminals.	Scarce use and limited relationships
		Serial Interdependencies Offering special rates to a number of them Close, long-term relationships towards co-creation of value only with a limited number of FF of equivalent power.		
	Pooled and Serial Interdependencies	*Pooled and Serial Interdependencies*	*Serial Interdependencies*	
Non-integrated global shipping lines	Close, contractual agreements towards value co-creation with TO mainly due to their power derived from their global operations	No relationships with small freight forwarders	Non-contractual agreements. Use of inland terminals for long periods of time. Adaptation to needs based on personal relationships.	Use of a limited number of them for long-periods of time. No contractual agreements. Adaptations based on personal relationships.

Semi-integrated shipping lines	Investments in Terminals or close, contractual agreements that aim to control operations in order to co-create value	*Pooled and Serial Interdependencies*	*Serial Interdependencies* Agreements on rates and secured capacity to a selected number of freight forwarders. *Pooled and Serial Interdependencies* Close relationships and co-creation of value with FF that service big in size shippers. *Reciprocal and Serial Interdependencies* Same as above	Use of inland terminals mainly to store empty containers picked up by FF *Serial Interdependencies* *Serial Interdependencies* Development and running of their own inland terminals. Also investment in inland terminals to gain control in management.	*Serial Interdependencies* Development of close, contractual agreements towards co-creation of value. In cases that services offered do not have sufficient value then they start operating subsidiaries offering truck, rail and barge services.

Table 9.2: (*Continued*)

	Terminal operators (TO)	Freight forwarders (FF)	Inland terminals	Rail, truck, barge companies
	Pooled and Serial Interdependencies		If not feasible, then development of contractual, close relationships leading to co-creation of value. One -year contracts with inland terminals imposed by the freight forwarders.	*Pooled and Serial Interdependencies*
Integrated shipping lines	Development and running of dedicated terminals. *Pooled and Serial Interdependencies* If not possible, then development of close, contractual agreements towards co-creation of value. *Pooled and Serial Interdependencies*	Same as above		Employment of their own means or development of close contractually based agreements. *Pooled and Serial Interdependencies*

operators and major shipping lines. The specific strategy increases the difficulty of advancing close relationships leading to co-creation of value. Moreover, port actors remain fragmented. Whenever involved port actors exploit strategies of vertical integration, opportunities for co-creating value along with other suppliers and customers emerge.

The presence of three types of interdependencies implies the need for more empirical data in order to recognise more port firms' strategies that address them. There is also a need to measure the correlation between the types of interdependencies and the relevant co-created value outcomes. The impact of the remaining relationship variables (for example, as recognised in Wilson, 1995) on port chains value offering also deserves analytical and empirical attention.

The great imbalances in terms of power and bargaining position being present in port settings make the development of close relationships more difficult and stand as adverse reasons towards co-creation of value practices. Relationships are also relative to the actors' strategic patterns. Different types of the same category of actors develop different types of relationships. In port settings there are cases where two port users share a common strategic objective but might pursue the fulfilment of this objective through largely distinctive strategies. Reciprocal and pooled interdependencies favour the development of close relationships between port stakeholders while cases of *derived relationships* may be developed. On the contrary the presence of serial interdependencies do not influence the co-creation of value practices. In general, shipping lines are more favourable to developing close relationships mainly due to the fact that they possess a significant power position in port settings.

Acknowledgments

The conducted research has been financially supported by the 'Training of Researchers-Operational Program "Competitiveness"' (PENED-03ED647) research project, co-financed by the General Secretariat for Research and Technology, Greek Ministry of Development and the Third European Community Support Program.

References

Anderson, E., & Weitz, B. (1989). Determinants of continuity in conventional industrial channel dyads. *Marketing science, 8*(4), 310–323.

Anderson, J. C., & Narus, J. A. (1991). Partnering as a focused market strategy. *California Management Review, 33*(3), 95–113.

Barber, E. (2008). How to measure the "value" in value chains. *International Journal of Physical Distribution & Logistics Management, 38*(9), 685–698.

Bichou, K., & Bell, M. Gh. (2007). Internationalization and consolidation of the container port industry: assessment of channel structure and relationships. *Maritime Economics & Logistics, 9*, 35–51.

Brooks, M. R., & Pallis, A. A. (2008). Assessing port governance models: Process and performance components. *Maritime Policy and Management, 35*(4), 411–432.

Carbone, V., & Martino, M. D. (2003). The changing role of ports in supply-chain management: an empirical analysis. *Maritime Policy and Management, 30*(4), 305–320.

De Martino, M., & Morvillo, A. (2008). Activities, resources and inter-organisational relationships: key factors in port competitiveness. *Maritime Policy and Management, 35*(6), 571–589.

Farrell, S. (2009). Factors influencing port efficiency — a case study of Dar Es Salaam, *Proceedings of the International Association of Maritime Economists (IAME) Conference,* (proceedings: CD-Rom), Copenhagen, June 24 – 26, 2009.

Ferrari, C., Parola, F., & Morchio, E. (2006). Southern European Ports and the Spatial Distribution of EDCs. *Journal of Maritime Economics and Logistics, 8*(1), 60–81.

Forsström, B. (2004). Value Co-creation through interdependence in the context of industrial buyer-seller relationships-findings from an empirical study, *Proceedings of the 20th annual IMP conference,* Copenhagen.

Forsström, B. (2005). *Value Co-creation in industrial buyer-seller partnership: Creating and exploiting interdependencies.* Turku, Finland: PHD Dissertation, Åbo Akademis Förlag — Åbo Akademi University press.

Graf, A., & Maas, P. (2008). Customer value from a customer perspective: a comprehensive review. *Journal für Betriebswirtschaft, 58,* 1–20.

Grönroos, C. (1997). Value-driven relational marketing: From products to resources and competencies. *Journal of Marketing Management, 13*(5), 407–419.

Gunasekaran, A., Patel, C., & Tirtiroglu, E. (2001). Performance measures and metrics in a supply chain environment. *International Journal of Operations & Production management, 21*(1/2), 71–87.

Hakansson, H. (1987). Product development in networks. In H. Hakansson (Ed.), *Technological development: A network approach* (pp. 84–128). New York: Croom Helm.

Hakansson, H., & Johanson, J. (1992). A model of industrial networks. In B. Axelsson & G. Easton (Eds.), *Industrial networks: A new view of reality.* London: Routledge.

Hakansson, H., & Persson, G. (2004). Supply chain management: The logic of supply chains and networks. *The International Journal of Logistics Management, 15*(1), 11–26.

Hall, P. V. (2004). Mutual specialization, seaports and the geography of automobile imports. *Tijdschrift voor Economische en Sociale Geografie, 95*(2), 135–146.

Hausman, A. (2001). Variations in relationship strength and its impact on performance and satisfaction in business relations. *Journal of Business and Industrial Marketing, 16*(7), 600–616.

Lewin, E. J., & Johnston, W. J. (1997). Relationship marketing theory in practice: A case study. *Journal of Business Research, 39*(1), 23–31.

Magala, M. (2008). Modelling opportunity capture: A framework for port growth. *Maritime Policy and Management, 35*(3), 285–311.

Martin, J., & Thomas, B. J. (2001). The container terminal community. *Maritime Policy and Management, 28*(3), 279–292.

Mohr, J. J., & Spekman, R. (1994). Characteristics of partnership success: Partnership attributes, communication behaviour and conflict resolution. *Strategic Management Journal, 15*(2), 135–152.

Notteboom, T. E., & Rodrigue, J. P. (2005). Port regionalization: towards a new phase in port development. *Maritime Policy and Management, 32*(3), 297–313.

Olivier, D., & Slack, B. (2006). Rethinking the port. *Environmental Planning A, 38*(8), 1409–1427.

Pallis, A. A., Vitsounis, T. K., & De Langen, P. W. (2010). Port economics, policy and management — Review of an emerging research field. *Transport Reviews, 30*(1), 115–161.

Pallis, A. A., Vitsounis, T. K., De Langen, P. W., & Notteboom, T. (2011). Port economics, policy and management — Content classification and Survey. *Transport Reviews, 31*(4), 445–471.

Ravald, A., & Grönroos, C. (1996). The value concept and relationship marketing. *European Journal of Marketing, 30*(2), 19–30.

Robinson, R. (2002). Ports as elements in value-driven chain systems: The new paradigm. *Maritime Policy and Management, 29*(3), 241–255.

Thompson, J. D. (1967). *Organizations in action.* New York: Mc Graw-Hill.

Tikkanen, H., Alajoutsijavri, K., & Tahtinen, J. (2000). The concept of satisfaction in industrial markets: A contextual perspective and a case study from the software industry. *Industrial Marketing Management, 29*, 373–386.

Turnbull, P., Ford, D., & Cunningham, M. (1996). Interaction, relationships and networks in business markets: An evolving perspective. *Journal of Business & Industrial Marketing, 11*(3/4), 44–62.

Van Der Horst, M. R., & de Langen, P. W. (2008). Coordination in Hinterland Transport Chains: A Major Challenge for the Seaport Community. *Maritime economics and logistics, 10*(1), 108–129.

Vitsounis, T.K. (2011) *Balanced port performance analysis: Port users and service providers interactions, generation of relationships, and measurement of perceived value.* Unpublished Ph.D. Thesis, registered at the University of the Aegean.

Wilson, D. T. (1995). An integrated model of buyer-seller relationships. *Journal of the Academy of Marketing Science, 23*, 335–345.

Woodruff, R. B. (1997). Customer value: The next source for competitive advantage. *Journal of the Academy of Marketing Science, 25*(2), 139–153.

Woodruff, R. B., & Flint, D. J. (2003). Research on business-to-business customer value and satisfaction, Evaluating marketing actions and outcomes. *Advances in Business Marketing and Purchasing, 12*, 515–547.

Chapter 10

Overview and Gaps in Container Terminal Industry Studies

Ioannis N. Lagoudis

Abstract

There is significant amount of literature tackling different issues related to the port industry. The present chapter focuses on a single business unit of seaports aiming at the documentation of works related to container terminals.

An effort to review, collect and present the majority of the works present in the last 30 years, between 1980 and 2010, has been made in order to picture the problems dealt and methods used by the authors in the specific research field. To facilitate the reader, studies have been grouped under five categories of addressed problems (productivity and competitiveness, yard and equipment utilization, equipment scheduling, berth planning, loading/unloading) and four modelling methodologies (mathematics and operations research, management and economics, simulation, stochastic modelling).

The analysis shows that most works focus on productivity and competitiveness issues followed by yard and equipment utilisation and equipment scheduling. In reference to the methodologies used managerial and economic approaches lead, followed by mathematics and operations research.

In reference to future research, two fields have been identified where there is scope of significant contribution by the academic community: container terminal security and container terminal supply chain integration.

The present chapter provides the framework for researchers in the field of port container terminals to picture the so far works in this research area and enables the identification of gaps at both research question and methodology level for further research.

Keywords: Container terminals; methodologies; literature review; supply chain; logistics; operations

Maritime Logistics: Contemporary Issues
Copyright © 2012 by Emerald Group Publishing Limited
All rights of reproduction in any form reserved
ISBN: 978-1-78052-340-8

10.1. Introduction

Seaport terminals, airport terminals and distribution centre terminals, which offer services to road and rail, are the three main types of nodes today. Each of these nodes offers specialised services and facilities to the different modes of transport. Their purpose is to minimise the turnaround time of the modes that make use of their sites and thus facilitate the operations of their customers. The reason for existence of the different types of terminals is based on the different characteristics that the modes they serve have. Based on their specifications these terminals adapt their infrastructure, services and facilities.

Ports' role in the distribution of goods and commodities is increasing constantly as the significance of the maritime transport industry in global transportation increases at a constant pace as the yearly average increase of 5% declares (UNCTAD, 2001–2010). The demand for sea transportation is estimated to further increase in the future as globalisation forces companies to adopt global strategies in order to expand their business. Figure 10.1 illustrates the investment decisions as reported by state agencies, port authorities and port operators between 2001 and 2010. It must be mentioned here that the information is not complete, as the main investment decisions have been adopted as reported in the Annual Reviews of Maritime Transport published by UNCTAD. In addition, the cancellations or postponement of any of these investments are not included as it is very difficult to trace any single development at a global level. Nevertheless having these limitations in mind, a very good presentation on the

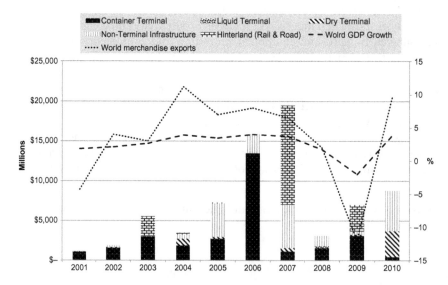

Figure 10.1: Investments in the port Industry
Source: Lagoudis and Rice (2010).

prevailing trends can be observed especially when compared with the global gross domestic product (GDP) and merchandise exports.

A number of additional observations need to be made at this point based on the presented data regarding the level and type of port investments announced:

- The majority of the investments are related to container terminals.
- Liquid and dry cargo terminals have the least reported investments.
- Non-terminal infrastructures refer to investments that have not been reported for specific terminals and may include dredging, waterfront improvements, acquisition of extra land for future terminal development etc.
- Hinterland investments are related to road and rail infrastructure for the improvement of intermodal improvements.
- Port investments follow the trend of the global economy especially when hinterland investments are excluded.

Port container terminals are the most integrated nodes of the sea transport process since containers are the most frequently used means of transport for the provision of door-to-door services. The minimisation of delays is of crucial importance in the daily operations, which requires detailed planning and accurate implementation by the operators. Based on the UNCTAD (2001–2010) Maritime Report delays derive mainly from strikes, industrial action outside the terminal, natural disasters and scarcity of specialised employees. In order to minimise delays apart from the heavy investment, container terminals have taken additional actions such as the mandatory $2 booking scheme to truck companies imposed by Southampton and a $47 penalty for late arrival and the creation of chassis pools, which increased space availability in US East Coast terminals and reduced truck turnaround and maintenance (UNCTAD, 2001–2010).

Due to the increasing role of port container terminals, there is significant literature tackling different issues of terminal efficiency and overall performance. Different methodologies have been adopted ranging from conceptual models to mathematical and operations research approaches examining different aspects of these terminals such as yard utilisation (Cullinane, Song, & Wang, 2005), storage space (Kim & Kim, 2002), equipment utilisation (Chen, 1999), berth allocation (Imai, Sun, Nishimura, & Papadimitriou, 2005) and other. This chapter focuses on container terminals aiming at presenting an, as much complete as possible, overview of the present studies in the literature in order to identify gaps and identify new areas of research.

10.2. Literature Overview

Studies on port container terminals have been categorised based on two criteria. The first criterion relates to the problems these address, and the second refers to the methodology used for the optimum solution. As seen in Table 10.1 studies have been grouped using five categories of addressed problems (productivity and competitiveness,

Table 10.1: Container terminal studies categorised by method and problem analysis.

Problem	Methodologies			
	Mathematics and operations research	Management and economics	Simulation	Stochastic
Productivity and competitiveness	Cullinane et al. (2005); Evers and Koppers (1996); Fu et al. (2007); Kim and Kim (2007); Koh (2001); Lee et al. (2006a); Legato and Monaco (2004); Rios et al. (2006); Yeo and Song (2006); Zeng and Yang (2002)	Ng (2006); Anderson et al. (2008); Anderson, Opaluch, and Grigalunas (2009); Baird (2006); Bichou and Bell (2007); Cochrane (2008); Cullinane and Song (1998, 2001); Cullinane and Wang (2006); Cullinane et al. (2004); De Souza et al. (2003); Dowd (1984); Dowd and Leschine (1990); Fleming (1997); Fung (2002); Ha (2003); Haralambides et al. (2002); Hayuth (1981); Hayuth and Fleming (1994); Heaver et al. (2001); Lam and Yap (2006, 2008); Lin and Tseng (2007); McCalla (1994, 1999); Monaco et al. (2009); Notteboom (1997, 2002); Nuefville and Tsunokawa (1981); Olivier (2005); Olivier et al. (2007); Peters (2001); Ramos-Real and Tovar (2010); Robinson (1985); Slack (1985); Song (2002); Song and Yeo (2004); Starr (1994); Teng et al. (2004);Turner et al. (2004); Veldman and Buckmann (2003); Veldman et al. (2005); Wang (1998); Wang and Slack (2000);	Kia et al. (2002); Kozan (1997); Lee et al. (2003); Luo and Grigalunas (2003); Shabayek and Yeung (2002); Tahar and Hussain (2000); Yun and Choi (1999); Zan (1999)	Cullinane et al. (2002); Cullinane and Song (2003); Cullinane et al. (2006); Lagoudis and Platis (2009); Notteboom et al. (2000)

			Wang and Cullinane (2006); Wiegmans et al. (2002); Wiegmans et al. (2008, 2009); Wu and Goh (2010); Yap et al. (2006)		Van Hee et al. (1988)
Yard and equipment utilisation	Bazzazi et al. (2009); Holguin-Veras and Jara-Diaz (1999); Kim (1997); Kim and Bae (1998); Kim and Kim (1998); Kim and Kim (1999b); Kim and Kim (2002); Kim and Park (2003); Kim et al. (2000); Lee et al. (2006b); Lee et al. (2008); Lehmann et al. (2006); Mattfeld and Orth (2006); Preston and Kozan (2001a); Preston and Kozan (2001b); Taleb-Ibrahimi et al. (1993); Van Hee and Wijbrands (1988); Zhang et al. (2002); Zhang et al. (2003);	Chu and Huang (2005); Chen (1998); Chen (1999); Chen et al. (2000); Choi et al. (2003); Ting et al. (2010)	Ballis, Golias, and Abacoumkin (1997); Castillo and Daganzo (1993); Dekker et al. (2006); Jula et al. (2006); Kim et al. (2006); Liu et al. (2002); Petering et al. (2009); Petering and Murty (2009); Petering (2009, 2011); Vis and Harika (2004); Yang et al. (2004)		
Equipment scheduling	Angeloudis and Bell (2010); Bish (2003); Briskorn et al. (2006); Cao and Uebe (1995); Cao et al. (2008); Chen and Yang (2010); Chung et al. (2002); Daganzo (1989); Goodchild and Daganzo (2006, 2007); Grunow et al. (2004); Grunow et al. (2006); Hartmann (2004); He et al. (2010); Kim and Kim (1997, 1999a, 1999c); Koo et al. (2004); Kozan and Preston (1999); Kozan and Preston (2006); Laik and Hadjiconstantnou (2008); Lau and Zhao (2008); Liang et al. (2009); Linn et al. (2003);		Goodchild and Daganzo (2006); Legato et al. (2009)		

Table 10.1: (*Continued*)

Problem	Methodologies			
	Mathematics and operations research	Management and economics	Simulation	Stochastic
	Liu et al. (2004); Narasimhan and Palekar (2002); Ng (2005); Nguyen and Kim (2009); Nishimura et al. (2005); Peterkofsky and Daganzo (1990); Tavakkoli-Moghaddam et al. (2009); Vis et al. (2001); Zhang and Kim (2009)			
Berth planning	Chang et al. (2010); Golias et al. (2009); Guan and Cheung (2004); Hansen et al. (2008); Imai et al. (2003, 2007a, 2008); Imai et al. (2005); Imai et al. (2007b); Kim and Moon (2003); Meisel and Bierwirth (2009); Moorthy and Teo (2006); Park and Kim (2002); Park and Kim (2003); Zhou and Kang (2008)		Dragovic et al. (2005); Guan and Yang (2010); Legato and Mazza (2001)	
Loading and unloading	Ambrosino and Sciomachen (2003); Chen et al. (1995); Guan and Liu (2009); Imai et al. (2002); Kang et al. (2008); Kim et al. (2004); Lee et al. (2007); Li and Vairaktarakis (2004); Mennis et al. (2008)		Chung et al. (1988)	
Conceptual models and literature review	Cheng et al. (2010); Gunther and Kim (2006); Martin and Thomas (2001); Ottjes et al. (2006); Steenken et al. (2004); Vis and de Koster (2003); Yi et al. (2000)			

Source: Author.

yard and equipment utilisation, equipment scheduling, berth planning and loading/ unloading) and four modelling methodologies (mathematics and operations research, management and economics, simulation and stochastic modelling).

A detailed presentation of these studies follows aiming at the illustration of the so far setting in the port container terminal literature.

10.2.1. Productivity and Competitiveness

10.2.1.1. Mathematical and operations research Among the studies which have adopted mathematical and operations research methodologies are those of Evers and Koppers (1996) using mathematics to develop a model for automatic traffic control in container terminals and Koh (2001), who developed an investment-planning model for container terminals with the assistance of a heuristic algorithm. The works of Cullinane et al. (2005) who examined the efficiency of container ports and terminal using mathematical programming and Kim and Kim (2007) who studied the optimal price policy a terminal should adopt for inbound containers are encapsulated in this category. Lee, Chew, Tan, and Han (2006a) developed a mathematical model to evaluate the impact of container throughput in Asian container terminals showing that improved service quality can boost demand. Rios, Maçada, & Gastaud (2006), Wang and Cullinane (2006) and Yeo and Song (2006) examined the improvement of container terminal efficiency with the assistance of operations research. In the first two studies, the authors used data envelopment analysis (DEA) whereas in the latter hierarchical fuzzy process (HFP) was selected to evaluate factors such as volume of cargo served, availability of equipment terminal area and other in order to measure the efficiency of different terminals. Fu, Li, Lim, and Rodrigues (2007) studied the space allocation for containers when arriving at different times during the planning period, and are made for different quantities and sizes of containers. Haralambides, Cariou, and Bennachio (2002) studied the effect of dedicated container terminals on the strategies of worldwide carriers using queuing theory. A hypothetical pricing rule is also developed which assists in the calculation of the costs stemming from the exclusive cooperation between carriers and ports. A different approach has been adopted by Legato and Monaco (2004) who considered the manpower planning problem in marine container terminals in order to evaluate the productivity of the terminal.

10.2.1.2. Management and economics A considerable amount of literature has focused on the measurement and identification of the level of efficiency of individual or groups of port container terminals. Among the studies which have adopted management and economics methodologies are those of Nuefville and Tsunokawa (1981) and Hayuth (1981) who studied the productivity levels of five major US container terminals of the East Coast in the former case and the factors that are critical in the creation of a container terminal as loading centre in the latter. With the assistance of economic analysis they intended to identify and justify between the investment in new, smaller in size, container terminals or in the improvement of the existing literature. Along the same lines is the work of Wu and Goh (2010) who compared the efficiency of port operations between emerging markets and the more advanced markets using DEA. Investment priorities for container terminals have also been investigated by McCalla (1994) in the presence of new developments in containerships. He used the Canadian ports of Halifax and Vancouver as case studies. Olivier, Parola, Slack, and Wang (2007) examined the prospects of further investments in the port container industry by the private sector in the modern internationalised market.

Heaver, Meersman, and Van de Voorde (2001) investigated the level of potential conflicts between port authorities and terminal operators and the level of competition among terminals aiming at the identification of feasible strategies that can be adopted by operators. Notteboom (2002) using the theory of contestable markets examined the level of contestability of the container handling industry in order to identify the factors that prevent players from entering or exiting the specific market. Along similar lines are the studies of Veldman and Buckmann (2003) and Veldman, Buckmann, and Saitua (2005), who worked on the level of competition container ports face with the use of logit models. Fung (2002) used a three-player oligopoly model to study the competitive conditions prevailing among Hong Kong, Hong Kong midstream and Singapore, whereas Yap, Lam, and Notteboom (2006), Song (2002) and Song and Yeo (2004) studied the competition conditions prevailing in Chinese ports. Lam and Yap (2008) focused on port competition in Southeast Asia for transhipment containers by an in-depth and quantitative analysis and similar work is found by Anderson et al. (2008) who developed a game-theoretic best response framework applying it on the ports of Busan and Shanghai. Lin and Tseng (2007) present five models of DEA to acquire a variety of complementary information about the operational efficiency of major container ports in the Asia-Pacific region and to identify trends in port efficiency. The works of Zeng and Yang (2002) and Hayuth and Fleming (1994) examined the significance of location factors for strategic decisions users make when selecting a container terminal for the movement of their products. Notteboom (1997) studied the load centre concept in European container terminals applying the Hirshmann–Herfindahl index on the Boston Consulting Group matrix.

The studies of Slack (1985), Wang (1998), Yap and Lam (2004), Teng, Huang, and Hunag (2004) and Lam and Yap (2006) with the use of economic theory examined inter-port competition in order to show the competitive advantage both the terminals and the users achieve. A location approach has been adopted by Fleming (1997) in order to identify the factors that make them excel among the global container terminal industry. Adjacent are the works of Koi Yu (2006) and Baird (2006) who compared competing container terminal location at a regional level in North Europe, Wiegmans, Ubbels, Rietveld, and Nijkamp (2002), Wiegmans, Hoest, and Notteboom (2008) and Wiegmans, Konings, and Priemus (2009) who investigated investment decisions related to container terminals and container terminal competition issues and Teng et al. (2004) and Starr (1994) who applied similar methodologies in North America. In the same category of analysis are the works of Cullinane and Song (1998) and Cullinane and Wang (2006) focusing on the analysis of business and functional problems that Korean container terminals are faced with in the former study and efficiency issues of European container terminals using cross-sectional data in the latter.

Dowd (1984) examined the pricing policies that can be adopted by container terminals focusing on the strategic decisions followed by container terminals in reference to leasing and their effectiveness. Similar is the study of Dowd and Leschine (1990) who studied possible criteria that can be used in order to measure terminal productivity. Productivity issues have been also dealt by Robinson (1985) and McCalla (1994). The former study evaluated the productivity of the first generation of Australian container terminals and the latter focused on the Canadian terminals aiming at speculating their future prospects. Similar is the approach by Ramos-Real and Tovar (2010) who used a cost function to investigate the competitiveness of Spanish container ports and by Anderson, Opaluch, and Grigalunas (2009) who used over 470,000 import shipment routing choices to determine how cost, time and schedule reliability affect cargo routers' port choices at the top 10 US ports.

A more managerial point of view has been adopted in the works of Cullinane and Song (2001), Cullinane, Song, Ji, and Wang (2004) and Peters (2001), who examined the organisational structure of Asian container ports. De Souza, Geraldo, Beresford, and Pettit (2003) studied the ownership trends and policies needed for fair competition levels to be achieved and maintained whereas, Wiegman et al.'s (2002) work focused on the Public Private Partnerships in Europe and their effect on the creation of competitive market conditions in the container industry. Bichou and Bell (2007) used structural equation modelling (SEM) to estimate the consolidation levels on the port container terminal industry and evaluate issues such as control, power and conflict. Finally, Ha (2003) focused on the quality factors of Korean container ports comparing them with top global operators, Cochrane (2008) examined the efficiency of different terminals with similar characteristics and throughput at a micro-level and Monaco, Moccia, and Sammarra (2009) studied the productivity of Gioia Tauro via the evaluation of both machinery and human element.

10.2.1.3. Simulation A number of studies use simulation techniques to examine container terminal productivity and efficiency. Kozan (1997) used simulation to study the efficiency of Australian container terminals. Zan (1999) analysed the interaction of port management policy, shipping companies and shippers via simulating the flow of container cargo. In their studies, Yun and Choi (1999) and Shabayek and Yeung (2002) intended to analyse the actual container terminal operations using Pusan and one of Hong Kong's container terminals in their studies respectively. Similar works have been made by Tahar and Hussain (2000), who examined the operations of the Malaysian Kelang Container Terminal aiming at improving the logistics operations and by Lee, Park, and Lee (2003) who developed a framework for efficient logistics planning. Finally, Luo and Grigalunas (2003) developed a model to estimate the impact on port demand and inter-port competition when fee changes take place in major US container terminals.

10.2.1.4. Stochastic modelling Finally, there are only a few studies, which have adopted stochastic modelling for tackling container terminal issues. Cullinane, Song, and Gray (2002) and Cullinane and Song (2003) used a stochastic frontier model to estimate the productive efficiency levels and proved that size and privatisation are positively correlated to improved productivity. Cullinane, Wang, Song, and Ping (2006) compared DEA and stochastic frontier analysis (SFA) to study the productivity of the technical infrastructure of container terminals. Similar work has been made by Notteboom, Coeck, and Van den Broeck (2000) using the same tool of stochastic frontier methodology to measure productive efficiency of European and Asian container terminals. Lagoudis and Platis (2009) used birth-and-death modelling in order to examine the improvement of container terminal operations in two stages of the container transportation process (loading/unloading and the stacking of containers in the container yard).

10.2.2.   Yard and Equipment Utilisation

10.2.2.1.   Mathematical and operations research   The studies that have dealt with yard and equipment utilisation issues can be grouped in two main categories in terms of methodologies. They mainly adopt either mathematical and operations research or simulation techniques. In the former group belongs the study of Taleb-Ibrahimi, Castilho, and Daganzo (1993) who described handling and storage strategies for export containers and measured terminals' performance based on the amount of space and number of handling moves. Similar works aiming at the determination of yard space and handling equipment have been made by Kim and Bae (1998), Kim and Kim (1998, 2002), Kim and Park (2003) and Kim, Park, and Ryu (2000). Ambrosino and Sciomachen (2003), Kim (1997) and Kim and Kim (1999b) investigated different stacking strategies and yard layouts that could lead to the minimisation of container re-handles, with the use of mathematical modelling. In the latter study, the focus was on import containers with different types of arrival rates: static, cyclic and dynamic.

Adjacent are the works of Preston and Kozan (2001a, 2001b), Lee, Chew, and Lee (2006b) and Lee, Wang, and Miao (2008) who studied the storage allocation problem in container hubs using two types of methodologies: algorithms (genetic and heuristic) and mix-integer programming. Along the same lines is the study of Van Hee and Wijbrands (1988) where they developed a decision support system for container terminal planning with the use of mathematics. The use of algorithms appears also in the studies of Vis, Koster, De Roodbergen, and Peeters (2001) who examined the number of automated guided vehicles a container terminal requires, Lehmann, Grunow, and Gunther (2006) who studied the deadlock handling problem that appears in automated container terminals, Bazzazi, Safaei, and Javadian (2009) who worked on a genetic algorithm to solve an extended storage space allocation problem and Mattfeld and Orth (2006) who addressed the problem of balanced distribution of vehicle movements in the container yard. Mathematical programming approaches are present in the studies of Zhang, Liu, Wan and Linn (2002) and Zhang, Liu, Wan, Murty, and Linn (2003) as well, who examined the problems of crane deployment and storage space allocation in container terminals.

10.2.2.2.   Management and economics   Management and economics approaches have been adopted by Chu and Huang (2005) who showed the trade-offs between terminal capacity and available yard handling systems and by Chen (1999), Chen, Lin, and Juang (2000) and Choi, Kim, Park, Park, and Lee (2003) whose studies examine the minimisation of unproductive moves with the assistance of statistical analysis and enterprise resource planning (ERP) methodology. Ting, Wang, Kao, and Pitty (2010) also provide a framework to improve yard crane operation efficiency in container terminals via a booking system for picking up import containers. Land utilisation has been dealt by Chen (1998) who investigated the reasons hidden behind the variations in the levels of utilisation achieved among container terminals of different geographic regions. Finally, Holguin-Veras and Jara-Diaz (1999) with the use of price differentiation theory developed a model for optimal space and pricing policy for priority systems in container terminals.

10.2.2.3. Simulation Among the studies that use simulation in the analysis of yard and equipment utilisation are the ones of Castillo and Daganzo (1993) who simulated handling strategies for the case of import containers and Dekker, Voogd, and Asperen (2006) who examined the methods of container stacking. Simulation has also been used in the studies of Kim, Jeon, and Ryu (2006), Yang, Choi, and Ha (2004) and Vis and Harika (2004) who intended to determine equipment productivity and efficiency and in the work of Kia, Shayan, and Ghotb (2002) who investigated methods of improving container terminal capacity. Liu, Jula, and Ioannou (2002), Petering, Wu, Li, Goh, and de Souza (2009), Petering (2009, 2011) and Petering and Murty (2009) also simulated different designs and layouts of automated container terminals and evaluated their performances. Finally, Jula, Chassiakos, and Ioannou (2006) simulated the optimisation of the reuse of empty container in order to minimise congestion in the ports of Los Angeles and Long Beach.

10.2.2.4. Stochastic Stochastic modelling is present in the work of Van Hee, Huitink, and Leegwater (1988) where they developed a decision support system for container terminal planning with the use of Markov models, queuing models and simple optimisation theory. This work is directly linked to the work of Van Hee and Wijbrands (1988) where as mentioned before a similar decision support system for container terminal planning was developed with the use of mathematics.

10.2.3. Equipment Scheduling

10.2.3.1. Mathematics and operations research Equipment routing and scheduling issues have been dealt mainly with mathematical and operation research methodologies and less with simulations ones. In the former category belong the studies of Bish (2003), who examined the scheduling of cranes for the provision of efficient service to containerships, Grunow, Gunther, and Lehmann (2004), Grunow, Gunther, and Lehmann (2006) and Vis et al. (2001) who analysed alternative strategies for AGVs scheduling and Hartmann (2004) and Nguyen and Kim (2009) who developed an algorithm for scheduling AGVs, straddle carries and stacking cranes for refrigerated containers and Kim and Kim (1997, 1999a, 1999c) focusing on the minimisation of container handling time in the yard. A hybrid algorithm is also used by He, Chang, Mi, and Yan (2010) and Liang, Huang, and Yang (2009) for yard crane scheduling in the former case and quay crane scheduling in the latter.

Additional studies using mathematical modelling are those of Daganzo (1989), Kozan and Preston (1999, 2006), Peterkofsky and Daganzo (1990), Cao and Uebe (1995), Cao, Lee, and Meng (2008), Narasimhan and Palekar (2002), Nishimura, Imai, and Papadimitriou (2005), Briskorn, Drexl, and Hartmann (2006), Linn, Liu, Wan, Zhang, and Murty (2003), Tavakkoli-Moghaddam, Makui, Salahi, Bazzazi, and Taheri (2009), Zhang and Kim (2009), Laik and Hadjiconstantnou (2008), Lau and Zhao (2008), Angeloudis and Bell (2010), Chen and Yang (2010), Koo, Lee, and Jang (2004), Liu, Jula, Vukadinovic, & Ioannou (2004), Ng (2005), Goodchild and Daganzo (2006, 2007) and Chung, Li, and Lin (2002) aiming at the routing and scheduling optimisation of the container terminal equipment.

10.2.3.2. Simulation In this category appears the study of Goodchild and Daganzo (2007) who with the use of simulation examined double-cycling versus single-cycling technique in order to evaluate terminal performance and the work of Legato, Canonaco, and Mazza (2009) who examined the assignment and deployment of rubber tired gantry cranes among yard blocks.

10.2.4. Berth Planning

10.2.4.1. Mathematics and operation research Berth planning has been discussed by Guan and Cheung (2004) with the use of mathematics and by Moorthy and Teo (2006) and Kim and Moon (2003) who used algorithms to study the economics of the home berth problem in the former study and the berth scheduling problem in the latter. Hansen, Uz, and Mladenovic (2008) have also examined the berth allocation problem with the assistance of a variable neighbourhood search (VMS) heuristic. In this work VMS is compared along with other methodologies (multi-start (MS), genetic search algorithm (GA) and memetic search algorithm (MA)) showing far better results. Imai, Nishimura, and Papadimitriou (2003), Imai et al. (2005), Imai, Chen, Nishimura, and Papadimitriou (2007a), Imai, Zhang, Nishimura, and Papadimitriou (2007b), Imai, Nishimura, and Papadimitriou (2008) and Park and Kim (2003) have used mathematical programming techniques to study berth allocation in container ports under different conditions and constrains such as the service priority rule and the limited crane and quay availability, whereas Park and Kim (2002) examined the transtainer routing problem in order to minimise the time containers are loaded from the yard to the ship with the use of an heuristic algorithm. Golias, Saharidis, Boile, Theofanis, and Ierapetritou (2009) have also examined the berthing problem aiming at the optimisation of costs related to vessel turnaround times. In their work a heuristic algorithm is used to minimise the costs related to fuel consumptions and vessel idle time. Similar work has been done by Chang, Jiang, Yan, and He (2010) using a series of heuristic algorithm examined the problem of berth planning and how this affects crane scheduling. Heuristics are also found in the work of Meisel and Bierwirth (2009) who proposed a problem formulation to increasing terminal productivity level when vessels are not berthed at the desired place as well as in the work of Zhou and Kang (2008) who worked on the berth and crane allocation problem.

10.2.4.1. Simulation Adopting a combination of simulation and queuing theory techniques Legato and Mazza (2001) and Dragovic, Park, Radmilovic, and Marac (2005) examined the performance of container terminals based on available infrastructure. Guan and Yang (2010) with the assistance of simulation evaluate the effect the different inspection measures imposed after the 9/11 attack have on berth planning and how these can create the least possible bottlenecks.

10.2.5. Loading and Unloading

10.2.5.1. Mathematics and operation research Among the studies that deal with the loading and unloading problem in port container terminals are those of Imai, Nishimura, Papadimitriou, and Sasaki (2002), Chen, Lee, and Shen (1995), Kim, Kang, and Ryu (2004) and Li and Vairaktarakis (2004). The first two studies use mathematical modelling to maximise the container terminal efficiency via the minimisation or re-handling moves, whereas the third and forth, with the use of algorithms, focus on the optimisation of the loading process of outbound containers and on the optimisation of the loading and unloading process of containerships respectively. Similar is the approach of Lee, Cao, and Meng (2007) who studied the handling sequence of holds for quay cranes assigned to a container vessel considering interference between quay cranes and of Kang, Medina, and Ouyang (2008) who worked on the optimisation of the size of transportation fleet (cranes and trucks) for unloading operations. Mennis, Platis, Lagoudis, and Nikitakos (2008) with the use of Markov theory and reliability models estimate the associated risks and costs that can result in delays due to machinery breakdowns during the loading and unloading process in the quay and finally, Guan and Liu (2009) focus on the terminal gate problem in order to examine the effect that 12,000 TEU vessels could have on the container terminal's hinterland connections.

10.2.5.2. Simulation Here only the work of Chung, Randhawa, and McDowell (1988) is present who developed a methodology to improve the loading process via the use of a buffer yard space, which enables yard and equipment utilisation.

10.2.6. Conceptual Models and Literature Review

Apart from the so far categorisation there are a number of studies that present different conceptual models for the operations of port container terminals. Among these are the works of Gunther and Kim (2006), Martin and Thomas (2001), Ottjes, Veeke, Duinkerken, Rijsenbrij, and Lodewijks (2006), Cheng, Tahar, and Ang (2010) and Yi, Kim, Choi, Park, and Lee (2000). Additionally, a review on port terminals can be found in the literature reviews of Steenken, Voß, and Stahlbock (2004), Dirk, Stefan, and Robert (2004) and Vis and de Koster (2003).

10.3.   Where Do We Stand?

As seen in Table 10.1 most of the research in the area of container terminal focuses on productivity and competitiveness issues followed by yard and equipment utilisation and equipment scheduling. Issues related to berth planning and loading/ unloading problems are limited compared to the rest of the research fields whereas there is a small but significant number of conceptual works as well. In reference to the methodologies used managerial and economic approaches lead followed by mathematics and operations research. Simulation and stochastic modelling approaches are also present at a lesser extend with the former applied in yard and equipment utilisation problems and the latter applied in productivity and competitiveness issues.

It is of interest to point out here that works are present as early as the 1980s but it is not before the mid-1990s when the maritime academic community started showing more interest in the port industry and more specifically in port container terminals. As presented in Figure 10.2 the works in academic journals are three times more between 2006 and 2010 compared to the respective time period between 1996 and 2000. Productivity and competitiveness issues are those that appear to attract more attention especially during the last decade followed by yard and equipment utilisation and berth planning.

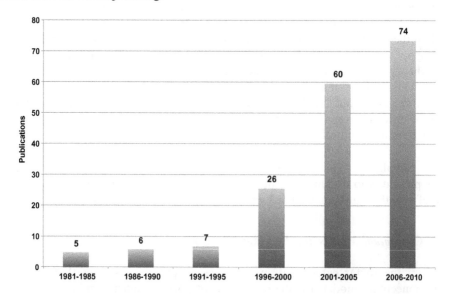

Figure 10.2: Literature evolution in publication numbers
Source: Author.

In terms of the academic journals where these works are published the ones related to the maritime industry stand out, with leading ones being *Maritime Economics and Logistics, Maritime Policy and Management* and *OR Spectrum. Computers and Industrial Engineering, Transportation Research Part B, Transportation Research Part E* and the *European Journal of Operations Research* follow (Figure 10.3 and Table 10.2).

10.3.1. The gap

In addition to the above studies, there are some new efforts present in the literature, which relate to niche issues stemming from the current political, economical, technological and business developments at a global level. The first group of works stems from the current developments in port security aspects. The works of Bichou (2011) and Guan and Yang (2010) are among the most recent works dealing with container terminal security aspects and the possible bottlenecks created.

The second type of problems, relate to supply chain aspects and the role of ports and container terminals in the design of modern supply chains. The works of Robinson (2002), Panayides (2006) and Parola and Sciomachen (2005) are among the first who tackled the problem at a port level. The aim of these works is to identify the current trends in modern supply chains and find ways of integrating port operations at the best level possible. More focused on container terminals due to the increasing role of containerised cargo in global trade are the works of Fan, Wilson, and Tolliver

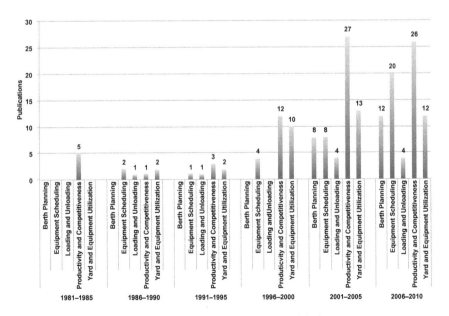

Figure 10.3: Key problems tackled
Source: Author.

Table 10.2: Journal publications.

Journal title	1981–1985	1986–1990	1991–1995	1996–2000	2001–2005	2006–2010	Total
Applied Economics					1		1
Computers and Industrial Engineering		1		5	2	6	14
Computers and Operations Research			1		1	1	3
Economic Geography	1						1
European Journal of Operational Research		2	1	1	6	2	12
IEEE Transactions on Intelligent Transportation Systems					1		1
IIE Transactions					1		1
International Journal of Decision Sciences, Risk and Management						1	1
International Journal of Logistics: Research and Applications						1	1
International Journal of Production Economics				2		3	5
International Transactions in Operational Research				1			1
Journal of Forecasting					1		1
Journal of Marine Science and Technology					1		1
Journal of Operational Research Society				1	2	1	4
Journal of Productivity Analysis					1		1
Journal of Transport Economics and Policy						1	1
Journal of Transport Geography				4	2	1	7
Logistics Information Management				1			1
Maritime Economics and Logistics				1	13	23	37
Maritime Policy and Management	4	1	3	7	7	3	25
OR Spectrum					8	10	18
Review of Network Economics						1	1
Systems Engineering – Theory & Practice						1	1

Table 10.2: (*Continued*)

Journal title	1981–1985	1986–1990	1991–1995	1996–2000	2001–2005	2006–2010	Total
Transport Reviews					1	1	2
Transportation						2	2
Transportation Planning and Technology					1		1
Transportation Research Part A				1	1	1	3
Transportation Research Part B		2	2	1	6	3	14
Transportation Research Part C						1	1
Transportation Research Part E					2	10	12
Transportation Science				1	2	1	4
Total	5	6	7	26	60	74	178

Source: Author.

(2009), Panayides and Song (2008), Van Der Horst and De Langen (2008), Notteboom and Rodrigue (2008) and Rodrigue and Notteboom (2009). In these works, the reader can find interesting aspects of containerised global supply chains with comparisons not only of different terminals but of trade routes and cargoes as well.

10.4.   Discussion and Conclusions

In this chapter, an effort to present the works focusing on port container terminals during the last 30 years has been made in order to create an as much as possible complete picture of the research that has taken place and identify future opportunities of research. From the journal papers found and incorporated here it is seen that the academic interest in this research area has boomed during the last decade with studies related to productivity and efficiency terminal issues attracting most of the attention. In reference to the tools used there is an increasing trend of mathematics and operations research methods with the use of algorithms assisting in the solution of equipment scheduling issues.

In terms of the journals publishing this type of works these are not restricted to maritime related ones even though these appear to dominate, with *Maritime Economics and Logistics* and *Maritime Policy and Management* standing out. There is significant dispersion of papers in journals like *OR Spectrum, Computers and Industrial Engineering, Transportation Research Part B, Transportation Research Part E*, the *European Journal of Operations Research, Transportation Science* and more (see Table 10.2 for details).

In reference to future research, two fields have been identified: container terminal security and container terminal supply chain integration. In the former case there are only a couple of works present recently focusing on how the new regulations imposed after the attacks of 9/11 will affect port and more specifically container terminal operations. In the latter case there are a few efforts present aiming at identifying the role of container terminals in modern supply chain strategies and how these can be further integrated. In both cases, there is significant scope for further research since globalisation demand effective and secure supply strategies.

References

Ambrosino, D., & Sciomachen, A. (2003). Impact of yard organisation on the master bay planning problem. *Maritime Economics and Logistics, 5,* 285–300.

Anderson, C., Opaluch, J., & Grigalunas, T. (2009). The demand for import services at US container ports. *Maritime Economics and Logistics, 11,* 156–185.

Anderson, C., Park, Y., Chang, Y., Yang, C., Lee, T., & Luo, M. (2008). A game-theoretic analysis of competition among container port hubs: The case of Busan and Shanghai 1. *Maritime Policy and Management, 35,* 5–26.

Angeloudis, P., & Bell, M. G. H. (2010). An uncertainty-aware AGV assignment algorithm for automated container terminals. *Transportation Research Part E, 46,* 354–366.

Baird, A. J. (2006). Optimising the container transhipment hub location in northern Europe. *Journal of Transport Geography, 14,* 195–214.

Ballis, A., Golias, J., & Abacoumkin, C. (1997). A comparison between conventional and advanced handling systems for low volume container maritime terminals. *Maritime Policy and Management, 24,* 73–92.

Bazzazi, M., Safaei, N., & Javadian, N. (2009). A genetic algorithm to solve the storage space allocation problem in a container terminal. *Computers and Industrial Engineering, 56,* 44–52.

Bichou, K. (2011). Assessing the impact of procedural security on container port efficiency. *Maritime Economics and Logistics, 13,* 1–28.

Bichou, K., & Bell, M. G. H. (2007). Internationalisation and consolidation of the container port industry: Assessment of channel structure and relationships. *Maritime Economics and Logistics, 9,* 35–51.

Bish, E. K. (2003). A multiple-crane-constrained scheduling problem in a container terminal. *European Journal of Operational Research, 144,* 83–107.

Briskorn, D., Drexl, A., & Hartmann, S. (2006). Inventory-based dispatching of automated guided vehicles on container terminals. *OR Spectrum, 28,* 611–630.

Cao, B., & Uebe, G. (1995). Solving transportation problems with nonlinear side constraints with Tabu search. *Computers and Operations Research, 22,* 593–603.

Cao, Z., Lee, D., & Meng, Q. (2008). Deployment strategies of double-rail-mounted gantry crane systems for loading outbound containers in container terminals. *International Journal of Production Economics, 115,* 221–228.

Castillo, B., & Daganzo, C. F. (1993). Handling strategies for import containers at marine terminals. *Transportation Research Part B, 27,* 151–166.

Chang, D., Jiang, Z., Yan, W., & He, J. (2010). Integrating berth allocation and quay crane assignments. *Transportation Research Part E, 46,* 975–990.

Chen, C. S., Lee, S. M., & Shen, Q. S. (1995). An analytical model for the container loading problem. *European Journal of Operational Research, 80,* 68–76.

Chen, G., & Yang, Z. (2010). Optimizing time windows for managing export container arrivals at Chinese container terminals. *Maritime Economics and Logistics, 12,* 111–126.

Chen, T. (1998). Land utilization in the container terminal: A global perspective. *Maritime Policy and Management, 25*, 289–303.

Chen, T. (1999). Yard Operations in the container terminal — A study in the "unproductive moves". *Maritime Policy and Management, 26*, 27–38.

Chen, T., Lin, K., & Juang, Y. C. (2000). Empirical studies on yard operations part 2: Quantifying unproductive moves undertaken in quay transfer operations. *Maritime Policy and Management, 27*, 191–207.

Cheng, J., Tahar, R., & Ang, C. (2010). Understanding the complexity of container terminal operation through the development of system dynamics model. *International Journal of Shipping and Transport Logistics, 2*, 429–443.

Choi, H. R., Kim, H. S., Park, B. J., Park, N. K., & Lee, S. W. (2003). An ERP approach for container terminal operating systems. *Maritime Policy and Management, 30*, 197–210.

Chu, C. Y., & Huang, W. C. (2005). Determining container terminal capacity on the basis of an adopted yard handling system. *Transport Reviews, 25*, 181–199.

Chung, R. K., Li, C-L., & Lin, W. (2002). Interblock crane deployment in container terminals. *Transportation Science, 36*, 79–93.

Chung, Y. G., Randhawa, S. U., & McDowell, E. D. (1988). A simulation analysis for transtainer-based container handling facility. *Computers Industrial Engineering, 14*, 113–125.

Cochrane, R. (2008). The effects of market differences on the throughput of large container terminals with similar levels of efficiency. *Maritime Economics and Logistics, 10*, 35–52.

Cullinane, K., & Song, D. W. (1998). Container terminals in South Korea: Problems and panaceas. *Maritime Policy and Management, 25*, 63–80.

Cullinane, K., & Song, D. W. (2001). The administrative and ownership structure of Asian container ports. *Maritime Economics and Logistics, 3*, 175–197.

Cullinane, K., & Song, D. W. (2003). A stochastic frontier model of the productive efficiency of Korean container terminals. *Applied Economics, 35*, 251–267.

Cullinane, K., Song, D. W., & Gray, R. (2002). A stochastic frontier model of the efficiency of major container terminals in Asia: Assessing the influence of administrative and ownership structures. *Transportation Research Part A, 36*, 743–762.

Cullinane, K., Song, D. W., Ji, P., & Wang, T. F. (2004). DEA windows analysis to container port production efficiency. *Review of Network Economics, 3*, 184–206.

Cullinane, K., Song, D. W., & Wang, T. (2005). The application of mathematical programming approaches to estimating container port production efficiency. *Journal of Productivity Analysis, 24*, 73–92.

Cullinane, K., & Wang, T. F. (2006). The efficiency of European container ports: a cross-sectional data envelopment analysis. *International Journal of Logistics: Research and Applications, 9*, 19–31.

Cullinane, K., Wang, T. F., Song, D. W., & Ping, J. (2006). The technical efficiency of container ports: Comparing data envelopment analysis and stochastic frontier analysis. *Transportation Research Part A, 40*, 354–374.

Daganzo, C. F. (1989). The crane scheduling problem. *Transportation Research Part B, 23*, 159–175.

De Souza, J., Geraldo, A., Beresford, A. K. C., & Pettit, S. J. (2003). Liner shipping companies and terminal operators: Internationalisation or globalisation? *Maritime Economics and Logistics, 5*, 393–412.

Dekker, R., Voogd, P., & Asperen, E. (2006). Advanced methods for container stacking. *OR Spectrum, 28*, 563–586.

Dirk, S., Stefan, V., & Robert, S. (2004). Container terminal operation and operations research — A classification and literature review. *OR Spectrum, 26*, 3–49.

Dowd, T. (1984). Container terminal leasing and pricing. *Maritime Policy and Management, 11*, 277–288.

Dowd, T., & Leschine, T. (1990). Container terminal productivity: A perspective. *Maritime Policy and Management, 17*, 107–112.

Dragovic, B., Park, N. K., Radmilovic, Z., & Marac, V. (2005). Simulation modelling of ship-berth link with priority service. *Maritime Economics and Logistics, 7*, 316–335.

Evers, J. J. M., & Koppers, S. A. J. (1996). Automated guided vehicle traffic control at a container terminal. *Transportation Research Part A, 30*, 21–34.

Fan, L., Wilson, W. W., & Tolliver, D. (2009). Logistical rivalries and port competition for container flows to US markets: Impacts of changes in Canada's logistics system and expansion of the Panama Canal. *Maritime Economics and Logistics, 11*, 327–357.

Fleming, D. (1997). World container port ranking. *Maritime Policy and Management, 24*, 175–181.

Fu, Z., Li, Y., Lim, A., & Rodrigues, B. (2007). Port space allocation with a time dimension. *Journal of the Operational Research Society, 58*, 797–807.

Fung, M. K. (2002). Forecasting Hong Kong's container throughput: an error-correction model. *Journal of Forecasting, 21*, 69–80.

Golias, M. M., Saharidis, G. K., Boile, M., Theofanis, S., & Ierapetritou, M. G. (2009). The berth allocation problem: Optimizing vessel arrival time. *Maritime Economics and Logistics, 11*, 358–377.

Goodchild, A., & Daganzo, C. (2007). Crane double cycling in container ports: Planning methods and evaluation. *Transportation Research Part B: Methodological, 41*, 875–891.

Goodchild, A. V., & Daganzo, C. F. (2006). Double cycling strategies for container ships and their effect on ship loading and unloading operations. *Transportation Science, 40*, 473–483.

Grunow, M., Gunther, H. O., & Lehmann, M. (2004). Dispatching multi-load AGVs in highly automated seaport container terminals. *OR Spectrum, 26*, 211–235.

Grunow, M., Gunther, H. O., & Lehmann, M. (2006). Strategies for dispatching AGVs at automated seaport container terminals. *OR Spectrum, 28*, 587–610.

Guan, C., & Liu, R. (2009). Container terminal gate appointment system optimization. *Maritime Economics and Logistics, 11*, 378–398.

Guan, Y., & Cheung, R. K. (2004). The berth allocation problem: Models and solution methods. *OR Spectrum, 26*, 75–92.

Guan, Y., & Yang, K. H. (2010). Analysis of berth allocation and inspection operations in a container terminal. *Maritime Economics and Logistics, 12*, 347–369.

Gunther, H. O., & Kim, K. H. (2006). Container terminals and terminal operations. *OR Spectrum, 28*, 437–445.

Ha, M. S. (2003). A comparison of service quality at major container ports: Implications for Korean ports. *Journal of Transport Geography, 11*, 131–137.

Hansen, P., Uz, C. O., & Mladenovic, N. (2008). Variable neighborhood search for minimum cost berth allocation. *European Journal of Operational Research, 191*, 636–649.

Haralambides, H., Cariou, P., & Bennachio, M. (2002). Costs, benefits and pricing of dedicated container terminals. *Maritime Economics and Logistics, 4*, 21–34.

Hartmann, S. (2004). A general framework for scheduling equipment and manpower at container terminals. *OR Spectrum, 26*, 51–74.

Hayuth, Y. (1981). Containerisation and the load centre concept. *Economic Geography, 57*, 160–176.

Hayuth, Y., & Fleming, D. K. (1994). Concepts of strategic commercial location: the case of container ports. *Maritime Policy and Management, 21*, 187–193.

He, J., Chang, D., Mi, W., & Yan, W. (2010). A hybrid parallel genetic algorithm for yard crane scheduling. *Transportation Research Part E, 46*, 136–155.

Heaver, T., Meersman, H., & Van de Voorde, E. (2001). Co-operation and competition in international container seaport: Strategies for ports. *Maritime Policy and Management, 28*, 293–305.

Holguin-Veras, J., & Jara-Diaz, S. (1999). Optimal pricing for priority service and space allocation in container ports. *Transportation Research Part B, 33*, 81–106.

Imai, A., Chen, H. C., Nishimura, E., & Papadimitriou, S. (2007a). The simultaneous berth and quay crane allocation problem. *Transportation Research Part E, 44*, 900–920.

Imai, A., Nishimura, E., & Papadimitriou, S. (2003). Berth allocation with service priority. *Transportation Research Part B, 37*, 437–457.

Imai, A., Nishimura, E., & Papadimitriou, S. (2008). Berthing ships at a multi-user container terminal with a limited quay capacity. *Transportation Research Part E, 44*, 136–151.

Imai, A., Nishimura, E., Papadimitriou, S., & Sasaki, K. (2002). The containership loading problem. *Maritime Economics and Logistics, 4*, 126–148.

Imai, A., Sun, X., Nishimura, E., & Papadimitriou, S. (2005). Berth allocation in a container port: Using a continuous location space approach. *Transportation Research Part B, 39*, 199–221.

Imai, A., Zhang, J., Nishimura, E., & Papadimitriou, S. (2007b). The berth allocation problem with service time and delay time objectives. *Maritime Economics and Logistics, 9*, 269–290.

Jula, H., Chassiakos, A., & Ioannou, P. (2006). Port dynamic empty container reuse. *Transportation Research Part E, 42*, 43–60.

Kang, S., Medina, J., & Ouyang, Y. (2008). Optimal operations of transportation fleet for unloading activities at container ports. *Transportation Research Part B: Methodological, 42*, 970–984.

Kia, M., Shayan, E., & Ghotb, F. (2002). Investigation of port capacity under a new approach by computer simulation. *Computers and Industrial Engineering, 42*, 533–540.

Kim, K. H. (1997). Evaluation of the number of rehandles in container yards. *Computers and Industrial Engineering, 32*, 701–711.

Kim, K. H., & Bae, J. W. (1998). Re-marshaling export containers in port container terminals. *Computers and Industrial Engineering, 35*, 655–658.

Kim, K. H., Jeon, S. M., & Ryu, K. R. (2006). Deadlock prevention for automated guided vehicles in automated container terminals. *OR Spectrum, 28*, 659–679.

Kim, K. H., Kang, J. S., & Ryu, K. R. (2004). A beam search algorithm for the load sequencing of outbound containers in port container terminals. *OR Spectrum, 26*, 93–116.

Kim, K. H., & Kim, H. B. (1998). The optimal determination of the space requirement and the number of transfer cranes for import containers. *Computers and Industrial Engineering, 35*, 427–430.

Kim, K. H., & Kim, H. B. (1999b). Segregating space allocation models for container inventories in port container terminals. *International Journal of Production Economics, 59*, 415–423.

Kim, K. H., & Kim, H. B. (2002). The optimal sizing of the storage space and handling facilities for import containers. *Transportation Research Part B, 36*, 821–835.

Kim, K. H., & Kim, K. Y. (1999a). Routing straddle carriers for the loading operation of containers using a beam search algorithm. *Computers and Industrial Engineering, 36*, 109–136.

Kim, K. H., & Kim, K. Y. (2007). Optimal price schedules for storage of inbound containers. *Transportation Research Part B, 41*, 892–905.

Kim, K. H., & Moon, K. C. (2003). Berth scheduling by simulated annealing. *Transportation Research Part B, 37*, 541–560.

Kim, K. H., & Park, K. T. (2003). A note on a dynamic space-allocation method for outbound containers. *European Journal of Operational Research, 148*, 92–101.

Kim, K. H., Park, Y. M., & Ryu, K. R. (2000). Deriving decision rules to locate export containers in container yards. *European Journal of Operational Research, 124*, 89–101.

Kim, K. Y., & Kim, K. H. (1997). A routing algorithm for a single transfer crane to load export containers onto a containership. *Computers and Industrial Engineering, 33*, 673–676.

Kim, K. Y., & Kim, K. H. (1999c). An optimal routing algorithm for a transfer crane in port container terminals. *Transportation Science, 33*, 17–33.

Koh, Y. K. (2001). Optimal investment priority in container port development. *Maritime Policy and Management, 28*, 109–123.

Koi Yu, A. N. (2006). Assessing the attractiveness of ports in the North European container transhipment market: An agenda for future research in port competition. *Maritime Economics and Logistics, 8*, 234–250.

Koo, P. H., Lee, W. S., & Jang, D. W. (2004). Fleet sizing and vehicle routing for container transportation in a static environment. *OR Spectrum, 26*, 193–209.

Kozan, E. (1997). Increasing the operational efficiency of container terminals in Australia. *Journal of Operational Research Society, 48*, 151–161.

Kozan, E., & Preston, P. (1999). Genetic algorithms to schedule container transfers at multimodal terminals. *International Transactions in Operational Research, 6*, 311–329.

Kozan, E., & Preston, P. (2006). Mathematical modelling of container transfers and storage locations at seaport terminals. *OR Spectrum, 28*, 519–537.

Lagoudis, I., & Platis, A. (2009). Using birth-and-death theory for container terminal strategic investment decisions. *International Journal of Decision Sciences, Risk and Management, 1*, 81–103.

Lagoudis, I. N., & Rice, J. B. (2010, June 22–24). Revisiting port capacity: A practical method for investment and policy decisions, ECONSHIP 2011, Chios, Greece.

Laik, N., & Hadjiconstantnou, E. (2008). Container assignment and yard crane deployment in a container terminal: A case study. *Maritime Economics and Logistics, 10*, 90–107.

Lam, J., & Yap, W. (2008). Competition for transhipment containers by major ports in Southeast Asia: Slot capacity analysis. *Maritime Policy and Management, 35*, 89–101.

Lam, J. S. L., & Yap, W. Y. (2006). A measurement and comparison of cost competitiveness of container ports in Southeast Asia. *Transportation, 33*, 641–654.

Lau, H., & Zhao, Y. (2008). Integrated scheduling of handling equipment at automated container terminals. *International Journal of Production Economics, 112*, 665–682.

Lee, D. H., Cao, Z., & Meng, Q. (2007). Scheduling of two-transtainer systems for loading outbound containers in port container terminals with simulated annealing algorithm. *International Journal of Production Economics, 107*, 115–124.

Lee, D. H., Wang, H. Q., & Miao, L. (2008). Quay crane scheduling with non-interference constraints in port container terminals. *Transportation Research Part E, 44*, 124–135.

Lee, L. H., Chew, E. P., & Lee, L. S. (2006b). Multicommodity network flow model for Asia's container ports. *Maritime Policy and Management, 33*, 387–402.

Lee, L. H., Chew, E. P., Tan, K. C., & Han, Y. (2006a). An optimization model for storage yard management in transshipment hubs. *OR Spectrum, 28*, 539–561.

Lee, T. W., Park, N. K., & Lee, D. W. (2003). A simulation study for the logistics planning of a container terminal in view of SCM. *Maritime Policy and Management, 30*, 243–254.

Legato, P., Canonaco, P., & Mazza, R. (2009). Yard crane management by simulation and optimisation. *Maritime Economics and Logistics, 11*, 36–57.

Legato, P., & Mazza, R. M. (2001). Berth planning and resources optimization at a container terminal via discrete event simulation. *European Journal of Operational Research, 133*, 537–547.

Legato, P., & Monaco, M. (2004). Human resources management at a marine container terminal. *European Journal of Operational Research, 156*, 769–781.

Lehmann, M., Grunow, M., & Gunther, H. S. (2006). Deadlock handling for real-time control of AGVs at automated container terminals. *OR Spectrum, 28*, 631–657.

Li, C. L., & Vairaktarakis, G. L. (2004). Loading and unloading operations in container terminals. *IIE Transactions, 36*, 287–297.

Liang, C., Huang, Y., & Yang, Y. (2009). A quay crane dynamic scheduling problem by hybrid evolutionary algorithm for berth allocation planning. *Computers and Industrial Engineering, 56*, 1021–1028.

Lin, L., & Tseng, C. (2007). Operational performance evaluation of major container ports in the Asia-Pacific region. *Maritime Policy and Management, 34*, 535–551.

Linn, R. J., Liu, J. Y., Wan, Y. W., Zhang, C., & Murty, K. G. (2003). Rubber tired gantry crane deployment for container yard operation. *Computers and Industrial Engineering, 45*, 429–442.

Liu, C., Jula, H., Vukadinovic, K., & Ioannou, P. (2004). Automated guided vehicle system for two container yard layouts. *Transportation Research Part C: Emerging Technologies, 12*, 349–368.

Liu, C. I., Jula, H., & Ioannou, P. A. (2002). Design, simulation, and evaluation of automated container terminals. *IEEE Transactions on Intelligent Transportation Systems, 3*, 12–26.

Luo, M., & Grigalunas, T. A. (2003). A spatial-economic multimodal transportation simulation model for US coastal container ports. *Maritime Economics and Logistics, 5*, 158–178.

Martin, J., & Thomas, B. J. (2001). The container terminal community. *Maritime Policy and Management, 28*, 279–292.

Mattfeld, D. C., & Orth, H. (2006). The allocation of storage space for transshipment in vehicle distribution. *OR Spectrum, 28*, 681–703.

McCalla, R. J. (1994). Canadian container ports: How have they fared? How will they do? *Maritime Policy and Management, 21*, 207–217.

McCalla, R. J. (1999). Global change, local pain: Intermodal seaport terminals and their service areas. *Journal of Transport Geography, 7*, 247–254.

Meisel, F., & Bierwirth, C. (2009). Heuristics for the integration of crane productivity in the berth allocation problem. *Transportation Research Part E, 45*, 196–209.

Mennis, E., Platis, A., Lagoudis, I., & Nikitakos, N. (2008). Improving port container terminal efficiency with the use of Markov theory. *Maritime Economics and Logistics, 10*, 243–257.

Monaco, M., Moccia, L., & Sammarra, M. (2009). Operations research for the management of a transhipment container terminal: The Gioia Tauro case. *Maritime Economics and Logistics, 11*, 7–35.

Moorthy, R., & Teo, C. P. (2006). Berth management in container terminal: The template design problem. *OR Spectrum, 28*, 495–518.

Narasimhan, A., & Palekar, U. S. (2002). Analysis and algorithms for the transfer routing problem in container port operations. *Transportation Science, 36*, 63–78.

Ng, A. (2006). Assessing the attractiveness of ports in the North European container transhipment market: An agenda for future research in port competition. *Maritime Economics and Logistics, 8*(3), 234–250.

Ng, W. (2005). Crane scheduling in container yards with inter-crane interference. *European Journal of Operational Research, 164*, 64–78.

Nguyen, V. D., & Kim, K. H. (2009). A dispatching method for automated lifting vehicles in automated port container terminals. *Computers and Industrial Engineering, 56*, 1002–1020.

Nishimura, E., Imai, A., & Papadimitriou, S. (2005). Yard trailer routing at a maritime container terminal. *Transportation Research Part E, 41*, 53–76.

Notteboom, E. (1997). Concentration and load centre development in the European container port system. *Journal of Transport Geography, 5*, 99–115.

Notteboom, T., Coeck, C., & Van den Broeck, J. (2000). Measuring and explaining the relative efficiency of container terminals by means of Bayesian stochastic frontier models. *Maritime Economics and Logistics, 2*, 83–106.

Notteboom, T., & Rodrigue, J. (2008). Containerisation, box logistics and global supply chains: The integration of ports and liner shipping networks. *Maritime Economics and Logistics, 10*, 152–174.

Notteboom, T. E. (2002). Consolidation and contestability in the European container handling industry. *Maritime Policy and Management, 29*, 257–269.

Nuefville, R., & Tsunokawa, K. (1981). Productivity and returns to scale of container ports. *Maritime Policy and Management, 8*, 121–129.

Olivier, D. (2005). Private entry and emerging partnerships in container terminal operations: Evidence from Asia. *Maritime Economics and Logistics, 7*, 87–115.

Olivier, D., Parola, F., Slack, B., & Wang, J. J. (2007). The time scale of internationalization: The case of the container port industry. *Maritime Economics and Logistics, 9*(1), 1–34.

Ottjes, J. A., Veeke, H. P. M., Duinkerken, M. B., Rijsenbrij, J. C., & Lodewijks, G. (2006). Simulation of a multiterminal system for container handling. *OR Spectrum, 28*, 447–468.

Panayides, P. (2006). Maritime logistics and global supply chains: Towards a research agenda. *Maritime Economics and Logistics, 8*, 3–18.

Panayides, P. M., & Song, D. W. (2008). Evaluating the integration of seaport container terminals in supply chains. *International Journal of Physical Distribution and Logistics Management, 38*, 562–584.

Park, K. T., & Kim, K. H. (2002). Berth scheduling for container terminals by using a sub-gradient optimization technique. *Journal of the Operational Research Society, 53*, 1054–1062.

Park, Y. M., & Kim, K. H. (2003). A scheduling method for berth and quay cranes. *OR Spectrum, 25*, 1–23.

Parola, F., & Sciomachen, A. (2005). Intermodal container flows in a port system network: Analysis of possible growths via simulation models. *International Journal of Production Economics, 97*, 75–88.

Petering, M. E. H. (2009). Effect of block width and storage yard layout on marine container terminal performance. *Transportation Research Part E, 45*, 591–610.

Petering, M. E. H. (2011). Decision support for yard capacity, fleet composition, truck substitutability, and scalability issues at seaport container terminals. *Transportation Research Part E, 47*, 85–103.

Petering, M. E. H., & Murty, K. G. (2009). Effect of block length and yard crane deployment systems on overall performance at a seaport container transshipment terminal. *Computers and Operations Research, 36*, 1711–1725.

Petering, M. E. H., Wu, Y., Li, W., Goh, M., & de Souza, R. (2009). Development and simulation analysis of real-time yard crane control systems for seaport container transshipment terminals. *OR Spectrum, 31,* 801–835.

Peterkofsky, R. I., & Daganzo, C. F. (1990). A branch and bound solution method for the crane scheduling problem. *Transportation Research Part B, 24,* 159–172.

Peters, H. J. F. (2001). Developments in global seatrade and container shipping markets: Their effects on the port industry and private sector involvement. *Maritime Economics and Logistics, 3,* 3–26.

Preston, P., & Kozan, E. (2001a). A Tabu search technique applied to scheduling container transfers. *Transportation Planning and Technology, 24,* 135–154.

Preston, P., & Kozan, E. (2001b). An approach to determine storage locations of containers at seaport terminals. *Computers and Operations Research, 28,* 983–995.

Ramos-Real, F., & Tovar, B. (2010). Productivity change and economies of scale in container port terminals A cost function approach. *Journal of Transport Economics and Policy, 44,* 231–246.

Rios, L. R., Maçada, A., & Gastaud, C. (2006). Analysing the relative efficiency of container terminals of mercosur using DEA. *Maritime Economics and Logistics, 8,* 331–346.

Robinson, R. (1985). Productivity of first-generation container terminals: Sydney, Australia. *Maritime Policy and Management, 12,* 279–292.

Robinson, R. (2002). Ports as elements in value-driven chain systems: The new paradigm. *Maritime Policy and Management, 29,* 241–255.

Rodrigue, J., & Notteboom, T. (2009). The terminalization of supply chains: Reassessing the role of terminals in port/hinterland logistical relationships. *Maritime Policy and Management, 36,* 165–183.

Shabayek, A. A., & Yeung, W. W. (2002). A simulation model for the Kwai Chung container terminals in Hong Kong. *European Journal of Operational Research, 140,* 1–11.

Slack, B. (1985). Containerization, inter-port competition, and port selection. *Maritime Policy and Management, 12,* 293–303.

Song, D. W. (2002). Regional container port competition and co-operation: The case of Hong Kong and South China. *Journal of Transport Geography, 10,* 99–110.

Song, D. W., & Yeo, K. T. (2004). A competitive analysis of Chinese container ports using the analytic hierarchy process. *Maritime Economics and Logistics, 6,* 34–52.

Starr, J. T. (1994). The mid-Atlantic load centre: Baltimore or Hampton roads? *Maritime Policy and Management, 21,* 219–227.

Steenken, D., Voß, S., & Stahlbock, R. (2004). Container terminal operation and operations research — A classification and literature review. *OR Spectrum, 26,* 3–49.

Tahar, M. R., & Hussain, K. (2000). Simulation and analysis for the Kelang container terminal operations. *Logistics Information Management, 13,* 14–20.

Taleb-Ibrahimi, M., Castilho, B., & Daganzo, C. F. (1993). Storage space vs. handling work in container terminals. *Transportation Research Part B, 27,* 13–32.

Tavakkoli-Moghaddam, R., Makui, A., Salahi, S., Bazzazi, M., & Taheri, F. (2009). An efficient algorithm for solving a new mathematical model for a quay crane scheduling problem in container ports. *Computers and Industrial Engineering, 56,* 241–248.

Teng, J., Huang, W., & Hunag, M. (2004). Multicritera evaluation for port competitiveness of eight East Asian container ports. *Journal of Marine Science and Technology, 12,* 256–264.

Ting, S. C., Wang, J. S., Kao, S. L., & Pitty, F. M. (2010). Categorized stacking models for import containers in port container terminals. *Maritime Economics and Logistics, 12,* 162–177.

Turner, H., Windle, R., & Dresner, M. (2004). North American container port productivity: 1984–1997. *Transportation Research Part E, 40*, 339–356.

UNCTAD. (2001–2010). *Review of maritime transport*. United Nations Conference on Trade and Development. Geneva. Retrieved from http://www.unctad.org/Templates/Page.asp?intItemID=2618&lang=1

Van Der Horst, M., & De Langen, P. (2008). Coordination in hinterland transport chains: A major challenge for the seaport community. *Maritime Economics and Logistics, 10*, 108–129.

Van Hee, K., Huitink, B., & Leegwater, D. (1988). PORTPLAN, decision support system for port terminals. *European Journal of Operational Research, 34*, 249–261.

Van Hee, K. M., & Wijbrands, R. J. (1988). Decision support system for container terminal planning. *European Journal of Operational Research, 34*, 262–272.

Veldman, S. J., & Buckmann, E. H. (2003). A model on container port competition: An application for the West European container hub-ports. *Maritime Economics and Logistics, 5*, 3–22.

Veldman, S. J., Buckmann, E. H., & Saitua, R. N. (2005). River depth and container port market shares: The impact of deepening the Scheldt river on the West European container hub-port market shares. *Maritime Economics and Logistics, 7*, 336–355.

Vis, I. F. A., & de Koster, R. (2003). Trans-shipment of containers at a container terminal: An overview. *European Journal of Operational Research, 147*, 1–16.

Vis, I. F. A., & Harika, I. (2004). Comparison of vehicle types at an automated container terminal. *OR Spectrum, 26*, 117–143.

Vis, I. F. A., Koster, R., De Roodbergen, K. J., & Peeters, L. W. P. (2001). Determination of the number of automated guided vehicles required at a semi-automated container terminal. *Journal of the Operational Research Society, 52*, 409–417.

Wang, J. J. (1998). A container load center with a developing hinterland: A case study of Hong Kong. *Journal of Transport Geography, 6*, 187–201.

Wang, J. J., & Slack, B. (2000). The evolution of a regional container port system: The Pearl River Delta. *Journal of Transport Geography, 8*, 263–275.

Wang, T. F., & Cullinane, K. (2006). The efficiency of European container terminals and implications for supply chain management. *Maritime Economics and Logistics, 8*, 82–99.

Wiegmans, B. W., Hoest, A. V. D., & Notteboom, T. E. (2008). Port and terminal selection by deep-sea container operators. *Maritime Policy and Management, 35*, 517–534.

Wiegmans, B. W., Konings, R., & Priemus, H. (2009). Critical mass for the development of a new container port in Vlissingen. *Maritime Economics and Logistics, 11*, 399–417.

Wiegmans, B. W., Ubbels, B., Rietveld, P., & Nijkamp, P. (2002). Investments in container terminals: Public private partnerships in Europe. *Maritime Economics and Logistics, 4*, 1–20.

Wu, Y. C. J., & Goh, M. (2010). Container port efficiency in emerging and more advanced markets. *Transportation Research Part E, 46*, 1030–1042.

Yang, C. H., Choi, Y. S., & Ha, T. Y. (2004). Simulation-based performance evaluation of transport vehicles at automated container terminals. *OR Spectrum, 26*, 149–170.

Yap, W., Lam, J., & Notteboom, T. (2006). Developments in container port competition in East Asia. *Transport Reviews, 26*, 167–188.

Yap, W. Y., & Lam, J. S. L. (2004). An interpretation of inter-container port relationships from the demand perspective. *Maritime Policy and Management, 31*, 337–355.

Yeo, G. T., & Song, D. W. (2006). An application of the hierarchical fuzzy process to container port competition: Policy and strategic implications. *Transportation, 33*, 409–422.

Yi, D. W., Kim, S. H., Choi, R., Park, N. K., & Lee, T. W. (2000). Developing a conceptual model for sharing container terminal resources: A case study of the Gamman container terminal. *Maritime Policy and Management, 27,* 155–167.

Yun, W. Y., & Choi, Y. S. (1999). A simulation model for container-terminal operation analysis using an object-oriented approach. *International Journal of Production Economics, 59,* 221–230.

Zan, Y. (1999). Analysis of container port policy by the reaction of an equilibrium shipping market. *Maritime Policy and Management, 26,* 369–381.

Zeng, Z., & Yang, Z. (2002). Dynamic programming of port position and scale in the hierarchized container ports network. *Maritime Policy and Management, 29,* 163–177.

Zhang, C., Liu, J., Wan, Y., & Linn, R. J. (2002). Dynamic crane deployment in container storage yards. *Transportation Research Part B, 36,* 537–555.

Zhang, C., Liu, J., Wan, Y., Murty, K. G., & Linn, R. J. (2003). Storage space allocation in container terminals. *Transportation Research Part B, 37,* 883–903.

Zhang, H., & Kim, K. H. (2009). Maximizing the number of dual-cycle operations of quay cranes in container terminals. *Computers and Industrial Engineering, 56,* 979–992.

Zhou, P. F., & Kang, H. G. (2008). Study on Berth and Quay-crane allocation under stochastic environments in container terminal. *Systems Engineering-Theory and Practice, 28,* 161–169.

PART II
GREEN AND SUSTAINABILITY ISSUES

Chapter 11

Corporate Social Responsibility in Maritime Logistics

Thomas Pawlik, Philine Gaffron and Patric A. Drewes

Abstract

This chapter discusses the concept of corporate social responsibility (CSR) within the context of the container liner shipping industry. It looks at the current practice of CSR in this industry and outlines the framework, the reasons and the drivers for companies to adopt and implement a CSR strategy. These include, among others, the increasing commitment to fostering CSR in the private sector at EU level, the changing expectations of customers — that is shippers — with regard to social and environmental standards of their contractors and suppliers, and the improving situation with regards to guidance and tools for adopting CSR and identifying and implementing the relevant measures (e.g. ISO 26000 and the European Commission's communication on CSR). The authors take the position that in an industry, which is as strongly consolidated as container liner shipping, the adoption and implementation of effective CSR strategies by a few companies at the top can have a profound impact on the industry as a whole. The Japanese NYK Group's CSR strategy is discussed in more detail to illustrate one of the best — if by no means perfect — examples in the current market. The chapter closes with a sector-specific definition of CSR for the container shipping industry.

Keywords: corporate social responsibility; container liner shipping; sustainability issues; NYK case study

11.1. Introduction

Although the concept of corporate social responsibility (CSR) can — and should — be applied to a wider range of maritime logistics sectors, we focus in this chapter on

Maritime Logistics: Contemporary Issues
Copyright © 2012 by Emerald Group Publishing Limited
All rights of reproduction in any form reserved
ISBN: 978-1-78052-340-8

container liner shipping. This is based on the leading idea that CSR is especially important in industries with a direct contact to consumers (B2C). Even though container liner shipping is a B2B industry, carriers are increasingly required by global brands as the users of liner services to get involved in the field of CSR. CSR activities within the liner shipping sector could, however, also be adapted to other maritime logistics sectors.

There is no single, universally accepted definition of the concept of CSR. Nevertheless, the idea that private businesses should aim for more than profit maximization has existed for almost as long as the idea of there being a private sector of commercial activities, which can produce profits for those involved. The question of whether CSR in general can be clearly defined and what might be a specific definition of CSR for maritime logistics in particular is discussed in Sections 11.3 and 11.5 of this chapter. As an entry point to the subject, we will use the European Commission's definition of 2006: 'Corporate social responsibility (CSR) is a concept whereby companies integrate social and environmental concerns in their business operations and in their interaction with their stakeholders on a voluntary basis' (Commission of the European Communities, 2006, p. 2).

Section 11.2 of this chapter provides a critique of current practice in the business, and highlights the importance of container liners in maritime logistics as well as the main sustainability issues, which speak in favour of considering CSR issues in this business. Section 11.3 looks at how the concept of CSR has developed and at the current state of the debate of this issue. In Section 11.4, we document the CSR strategy of the Nippon Yusen Kabushiki Kaisha (NYK) line as a case study and provide a CSR definition targeted towards container liner shipping as well as concluding remarks in Section 11.5.

11.2. Necessity for CSR in Maritime Logistics

11.2.1. CSR in Practice: Samples from Top Container Shipping Lines

Considering the voluntary aspect of CSR, it is interesting to look at the extent to which top companies in the maritime logistics sector have embraced the concept in their activities. The following will present a snapshot of instances of CSR in the main public communication tools of the world's top five container shipping lines. In May 2011, these were APM-Maersk, Mediterranean Shipping Company (MSC), CMA CGM Group, Evergreen Line and Hapag-Lloyd in descending order.[1]

Maersk devotes one section of its home page to *sustainability*,[2] which in turn contains a link to a page on social responsibility[3] that covers the topics of *global*

---

1. Retrieved from http://www.alphaliner.com/top100/index.php. Accessed on 9 May 2011.
2. Retrieved from http://www.maersk.com/SUSTAINABILITY/Pages/Welcome.aspx Accessed on 16 May 2011.
3. Retrieved from http://www.maersk.com/Sustainability/SocialResponsibility/Pages/SocialResponsibility .aspx. Accessed on 16 May 2011.

labour principles, diversity, disaster response programme and *community.* A separate page deals with *climate and environment.*[4] In its Sustainability Report 2010 (A.P. Moller-Maersk, 2011), the company sets the target of completing training on the so-called Maersk Global Labour Principles for 400 general and human resource managers in 2011 (*ibid.*, p. 30). There is a further 2011 target for the involvement of women in Maersk headquarters, which are situated in Denmark: 18% of general managers, 10% of directors and 6% of vice presidents (compared to 18%, 8% and 4% respectively; *ibid.*, p. 33). Maersk further participates in the United Nations Global Compact LEAD programme, which is designed to challenge companies to implement a Blueprint for Corporate Sustainability Leadership (United Nations, 2010) that builds on and extends the 10 UN Global Compact principles in the areas of human rights, labour, environment and anti-corruption.[5]

The Maersk Sustainability Report 2010 (A.P. Moller-Maersk, 2011) contains no environmental targets for 2011, but the company reports a target of a 10% reduction of green house gas (GHG) emissions by the year 2012 as compared to the 2007 baseline. This had already been exceeded by 3% at the end of 2010 (*ibid.*, p. 11). Much of this reduction is attributed to the adoption of slow steaming, which according to the report 'began as a cost-saving initiative in 2008 but is now a core operating principle of Maersk Line, in spite of the market turn-around in 2010' (*ibid.*, p. 53).

The MSC provides no information relating to sustainability or CSR on its website.[6] Also, no company reports for 2010 could be found online or in libraries that might have contained such information.

The CMA CGM Group includes a section entitled *environment* on its website[7] where it provides information on its *air quality objective.* Associated measures include electronic fuel injection systems and connectors for cold-ironing on new ships from 2009 and the use of bunker fuel with a lower sulphur content than is internationally stipulated (2.7% as opposed to 4.5%). The company also reports on its *sea objective* (relating to the protection of the marine environment through, for example, using non-tributylin anti-fouling) and on further solutions associated with the group's containers (such as the use of bamboo flooring in almost 10% of its containers in 2009[8]). While these sections report on measures to reduce emissions or waste for example, they generally do so without any quantification or the setting of specific targets for activities in these areas. Again, no reports on or references to CSR activities were found.

---

4. Retrieved from http://www.maersk.com/Sustainability/ClimateEnvironment/Pages/ClimateEnvironmen t.aspx. Accessed on 16 May 2011.
5. Retrieved from http://www.unglobalcompact.org/AboutTheGC/TheTenPrinciples/index.html. Accessed on 18 May 2011.
6. http://www.mscgva.ch/index.html. Accessed on 16 May 2011.
7. http://www.cma-cgm.com/AboutUs/Default.aspx. Accessed on 16 May 2011.
8. http://www.cma-cgm.com/Environment/Solution/Ecocontainers.aspx. Accessed on 16 May 2011.

The website of the Evergreen Line contains the link *Environmental Guardians*. The associated pages open with a quote from the Evergreen Group Chairman: 'We will not wait for legislation to be introduced. We will use the latest technology as soon as it is available so as to minimize the impact of container shipping operations both on marine life, on port communities and on humanity worldwide'.[9] The pages contain information on an array of environmental measures such as the environmental features of Evergreen ships (including bilge water separators and recycle bins), measures to reduce engine emissions and measures associated with *ship recycling*. Much of this information is qualitative rather than quantitative and not associated with concrete targets. No direct references to labour issues or CSR were found.

The Hapag-Lloyd A.G.'s Annual Report 2010 (2011) refers to an Ethics Guideline, which was issued in the year 2010 with the basic objective 'to encourage employees to treat one another fairly, respectfully and in accordance with prevailing laws' and is also applicable to relations outside the Hapag-Lloyd Group (*ibid.*, p. 55). The company has been certified according to ISO 14001 since 2003. The company reports a 12% reduction of carbon dioxide (CO_2) emissions between 2006 and 2009 per TEU km (*ibid.*, p. 57), but no future targets are mentioned. Slow steaming as well as retroactive reduction of the engine outputs of 21 vessels of the Hapag-Lloyd fleet (so-called derating) are listed as contributors to this reduction among other measures (*ibid.*, pp. 57–58). The company's website contains a section on sustainability,[10] which gives information on measures relating to *vessel technology* (e.g. silicone-based hull coatings and electronic fuel injection); measures *on board* (e.g. measures relating to ship recycling and a 'no garbage over board' policy); use of more 'quickly renewable woods' (*sic.*),[11] as container flooring; *shore-based contributions* such as stowage planning to optimize trim and thus fuel consumption and a yield management system to avoid empty container moves. The sustainability section also lists the voluntary emission reduction schemes that the company participates in in various international ports and provides information on environmental awards and certificates. The section on *Philosophy* contains a reference to the company's commitment to its CSR, but no formalised measures, programmes or targets are linked to this concept.[12]

As stated earlier, this overview is a snapshot and not a comprehensive review of CSR-related activities of the companies listed (see Drewes, 2011 for a more comprehensive treatment of this issue). However, it does show that at the time of writing, the world's top five container shipping lines firstly place very different emphasis on implementing and communicating CSR-related measures. Secondly, the main focus lies on environmental issues such as engine emissions or marine pollution. Emission issues are often directly related to fuel consumption and, in times of rising energy costs, thus also to a company's economic efficiency. They are also often

---

9. http://www.evergreen-line.com/tbi1/jsp/TBI1_Index.jsp (16.5.2011).
10. http://www.hapag-lloyd.de/en/about_us/environment_overview.html (18.5.2011).
11. http://www.hapag-lloyd.de/en/about_us/environment_container.html (18.5.2011).
12. http://www.hapag-lloyd.com/en/about_us/philosophy.html (18.5.2011).

covered by international rules and regulations (e.g. the *International Convention on the Control of Harmful Anti-fouling Systems on Ships* (AFS), in force since 17 September 2008). Social issues, which are also an important aspect of CSR (cp. Commission of the European Communities, 2006), receive much less coverage. Thirdly, the majority of CSR-related activities are reported *ex post* and are not related to any future targets.

11.2.2. The Role of Container Liner Shipping within Maritime Logistics and Shippers' Expectations

Since the maturing of the container shipping industry in the 1980s, its share within the whole system of maritime transport has constantly grown (see Figure 11.1). Compared to other shipping markets, containerized liner shipping services are in many cases more closely linked to and thus a critical part of their customers' supply chains. Major customer groups are, among others, large logistics service providers, global retailers and companies embedding liner services in their globally spread production networks.

From a generic operations management point of view, ocean carriers strive for the following basic performance objectives: quality, speed, dependability, flexibility and cost (Slack & Chambers, 2007). In the context of liner shipping these generic objectives are reflected *inter alia* by the criteria of maritime awards. They are generally awarded by maritime media to highlight above average achievements in

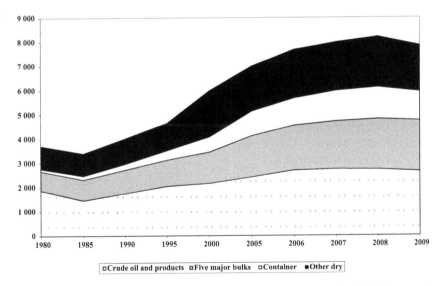

Figure 11.1: Development of volume (millions of tons loaded) in international seaborne trade, selected years from 1980 to 2009
Source: UNCTAD secretariat (2010).

respect to performance objectives which the market considers to be of relevance and can thus be used as a proxy for generally accepted shippers' requirements. The Container Shipping Line Award, for example, is part of the Asian Freight & Supply Chain Awards. It embraces the categories 'maintenance of schedule integrity, effective and easy to use IT systems backed by efficient and professional customer service systems, comprehensive ports of call on the specific trade and a competitive freight rate for level of service delivered'[13] (*Cargonews Asia*, 2011).

The relative importance of specific shippers' requirements might change subject to market conditions (Brooks & Trifts, 2008). High volume shippers usually launch global tenders for selecting their carriers. Such tenders can take several rounds with the first round focussing on freight rates and services, followed by more refined processes in the second round (Beddow, 2011). In regard to quality and environmental management, a growing number of shippers expect their supply chain partners to be audited in accordance with the ISO 9001 and ISO 14000 regulations (Celik, 2009). Companies without such systems might not even be taken into closer consideration in the carrier selection process. A comparable development can be expected in the near future in the wider field of CSR: 'Many users of shipping services want to ensure their goods are being shipped in a "socially responsible" way and shipping companies increasingly will need to demonstrate they are doing so' (Matthews, 2010, p. 4).

During the last years, the liner shipping industry has undergone a number of structural changes, including various mergers and takeovers. In spring 2011, the Top 10 carriers already had a total market share in terms of operated TEU capacity of more than 60% (see Table 11.1).

Table 11.1: TOP 10 carriers (market share and total operated TEU capacity) as per 9. May 2011.

Rank	Operator	Market share (%)	TEU
1	APM-Maersk	15.4	2,284,967
2	Mediterranean Shg Co	13.4	1,981,188
3	CMA CGM Group	8.5	1,261,443
4	Evergreen Line	4.1	612,911
5	Hapag-Lloyd	4.0	590,780
6	COSCO Container L.	4.0	589,762
7	APL	4.0	587,983
8	CSAV Group	3.8	559,722
9	Hanjin Shipping	3.6	527,269
10	CSCL	3.3	486,897
	Total	64.1%	8,951,220

Source: Alphaliner (http://www.alphaliner.com/top100/index.php (09.05.2011)).

---

13. http://www.cargonewsasia.com/afsca/index.html (17.5.2011).

Due to this particular market structure, CSR activities of the TOP carriers might easily influence the whole industry and can be emulated by smaller shipping companies as well (Sweeney & Coughlan, 2008).

11.2.3. Sustainability Issues within Container Shipping

The construction, operation (at sea and in ports) and retirement of a container ship are all associated with questions of sustainability from both the environmental and the social perspective. Most frequently considered are the engine emissions created during operation. In 2000, they amounted to about 2.7% of all anthropogenic CO_2 emissions. This value represents a best available estimate based on different methods of calculation (Eyring et al., 2010) and is not high in relative terms — though it does equal about 780 Megatons per year with an upward tendency (*ibid.*). Since about 70% of ships' emissions occur within 400 km of coastlines, other pollutants such as NO_x, SO_2 and particulate matter (PM) contribute to local and regional pollution both in ports and in coastal areas and thus to associated risks to human health and ecosystems (*ibid.*). According to current estimates, PM emissions from shipping could have contributed to about 60,000 premature deaths in 2000 with a projected increase of 40% by 2012 (Eyring et al., 2010). Thus, as the United Nations Conference on Trade and Development puts it 'Environmental considerations are also gaining momentum [in the maritime transport sector] in view of sustainable development objectives, the climate change challenge and concerns over growing air pollution' (UNCTAD, 2008, p. 9).

Another environmental issue is the problem of introducing marine organisms into new habitats and ecosystems through ballast water (Hoffmann, 2007). Such so-called neophytes can upset existing biological equilibria with negative effects on local biodiversity and can also have severe negative economic effects for example through damaging commercial fisheries, local tourism or even infrastructure (de Poorter, Darby, & MacKay, 2009)). The International Union for Conservation of Nature considers this phenomenon to be as threatening to the world's oceans as overfishing, habitat destruction, pollution and climate change (*ibid.*). There is also an IMO convention covering this issue, the 2004 *International Convention for the Control and Management of Ships' Ballast Water and Sediments* (BWM)[14] which will enter into force 12 months after the ratification by 30 states (representing at least 35% of the world's merchant shipping tonnage).

Further environmental issues associated with the operation of container ships include noise (which affects marine mammals at sea and human populations in the vicinity of ports), the (partly illegal[15]) dumping at sea of ships' waste (sewage, garbage)

---

14. http://www.imo.org/About/Conventions/ListOfConventions/Pages/International-Convention-for-the-Control-and-Management-of-Ships%27-Ballast-Water-and-Sediments-%28BWM%29.aspx (18.5.2011).

15. The International Convention for the Prevention of Pollution from Ships' (MARPOL) Annex V (in force since December 1988) prohibits disposal of plastics anywhere at sea and restricts discharge of other wastes in coastal waters and so-called special areas such as the Mediterranean, Baltic and North Seas.

and the risk of bunker fuel spills following accidents. Another important issue is that of hinterland transport to and from ports. This often relies on trucking, which causes both local noise and air pollution as well as emissions of GHGs. Congestion and accidents are also associated with container transport in the hinterland of ports.

The scrapping or recycling of ships has been a further cause for environmental concerns, as the shipbreaking normally takes place on land and often in developing countries, which have much lower standards for dealing with the hazardous wastes associated with the decommissioning of ships (Chang, Wang, & Durak, 2010). This may often lead to the environmentally harmful disposal of such substances. It also places the workers at much higher risks from occupational accidents (*ibid.*) and ship recycling is also associated with general concerns over labour rights. The *Hong Kong International Convention for the Safe and Environmentally Sound Recycling of Ships* was adopted in 2009 but has not yet entered into force (and would furthermore only apply to ships of 500 gross tons or above).

Employment conditions, including wages, working hours and other contractual agreements as well as health and safety issues at work, training and accommodation are also areas of potential concern during both the construction and operation of container ships. The United Nations' (UN) International Labour Organisation has passed the *Maritime Labour Convention* in 2006 (International Labour Conference, 2006), which covers these and further issues with respect to seafarers' rights. However, at the time of writing, it had not been ratified by enough UN member states to have entered into force.

All the issues mentioned above are to some extent also covered in the new ISO standard on social responsibility, ISO 26000 (International Organization for Standardization, 2010). Unlike other ISO standards, like for example the 14000 series relating to environmental management, ISO 26000 is not intended as a basis for certification. Instead, it is meant as a comprehensive guidance document for public as well as private organizations of all sizes wishing to become (more) effective in fulfilling their social responsibility — which unlike in the European Commission definition cited above is *not* considered to be a voluntary commitment but a duty resulting from the fact that all organizations affect and change society through their actions (Roloff, 2011).

11.2.4.   Value Drivers for CSR

For some years now, the business case for CSR has been gaining importance. Decision-makers on all levels need insights into how CSR activities and business performance are linked. Although specific links might differ from industry to industry, and even from company to company, it is possible to relate various CSR dimensions to measures of business performance. It can for example be assumed that

---

Annex VI (in force since September 2003) prohibits the discharge of untreated sewage within a specified distance from land.

there is a strong positive impact on the performance measure *brand value and reputation* from the following CSR dimensions: (1) ethics, values, principles, (2) accountability and transparency, (3) eco-efficiency, (4) social development, (5) human rights and (6) a company's CSR engagement with external stakeholders (Blowfield & Murray, 2011). In order to get a deeper understanding of the links between CSR activities and business performance, Perrini, Russo, Tencati, and Vurro (2009) suggest a framework of analysis to differentiate between six categories of value drivers, having their roots in different spheres (organizational, customer, society, natural environment, innovation and corporate governance). These drivers are influenced by a company specific set of CSR values, beliefs and attitudes and impact revenue-related or cost-related outcomes (Perrini et al., 2009; see Figure 11.2).

This generic framework of CSR-related performance drivers can easily be adapted to the liner shipping industry. A committed workforce for example is regarded as a prerequisite for a company's commercial success and also has a positive impact on the cost of labour (e.g. in terms of reduced absence from work). In an industry in which labour shortage is a crucial issue (BIMCO/ISF, 2011), responsible human resource management policies and practices might lead to competitive advantages in recruiting talented seafarers as well as onshore employees. According to a global consultancy survey, 88% of the respondents (3906 so-called *millenials*, i.e. graduates who entered the workforce after 1 July 2000) said 'they will choose employers who

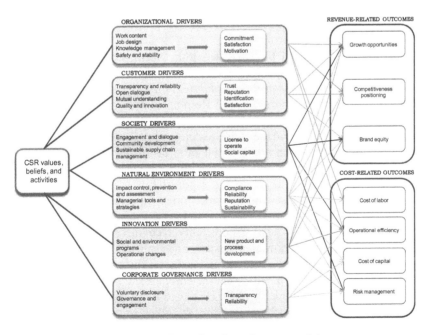

Figure 11.2: CSR-related performance drivers
Source: Adapted from Perrini et al. (2009).

have corporate social responsibility (CSR) values that reflect their own and 86% would consider leaving an employer if CSR values no longer matched their expectations' (PricewaterhouseCoopers, 2008).

11.3. Initial Roots and *Status Quo* of CSR

11.3.1. Initial Roots of a CSR

The initial roots of the concept of CSR can be traced back to the ancient Greeks. Back in those days, certain entrepreneurs or companies with a philanthropic attitude already supported people in need with money and food. These companies thus adopted a role as a social actor within the social system (Eberstadt, 1977).

Similar developments were observed during industrialization in the 19th century. The economic structure of society changed. The market power increasingly shifted from small and medium-sized enterprises (SMBs) to larger companies. Those companies also began to tackle questions of social responsibility and began looking for ways to serve the public good. This often included supporting local institutions with financial donations (Carroll & Buchholtz, 2006).

During the early 1930s, politicians increased their influence on the economic process. Topics like retirement provisions, safety and health care for employees were moved onto the agenda of private companies (Carroll & Buchholtz, 2006).

11.3.2. Status Quo *of the International CSR Debate*

11.3.2.1. The scientific roots of the CSR debate in North America The scientific debate concerning the concept of CSR has its roots in North America.

Bowen with his writing on *Social Responsibilities of the Businessman* (1953) can be regarded as the 'Father of Corporate Social Responsibility' (Carroll, 1999, p. 270). He defined the social responsibility of managers and stipulated that 'it refers to the obligations of businessmen to pursue those policies, to make those decisions, or to follow those lines of action which are desirable in terms of the objectives and values of our society' (Bowen, 1953, p. 6). The definition emphasized the obligation of managers to take social as well as economic responsibility.

In the 1960s, the focus of the scientific debate shifted from the social responsibility of the manager to corporate actions and their impact on the social system. Walton (1967) enunciated: 'corporate social responsibility recognizes the intimacy of the relationships between the corporation and society and realizes that such relationships must be kept in mind by top managers as the corporation and the related groups pursue their respective goals' (p. 18). Walton emphasized a present relationship between enterprises and stakeholder groups. He added that possible costs could arise from actions guided by CSR which are not directly linked to an immediate payback (Walton, 1967).

Carroll (1979) defined the requirements of society regarding enterprises. He structured CSR into four categories: *Economic Responsibility, Legal Responsibility, Ethical Responsibility* and *Discretionary Responsibility*. The economic responsibility —

to make a financial profit — and the legal responsibility — to obey the law — were categorized as fundamental responsibilities. Besides that, society expects enterprises to take on ethical responsibilities. These responsibilities encompass certain behaviour patterns which are expected by society and exceed the legal stipulations. Furthermore, it is requested by society that enterprises are good corporate citizens and take on other discretionary responsibilities (Carroll, 1979, 1991).

In the framework of more comprehensive scientific concepts, further definitions of the CSR concept were developed (Carroll, 1991; Frederick, 1978; Wood, 1991). Overall, a consensus of a generally accepted definition of the CSR concept was not reached within the international debate. However, a broadly accepted definition of the CSR concept was formulated within the mainly political CSR debate in Europe, which is illustrated in the following section.

11.3.2.2. The political nature of the CSR debate in Europe   At the Lisbon Summit in 2000, the European Council developed an economic development strategy for the European Union (EU). This so-called Lisbon Strategy defined the objective of the EU, 'to become the most competitive and dynamic knowledge-based economy in the world, capable of sustainable economic growth with more and better jobs and greater social cohesion' (European Commission, 2001a, p. 2). For the first time, companies were requested to make a contribution to sustainable development. In July 2001, the Green Paper *Promoting a European framework for CSR* concretised the Commission's CSR requirements. The European Commission defined CSR 'as a concept whereby companies integrate social and environmental concerns in their business operations and in their interaction with their stakeholders on a voluntary basis' (European Commission, 2001b, p. 6). Furthermore, the European Commission stated that 'being socially responsible means not only fulfilling legal expectations, but also going beyond compliance and investing "more" into human capital, the environment and the relations with stakeholders' (European Commission, 2001b, p. 6).

A politically driven interpretation process followed the publication of the CSR Green Paper. In July 2002, the results of this process were published in the Commission's Communication on CSR (European Commission, 2002). The major results were that CSR is not obligatory and goes beyond legal obligations, regards the economic, social and environmental dimension and should be integrated within an enterprise on a strategic as well as operative level (European Commission, 2002).

In 2002, the European Commission initiated the European Multistakeholder Forum (EMF). The overall aims of the EMF were 'to foster corporate social responsibility' (2004, p. 2) and to 'promote innovation, transparency and convergence of CSR practices and instruments' (2004, p. 2). The EMF represented the first European platform to support a 'dialogue between the business community, trade unions, civil society organizations and other stakeholders' (2004, p. 2). The work of the EMF was successful as the EMF achieved a consensus on CSR between different stakeholder groups (2004).

In 2003, the High Level Group of Government Representatives on CSR was set up additionally to the EMF. The purpose was to ensure a regular knowledge interchange between the member states of the EU, EU institutions, CSR Europe[16] and other stakeholder groups (European Commission, 2003).

In 2006, the European Alliance for CSR was developed as a business-lead initiative. The major aim of the alliance was to affiliate existing and new CSR initiatives of small and medium-sized enterprises (SMEs) and large enterprises as well as their stakeholder groups. The main activities of the alliance were defined as 'raising awareness and improving knowledge on CSR and reporting on its achievements, helping to mainstream and develop open coalitions of cooperation and ensuring an enabling environment for CSR' (European Commission, 2006, p. 11). The results of the European Alliance for CSR, which together form a toolbox for a competitive and responsible Europe, were presented in 2008 (European Commission, 2011a).

In 2010, the European Commission decided to renew the EU Lisbon Strategy. The major aim is now 'to promote CSR as a key element in ensuring long-term employee and consumer trust' (European Commission, 2011b).

11.4. Good-Practice Case Study: CSR within the NYK Line

The NYK Group is a transport and logistics company which employs 55,000 people on- and offshore. Major business segments of the company are the *Logistics Business*, *Terminal and Harbour Transport Business* and the *Liner Trade Business*. The headquarters of the company are based in Tokyo, Japan (NYK Group, 2010a).

The NYK Group successfully integrated CSR on a strategic and operative level. This is also acknowledged by the inclusion of NYK in the social responsible investment (SRI) portfolios by a number of rating agencies and other institutions as a group of companies that actively promote CSR activities, for example the FTSE4Good Global Index, the Dow Jones Sustainability World Index and the Global 100 Most Sustainable Corporations in the World Index (NYK Group, 2010b).

11.4.1. The NYK Strategy is Based upon CSR

NYK develops company strategies on a three-year basis. Within a difficult economic environment, NYK published the strategy *Revision of New Horizon 2010* which regarded the time horizon from 2008 till 2010. Due to this reason the strategy was also called *Emergency Structural Reform Project Yosoro*[17] (NYK Group, 2009c).

The strategy is structured into the three core elements: growth, stability and environment, as Figure 11.3 illustrates. The strategy *Revision of New Horizon 2010* sets as the basis a commitment to strengthening CSR Management which is thus incorporated into the group's overall development strategy (NYK Group, 2009c).

---

16. The CSR Europe is a European business network for corporate social responsibility (CSR) which was founded in 1995. The members of the CSR Europe are around 70 multinational companies and 27 national partner organisations across Europe. The mission of the CSR Europe is to act as the European platform for companies and their stakeholders to exchange and cooperate to make themselves and Europe global leaders in sustainable competitiveness and societal wellbeing (CSR Europe, 2011).
17. NYK translates the term "Yosoro"as "Steady at full steam ahead!".

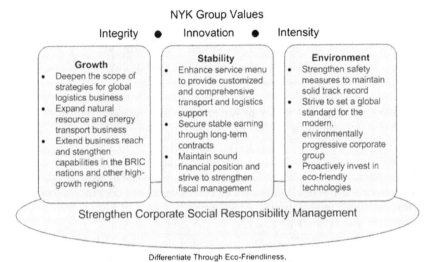

Figure 11.3: NYK Strategy *Revision of New Horizon 2010*
Source: NYK Group (2009c, p. 1).

The strategic elements *Stability* and *Environment* are intended to integrate the ecological and social dimension into the company strategy (NYK Group, 2009c).

The development process of the strategy *Revision of New Horizon 2010* was guided by the company president's office which initiated several company meetings with experts from different departments. Regional data such as market data and customer requirements, which may regionally differ, was provided by the regional offices. At the end of the development process, the company president's office decided about the content of the company strategy (Horimoto & Usami, 2009).

In summary, the following success factors were identified concerning the development process of the NYK company strategy (Horimoto & Usami, 2009):

1. The commitment of the top management to a CSR enabled the integration of a CSR management as a basis of the NYK strategy.
2. The integration of several departments into the development process of the strategy assured detailed know-how — also on an operative level — within the development process of the strategy.
3. The support of the regional offices was necessary for the budgeting process.

Neither specific barriers nor strategies to overcome them were named in the context of the development process of the NYK strategy.

11.4.2. Management System Supports CSR on an Operative Level

NYK implemented CSR on an operative level. The implementation process is supported by management systems. NYK has developed an environmental management system (EMS) and a safety management system (SMS). Both systems are interlinked and are considered a single unit (NYK Group, 2010b).

The core elements of the management system are vision, strategy and policy, organizational design, communicational design and controlling which are broadly illustrated in the following section (Drewes, 2011).

11.4.2.1. Vision, strategy and policy of the management system Within the EMS, the NYK Group has published a corporate vision, which is defined as follows: 'Contribute to the global environment and the creation of sustainable societies by managing environmental risks and arriving at an optimal balance between environment and economy' (NYK Group, 2009b, p. 43). The aim of the vision appears to be to emphasise to all internal and external stakeholders that the company is willing to contribute to sustainable development.

This long-term vision shall be reached by three environmental strategies. These strategies involve the implementation of measures to reduce GHG emissions, the promotion of a social contribution through activities that protect the natural environment and the strengthening of the environmental management throughout the NYK Group (NYK Group, 2009b).

The vision and the strategy of the EMS are based on the following NYK Green Policy, which consists of basic CSR guidelines for the employees of the NYK Group (NYK Group, 2009b):

1. preserve the marine and global environments by making continual improvements in operations,
2. comply with all relevant laws, ordinances, regulations, etc.; formulate and enforce voluntary standards,
3. ensure the safety of ocean, land and air transportation services,
4. prevent and suppress global warming and air and marine pollution,
5. adopt environment-friendly technologies,
6. conduct employee education programmes that increase environmental awareness,
7. disclose environmental information; contribute to society through environmental conservation.

Regarding the SMS, NYK has not developed a vision, strategy and policy. This indicates that the management system of NYK focuses more on the environmental dimension of a CSR.

The implementation of the CSR is assured through an integrated organizational design, which is explained in the following section.

11.4.2.2. Organizational structure of the management system The Safety and Environmental Management Committee (SEMC), which is based in the company headquarter in Tokyo, Japan, is responsible for the CSR, as shown in Figure 11.4. The main tasks of the SEMC are the development of policies as well as activity and financial plans. The president of the NYK Group is the head of the SEMC (NYK Group, 2008).

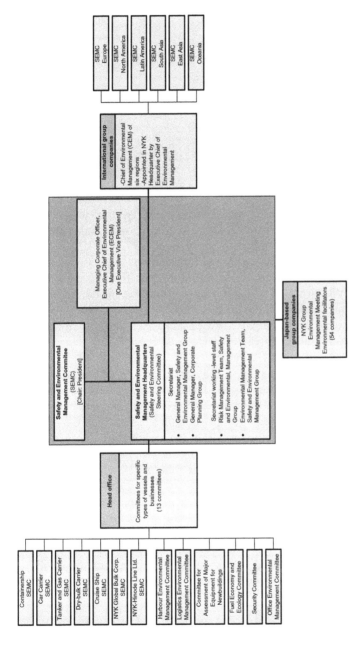

Figure 11.4: Organizational structure of the management system
Source: NYK Group (2004, p. 11; 2006, p. 23; 2007, p. 23; 2009b, p. 43).

Figure 11.5: Global Safety and Environmental Management Committee (SEMC)
Source: NYK Group (2009b, p. 29).

The SEMC is directly in charge of the committees for specific types of vessels and businesses, the environmental facilitators and the chiefs of environmental management (CEM), as shown in Figure 11.4.

The committees for specific types of vessels and businesses are based at the headquarters of the company, with overall responsibilities for their name giving activities throughout the NYK Group. Their major responsibility is the development of activity and financial plans which are more detailed than those plans developed by the SEMC. The implementation of the activity plans is supported and monitored in regular meetings (NYK Group, 2008, 2009b).

The environmental facilitators are 54 deputies which belong to NYK Group companies. They are responsible for the support, coordination and communication concerning environmental measures within Japan. The knowledge about successful measures is transferred to non-Japanese branches and daughter companies of the NYK group. The environmental facilitators meet on a regular basis within the NYK environmental management meeting which represents a communication platform for the involved parties (NYK Group, 2008, 2009b).

Six CEM were nominated within the NYK Group. The CEM work under the direct responsibility of the executive chiefs of environmental management (ECEM). Each CEM is in charge of specific regions. The responsibility areas are structured into Europe, North America, Latin America, South Asia and Oceania, as shown in Figure 11.5.

The CEM are responsible for the compliance with the certified processes of the management system. Regional meetings and audits are part of regular practice (NYK Group, 2009b).

11.4.2.3.   Communication strategy of the management system   NYK has developed a communication strategy which particularly aims at a continuous dialogue with stakeholder groups. This dialogue is intended to assure an *ex-ante* identification of sustainability issues. The target group consists of stakeholders such as customers, clients and business partners (NYK Group, 2010b).

The communicators are especially the CSR management headquarter, the public relations department, the CSR coordination team and the investors relations group/ team (NYK Group, 2010b).

Different kinds of media such as the internet (website, e-mail, newsletter), print products (company magazines, flyers) and DVDs (company movies) are applied to reach the different target groups. In addition, company events like seminars are especially carried out for employees to promote CSR activities.

11.4.2.4. CSR controlling: key environmental and social indicators In addition to economic targets, NYK has formulated environmental and social targets which are monitored by the controlling department with the support of indicators. The following provides a brief summary of the most important targets and the corresponding indicators.

According to the NYK environmental strategy, the major environmental target is the reduction of the greenhouse gas CO_2. Regarding the container shipping segment NYK has thus formulated the following environmental CO_2 reduction targets (NYK Group, 2009a):

– Reduction of CO_2 emissions by 100% till 2050 on the basis of 2008.
– Reduction of CO_2 emissions by 69% till 2013 on the basis of 2008.

The indicator used by NYK to monitor the degree of achievement of these targets is g CO_2/tkm. This indicator was chosen as it illustrates the eco-efficiency of the fleet in operation.

Within the container shipping segment, NYK has furthermore defined zero downtime of vessels as the most important social target. The downtime represents the time that vessels are stopped due to accidents or other problems. This indicator illustrates the degree to which NYK has achieved safe ship operation. An Emergency Response Network in six regions around the world was developed to enable NYK to quickly respond and minimize damage in case of an abnormal event (NYK Group, 2010b).

11.4.2.5. NYK Eco Ship 2030 as an intended path to zero emission shipping A substantial contribution to the long-term NYK CSR targets is planned to be made through the realization of the NYK Eco Ship 2030, which is illustrated in Figure 11.6. The study shows the conceptual design of a container ship. The development of the concept was carried out by the NYK research institute Monohakobi Technology Institute (MTI), the Finnish company Elomatic and the Italian ship designer Garroni Progetti p.r.l. (Mizuno, 2009).

The NYK Eco Ship 2030 combines several innovative eco-friendly technologies which can be clustered into measures to reduce power requirements, measures to enable the use of renewable power sources and the use of new technologies to generate power. The measures to reduce power requirements are for example reduction of weight, reduction of power required for the ships' on-board use, reduction of frictional resistance, reduction of wind resistance, an increase in propulsion efficiency, an increase in motor efficiency and the development of an optimized hull form. The use of renewable power sources considers for example solar

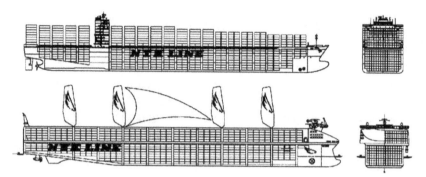

Figure 11.6: NYK Eco Ship 2030
Source: Mizuno (2009, p. 24).

and wind power. New technologies to generate power include the use of alternative fuels such as hydrogen and liquid natural gas (Mizuno, 2009).

In consideration of the CSR activities of the top five liner shipping companies at the time of writing (see Section 11.2.1) NYK seems to be a first mover in this respect. NYK has integrated CSR on a strategic and operative level, which is not state-of-the-art within the container shipping industry in general. There are still various sustainability issues outlined above (Section 11.2.3), however, which are not evidently covered by the NYK activities regarding CSR.

11.5.　CSR in Container Shipping — Implications

The concept of CSR encompasses a wide range of issues such as the protection of natural environments and non-renewable resources, the reduction of GHG emissions, the protection of workers from professional hazards and the implementation of high employment standards for the entire work force. Many of these are covered to some extent by existing legislation in some parts of the world but the legal standards differ widely on an international scale and are in some cases also non-existent. It follows that adhering to the respective laws and regulations of a company's home country or the ships' flag countries and port countries is — while highly desirable — not sufficient to attain a high level of CSR in international container shipping. It is at present still a voluntary concept, though, when viewed as a comprehensive package covering all social and environmental consequences of a company's decisions and activities.

The snapshot analysis at the beginning of this chapter has shown that the top carriers' main focus in reporting on CSR activities lies on environmental issues. Given the impact of maritime shipping on the natural environment this can be interpreted as a proactive approach with regards to the growing demand for transparency, both in the market and at the political level. However, tackling environmental challenges is only one element of CSR — social issues should be equally important.

Currently, the UN Global Compact (United Nations, 2010) is a universally accepted framework for companies committed to CSR. For a network industry like liner shipping with its high degree of outsourcing and subcontracting, some of the 10 principles of the UN Global Compact could represent demanding benchmarks, though. Nevertheless, at the time of writing, a small number of container shipping lines (COSCO, NYK, Maersk, Mitsui O.S.K) were in fact participating in this global initiative. Current developments point in the direction, that the integration and communication of a comprehensive CSR strategy on both the visionary, strategic and operative levels of a company will become increasingly important in the maritime industry. As is already the case with individual issues such as the quality of bunker fuel or anti-fowling, current trends mean that over time, CSR activities that a short while ago were mostly a voluntary commitment by selected companies are fast becoming standard customer demands. Stakeholder dialogue is thus also gaining in importance since especially shippers are increasingly integrating sustainability issues into their calls for tender. Ultimately, many elements of CSR are even likely to become regulatory requirements on a much wider scale than is currently the case.

A successful CSR has to be integrated on all levels of a company. Top management and all employees need to be sensitized to the CSR concept and the corresponding value drivers. A general standard for holistic CSR accounting should also be developed to assure comparability. Although the aforementioned ISO 26000 (Section 11.2.3) is currently not intended as a basis for certification, it may over time become one of the main sources for such a CSR accounting standard — along with the UN Global Compact and the European Commission's CSR Green Paper for example.

Finally, on the basis of the European CSR in the CSR Green Paper (European Commission, 2001b, p. 6), we propose in the following as a sector-specific definition of CSR for the container shipping industry:

> Corporate Social Responsibility (CSR) in Container Shipping is a concept according to which liner shipping companies integrate all relevant sustainability issues in their business operations on a visionary, strategic and operative level while considering a constant interaction with their stakeholder groups on a voluntary basis. CSR activities of liner shipping companies especially take into account the particular environmental impact of container shipping on the seven seas, the world's coastlines and in regard to hinterland transport. Furthermore, the Container Shipping CSR concept considers the global scope and the networking structure of the industry as well as the high degree of outsourcing and sub-contracting. The concept also encompasses the entire life cycle of the vessels used, from building via operation to ship breaking and recycling. Due to the special working conditions of seafarers, CSR in Container Shipping puts a strong emphasis on labour related issues, including cross-cultural and diversity considerations.

Future research on this issue should firstly focus on looking at which CSR measures can achieve — and have already shown — the greatest results towards an improvement of the environmental and social impacts of container liner shipping and maritime logistics in general. The conditions for their successful implementation should be documented, both from case studies and from theoretical considerations. Such documentation should include information on technical and operational requirements as well as the stakeholder dialogues inside the company and with external parties that have shown to both firmly anchor the measures in business and operations practice as well as in the awareness of the market.

Furthermore, the main scientific question is how sustainability issues should be integrated in the decision-making processes on the visionary and strategic level of liner shipping companies. Within this research field, especially qualitative research methods should be applicable due to the highly consolidated market structure.

11.6. Conclusions

The leading liner shipping companies are tackling the major sustainability issues on an operative level. Nevertheless, the majority of liner shipping companies have not integrated sustainability issues in the visionary and strategic decision-making processes. This is also a consequence of the high variety of CSR interpretations. Managers have problems to derive concrete management actions. It is the challenge of scientific research to focus on this problem and to provide the liner service industry with industry-specific solutions for a comprehensive CSR.

References

BIMCO/ISF-Baltic and International Maritime Council, Dalian-Haishi-Daxue & Institute for Employment Research. (2011). *BIMCOISF manpower 2010 update: The worldwide demand for and supply of seafarers: main report.* Bagsvaerd: Bimco.

Beddow, M. (2011). Twists & turns. *Containerisation International, 5,* 48–49.

Blowfield, M., & Murray, A. (2011). *Corporate responsibility: A critical introduction* (2nd ed.). Oxford: Oxford University Press.

Bowen, H. R. (1953). *Social responsibilities of the businessman.* New York, NY: Harper and Brothers.

Brooks, M. R., & Trifts, V. (2008). Short sea shipping in North America: Understanding the requirements of Atlantic Canadian shippers. *Maritime Policy and Management, 35*(2), 145–158.

Cargonews Asia. (2011). Retrieved from http://www.cargonewsasia.com/afsca/index.html. Accessed on 17 May 2011.

Carroll, A. B. (1979). A three-dimensional conceptual model of corporate performance. *Academy of Management Review, 4*(4), 497–505.

Carroll, A. B. (1991, July–August). The pyramid of corporate social responsibility: Toward the moral management of organization stakeholders. *Business Horizons, 34,* 39–48.

Carroll, A. B. (1999). Corporate social responsibility: Evolution of a definitional construct. *Business & Society, 38*(3), 268–295.

Carroll, A. B., & Buchholtz, A. K. (2006). *Business & society: Ethics and stakeholder management*. Mason, USA: South-Western.

Celik, M. (2009). Designing of integrated quality and safety management system (IQSMS) for shipping operations. *Safety Science, 47*(5), 569–577.

Chang, Y-C., Wang, N., & Durak, O. (2010). Ship recycling and marine pollution. *Marine Pollution Bulletin, 60*(9), 1390–1396.

Commission of the European Communities. (2006, March 22). Implementing the partnership for growth and jobs. Making Europe a pole of excellence on corporate social responsibility. 136 final.

Drewes, P. (2011). Corporate sustainability management in container shipping. PhD Dissertation. Hamburg.

Eberstadt, N. (1977). What history tells us about corporate responsibilities. In A. B. Carroll (Ed.), *Managing corporate social responsibility* (pp. 17–22). Boston, MA: Little, Brown Book.

European Commission. (2001b). Communication from the commission: A sustainable Europe for a better world: A European Union strategy for sustainable development. Brussels.

European Commission. (2001a). *Green Paper — Promoting a European framework for Corporate Social Responsibility*. Brussels.

European Commission. (2002). *Communication from the commission concerning corporate social responsibility: A business contribution to sustainable development*. Brussels.

European Commission. (2003). High Level Group of National Social Representatives on CSR: Proposal for a Mandate. Bruessels.

European Commission. (2006). *Communication from the Commission to the European parliament, the council and the European economic and social committee: Implementing the partnership for growth and jobs: Making Europe a pole of excellence on corporate social responsibility*. Brussels.

European Commission. (2011a). *Sustainable and responsible business: European alliance for corporate social responsibility (CSR)*. Retrieved from http://ec.europa.eu/enterprise/policies/sustainable-business/corporate-social-responsibility/european-alliance/index_en.htm. Accessed on 23 May 2011.

European Commission. (2011b). *Sustainable and responsible business: Corporate social responsibility (CSR)*. Retrieved from http://ec.europa.eu/enterprise/policies/sustainable-business/corporate-social-responsibility/index_en.htm. Accessed on 25 May 2011.

European Multistakeholder Forum on CSR. (2004). *Final results & recommendations*. Brussels.

Eyring, V., Isaksen, I. S. A., Berntsen, T., Collins, W. J., Corbett, J. J., Endresen, O., Grainger, R. G., et al. (2010). Transport impacts on atmosphere and climate: Shipping. *Atmospheric Environment, 44*(37), 4735–4771.

Frederick, W. C. (1978). *From CSR1 to CSR2: The maturing of business-and-society thought*. Pittsburgh, PA: Graduate School of Business, University of Pittsburgh.

Hapag-Lloyd, A. G. (2011). *Annual Report 2010*. Hamburg. Retrieved from http://www.hapag-lloyd.de/downloads/news/hapag_lloyd_annual_report_2010_en.pdf. Accessed on 18 May 2011.

Hoffmann, C. (2007). Die Invasion aus dem Tank — das Problem mit dem Ballastwasser. *Umwelt, 2*, 107–109.

Horimoto, M., & Usami, Y. (2009). Personal communication from 17.11.2009. Tokyo.

International Labour Conference. (2006). *Maritime Labout Convention 2006*. UN International Labour Organization. Retrieved from http://www.ilo.org/wcmsp5/groups/public/@ed_norm/@normes/documents/normativeinstrument/wcms_090250.pdf. Accessed on 20 May 2011.

International Organization for Standardization. (2010). *International standard ISO 26000. Guidance on social responsibility* (1st ed.). Geneva: International Organization for Standardization.

Matthews, S. (2010, May 25). Shipping sees the broader benefits of acting responsibly. *Lloyd's List*, p. 4.

Mizuno, K. (2009). *Advanced technologies in shipping.* Retrieved from http://www2.ir3s. u-tokyo.ac.jp/esf/images/activity/symposium_04_mizuno.pdf. Accessed on 2 June 2011.

Moller, A. P. — Maersk. (2011). *Sustainability Report 2010 — Setting the course.* Copenhagen: A. P. Moller — Maersk. Retrieved from http://www.maersk.com/Sustainability/Docu ments/Maersk_Sustainability_Report_2010.pdf. Accessed on 16 May 2011.

NYK Group. (2004). *Social & environmental report* 2004. Tokyo.

NYK Group. (2006). *CSR report 2006.* Tokyo.

NYK Group. (2007). *CSR report 2007.* Tokyo.

NYK Group. (2008). *CSR report 2008.* Tokyo.

NYK Group. (2009a). *Annual report 2009.* Tokyo.

NYK Group. (2009b). *CSR report 2009.* Tokyo.

NYK Group. (2009c). *Revision of New Horizon 2010.* Retrieved from http://www.nyk.com/ english/ir/manage/plan/pdf/new_horizon2010_2009.pdf. Accessed on 25 May 2011.

NYK Group. (2010a). *Annual report 2010.* Tokyo.

NYK Group. (2010b). *CSR report 2010.* Tokyo.

Perrini, F., Russo, A., Tencati, A., & Vurro, C. (2009). *Going beyond a long-lasting debate: What is behind the relationship between corporate social and financial performance?* Working Paper. Retrieved from http://www.investorvalue.org/docs/GoingBeyondALongLastingDe bate.pdf. Accessed on 15 May 2011.

de Poorter, M., Darby, C., & MacKay, J. (2009). *Marine menace. Alien invasive species in the marine environment.* Gland: International Union for Conservation of Nature. Retrieved from http://data.iucn.org/dbtw-wpd/edocs/2009-011.pdf. Accessed on 12 May 2011.

PricewaterhouseCoopers. (2008). *Managing tomorrow's people. Millennials at work: Perspectives from a new generation.* Retrieved from http://www.pwc.com/managingpeople2020. Accessed on 30 May 2011.

Roloff, J. (2011). Zur Bedeutung des Leitfadens ISO 26000. Meilenstein oder Fußnote auf dem Weg zur gesellschaftlich verantwortungsvollen Unternehmung? *Forum Wirtschaftsethik, 19*(1), 29–40.

Slack, N., & Chambers, S. (2007). *Operations management.* Harlow, UK: Prentice Hall.

Sweeney, L., & Coughlan, J. (2008). Do different industries report corporate social responsibility differently? An investigation through the lens of stakeholder theory. *Journal of Marketing Communications, 14*(2), 113–124.

United Nations. (2010). *Blueprint For corporate sustainability leadership.* UN Global Compact Office. Retrieved from http://www.unglobalcompact.org/docs/news_events/8.1/Blue-print.pdf. Accessed on 18 May 2011.

UNCTAD Secretariat (2010). *Review of maritime transport 2010.* New York, NY: United Nations.

Walton, C. C. (1967). *Corporate social responsibilities.* Belmont, CA: Wadsworth Publishing Company Inc.

Wood, D. J. (1991). *Corporate social performance revisited.* Veröffentlichungsreihe der Abteilung Organisation und Technikgenesung des Forschungsschwerpunkts Technik-Arbeit-Umwelt des Wissenschaftszentrums Berlin für Sozialforschung (FS II 91-101), pp. 1–34.

Chapter 12

Green Maritime Logistics and Sustainability

Haakon Lindstad, Bjørn E. Asbjørnslett and Jan Tore Pedersen

Abstract

The environmental consequences of international trade and transport have gained importance as a result of the current climate debate. Products are increasingly being produced in one part of the world, transported to another country and then redistributed to their final country of consumption. Since more than 80% of world trade tonnage measured in metric tons is carried by seagoing vessels, maritime transport will continue to be a core part of most supply chains while rail and road mainly are used for hinterland transport and to and from ports. This chapter presents a methodology for assessing the environmental impact of maritime transport and transport in general, with a specific focus on greenhouse gas emissions. The first section gives an introduction to why Green Maritime Logistics and Sustainability are important topics, while the second offers a framework for measuring greenhouse gas emissions (GHG) for transport systems. The third section presents a model for measuring seaborne transport and its greenhouse gas emissions, and in the fourth section we compare greenhouse gas emissions from different modes of transportation.

Keywords: Maritime transport; energy efficiency, benchmarking; logistics

12.1. Introduction

Since the late 1980s and until 2007, the rate of growth in world trade was higher than in any other period during the last 200 years, and trade and transport volumes nearly doubled, while world energy consumption rose from 8732 MTOE (million tons of oil equivalent) in 1990 to 12,013 MTOE in 2007 (IEA, 2009) of which 20% (Second IMO GHG Study, 2009) was consumed by the transport sector. This increased the

Maritime Logistics: Contemporary Issues
ISBN: 978-1-78052-340-8

challenges related to available energy sources and raised emissions of greenhouse gases, since 80% (IEA, 2009) of the energy consumed by this sector comes from burning fossil fuel. When energy is generated by burning fossil fuel, the outputs are energy as such and CO_2, which is the main manmade greenhouse gas. Greenhouse gases are essential for maintaining the temperature of the Earth. However, excess production of greenhouse gases can raise the temperature and cause climate change which is widely regarded as one of the gravest threats to the environmental sustainability of the planet, the well-being of its people and the strength of its economies.

According to the IMO (Second IMO GHG Study, 2009), maritime transport emitted 1046 million tons of CO_2 in 2007, representing 3.3% of global greenhouse gas emissions. These emissions are expected to increase by 150–250% by 2050 if no action is taken (i.e. 'business as usual' scenarios with a tripling of world trade). A controversial issue is how reductions in greenhouse gas emissions are to be made by individual sectors. Given a scenario in which all sectors accept the same percentage reductions, total shipping emissions in 2050 would have to be no greater than 15–50% of current levels, based on the required 50–85% reduction target set by the IPCC (2007). Moreover, if the demand for sea transport follows the predicted tripling of world trade (Lindstad, Asbjørnslett, & Strømman, 2011), it can easily be deduced that the amount of CO_2 emitted per ton-nm (1 nm $= 1.852$ km) will then (as a minimum) have to be reduced from 25 to 4 g of CO_2 per ton-nm by 2050. This is a reduction by a factor of five, which is a substantial challenge.

Traditionally the evaluation of the different transport options has been based on a combination of cost and logistics requirements, where the typical cost considered has consisted of the direct costs of the vessel, its fuel, terminal handling, hinterland transport and the capital cost of the goods transported. While more recently we have observed a growing interest in including environmental impact when assessing alternative transport options, the simplified version usually employed is to take only the CO_2 emitted to the atmosphere into consideration. The World Business Council has published approximate values that basically provide only an average figure for sea transport, while Psaraftis and Kontovas (2009) estimate gram CO_2 per ton-km per vessel type and size. Lindstad and Mørkve (2009) have developed this further in a methodology for how to map and measure the CO_2 footprint along the logistics chain.

Within the European Union, awareness of the environmental consequences of intensifying international trade has grown during the past two decades. For this reason, the European Commission (EC) has suggested incorporating all external costs into assessments of the total environmental impact and cost of transport. Examples of socio-environmental impact areas affected by transport are: costs of maintaining infrastructure, accidents, effects on human health, damage to buildings and nature. Life Cycle Assessment (LCA) is the leading methodology for evaluation of environmental impact. LCA has been developed as a tool for evaluating the environmental effects of a specific economic activity. LCA is usually performed as a 'bottom-up' process analysis, based on linking the specific processes involved in a supply chain. A significant advantage of such process analysis is precisely its capability for detail.

However, employing LCA to assess the total environmental impact of transport, and maritime transport in particular goes beyond the forefront of current research. The focus of the rest of this chapter will therefore be on measuring the environmental performance of maritime transport in a comprehensive and uniform way to calculate the greenhouse gas emissions.

12.2. Measuring Greenhouse Gas Emissions and Energy Consumption in Transport Systems

The results of energy consumption and emissions analyses can be presented in two different ways: the energy consumption and emissions for the defined system regardless of volume transported, that is a system focus, for example on emissions generated by a single transport company. Alternatively, the energy consumption and emissions per unit of product passing through the system can be calculated, that is a product focus. When we focus on measuring the performance of a system with respect to energy consumption and emissions we need to know how efficiently a unit of product is moved within the defined system boundaries. The common unit used to estimate environmental performance is CO_2 emitted per unit or ton of cargo or CO_2 emission related to the transport work done, that is CO_2 per ton-nm or ton-km. The general approach used when calculating the CO2 per ton-nm or ton-km is:

- Calculate the amount of fuel used on the voyage and multiply it by its carbon content, and the result is the CO_2 emitted on that voyage.
- Multiply the tonnage of the cargo transported by the distance to give the transport work performed in ton-nm or ton-km.
- The CO_2 per ton-km is obtained by dividing the total CO_2 emitted on the voyage by the transport work performed.

For qualified suggestions to be made about the effects of introducing measures in a maritime logistics chain for improving GHG emissions and energy consumption of alternative chains, accurate estimates, or benchmarks, of the current situation are a prerequisite. There are two main approaches to performing such benchmarking studies. First, we can compare the performance of each link (nodes and legs) in the chain separately, for example individual means of transport, terminals and warehouses. Secondly, we can look at larger parts or the whole of a logistics chain. Figure 12.1 illustrates the two approaches; the 'vertical' approach, looking at one process, for example a single leg or node, and the 'horizontal' approach, that is looking at the whole of a logistics chain.

Each of these approaches has its challenges and possible pitfalls when the 'as-is' or benchmarks are being estimated. However, the complexity of calculating energy consumption and CO_2 emissions increases when the focus is shifted from a single mean of transport or fleet of transport means to a total transport chain that includes terminal handling and warehousing or a total value chain that also includes

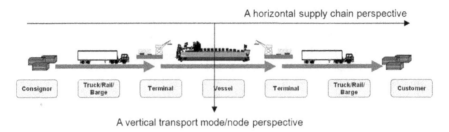

Figure 12.1: Two main approaches to benchmarking studies

production. Several parameters need to be included in estimating CO_2 emissions by alternative logistics systems. The main parameters to be included are:

- Technological characteristics: Type of fuel, size of engine (type and power), vessel/ vehicle capacity (payload), engine load and energy requirements under different operational conditions, fuel consumption under different operational conditions.
- Operational characteristics: Degree of utilization, round trip (loaded and in ballast, repositioning, etc.), vessel/vehicle speed — average and range, specific engine load, specific fuel consumption/energy use, distance sailed/travelled, transport route (origin–destination matrix).

Since more than 80% of world trade (measured in metric tons) is carried by seagoing vessels, shipping is a part of most supply chains, while rail and road are mainly used for hinterland transport to and from ports. Both rail and road solutions are compared to seagoing vessels quite standardized, with more or less given figures for capacity and speed per unit. However there is a clear distinction between ordinary freight trains and trains transporting bulk products like iron ore, coal and grain, where the latter have larger capacity and much lower energy consumption per ton-km.

The maritime fleet on the other hand consists of vessels where the same cargo types can be carried by vessels of different types and sizes as shown in Table 12.1. The size of the vessels range from a few thousand up to hundreds of thousands of tons. Vessels use a wide range of cargo handling technologies, and their service speed, which is 90–95% of maximum speed, lies in the range of 10–12 knots to 25–30 knots (1 knot = 1 nm/hour = 1.8512 km/hour). The choice of all these variants that can appear in the same type of logistics chain will have an impact on the carbon footprint of the logistics chain.

12.3. A Model for Measuring Seaborne Transport and Its Greenhouse Gas Emissions

As described above, the maritime fleet consists of vessels that range widely in size, speed and handling technology. Transport distances also range from a few to more than 10,000 nm. To handle this variety, models are needed. A typical approach has been to build a simplified model for each shipping segment and then use it as a basis

Table 12.1: Matrix of vessel/cargo alternatives.

Cargo type	Ship types									
	Dry bulk	Open hatch	Reefer	Container	Crude oil	OBO	Product/Chemical	RoRo	LNG	LPG
Coal	X					X				
Iron ore	X	X				X				
Steel products	X	X		X				X		
Grain	X	X		X				X		
Cement and Clinker	X	X		(x)		X		(x)		
Fertilizer	X	x		(x)			x	(x)		
Aluminium	X	x		(x)						
Other dry bulk	X	x		(x)		X		(x)		
Crude oil					X	X				
LNG									X	
LPG				X						X
Clean petrol products				X			x	X		
Chemicals				X			x	X		
Vegetable oils				X			x	X		
Forest products		x		X				X		
Fruit and vegetables			X	X				X		
Frozen products			X	X				X		
FMC products				X				X		
Machines/Equipment		x		X				X		
Project cargo		x						X		
Cars				x				X		
Trailers		x						X		
Trucks/Heavy machinery		x						X		

for decision support regarding the balance between supply and demand, contracts and fleet renewals.

The approach to more detailed figures for CO_2 emissions from shipping outlined below is based on a model that simulates how different vessels types have been used in different trades. The model is based on a combination of exact and estimated data. The exact data is the world fleet as listed in 2007 in the Lloyds Fairplay database (now the IHS database) divided into vessel type and size groups. The development of the model started with an analysis of the dry-bulk shipping segment, focusing on the vessels used and cargo flows, including movement patterns (origin and destination) of the main dry-bulk commodities transported. Dry-bulk commodities are in solid form and can be handled mechanically by grabs, conveyor belts, bucket units or pneumatic systems. Typical dry-bulk commodities are iron ore, coal, grain, cement, fertilizer and aggregate. General bulk carriers have a single deck and vertical access is through the cargo hatches. The transport work performed (billion ton miles) by dry-bulk carriers represents nearly 40% of the total marine transport work performed.

The largest vessels in the dry-bulk segment are the Capesize vessels, which cannot only pass through the Suez Canal partly loaded. The average size of a Capesize vessel is 172,000 dwt. The main Capesize trades are from Australia to Japan/Korea/China in Asia or to Western Europe, and from Brazil to Asia and Western Europe. A typical sailing pattern is from Western Australia to Western Europe with cargo, then in ballast to Brazil before returning to Asia with cargo. Another sailing pattern is from Australia to Japan/Korea/China with coal or iron ore and then in ballast back. The average sailing distance is 7500 nm one way and these vessels will inaverage do six voyages a year with cargo and five in ballast due to imbalance in trades. Post-Panamax vessels are smaller than Capesize, and are too large to transit the Panama Canal before its extension opens in 2014. Panamax vessels are the largest vessels which can currently transit the Panama Canal as it exists today. Panamax vessels are used both for major and minor bulk products in North–South and East–West trades, and in the same trades as the Capesize vessels. Their average sailing distance is 5500 nm on the cargo legs and they make an average of eight voyages with cargo per year. The ratio between cargo sailings and ballast sailings, 8:5, is better than that of the Capesize vessels. The main reason for this is that it is easier to find return cargo. The Handymax vessels have the same beam as the Panamax class and are able to utilize the maximum dimensions of the Panama Canal, but their shorter length enables them to serve a number of ports and terminals that are not capable of accommodating Panamax vessels. Another advantage of Handymax vessels over Panamax is that they take smaller cargo batch sizes and thus can serve more customers.

Table 12.2 summarizes the main characteristics of the operational patterns of dry-bulk carriers. The matrix shows vessel type in the first column, number of vessels in the second column, average dead weight (dwt) in the third column, average distance per one way voyage in the fourth, average speed in the fifth, then follows days per laden voyage, annual number of cargo voyages, days per ballast voyage, annual number of ballast voyages, average engine size, annual billion ton miles and grams CO_2 per ton-km as a function of cargo transported and operational patterns. The gram CO_2 per ton-km is lowest for the Capesize vessels with 4 g/t compared to

Table 12.2: Operational patterns of dry bulk carriers.

	No. of ships	dwt	Distance per voyage	Speed	Days per laden voyage	Cargo voyages	Days per ballast voyage	Ballast voyages	Engine size (kW)	Billion ton miles	Gram CO_2 per ton km
Dry bulk Capesize 120+	782	172,251	7,500	14.4	33	6	30	5	15,427	5,769	4
Dry bulk 80–120'	119	93,752	6,500	14.4	29	7	26	5	11,969	478	5
Dry bulk Panamax 60–85'	1,447	72,219	5,500	14.4	28	8	25	5	9,801	4,173	6
Dry bulk Handymax 35–60'	1,937	46,069	5,000	14.4	25	9	22	5	8,214	3,643	7
Dry bulk Handysize 15–35'	1,920	26,071	3,000	14.3	16	15	14	7	6,656	1,944	11
Dry bulk coastal 0–15'	1,318	4,307	787	11.8	6	36	5	20	1,949	130	50

50 g/t for the dry-bulk coastal carriers; a ratio of 1 to 12. Apart from the relatively high CO_2 values for the coastal ones all the others are within the range of 4–11 g/tkm, which clearly shows that dry-bulk carriers transport cargo in an energy-efficient way as far as their low emissions are concerned.

Another shipping segment of specific interest is container vessels, which are employed in regular liner services with fixed schedules. The largest vessels in the container segment used to be the 8500 TEU+ , which were capable of carrying 8500 or more 20-foot container units or more. The 4500–5500 TEU vessels are the largest ones that can go through the existing Panama Canal, while the 2014 extension of the Canal will enable container vessels up to 7500 TEU to do so. Recently some operators have ordered vessels of up to 18,000 TEU, while others have expressed serious doubt about both the benefits to society and the profitability of vessels above 10–12,000 TEU. The following description is based on how it is done at present, where the 8500 TEU+ and the 5500–8500 TEU vessels actually represent a single operational vessel segment. These vessels typically have an average voyage length of 31 days. Since they are employed in liner trades with fixed schedules, eight vessels are needed in a trade to enable weekly departures on the same weekday if the voyage length one way is 28 days. Nine vessels are needed for a voyage length of 31 days and 10 for a voyage length of 35 days. The most common operational pattern for these largest vessels is to use them in 'pendulum operation': from Europe to Asia and back, Asia to North America and back, and from Europe to East Coast North America.

The next size segment is the 3000–5500 TEU vessels, better known as Panamax container vessels, however not all vessels in this group can pass the canal since either their beam or length exceeds the Panama Canal dimensions. Typical operation patterns are from Asia to the east coast of America and from Europe to the west coast of North America, both through the Panama Canal. In addition to the service through the Canal, these vessels are used in north–south trades and to some extent in the same services as the post-Panamax vessels. A 2000–3000 TEU vessel is a typical intermediate container vessel. These vessels are employed in coastal roundtrip services such as in the Mediterranean, and in regions where the cargo flow does not justify a larger vessel. Small container ships ranging from 150 to 2000 TEU are used in feeder operations between large continental hubs to smaller hub and ports where the containers are unloaded and transported to the final receiver by road or rail.

Table 12.3 summarizes the main characteristics of the operational pattern for the container carriers. The matrix shows vessel type in the first column, number of vessels in the second column, average dead weight (dwt) in the third column, average utilization when loaded in the fourth column, average service speed in the fifth, then follows days per laden voyage, annual number of cargo voyages, days per ballast voyage, annual number of ballast voyages which is in general zero in the container segment, average engine size, annual billion ton miles and gram CO_2 per ton-km as a function of cargo transported and operational patterns. The 15 g of CO_2 emitted per ton-km is lowest for the 8500 TEU+ vessels, compared to 43 for the smallest vessels below 1000 in the European Union; a ratio of 1 to 3.

To provide an overview of the more detailed level of our model, we show an example from the container segment 8500 TEU+ vessel class in Table 12.4.

Table 12.3: Operational patterns of container carriers.

	No. of ships	dwt	Utilization when loaded (%)	Distance per voyage	Speed	Days per laden voyage	Cargo voyages	Days per ballast voyage	Ballast voyages	Engine size (kW)	Billion ton miles	Gram CO_2 per ton km
Container 8500 TEU+	206	105,995	70	11,000	25.1	31	11	27	0	67,369	1,483	15
Container 5500–8500 TEU	175	80,084	70	11,000	25.3	31	11	27	0	60,277	949	18
Container 3000–5500 TEU	1,068	55,297	70	7,000	23.3	24	14	20	0	37,208	3 224	18
Container 2000–3000 TEU	789	33,243	70	2,500	20.9	10	32	9	0	20,000	1,193	18
Container 1000–2000 TEU	832	20,512	70	1,000	19.0	8	45	6	0	12,662	430	26
Container 0–1000 TEU	1,328	9,149	70	650	16.5	6	49	5	0	6,231	223	43

Table 12.4: Vessel model with example of a container segment.

	No. of ships	dwt	Net payload capacity	Utilization when loaded	Distance per voyage	Speed	Loading and unloading rates in Ton or	Theoretical load and discharge times per	Additional port time and slow zones per voyage	Days per laden voyage	Cargo voyages	Ballast voyages
8500 TEU++	206	105,995	85,000	70%	11,000	25	200	4.6	4.0	31	11	0

	dwt utilization per year	Engine size (kW)	Gram fuel per kWh	Fuel per ship in ton	Cargo in million ton	Fuel in million ton	Gram fuel per ton nm	Gram CO_2 per ton nm	Total CO_2 emission in million ton	Days at sea with service speed	Days in port & slow zones	Days waiting repair, crew limits	Billion ton miles
8500 TEU++	56%	67,369	190	64,281	135	13.2	9	28	42	251	94	19	1,483

Based on the above analysis structure a detailed calculation of emission factors can be derived for ship types and sizes. Table 12.5 shows the full picture by vessel type for all the main cargo vessels.

The main observations from Table 12.5 are that the largest vessels are primarily used on the long voyages, while the smallest are mostly used on the short voyages. Most freight work is performed by the largest vessels including Panamax size groups, while the 'coastal vessels' below 15 000 dwt perform some 5% of all sea transport work. The largest vessels of all types emit less CO_2 per ton-nm sailed, where the ratio of largest to smallest is 1:13 in dry bulk (7–91 g of CO_2 per ton-nm) and 1:3 in the container segment (28–80 g of CO_2 per ton-nm).

12.4. Comparing Greenhouse Gas Emissions of Different Transport Modes

The transport efficiency of all transport modes is affected by many of the same factors as in shipping. This means that the efficiency depends on the load factor, cargo type and vehicle efficiency. For all surface transport modes heavier cargo usually improves the cargo/vehicle weight ratio, resulting in better CO_2/ton-km values. Theoretical consumption and emissions figures can be calculated for both road and rail transport, while inland waterways figures can be established in the same way as for sea transport. Average figures can be estimated on the basis of statistics from Eurostat and the EC and similar bodies in the United States and Japan.

In Table 12.6 we have used the main figures from the European White paper on Transport (2006) in combination with Eurostat figures to calculate and compare the average energy efficiency of road, rail and inland waterways transportation.

The table shows that the average emission figures are 156 g CO_2 per ton-km for road transport, 81 for rail and 68 for inland waterways. The European road transport figure is at a similar level to the 153 g CO_2 per ton-km published in the United States by the National Transport Statistics (2007) and the 144 g CO_2 per ton-km published in National Japanese statistics.

The theoretical figure for road transport based on modern truck and trailer combinations and fully utilizing the 40 ton total weight permitted within the European Union makes it possible to transport 26 tons of payload (net cargo weight) per cargo unit. Such modern truck and trailer combinations typically use 300 g of fuel per km on long-distance intra European transport, based upon maximum speeds of 90 km per hour, which is the European speed limit for trucks. With 70% utilization, which is a level commonly achieved on long-haul transport on round trips basis, we calculate the emissions per km to be ((320 g × 3.15 g CO_2 per g fuel)/26 ton)/ $0.7 = 54$ g CO_2 per ton-km. This is no more than a third of the average European figure of 156 g CO_2 per ton-km, which means that trucking activity must be less efficient than the average, regarding both fuel consumption per kilometre and vehicle utilization. Calculating the relative inefficiency of road transport is difficult, but if we make the assumption of a normal distribution around 156 g per ton-km, the typical range then becomes from 54 to 258 g per ton-km.

Table 12.5: Operational and technical characteristics of the different vessel types and calculation of bunker consumption figures.

	No of ships	Average dwt	Net pay-load capacity	Utilization when loaded	Dist-ance per voyage	Speed	Days per voyage	Cargo voyages	Balast voyages	dwt utilization per year	Days at sea, service speed	Engine size [kW]	Gram fuel per kWh	Fuel per ship in ton	Cargo in million ton	Billion ton miles	Fuel in million ton	Gram CO_2 per ton km
General Cargo Fleet																		
G.Cargo 15'++	1,215	25,341	24,000	90%	3,000	15	16	15	8	56%	186	8,080	190	7,450	394	1,181	9.1	13
G.Cargo 10'–15'	710	12,434	11,400	90%	2,000	15	11	22	12	53%	188	5,666	190	5,300	160	321	3.8	20
G.Cargo 5'–10'	2,654	6,957	6,400	85%	1,000	13	6	36	20	50%	174	3,280	210	3,181	520	520	8.4	28
G.Cargo 1'–5'	7,806	2,545	2,300	85%	500	12	5	44	25	49%	123	1,328	230	1,130	671	336	8.8	45
G.Cargo 500–1'	2,482	713	600	85%	350	10	5	46	26	46%	102	560	230	424	58	20	1.1	88
G.Cargo 0–500	2,413	196	150	85%	200	10	2	68	40	41%	93	369	230	239	21	4	0.6	234
Total General C.	17,280	4,641				12						2,142			1,824	2,382	31.7	23
Dry Bulk fleet																		
Capesize 120'++	782	172,251	169,000	97%	7,500	14	33	6	5	52%	239	15,427	190	16,597	769	5,769	13.0	4
Post P. 85'–120'	119	93,752	91,000	97%	6,500	14	29	7	5	55%	226	11,969	190	12,328	74	478	1.5	5
Panamax 60'–85'	1,447	72,219	69,000	95%	5,500	14	28	8	5	56%	206	9,801	190	9,573	759	4,173	13.9	6
Handymax 35'–60'	1,937	46,069	44,000	95%	5,000	14	25	9	5	58%	202	8,214	190	7,922	729	3,643	15.3	7
Handysize 15'–35'	1,920	26,071	25,000	90%	3,000	14	16	15	7	59%	192	6,656	190	6,299	648	1,944	12.1	11
Coastal 5–15'	464	9,318	8,600	85%	1,500	13	10	22	11	52%	156	3,565	210	3,168	75	112	1.5	22

Small Bulk 0–5'	854	1,585	1,400	85%	400	11	4	44	25	48%	105	1,071	230	787	45	18	0.7	64
Total Dry Bulk	7,523	52,549				14						7,922			3,098	16,137	57.9	6
Reefer fleet																		
Reefer 15'++	22	16,075	14,500	85%	4,000	21	14	16	10	47%	205	14,972	210	16,225	4	17	0.4	35
Reefer 10–15'	203	11,691	10,500	85%	3,000	20	11	20	12.5	47%	199	11,037	230	12,801	36	109	2.6	41
Reefer 5–10'	372	7,155	6,400	85%	2,000	18	9	25	17	45%	197	6,387	230	7,349	51	101	2.7	46
Reefer 0–5'	629	1,952	1,700	85%	1,000	13	6	34	23	44%	179	1,901	230	1,950	31	31	1.2	68
Total Reefer	1,226	5,397				16						5,134			122	258	6.9	46
Container fleet																		
8500 TEU	206	105,995	85,000	70%	11,000	25	31	11	0	56%	251	67,369	190	64,281	135	1,483	13.2	15
6500 TEU	175	80,084	64,000	70%	11,000	25	31	11	0	56%	250	60,277	190	57,088	86	949	10.0	18
4000 TEU	1,068	55,297	44,000	70%	7,000	23	24	14	0	56%	226	37,208	190	32,152	461	3,224	34.3	18
2300 TEU	789	33,243	27,000	70%	2,500	21	10	32	0	57%	215	20,000	190	16,388	477	1,193	12.9	18
1400 TEU	832	20,512	16,400	70%	1,000	19	8	45	0	56%	174	12,662	190	7,988	430	430	6.6	26
700 TEU	1,161	10,022	8,000	70%	700	17	7	48	0	56%	152	6,794	210	4,245	312	218	4.9	38
200 TEU	167	3,080	2,300	70%	300	13	5	55	0	52%	107	2,319	230	1,228	15	4	0.2	79
Total	4,398	34,186				20						22,517			1,915	7,501	82.3	19
Crude oil tanker fleet																		
Crude oil 200++	506	295,237	289,000	99%	9,000	15	42	4.5	4.5	48%	262	24,829	200	25,537	651	5,863	12.9	4
Crude oil 120–200'	356	151,734	147,000	99%	6,000	15	29	6.4	6.4	48%	245	17,162	200	17,352	332	1,989	6.2	5
Crude oil 75–120'	660	103,403	100,000	99%	2,500	15	16	11.5	11.5	48%	211	12,728	260	13,570	751	1,879	9.0	8
Crude oil 50–75'	198	66,261	64,000	99%	1,000	15	11	17	17	48%	170	10,571	260	7,822	213	213	1.5	12
Crude oil 15–50'	212	38,631	37,500	99%	800	14	10	18	18	48%	158	7,707	260	5,170	142	113	1.1	16

Table 12.5: (Continued)

	No of ships	Average dwt	Net pay-load capacity	Utilization when loaded	Dist-ance per voyage	Speed	Days per voyage	Cargo voyages	Balast voyages	dwt utilization per year	Days at sea, service speed	Engine size [kW]	Gram fuel per kWh	Fuel per ship in ton	Cargo in million ton	Billion ton miles	Fuel in million ton	Gram CO$_2$ per ton km
Crude oil 0–15'	121	3,638	3,500	98%	300	12	6	25	25	47%	110	1,926	260	934	10	3	0.1	62
Total Crude oil	2,053	142,914				15						15,125			2,100	10,061	30.8	5
Oil products tanker																		
Products 75'++	47	112,054	108,000	85%	5,000	15	29	8.5	4	56%	226	14,582	260	16,357	37	183	0.8	7
Products 25–75'	630	51,120	49,000	85%	4,000	15	24	9.5	5	53%	223	9,532	260	10,292	249	997	6.5	11
Products 15–25'	107	18,418	18,000	80%	1,500	14	15	15	8	51%	171	5,616	260	4,477	23	35	0.5	24
Products 10–15'	98	12,318	12,000	80%	700	13	13	18	10	50%	144	3,847	260	2,399	17	12	0.2	34
Products 5–10'	471	6,540	6,200	80%	400	12	11	20	12	47%	137	2,742	260	1,373	47	19	0.6	59
Products 0–5'	3,553	1,712	1,500	80%	100	11	7	26	16	43%	86	1,118	260	354	111	11	1.3	193
Total oil products	4,906	10,154				12						2,725			484	1,257	9.9	13
Chemical tankers																		
Chemical 40'++	533	47,614	45,000	85%	5,000	15	25	10.5	3	62%	241	9,361	260	11,274	214	1,070	6.0	10
Chemical 25–40'	469	34,686	33,000	80%	4,000	15	22	12.5	3	61%	230	8,930	260	10,087	155	619	4.7	13
Chemical 15–25'	370	18,987	18,200	80%	1,500	14	21	11	5.5	51%	239	6,409	260	3,357	59	89	1.2	24
Chemical 5–15'	1,028	9,161	8,800	80%	700	13	9	24	12	51%	166	3,695	260	2,360	174	122	2.4	34

Category																		
Chemical 0–5'	1,468	1,984	1,800	80%	250	12	6	36	18	48%	129	1,278	260	644	76	19	0.9	85
Total Chemical	3,868	15,771				13		11.5				4,478			678	1,919	15.4	14
RoRo fleet																		
RoRo 35'++	20	44,603	38,000	70%	8,500	18	31	20		60%	258	20,226	190	20,993	6	52	0.4	14
RoRo 25'–35'	49	28,403	24,000	70%	4,000	19	18	35		59%	212	16,492	190	14,791	16	66	0.7	19
RoRo 15'–25'	360	18,565	15,600	70%	1,500	19	10	50		59%	158	13,854	190	9,935	138	206	3.6	29
RoRo 5'–15'	678	9,844	8,100	70%	700	18	6	95		58%	116	9,735	210	6,559	192	135	4.4	56
RoRo 0'–5'	1,303	1,292	1,000	70%	300	12	3			54%	111	2,502	230	1,838	87	26	2.4	157
Total RoRo	2,410	7,189				16						7,484			439	485	11.6	41
LNG fleet																		
LNG 60'++	229	76,346	75,000	99%	8,000	20	31	6	6	49%	254	27,087	285	37,403	102	816	8.6	18
LNG 30'–60'	18	44,574	43,000	99%	5,000	18	24	8	8	48%	243	15,969	285	20,551	6	31	0.4	21
LNG 15'–30'	8	24,386	23,000	99%	1,500	18	14	14	14	47%	172	12,536	285	10,438	3	4	0.1	37
LNG 0'–15'	10	8,609	8,200	99%	700	16	9	18	18	47%	100	5,798	285	3,655	1	1	0.0	61
Total LNG	265	70,063				19						25,051			112	852	9.1	18
LPG fleet																		
LPG 45'++	118	53,262	51,000	99%	5,000	17	21	9	9	47%	277	13,401	230	16,207	54	268	1.9	12
LPG 25'–45'	68	33,570	32,000	99%	2,500	17	15	13	13	47%	233	11,298	230	10,575	28	70	0.7	17
LPG 15'–25'	60	19,264	18,300	99%	1,500	16	11	17	17	47%	201	8,657	230	6,902	18	28	0.4	25
LPG 5'–15'	205	7,985	7,600	99%	700	15	7	24	24	47%	153	4,857	260	3,458	37	26	0.7	47
LPG 0'–5'	652	2,116	2,000	99%	200	13	4	37	37	47%	74	1,825	260	926	48	10	0.6	107
Total LPG	1,103	11,551										4,586			185	401	4.4	18
Totals	45,032														10,957	41,253	260	11

Table 12.6: Key European transport figures and energy efficiency and emissions.

Key European freight transport figures 2004

	Road	Rail	Inland waterways
btkm (billion ton km)	1,684	379	129
Billion Vehicle km	169	2.046	0.320
Million Ton transported	15,202	828	465
Yearly no. of voyages/journeys in millions	1520.2	4.5	1.2
Average travel distance in km per voyage	111	457	277
Average amount in ton per voyage	10	185	403
Fuel Consumption in gram per ton km	50	26	22
Fuel consumption best case	12	10	10
Mtoe-Calculated Million ton oil equivalents (9)	83	10	3
Gram CO_2 per ton km	156	81	68

Calculating the theoretical rail figures is more complicated than the road figures, because there are wide differences in the maximum length of cargo trains from one country to another and because the topography varies. We tend to find the lowest train figures in the United States, where low-speed trains move bulk cargo over thousands of kilometres across nearly flat terrain as in the Mid West, more or less without curves or stops. The lowest published US figures indicate values down to 10–14 g CO_2 per ton-km (National Transportation Statistics, 2007) for bulk train combinations, which is less than 20% of the average European figure shown in Table 12.6. If we make the assumption that similarly low figures are achieved in the most efficient part of industrial bulk transport on the European railways, we can employ the same assumption as for road transport to establish the range for the rail transport. This gives a normal distribution around 81 g CO_2 per ton-km with a range of 14–148 g CO_2 per ton-km.

For transport on the inland waterways, the average value from table 12.6 is 68 g CO_2 per ton-km. Table 12.5 shows no values for inland waterway barges, but we have values for sea river vessels, which can operate both on inland waterways and along the coast, and can even cross the North Sea. For the different sea river groups we get values of 20 g CO_2 per ton-km for those above 5000 dwt and 44 g CO_2 for those between 1000 and 5000 dwt. Since the largest sea river vessel cannot be used on much more than the Rotterdam/Antwerp–Duisburg trades it would seem to be reasonable to use 30 g CO_2 per ton-km as the lower limit. If we make the same normal distribution assumption as for road and rail transport we get a distribution around 68 with a range of 30–106 g CO_2 per ton-km.

By using these figures for road, rail and inland waterway transport in combination with the sea transport figures per vessel segment it is easy to make a straightforward comparison, as illustrated in Figure 12.2. As the figure shows, the weighted average for all vessel types is undoubtedly lower than the average value for road transport,

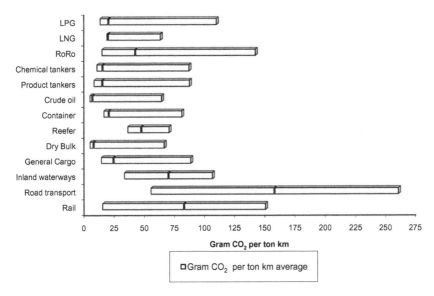

Figure 12.2: Gram CO_2 per ton-km for all surface transport modes

rail and inland waterway barges. What may be surprising is that both road and rail transport can be more competitive regarding energy usage and emissions than sea transport. The main reason for this is that smaller vessels, that is those below 5000 dwt, tend to be much less energy-efficient than the larger ones, as shown in Figure 12.2.

References

European Commission. (2006). *White paper on transport, time to decide.* Retrieved from http://ec.europa.eu/transport/white_paper

IEA. (2009). World Energy Outlook 2009, International Energy Agency Publications, 9 rue de la Fédération, 75739 Paris Cedex.

IPCC. (2007). Contribution of Working Groups I, II and III to the fourth assessment report of the Intergovernmental Panel on Climate Change, Geneva.

Lindstad, H., & Mørkve, O. T. (2009). A methodology to asses the energy efficiency and the environmental performance of maritime logistics chains. *Proceedings of the 10th international marine design conference*, Trondheim, May 26–29 2009, IMDC09&Tapir Academic Press, ISBN 978-82-519-2438-2.

Lindstad, H., Asbjørnslett, B. E., & Strømman, A. H. (2011). Reduction in greenhouse gas emissions and cost by shipping at lower speeds. *Energy Policy Journal, 39*, 3456–3464.

Lloyds Fairplay. (2007). *SeaWeb database.* Retrieved from www.lrfairplay.com

Psaraftis, H., & Kontovas, C. (2009). CO_2 emissions statistics for the world commercial fleet. *WMU Journal of Maritime Affairs, 8*, 1–25.

Second IMO GHG Study. (2009). International Maritime Organization (IMO) London, UK, April 2009; Buhaug, Ø., Corbett, J. J., Endresen, Ø., Eyring, V., Faber, J., Hanayama, S., Lee, D. S., Lee, D., Lindstad, H., Markowska, A. Z., Mjelde, A., Nelissen, D., Nilsen, J., Pålsson, C., Winebrake, J. J., Wu, W., Yoshida, K.

Chapter 13

Maritime Logistics in EU Green Ports and Short Sea Shipping

Alexandros M. Goulielmos, Venus Y. H. Lun and Kee-Hung Lai

Abstract

To examine the EU 'Short Sea Shipping' (SSS), its 'motorways of the sea (MoS)' and green ports, within short sea maritime logistics.

To present past research and report recent developments speculating on future trends.

The dominance of SSS over road is questioned; as road transport has expanded, hubs are expected to become larger and fewer with feeders. Road transport is not certain to follow SSS and its four motorways. This result was responsible for the relocation of industry from West to East and North–East inter-port competition.

The SSS ship size and port are undefined; specific data on these concepts are unavailable.

'Door-to-door' services are highly sought after in this sector, but difficult to establish.

The green element introduced here, mainly for ports, will dominate future discussions because of the high importance given to climate change.

This chapter outlines for the first time the development of the policy on EU Eco-ports, the relocation of industry, the West–East port competition, the MoS and the long-term deterioration of SSS logistics which is likely to persist in the future.

Keywords: EU short sea shipping; logistics; motorways of the sea; relocation of industry; West–East port competition; green ports

Maritime Logistics: Contemporary Issues
Copyright © 2012 by Emerald Group Publishing Limited
All rights of reproduction in any form reserved
ISBN: 978-1-78052-340-8

13.1. Introduction

The development of the maritime logistics hub and its implications for container ports were analyzed in a recent seminal conceptual article by Nam and Song (2011). Maritime logistics deal with maritime transport as manifested in shipping and ports, traditional logistics functions and integrated logistics activities. Nam and Song (2011, p. 270) saw the need to 'critically review the concepts and definitions associated with the existing hub literature applicable to maritime transport and logistics by synthesizing the existing studies and perspectives'.

In this chapter, Short Sea Shipping (SSS) is presented as the means to accomplish the spoke in the hub-and-spoke concept. Hub-and-spoke distribution systems first appeared in the US airline industry soon after its deregulation. The pattern led large liner and container companies to consolidate shipments on a massive scale at major terminals, the hubs, and redistribute smaller shipments to their respective destinations in the a fashion of radial links, or spokes. The ships used to realise this concept were the feeder ships. This model of transportation network is particularly evident in the Mediterranean area. Naturally, the success of SSS will depend on how faithfully container companies apply the hub-and-spoke concept on the one hand, and how the EU will avoid the diversion of traffic onto the roads on the other. We explore these issues in this chapter.

Given that the main advantage of SSS is the reduction of pollutants to the environment compared with road, an important element in the maritime environment is the emerging European Green Revolution in ships and ports. It is extraordinary how fast new terminology emerges, and discussion in the EU already addresses the question of greener competition. It is unclear whether this will mean establishing green maritime logistics hubs in the EU and in what respects these will be innovative. The rapid environmental deterioration over the last few decades has drastically increased corporate awareness of environmental responsibility on the part of large companies (Du Pont, Coca-Cola, PepsiCo, Procter and Gamble, H. J. Heinz). Though a growing number of companies developed environmentally green products (Li, 2007, p. 75), green services, especially from ships and ports, are still in their early stages of development.

As Min and Galle (2006) argued, the formulation of a green purchasing strategy may result in increased material costs and fewer qualified suppliers. As shown in this chapter, of 1000 EU ports only 156 ports have shown their determination to become green. Shore companies are now developing strategies to diminish the sources of upstream waste by reducing (1) items difficult to dispose of, or harmful to ecosystems, (2) the use of hazardous raw materials and (3) unnecessary packaging by increasing the use of returnable containers and biodegradables. The EU is currently concerned with recycling of old ships (scrapping). As Li (2007, p. 76) suggested, current green purchasing strategies seem to be reactive in that they try to avoid violations to existing legislation on the environment, rather than embedding proper goals within the long-term corporate policy. On shore, the link between green purchasing and supplier quality assurance is still weak. This is also the case in EU Eco-ports or feeder ports.

Maritime logistics may be divided into deep-sea logistics and short sea logistics, in particular, European short sea logistics. This is an effort to introduce maritime logistics even when an ocean carriage is not always involved by definition (in contrast with Nam & Song, 2011, p. 275, with reference to Song & Panayides, 2008). This chapter will focus on European short sea logistics as seen from the perspective of ports and ships.

13.2. Background Research on EU Short Sea Shipping

The history of the EU shipping policy can be traced back to 1957 (Paixao & Marlow, 2001). Between 1985 and 1994, the EU tried to establish pollution prevention policies by founding an EU register of ships (EUROS) to incorporate the IMO's work on quality shipping, which would have led to the elimination of sub-standards ships. This policy failed. From 1995 to 2001, the dominant EU policy was in favour of SSS, which was based on (1) spare transport capacity, (2) providing an opportunity to improve quality, efficiency and the infrastructure of ports, (3) integrating SSS-EU-10 into common transport policy dealing with externalities, (4) reducing congestion caused by road transport and (5) the fact that a number of ports[1] were already able to receive sea-river ships. Support of SSS intensified, as a sustainable mobility policy had emerged as manifested in the Brundtland Report[2] in 1987. In 1997, the EU Commission Green Paper on ports treated ports as part of the intermodal chain for the first time, and described them as 'inland and intermodal terminals' in the provision of just-in-time logistics. This was important as it finally integrated ports with the sea and with other ports and created the idea of the motorways of the sea (MoS).

Paixao and Marlow (2002) described the weaknesses of short sea shipping in Europe (SSS-EU) by outlining the (1) poor port environment, (2) low quality of service, (3) inefficient port operations, (4) unreliable vessel schedules, (5) excessive paperwork and (6) high administrative costs. On the other hand, advantages included (1) benefits to the environment, (2) lower energy consumption, (3) economies of scale and (4) lower costs for infrastructural expansion. In addition, Paixao and Marlow (2005) argued that the desired shift from road transport to SSS-EU did not come all about by 2002. The key attributes affecting the success of shifting to SSS-EU included quality of service (e.g. notice of cargo availability, time of collection/delivery), frequency and regularity of service, transport safety (e.g. technical ability), transport documentation, reliability (i.e. consistency in delivery time/drop-off), carrier's willingness to establish long-term relations and competitive prices for

---

1. Rotterdam and Antwerp, unlike Hamburg and Bremerhaven, had substantial *barge* activity (Notteboom, 2009) from the hinterland region (Perakis & Denisis, 2008).
2. *Our Common Future*, UN, 1987, World Commission on Environment and Development. Brundtland was the Norwegian Chairman of this commission.

equivalent quality and value for money. The low quality of SSS-EU did not stimulate the transfer of goods to sea.

Trujillo and Tovar (2007) analyzed the economic efficiency of ports with reference to the 1997 Green Paper'[3] and the 2004 liberalization of port services. The EU Commission re-engaged in promoting SSS-EU in 1999. SSS-EU was considered less polluting and more cost-effective. The growth of SSS could reduce road traffic congestion and provide better connections between continental and peripheral countries and islands.

On the other hand, Perakis and Denisis (2008) pointed out that the use of container barges in inland waterways did represent progress and a successful development of SSS-EU. For example, in Rotterdam 25% of the box traffic was on container barges, which as a corollary meant that speed is not the crucial factor in these operations.

In 2001, SSS-EU had a 40% share of transport in terms of ton-km, and it has increased since then by more than 1%. There is also the distance element. SSS-EU is dominant for transport distances of 1385 km or more, while road transport dominates for distances below that. Rail transport handles a small share of freight in the EU. SSS in the Baltic region is expected to grow as road conditions have in the meantime deteriorated.

Ng (2009) examined whether SSS-EU will be able to compete with other means of transport focusing on Baltic region. His findings suggested that SSS in the Baltic region was inefficient. Ng concluded that, for containerized general cargo in North Europe and in the Baltic, road transport was a superior transport mode in inland regions, as well as in Poland, Ukraine and Southern Lithuania. Among ports, Riga was found to be a genuine SSS port and its potential is partly determined by geography and partly by achieving rates of 30 containers per hour.

Medda and Trujillo (2010) found that road transport met the needs of a modern economy in such activities as global sourcing, just-in-time delivery and a fragmented production chain. However, road transport created congestion, which, in turn, threatened road transport and the growth of the European economy. The key-policy question is whether SSS can alleviate traffic congestion and enhance economic development. SSS-EU offers higher fuel economy, lower emissions of harmful pollutants and is the most sustainable and economically competitive mode of transport. In order for SSS-EU to substitute road transport, it must achieve the following targets by offering (1) lower cost and/or transport time, (2) door-to-door service, (3) better ports[4] (plus telematics and control systems for cargo handling), (4) high-performance corridors between ports, (5) internalization of external costs for at least sea and road, (6) legislation for a congestion fee in roads, (7) fiscal measures promoting SSS-EU, (8) initiatives such as 'Marco Polo' and 'Eco-bonus',

---

3. 'On ports and maritime infrastructures'.
4. More than 1000 ports in the EU handled 3.5 billion tons p.a. and 350 million passengers in 2003, but only 9 had ISO 9000 (Pantouvakis & Dimas, 2010).

(9) *the necessary intermodal capacity and logistics* and (10) proper legislation and management of SSS-EU.

13.3. European Short Sea Shipping and its Importance for the EU

The EU continued to sponsor SSS-EU after 1992 when PACT[5] project (1992–2000) was replaced by the 'Marco Polo Project', in an effort to boost inter-modality. To facilitate SSS, the EU established 16 national promotion SSS centres, which collected data, reduced paperwork and enhanced port infrastructure, between 2003 and 2006. In 2004, 'Marco Polo II'[6] extended this work to promote the 'MoS' in four European regions (2007–2013). This policy has also developed to include countries bordering with EU, in an effort to shift cargo from road to sea. The next project, which was the 'CREATE3S' paid attention to the development of a standardized SSS vessel capable of fast loading/unloading to minimize port time.

In 2009, EU confirmed its support for SSS, and stated that it is expected for SSS to grow by 2018.[7] To this end, the EU will (1) help to make SSS more attractive, (2) prepare a sea space without any barriers, (3) maintain a port policy, as it did since 2007, (4) focus on the trans-European transport networks and (5) seek compliance with environmental regulations in any port development. This is the European strategy, requiring compliance also with the environmental code of the European Sea Ports Organization (ESPO). A third version of this code is expected at the end of 2011.

SSS-EU can be defined as shipping that deals with the movement of cargo and passengers by sea, between ports situated in 'geographical Europe', or 'between those ports situated in non-European countries, having a coastline on the enclosed seas bordering Europe' (Medda & Trujillo, 2010). SSS can be further distinguished from deep-sea shipping (DSS), whenever an *ocean* is crossed. Geographically, the SSS-EU fleet connects 14 important areas in 6 geographical groups: (1) North Sea/NE Baltic, West and East-Kattegat/Baltic entrance, (2) Ireland/UK West, UK East, Channel UK and Channel mainland, (3) Atlantic, (4) West Mediterranean (Med) France-Italy and Spain, (5) West Med Adriatic and (6) Black Sea (West). The Atlantic and the Black Sea account for relatively little traffic at the moment.

Four hundred and forty-eight million tons of goods were transported through the 260 ports by 'deep-sea' and 'short-sea' RoRo ships in Europe in 2006 (EUROSTAT, 2007). The EU RoRo market consists of the RoRo[8] and RoPax[9] vessels and the

---

5. 'Pilot action for combined transport'.
6. COM 478/14-07-2004 final.
7. 'Strategic goals and recommendations for the EU's maritime transport policy until 2018'.
8. Ships receiving cars and passengers in/out 'on wheels'; designed for passengers/tourists wishing to have their car at destination, as well as door-to-door transport of freight loaded on trucks.
9. Ropax is a ferry offering sufficient freight trailer capacity, and as a result a lower passenger and cabin space.

feeder services. These ships, depending on their size (around 10,000 gt), belong to SSS. By the same token, these belong to the spoke length of the logistics system. In the current economic crisis, ferries now prefer freight to passengers, with the exception of the Sweden–Finland connection and cruise ferry activity (Notteboom, 2009). The main markets are the English Channel, Baltic and Mediterranean in a North–South pattern (N. Italy–Sicily; Italy–Greece; France–Corsica–N. Africa).

In 2009, a substantial part of SSS-EU involved box traffic, which was transhipped. Transhipment is a dominant factor in Mediterranean ports, for it constitutes 85–95% of all traffic. Transhipment is the other name for spoke traffic in the logistics network.

13.4. European Hubs

Worth noting for our further discussion to have it in the back of our mind is what Notteboom (2011) argued about the Anglo-Saxon and Asian perspectives on ports. The Anglo-Saxon view is that the criteria of the investors have precedence over those of the community, and a port should be self-sufficient. The Asian view is that the ports are facilitators of the economy and stimulate exports, and thus the community's criteria take precedence over those of the terminal operators. The continental European perspective, as described by Bennathan and Walters (1979), is closer to the Asian view, and considers ports to be part of the social infrastructure, and that a port should be assessed in terms of its contribution to the development of its region.

One of the main characteristics of Europe is its extensive coastline, ranging from the Baltic to the Mediterranean and Black Seas. This European port system appears naturally heterogeneous, having all sizes of ports, servicing specific hinterlands, various types of goods and of different quality due to different locations. Moreover, Europe is one of the world's main import and export market, where in 2008 received 91 million TEUs in its 130 container ports (Notteboom, 2009).

Freight traffic in the top 27 ports is shown in Figure 13.1. All European ports together handled 3.8 billion tons in 2008. This has an increase of 14.5% since 2003. The top 20 had a 20% increase since 2002. In particular, EU and Norway transported 3.21 billion tons in 2008, while only 6 countries[10] contributed to a total of 82% of this, or 3 billion tons.

EU hubs can be classified into four main categories according to their demand: (1) pure transhipment hubs: Gioia Tauro, Marsaxlokk and Algeciras, (2) pure gateways: Genoa and Barcelona, (3) dominant gateways/transhipment centres: Hamburg, Rotterdam, Le Havre and Antwerp and (4) stand-alone gateways: Marseille, Liverpool, Bilbao, Naples, Piraeus, Thessaloniki, Malaga and Klaipeda. A total of more than 3,359,000 TEU was serviced by these last eight ports in 2007.

---

10. The Netherlands 17.3%, UK 16.3%, Italy 14.5%, Spain 12.8, France 10.7% and Germany 10.2%.

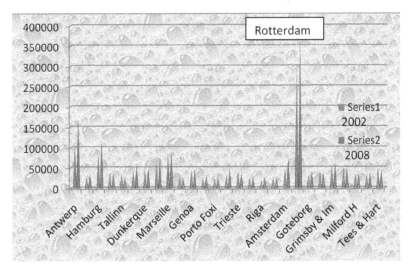

Figure 13.1: Freight Traffic of the Top EU-SSS Ports between 2002 and 2008
(in 1000 tons)
Source: EUROSTAT 07/10/2010 htpp://appsso.eurostat.ec.europa.eu/nui/show.doa
sic=true Ports not shown by name are: Zeebrugge, Wilhelmshaven, Algeciras,
Le Havre, Augusta, G. Tauro, Taranto, Venice, Klaipeda, Rotterdam (top), Forth,
London and Southampton.

In general, there has been a consistent growth in container traffic since 1985
(from about 7% in 1985–1995 to 10.5% in 2005–2007), with half of all boxes to
have landed in the Hamburg-Le Havre region ('the North'). Between 1980 and
2000, Mediterranean ports ('the South') grew faster than the North, due to
transhipment. This is the most perfect manifestation of the spoke structure
mentioned above. Between 2000 and 2010, the ports in the United Kingdom and
Mediterranean experienced a fall, while the Baltic and Black Sea emerged stronger.
The emergent rise of Baltic and Black Sea ports, which is due to relocation of
industry from 'Western Europe' to 'East Europe', means that the situation of
SSS-EU will deteriorate overall as a dominance of the hub concept prevails over
the spoke.

As shown in Figure 13.2, the RoRo traffic of the 448 million tons in 2006 was
distributed almost equally between only four port areas. Cargo concentration
counted in ports (HH-index/normalized) found high (>0.18). The 15 top EU box
ports share 69% (or 63 million TEUs) of the cargo volume. Despite the dominance
of Rotterdam in 2008, Hamburg and Antwerp remained competitive in 'North'.
In 2006, the RoRo ports in United Kingdom and Ireland handled a quarter of all
cargo or 114 million tons. Baltic was a larger market, with 125 million tons, and this
is where there needs to be increased effort to ensure the success of SSS-EU.

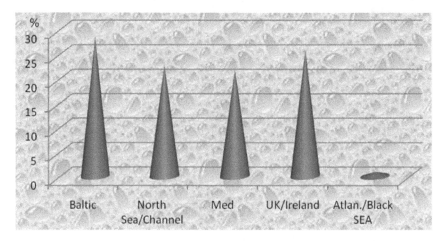

Figure 13.2: Areas of RoRo Traffic in 2006 in the EU

Economies of port density[11] (EPD) in box traffic occur if there are cost savings accruing to carriers from the heavy load placed on one destination port. In Europe, 12 large container ports serve all EU hinterlands (Notteboom, 2009) with 65.2 million TEU out of 91 (72%). This trend will be intensified in future, making large ports larger as economies of density derived from economies of scale on each route encourage box carriers to concentrate further.

It is thus our estimation that hubs will diminish in number during crisis years in the EU and given the relocation of industry noted below, as well as the aggressive marketing of ports in the North, road transport will gain market share at the expense of SSS. As mentioned above, there is no doubt that whatever activity or sector we examine, its sustainability matters first. We will next examine this issue.

13.5. The Issue of Sustainable Transport in EU

Since the EU has extended to 27 countries, transport of goods across Europe has grown dramatically with a substantial part of that growth taking place in road transport. In 2008, there were 47 million goods vehicles on European roads, an increase of 8 million since 2000. Europe has reached a state of transport hypertrophy, where the external costs of transport, in the cost of accidents, pollution, emission of greenhouse gases and degradation of the environment, exceed the contribution that transport makes to the economy (Hoyos, 2009). In 2000, the external costs of transport were 7.3% of GDP, or €650 billion per year. Of that total, the external

---

11. These are economies of scale along a given route. Average cost falls as traffic volume on the route increases. This traffic is measured as revenue-TEU miles. This is the number of TEUs on the route times the number of miles (Besanko, Dranove, Shanley, & Schaefer, 2010, p. 48).

costs related to the transport modes of sea and rail transport are comparatively low. Nash, Sansom, and Still (2001) argued that if prices are equal to marginal social costs, then socially optimal, fair and efficient pricing could result in a shift to a more environmentally friendly model of transport, and with more goods transported by rail and sea. The International Maritime Organization (IMO) suggested in 2008 that greenhouse gases should be reduced by between 50% and 85% by 2050 to limit the rise in global temperature to 2 °C. Various methods have been suggested to reduce maritime emissions (Eide, Endresen, Skjong, Longva, & Alvik, 2009; Eide, Longva, Hoffmann, Endresen, & Dalsoren, 2011; Longva, Eide, & Skjong, 2010; Tzannatos, 2010a). Reducing the speed of ships would reduce emissions, but this would result in a loss of shipping capacity. There is an urgent need to balance sustainable development of the society and firm performance.

Sustainable mobility is the process of reducing the irreversible environmental degradation produced by transport, while at the same time satisfying the social need for accessibility. In order to achieve sustainable mobility, a holistic approach has to be taken to mitigate environmental damage. A holistic approach to sustainable mobility must achieve four goals: (1) reduce the need for transport, (2) rebalance the modal allocation towards ship and train, (3) improve the eco-efficiency of trips and (4) match land use to transport policy through land planning, industrial and energy policies (Hoyos, 2009). These four goals indicate the importance of a holistic and cross-disciplinary analysis, where policies that affect mobility are all taken into account.

13.6.   The Relocation of Industry in EU

There is a trend for industry to get moved from 'Central Europe' to 'Central and East Europe (CEE)'. This development will modify the traffic in the established hubs and it will affect spokes as well. We may underline in this respect that European power plants and steel mills are located in or near ports (Notteboom, 2009), as can be seen in the case of the ArcelorMittal Steel Group. Maritime flat carbon steel mills are in the ports of Dunkirk, Ghent, Fos, Gijon and Bremen. Other plants are less than 100 km from major import ports. Europe still depends on coal for electricity production, and on iron ore. The liquid sector (with 116 refineries or an 18% share in the world in 2007) is also located close to seaports with 1.59 billion tons of traffic, dominated by Rotterdam. This port is also well connected with the major petrochemical clusters (4 world-scale oil refineries) and 40 chemical and petrochemical companies. In addition, Antwerp supplies five refineries by pipeline. The ports of Marseilles, Le Havre, Wilhelmshaven, Tees and Hartlepool, Milford Haven, Forth, Southampton, Trieste and Augusta are also involved. The ports in the United Kingdom and Norway are influenced by the North Sea oil fields, as is well known.

Theory of location economics suggests that the existence of a port attracts industry. Many of Europe's largest cities benefited from the presence of a good harbour or of access to a major waterway (Fujita, Krugman, & Venables, 1999).

Ports and transportation hubs become urban centres, or big cities become ports. As we have implicitly argued there is a 'North–East port war' and it will be interesting to see who will win. The outcome of this war will have repercussions on the logistics pattern known so far.

Maritime logistics is an issue that has dominated literature (Nam & Song, 2011, p. 270) and it requires user's satisfaction/requirements which is the door-to-door service. This idea is incorporated into the MoS, to which we come next.

13.7.   The Motorways of the Sea (MoS)

Road freight in the EU is forecast to grow by about 60% by 2013 to 20.5 billion ton-km per year, with accidents, congestion, unreliability in the supply chain and logistics processes and environmental damage increasing proportionately (Baird, 2007). It is suggested that there should be MoS as an alternative to long-distance road transport. SSS-EU has been promoted by the EU Commission since 1992, as noted above. In 2004, the Commission realized that SSS-EU needed a further boost.[12] SSS-EU was considered to be the only transport mode that could cope with rapid economic growth. Moreover, SSS-EU could help the modal shift from road, reduce environmental damage and foster cohesion. This may in part be due to the expansion of EU to island countries (Malta, Cyprus, and UK and Ireland before them) and to peninsular countries — a characteristic of almost all EU nations and Greece. SSS flows are recognized to form an indispensable and growing segment in the connectivity between European regions.

The new term, the MoS, was introduced (Baird, 2007) to emphasize door-to-door logistics chains for SSS-EU and also to specify origins destinations. Europe has the advantage of being surrounded by sea (over two-thirds of borders are coastal) on three sides being a peninsula, and by two oceans (Arctic and Atlantic). Industries, as well as big cities and civic centres, are never more than 200 km from the coast. As a result, 90% of cargo to Europe comes by sea. More specifically, and in an effort to cultivate the metaphor between road highways and SSS-EU routes, the EU designated four MoS or seaways. The four EU motorways are illustrated in Figure 13.3.

In 2004, the EU set itself the target of achieving: (1) a modal shift of cargo from road to sea, (2) reduced barriers to intermodal transportation, (3) door-to-door transport, (4) reduced demand for freight transport and (5) enhanced knowledge of the functioning of the whole logistics sector. This means that SSS-EU (Baird, 2007) must offer the same overall service packages as road transport in the long-distance road haulage sector. Truckers now use articulated vehicles to carry the majority of freight. To promote SSS-EU, Baird (2007) argued that (a) road tolls, such as those

---

12. COM, 2004, 453 and 478.

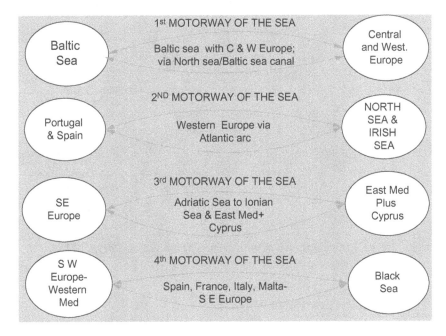

Figure 13.3: The Four MoS

used in Italy, can play a partial role in promoting SSS, (b) a sea route can offer a distance advantage over road (as in Genoa-Palermo, Genoa-Barcelona), (c) modern ship technology (like fast-conventional RoRo/Ropax ferries) can increase payloads and (d) speeds of 22 knots or above are required, although present high oil prices militate against this, with multiple trailer decks (i.e. 300 or more trailers per ship) and on-board passengers. There are also examples of bad practice in Scotland and Sweden. The EU aims: (1) to be fully integrated in the intermodal door-to-door supply chain, (2) to modernize the image of SSS, (3) to abandon complex administrative procedures and (4) to promote high port efficiency. On the other hand, ESPO (2011) argued that the MoS should be reviewed because the policy will not be successful if (1) it distorts of competition, (2) is unnecessarily complex, (3) is fragmented and (4) leads to a lack of synergy. ESPO argues that the MoS should not be part of the port-to-port connections, but should be port-to-hinterland connections, and to avoid congestion.

The Marco Polo II target is to shift more than 140 billion ton-km of freight off the road (i.e. 7 million truck journeys of 1000 km) and to reduce CO_2 emissions by 8400 million kilograms or €5 billion external benefits. These targets are across the 25 members of the EU together with the candidates for EU enlargement. To avoid traffic congestion in the MoS, there needs to be increased infrastructure funding from the private sector. The MoS are expected to offer high-quality logistics services based on SSS-EU transport, which will be comparable with road motorways.

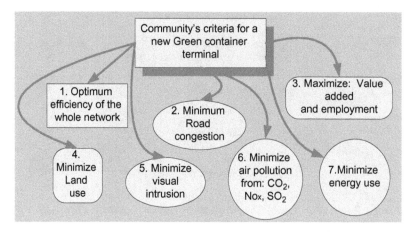

Figure 13.4: Community Requirements for a Green Port, 2011
Source: inspired by Notteboom (2011).

13.8.   Developing Green Ports in the EU

In order to develop a green port, the criteria that a community places now on a new terminal are shown in Figure 13.4, which captures all the essential properties of a modern port from an economic and environmental point of view. This can also be used as a yardstick for old ports, as it indicates the competitive advantage that new, green ports will have in future. Old ports should also meet these standards to maintain inter-port competition (with the possible exception of number 5, which is a historical event). This model lacks a profit objective (or a break-even objective).

In the EU, ESPO deals with Eco-ports. To date, the ports have become aware of the new requirements and now share knowledge and have implemented environmental management systems (EMS). European ports have set priorities (ESPO Annual Report[13]) on such green topics as (1) noise, (2) air quality, (3) waste management, (4) disposal due to dredging, (5) stakeholder's support to develop green ports, (6) energy saving, (7) land use and water treatment due to port expansion and (8) climate change.

ESPO plans to speed up its cooperation with Eco-ports and to manage this brand and network and to integrate them in it. ESPO will provide a 'self-diagnostic method (SDM)' and a port environmental review system. The Eco-Ports label will be given only if a port submits an SDM. Workshops will be organized for ports by ESPO.[14] Climate change is monitored by the World Port Climate Initiative (WPCI). WPCI works on the environmental ship index (ESI). This is a voluntary system. It is hoped that a database and an ESI website will be soon prepared by the International Association of Ports and Harbours (IAPH). Similarly, the issues of carbon footprint

---

13. ESPO's annual report 2009–2010/sustainable development.
14. One took place in March 2010 in Kotka (Finland).

and onshore power supply are matters of concern to ESPO. ESPO and the European Countries Ship-Owners Association (ECSA) are attempting to persuade the EU Commission that there should be a VAT exemption for electricity provided through onshore power supply systems.

The IMO has decided that, by 2015, the sulphur content of marine fuel should be reduced to 0.1% in certain designated sulphur emission control areas (SECAs). This created concerns, especially in Baltic ports. There are also EU Commission guidelines on the application of the Birds, Habitats and Water Framework which will be published at the end of 2011. The Commission is also working actively in the area of Maritime Spatial Planning for the rational and sustainable use and management of European seas.

ESPO is now revising its Environmental Code of Practice and a new edition at the end of 2011 will guide port authorities on how to deal with environmental issues and improve sustainability. One hundred and fifty-six ports contribute to the Eco-ports Foundation, many of them involved in SSS. The ports of seven countries that dominate in number of ports (70.5%) are the United Kingdom, with 34 ports (22%); Denmark, 20 ports (13%); Spain, 17 ports (11%); Italy, 11 ports (7%); France, 10 ports (6.4%); Sweden, 9 ports (5.8%) and Finland, 9 ports (5.8%).

The procedure to become a green port/Eco-port is to submit an SDM, which involves preparing a checklist to assemble facts and figures for the area of the port. It involves a six-step approach for Port Environmental Management (PEP) as follows: (1) identify the port's 10 top environmental risks, (2) plan improvements/investment for the identified priorities, (3) carry out plans to improve the port's environment, (4) monitor progress on PEP, (5) publish a periodic report to stakeholders and (6) apply for certification. An Eco-port needs to prepare a database of best practice, conferences and workshops, training, collaborative developments and implementation projects. It must also set uniform key performance indicators, enabling benchmarking in energy use, water quality and noise. The Eco-port Environmental Certificate will be reviewed by Lloyd's Register.

Ports in the United States have promoted a green image since 2005. A Green Image Port is one that cares for the following aspects: (1) sustainability, (2) air, (3) water, (4) wildlife, (5) soils and sediments and (6) the community around the port. The environment has become an element in port economics, as manifested by the location criteria used very recently in the construction of a new container port mentioned above (Diagram 4). The various stresses and burdens on the environment can now be measured (Eide et al., 2009, 2011; Psaraftis & Kontovas, 2009; Tzannatos, 2010a, 2010b). Ports have to fulfil their sustainability obligation. The development of a sustainable transport system is expected to protect the environment, delivering it intact to future generations.

13.9. Conclusions

The EU has had a constant vision of European shipping since 1992. This vision has been supported by the PACT project (1992–2000), the Marco Polo Projects I and II

(2003–2013) boosting inter-modality and CREATE3S for the SSS standardized vessel. This shipping, serving an EU of 27 nations, or over 40% of internal traffic, is the only hope for the EU to save the roads from congestion, given the ever increasing trade created. The ship types that will be increasingly important in these new logistics patterns are the RoRo, RoPax and Feeders, moving 448 million tons of trade over 260 ports. Between 1980 and 2000, the South grew faster than that in the North, due to transhipment, but their performance was worse between 2000 and 2010.

The vision, however, remains valid and beyond 2011, to 2018, reinforced by the concept of the four MoS. Though the European shipping sector is undefined so far, this chapter assumed that ships of round 10,000 Gt belong to this sector. The chapter clearly discussed the spoke length of container transport, or the distance travelled by feeder shipping in large hubs like Algeciras, Rotterdam, Antwerp, Hamburg, Marsaxlokk and Le Havre.

The statistics show that the 2008 crisis compelled ships to concentrate on fewer hubs based on economies of density, and thus less European shipping activity, though hopes are now high for the development of the Baltic.

Most analysts are in favour of SSS-EU and its promotion. A minority specify detailed pre-conditions under which this can be successful. However, it seems that the policy-makers have not provided suitable incentives, and SSS-EU ports have not exerted themselves so far. The long desired modal shift has not been achieved. This issue depends on the speed of adaptation of SSS-EU to the model that is desired by the EU community.

Despite the failure of the undertaking to establish the main logistics arms in SSS, which is sea door-to-door transportation, this chapter identified recent developments that may prolong the dominance of road transport. The traffic will land first at certain of the 130 main Western European container hubs (91 million TEUs in 2006), but part of it will land in CEE. This chapter shows the West–East inter-port competition. Sea transhipment will probably be replaced by road transhipment.

Recently, 156 European ports have prepared to gain the title of Eco-port. But with green ships and green ports, and lower Green House Gasses (GHG) emissions, sea transport will most probably win in the end. The EU has expanded over the years from 10 member countries to 27. Europe envisaged SSS-EU being useful in 1992 and in 1995. Given the expansion of trade stimulated by removing tariff barriers, following the institution of the Single Market, and the limited capacity of the roads, the natural way out of this impasse would be SSS. Europe is one corner of the world trade triangle (United States–China–Europe). Moreover, transport mobility was one of the dreams of those who created the Single Market. Given the impact of congestion on the roads, SSS-EU is a worthwhile alternative. This is the dominant reason for supporting the promotion of SSS-EU.

The relocation of industry is expected to play a role in expanded Europe. While this is necessary, it is not a sufficient condition for ports in CEE to grow because aggressive ports in Western Europe get a share of this traffic. A 'West–East War' has started. This traffic must be moved by environmentally friendly means, such as rail and/or SSS-EU. However, the hegemony of ports in the extended Rhine–Scheldt delta and Helgoland bay (the 'North') with 57.4% share in 2008 is undisputable. Here the "North–South War" continues.

Meanwhile, SSS-EU blossoms when plenty of feeder services are established within the general box transportation, as in the Mediterranean. This depends on carriers' policies, however, and whether they wish to perform direct calls with no further sea transhipment. Ownership of certain terminals creates EPD. The trend, however, in 2008 was towards direct calls and sea feeders were not used, but this may be an ephemeral phenomenon due to current crisis in Europe.

Ports are 'gates of externalities' and 'doors of sustainability'. They welcome sea transport vessels, carrying vital cargoes into a nation's area or a port's hinterland. Vessels pollute a port's air and water (estimated at 3% of global CO_2 emissions in 2008). Moreover, ports are (or must be) the end destination of other means of transport like rail, trucks, air (and inland waterways/barges). All means of transport pollute and create congestion, but congestion, being principally a problem created by trucks in the road networks of the EU, is the target of EU maritime policy.

The metaphor of the MoS is useful in cultivating the idea in the mind of users that road and sea are equivalent alternatives (perfect psychological substitutability), but this is hardly sufficient for the policy to be successful. The seaways, as they are called in United States, the MoS, as they are called in Europe, are not free, as EU policy-makers seem to think, but need a share of public investment. The sea needs infrastructure, though it seems to have enough space to expand. Ports, however, often cannot expand, except towards sea, as they are restricted by their cities. Ships' journeys, to be equivalent to road journeys, must spend the same time at sea and in port, as trucks spend on the roads, in checkpoints and at traffic lights. This obviously is not compatible with any bureaucratic customs procedures and endless paperwork in ports. For SSS-EU to take cargo off the road it must achieve the same quality and timely procedures as far as customs and paperwork/bureaucracy and information flow (including electronic devices) are concerned, as well as the satisfaction of user in a door-to-door and just-in-time operation.

Acknowledgements

This research was supported in part by The Hong Kong Polytechnic University under grant number J-BB7L. The authors would like to thank our research assistant, Mr Michael Ng, for his able assistance in the development of this chapter. Thanks are also due to the editor, Prof. Song, Dong-Wook, for his valuable comments.

References

Baird, A. J. (2007). The economics of motorways of the sea. *Maritime Policy and Management*, *34*(4), 287–310.

Bennathan, E., & Walters, A. A. (1979). *Port pricing and investment policy for developing countries*. Oxford, UK: Oxford University Press.

Besanko, D., Dranove, D., Shanley, M., & Schaefer, S. (2010). Economics of Strategy (5th ed.). New York, USA: Wiley. International Student edition. ISBN 978-0-470-484838.

Eide, M. S., Endresen, O., Skjong, R., Longva, T., & Alvik, S. (2009). Cost-effectiveness assessment of CO_2 reducing measures in shipping. *Maritime Policy and Management, 36*(4), 367–384.

Eide, M. S., Longva, T., Hoffmann, P., Endresen, O., & Dalsoren, S. B. (2011). Future cost scenarios for reduction of ship CO emissions. *Maritime Policy and Management, 38*(1), 11–37.

ESPO. (2011). *Annual report 2009–2010.* Retrieved from http://www.espo.be/images/stories/Publications/annual_reports/annualreport2010.pdf. Accessed on 12 July 2011.

EUROSTAT. (2007). *European transport statistics.* Retrieved from http://appsso.eurostat.ec.europa.eu

Fujita, M., Krugman, P., & Venables, A. J. (1999). *The spatial economy: Cities, regions, and international trade* (ISBN 978-0-262-56147-1). Cambridge, MA: The MIT Press.

Hoyos, D. (2009). Towards an operational concept of sustainable mobility. *International Journal of Sustainable Development Planning, 4*(2), 158–173.

Li, L. (2007). *Supply chain management: Concepts, techniques and practices enhancing value through collaboration.* Singapore: World Scientific.

Longva, T., Eide, M. S., & Skjong, R. (2010). Determining a required energy efficiency design index level for new ships based on a cost-effectiveness criterion. *Maritime Policy and Management, 37*(2), 129–143.

Medda, F., & Trujillo, L. (2010). Short-sea shipping: An analysis of its determinants. *Maritime Policy and Management, 37*(3), 285–303.

Min, H., & Galle, W. P. (2006). A US survey on green purchasing. *International Journal of Purchasing and Materials Management, 33*(3), 10–18.

Nam, H. S., & Song, D. W. (2011). Defining maritime logistics hub and its implication for container port. *Maritime Policy and Management, 38*(3), 269–292.

Nash, C., Sansom, T., & Still, B. (2001). Modifying transport prices to internalize externalities: Evidence from European case studies. *Regional Science and Urban Economics, 31*, 413–431.

Ng, A. K. Y. (2009). Competitiveness of short sea shipping and the role of port: The case of North Europe. *Maritime Policy and Management, 36*(4), 337–352.

Notteboom, T. (2009). *Economic analysis of the European seaport system.* 14th May report for ESPO, p 64. Retrieved from http://www.espo.be/images/stories/Publications/studies_reports_surveys/ITMMAEconomicAnalysisoftheEuropeanPortSystem2009. Accessed on 12 July 2011.

Notteboom, T. (2011). An application of multi-criteria analysis to the location of a container hub port in South Africa. *Maritime Policy and Management, 38*(1), 51–79.

Paixao, A. C., & Marlow, P. B. (2001). A review of the European Union shipping policy. *Maritime Policy and Management, 28*(2), 187–198.

Paixao, A. C., & Marlow, P. B. (2002). Strengths and weaknesses of short sea shipping. *Marine Policy, 26*(3), 167–178.

Paixao, A. C., & Marlow, P. B. (2005). The competitiveness of short sea shipping in multimodal logistics supply chains: Service attributes. *Maritime Policy and Management, 32*(4), 363–382.

Pantouvakis, A., & Dimas, A. (2010). Does ISO 9000 series certification matter for the financial performance of ports? Some preliminary findings from Europe. *Maritime Policy and Management, 37*(5), 505–522.

Perakis, A. N., & Denisis, A. (2008). A survey of short sea shipping and its prospects in the USA. *Maritime Policy and Management, 35*(6), 591–614.

Psaraftis, H. N., & Kontovas, C. A. (2009). A web-based open emissions calculator. *International Journal of Ocean Systems Management, 1*(2), 188–199.

Song, D.-W., & Panayides, P. M. (2008). Global supply chain and port/terminal: Integration and competitiveness. *Maritime Policy and Management, 35*(1), 73–87.

Trujillo, L., & Tovar, B. (2007). The European port industry: An analysis of its economic efficiency. *Maritime Economics & Logistics, 9*(2), 148–171.

Tzannatos, E. (2010a). Cost assessment of ship emission reduction methods at berth: The case of the Port of Piraeus, Greece. *Maritime Policy and Management, 37*(4), 427–445.

Tzannatos, E. (2010b). Costs and benefits of reducing SO_2 emissions from shipping in the Greek seas. *Maritime Economics & Logistics, 12*(3), 280–294.

Chapter 14

Assessing the Environmental Impact
of Maritime Operations in Ports:
A Systems Approach

John Dinwoodie, Sarah Tuck and Harriet Knowles

Abstract

This chapter presents a framework which is accessible to port authorities to assess the potential environmental impact of maritime operations. Pursuant on globalisation, increased numbers of ship movements have generated more frequent routine maritime operations in ports but few formal approaches exist for assessing their environmental impact, which potentially could be significant. In a novel framing of environmental assessment a business process modelling technique is deployed in a systems approach which highlights inputs, service processes and outputs. In an initial focus, primary processes at strategic level are defined which affect the environmental assessment of present and future operations and their potential impacts. Later, tactical service processes define the integrity of processes that guarantee service level and quality. Finally, outputs are defined by operational processes. The contribution of applying the systems approach to plan more sustainable maritime operations is assessed in a case study of Falmouth Harbour Commissioners (FHC) which regulates much of Falmouth Harbour and hosts the UK's largest offshore marine bunkering operation. Following EU designation of a North Sea Sulfur Oxide Emissions Control Areas (SECA) Falmouth recently recorded a significant rise in the number of vessels calling, and volume of fuel sold as more passing vessels take onboard low-sulfur fuel. The systems approach which empowers FHC to mitigate potential risks and assess development proposals pro-actively is easily transferable to other ports.

Keywords: Port management; maritime operations; systems approach; environmental management; sustainable port development; port logistics

Maritime Logistics: Contemporary Issues
Copyright © 2012 by Emerald Group Publishing Limited
All rights of reproduction in any form reserved
ISBN: 978-1-78052-340-8

14.1. Introduction: Maritime Operations in Ports

As ports offer more value adding logistics services within integrated logistics networks (Notteboom & Rodrigue, 2005), international supply chains have dramatically increased the range and complexity of maritime operations undertaken in them. As the risk of adverse environmental impacts has burgeoned, so have the regulatory framework required to manage them, stakeholder pressures and administrative burdens on port authorities to ensure compliance. To assist them, this chapter proposes and applies a system's framework within which to plan assessment of the potential environmental impact of routine maritime operations which are subject to specialist regulations, conventions and guidelines and environmental legislation which guides port authorities.

Maritime operations embrace multifarious routine procedures which a ship must undergo whilst in port to operate effectively including marine fuel bunkering, ballast water exchange and anchoring. Each operation is guided by specialist regulations, conventions and guidelines and may *inter alia* impact on environmental aspects including emissions to air, soil and sediments, discharges to water, noise, waste production, changes in terrestrial habitats and marine ecosystems, odour, resource consumption and port development on land or sea (Darbra, Ronza, Stojanovic, Wooldridge, & Casal, 2005). Research to assess the potential environmental impacts of bunkering operations has analysed the risks of oil spills (Edoho, 2008) and petroleum waste management and site remediation policies (Qin, Huang, & He, 2009) and penalties to deter pollution risks (Weber & Crew, 2000). Anchoring may impact the seabed and ballast water exchange biodiversity (Fernandez, 2008). Port authorities urgently require practical support to assist them to discharge their responsibilities.

This chapter reviews environmental management in ports including extant tools and UK practice. A methodology section introduces the systems approach and an environmentally sensitive case context of Falmouth Harbour where it is applied to offshore marine bunkering operations. Processes at strategic, tactical and operational level are analysed before the usefulness of the systems approach is appraised.

14.2. Environmental Management in Ports

14.2.1. Some Extant Tools to Assist Environmental Management in Ports

Intra-firm development of environmental awareness is a process which involves understanding of corporate environmental impacts and management of them (Hannon & Atherton, 1998). At any one time, individual organisations are at different stages of both. Some early work investigated environmental management practice in ports, aiming to develop effective Environmental Management Systems (EMS) to assist ports to manage environmental risks successfully and improve their performance. A case study of three Fal estuary ports which established a joint EMS changed managers' awareness (Paipai, 1999, p. 45). Later, ongoing pursuit of continuous improvement engendered new approaches in which ports have shifted from investigating the need for environmental management to deploying tools and methodologies to encourage better performance, such as those embodied in the EcoPorts project (EcoPorts, 2006).

ISO14001 (Saengsupavanich, Coowanitwong, Gallardo, & Lertsuchatavanich, 2009) promotes continual improvements by encouraging EMS adoption and implementation. These systems and standards assist firms to systematically develop a formalised management process, and evaluate the effectiveness of their activities, operations, products and services, but require specialist resources and sustained involvement. Continuous monitoring improves understanding and assists risk management, supported by appropriate data collection techniques and record keeping (Darbra, Pittam, Royston, Darbra, & Journee, 2009). Multi-site applications of standardised procedures within Associated British Ports which identify environmental issues and their associated risks before ranking each by significance, assessing the probability of occurrence and magnitude of consequences (Darbra et al., 2005, p. 867) offer some scale economies.

14.2.2. EcoPorts Initiatives

The EcoPorts Foundation aims to help develop practical solutions for ports seeking to improve their environmental performance and to share knowledge and expertise 'to create a level playing field by limiting poor environmental practice as a competitive factor between port administrations' (ESPO, 2003, p. 8). For larger ports initiatives demonstrate a capability to self-regulate and EcoPorts offers an intermediary between the EU and its members on environmental issues, but not for non-members. EcoPorts tools assist ports to develop an Environmental Management and Information System to plan and assess environmental issues, monitor compliance and assess impacts. They include:

- Self Diagnosis Method (SDM). At entry-level tool to identify environmental risks and establish priorities for action and compliance (Darbra, Ronza, Casal, Stojanovic, & Wooldridge, 2004). A port manager can quickly complete a simple checklist, pay a fee, receive benchmark guidance on the port's environmental performance, an analysis report showing the port's strengths, weaknesses, opportunities and threats and strategic advice. However, because the analysis is exogenous the port manager's understanding, awareness and commitment may remain limited.
- Port Environmental Review System (PERS). Over time, updated past comparisons of performance allow for progress reports to build evidence of the effectiveness of a port's environmental management policies. PERS assists ports to implement an EMS through developing various components of it. Measurement of environmental performance is possible through an independent review which consists of guidelines and example documents, but this requires time, incurs costs and being external, may limit internal commitment to its findings.

- Strategic Overview of Environmental Aspects (SOSEA). SOSEA aims to identify 'significant' environmental aspects which stem from operations and guides a port in gathering information to manage its liabilities and responsibilities (Darbra et al., 2005). This assists long-term environmental strategic development by highlighting the current situation and policies, thereby strategically increasing the port's environmental awareness. An initial SOSEA assessment proceeds by indicating whether each of the 12 environmental aspects applies to a range of listed activities which include bunkering. An aspect (such as discharges to water) is considered 'significant' if either, after the number of ticks has been summed for each aspect, the number against it exceeds half of the maximum number of ticks recorded for any aspect, or, if a breach of legislation is considered to be 'significant'. For each significant aspect, further questions then relate to how it is managed and what environmental actions have been taken (Darbra et al., 2005).

If a port attains ISO14001, additional demanding certification in the Eco-Management Scheme and Audit Scheme (EMAS; IEMA, 2010) requires preparation of an environmental review and environmental statement detailed in regulation EC1221/2009.

14.2.3. Practice in Europe's Largest Port Industry

A case application presented below is set within the UK, Europe's largest ports sector (Oxford Economics, 2009), comprised of 650 statutory harbour authority ports which typically handle 95% of national imports and exports by volume and 75% by value (Department for Transport, DfT, 2006, p. 1). The UK government seeks to promote high environmental standards and support sustainable port development (DfT, 2000) but not intervene in commercial activities. Port authorities have a statutory duty to meet social and environmental obligations while embedding corporate social responsibility (CSR) concepts in their management systems and undertaking routine operations and development projects commercially (Pettit, 2008). 'Environmental assessment' does not imply monetary or quantitative evaluation of potential impacts but experts may need to assess whether potential impacts are likely to be 'significant', depending on the scale of projects, local environmental sensitivity and complexity of impacts (Paipai, 1999). Port developments that generate environmental concern are subject to Environmental Impact Assessment (EIA) methodologies (Darbra et al., 2005) to assess the potential impact on marine and terrestrial habitats (UNESCAP, 2009). Where assessments identify adverse impacts, mitigation requires management plans to conserve and protect public access to features of natural beauty or historic interest. Public bodies and harbour authorities prepare these for Sites of Special Scientific Interest (SSSIs; DfT, 2000). A qualitative scoping study is required if developments will impact *inter alia* on biodiversity or water (DfT, 2002).

EC Directive 85/337 (later altered by EC97/11) advises ports, to conduct an environmental audit covering *inter alia*, handling and storage areas of prescribed materials, waste emissions, spoil disposal areas, fishing, wetlands and zones of specific scientific or cultural interest. This directive exhorts prioritisation of issues for environmental protection and compliance with conventions and codes covering marine pollution and dangerous goods. In the UK, environmental standards for port operations are notified to port authorities to ensure that standards, guidance and best practice are widely available and assist compliance (DfT, 2000). Environmental audits are discretionary, but port managers are liable for environmental damages with consequent punitive damages. Over time, port managers have influenced legislation through consultation and agreement which underpins guidelines and best practice, supported by requirements to protect and manage nationally important sites. Practitioners have contributed to benchmarks, initiatives, projects, management schemes, training, monitoring, research and collaborative involvement (Paipai, 1999) and the British Ports Association (BPA, 2009) Environmental Code of Practice (ECP) aimed to raise environmental awareness amongst port employees and users. Government intervention offers statistical information, general guidelines, control on the development planning process and rules for project appraisal and commercial independence (Gilman, 2003).

Understanding of the process whereby environmental awareness in ports is established and developed underpins practical development and adoption of environmental management procedures but alongside business process thinking, is rarely reported (Peris-Mora, Diez Orejas, Subirats, Ibanez, & Alvarez, 2005; Dinwoodie, Tuck, Knowles, Benhin, & Sansom, 2011). Consequently, many specialist tools remain accessible only to EcoPorts members or ports which possess sufficient resources to employ environmental experts. A recent survey of 100 UK ports (Royal Haskoning, 2009) reported ISO14001 certification in only 32, PERS certification in 24 and EMAS in 19. Initiatives are unlikely to have embraced many of the 500 UK ports not surveyed. A further 32% of sampled ports plan to outsource environmental management functions and 22% plan to recruit an environmental specialist. Relatively few port managers apparently own the process of environmental management.

14.3. Methodology

14.3.1. The Systems Approach

Twin traditions of science and management influence a system's approach to environmental management in ports. Concepts of General Systems Theory emanating from biology and the physical sciences quickly infiltrated management studies (e.g. Kast & Rosenzweig, 1972; Churchman, 1979), but applications of management systems to the management of scientific processes are sporadic (Buckley, 1968; Pidd, 2004). Recent applications of systems thinking in environmental management, typically context dependant, span environmental planning (Korhonen, 2007) and a framework for evaluating natural resource management policy initiatives (Bellamy, Walker, McDonald, & Syme, 2001). The latter typifies the approach, progressing through stages of issue characterisation, defining objectives, assumptions, evaluation criteria and methods, process of implementation, outcomes and case study applications.

Early literature relating a systems approach to organisational effectiveness is exemplified by a progression from problem conceptualisation through performance analysis to monitoring (Fox, 1974). A hierarchy of systems and subsystems, which are themselves intellectual constructs, is formulated during problem definition. After system components have been defined and flows and objectives identified, the impact of systematic interventions on total system performance indicators is analysed. Finally a monitoring process generates archives of measurements which record the operation and functioning of different types of systems. Recent applications have featured organisational effectiveness at seaports (Cetin & Cerit, 2010).

Systems applications in maritime business often conceptualise ports as open systems which interface with the complex dynamics of international trade, supply chain systems and technological change. A typical conceptual formulation defines a system comprised of:

- a holistic unit made up of components;
- flows between components and flows interacting with the system's environment, of mass, energy and information and
- the system's functional purpose.

The formulation is underpinned by Churchman's (1979) delineation of system objectives and performance measures; system resources; the system's environment; the activities, goals and performance of system components; and system management. Studies in management have identified concepts including hierarchy, inputs, outputs and transformation processes, chains of effect, relaxation time between action and effect, feedback both positive and negative, systems dynamics and cybernetic intervention, which have stimulated specialist studies or academic sub-disciplines (Pidd, 2004). Recent ports studies have attempted to define performance using measures of finance, efficiency or effectiveness (Yeo, Roe, & Dinwoodie, 2008; Yeo, Song, Roe, & Dinwoodie, 2010), or adopted a functionalist stance (Verhoeven, 2010). However, recent studies of environmental management and performance in ports have typically engaged either academic scientists or bespoke applications of tools available only within member-based organisations. A consequent practitioner vacuum invites development of a systematic management framework, accessible to all managers and ports. Concepts drawn from business systems engineering, described below, underpin such a framework.

14.3.2.   A Business Process Approach

To encourage local awareness and commitment to environmental management by port authorities requires a process which individual managers can initiate, undertake and own, which should be staged (Paipai, 1999). The systems approach commences by formulating strategy, progresses via the tactics required to establish processes and finally defines the tasks required to operate it. Because the environmental impacts of maritime operations extend beyond the immediate control of port authorities, a holistic approach is essential. To meet these criteria a systems approach was applied to assist observation, understanding and analysis of the issues involved.

Business systems engineering aims to understand, document, simplify and optimise processes and more specifically, process mapping focuses on the stages of understanding and documenting. Lagoudis, Lalwani, and Naim (2004, p. 58) defined a system as a 'group of interacting, interrelated or interdependent elements, forming a complex whole' and Parnaby's (1979) input–output process modelling technique aims to identify functional units and flows that define processes in a company by defining the problem, system boundaries, function and variable flows. The technique proceeds by identifying processes at a strategic level, which affect present and future operations and their potential impacts. Next, it defines service processes which are tactical, in which service level and quality are guaranteed through the integrity of processes. At output level, operational processes are defined. The levels also interact.

The systems approach aims to identify the inputs needed by a port authority to assess the environmental impact of maritime operations in the maritime environment, analyse the service processes that take place in everyday operations and determine the final result or output of these processes (Dinwoodie et al., 2011). Decisions are required at strategic, tactical and operational levels, representing system inputs, services and outputs (Table 14.1). At strategic level, decisions (S1–S7) incorporate overall determination of objectives. At tactical level (T1–T7) decisions

Table 14.1: Systems framework overview.

Strategic level		Tactical level		Operational level	
Input		Service processes		Output	
S1	Mission statement	T1	Local familiarisation	O1	Internal monitoring, reporting, archiving
S2	Physical conditions	T2	Operational conventions	O2	External communication, dissemination
S3	Governance issues	T3	Networking	O3	Recommendations
S4	Stakeholders	T4	Consultation	O4	Mitigations
S5	Local data	T5	Reviewing, monitoring	O5	Sustainability
S6	Management system	T6	Hire expertise	O6	Awareness
S7	Resource assessment	T7	Reporting		

required to achieve the overall objectives. The operational level (O1–O6) requires decisions which keep the system within constraint limits and in accord with objectives. This chapter reports application of the systems framework to offshore marine bunkering operations, a maritime operation with potentially devastating environmental impacts.

Direct comparison with existing tools is inappropriate because the systems approach focuses on processes needed for assessment at strategic, tactical and operational levels and some components may be revisited at different levels. Stakeholders for example are engaged as inputs (S4), processes (T1, T3 and T4) and outputs (O6) and communication comprises processes (T1, T3, T4 and T6), and outputs (O1, O2 and O6). Indicative mapping of levels (Tables 14.4–14.6) against the SDM (Darbra et al., 2004) and ISO14001 (ISO14000, 2009) reveals less emphasis on individual responsibilities or targets. This reflects the systems approach objective of identifying inputs required to assess potential environmental impacts, rather than environmental management *per se*. The oblique mapping reveals proximate correspondence of categories (Table 14.3, S2) or actions (S6i) or null links (Table 14.5, O3ii).

In case-based research, the case is the prime focus of interest and because ports are unique, a case study research strategy allows the systems approach, as the phenomenon under study, to remain embedded within this unique context (Dinwoodie & Xu, 2008). However, if the systems approach is sufficiently robust to assist assessment in an environmentally sensitive area, it should be transferable elsewhere. The case context of FHC, home of the UK's largest offshore terminal for marine oil and fuel, is appropriate.

14.3.3.   The Case Context: Falmouth

FHC manage a UK trust port, an independent statutory body controlled by an independent board and without shareholders or owners, which seeks to proactively develop a sustainable approach to port operations and development opportunities. Located within the Fal Estuary in Southwest England, this natural deepwater harbour attracts all sizes of vessel for safe anchoring and bunkering facilities (Falmouth Port, 2003). Falmouth hosts a historic built environment, spectacular natural setting, rich water ecosystem and valuable habitat. Regional development plans emphasise environmental sustainability and regional distinctiveness through prioritising waterfront and harbour regeneration (Cornwall County Council, 2005). The Bay and Estuary incorporate SSSIs, Areas of Outstanding Natural Beauty (AONB), Special Areas of Conservation (SAC) and Heritage Coasts and port authorities must ensure that marine operations do not harm these (Falmouth Port, 2009). Four harbour authorities operate within the boundaries of the Fal estuary where FHC have responsibility for areas where bunkering operations frequently take place (World Port Source, 2005; Falmouth Port, 2003 show maps). All profits arising from commercial activities are reinvested in port development (Falmouth Port, 2007). Port management is open to public examination and responsible to interested stakeholders (DfT, 2000). Applicable safe standards are implemented through compliance with the Port Marine Safety Code (PMSC, Falmouth Port, 2009).

Falmouth's offshore marine bunker station borders the world's busiest shipping lanes and post-August 2007 5 degree west SECA zone. Falmouth Oil Services Limited (FOS) the marine oil terminal bunkering operator deploys barges, road tanks or pipe, to supply fuels and lubricants to vessels and deliver gas, oil and fresh water. As owner and operator of a 50-kt shore-side bunker station FOS stores fuel for delivery to vessels anchored alongside or sheltering locally (Falmouth Port, 2003). FOS manages fuel deliveries, supported by a large independent bunker supplier and barge operator, which arranges bunker sales. The oil terminal contains three tank farms, clean oil and fuel oil loading racks, slop reception and processing facility (FOS, 2009). Ship arrivals to load Low Sulfur Fuel Oil spiralled post-2007 as ships comply with SECA zone emissions regulations (see DfT, 2009, Table 3.6), serviced by two bunker barges. Barges handle fuel, gas, lube oil and slops for vessels. FOS' Quality Management System commits to standard personnel training and regular exercises to ensure that all personnel and equipment are fully prepared. Policies span quality, environment and oil pollution and each commits to continual improvement and strives to exceed mandatory requirements (FOS, 2009).

FHC environmental policy is to maintain and improve the port environment by working with environmental agencies in accordance with UK environmental legislation and international conventions. Staff education and training aims to conserve and enhance the local environmental quality and an ECP guides human activities which could cause negative impacts. Harbour authorities provide waste reception facilities. The EMS details legislation and regulations notified by trade associations including BPA, EcoPorts, and government bodies. All internal or external communications are recorded including complaints and environmental correspondence pertaining to port operations and commercial activities, and consultants should be appointed to audit and review activities or conduct an EIA if impacts are significant. All targets and objectives focus on mitigation and applicable safe standards are required to comply with the PMSC (Falmouth Port, 2009).

14.3.4. Offshore Marine Bunkering

Historically, heavy fuel oil powered ships' bunkers stored residual low-grade fuel oil with high sulfur contents (Alizadeh & Nomikos, 2004). In 1997, the International Maritime Organisation (IMO) adopted MARPOL 73/78, an International Convention for the Prevention of Pollution from Ships Annex VI, Regulations for the Prevention of Air Pollution from Ships, limiting mass/mass of sulfur content for marine fuel oil to control sulfur oxides (SOx) emissions from ships (IMO, 2011; Table 14.2). Lower limits applied to North Sea, Baltic Sea and North American SECAs (Wang & Corbett, 2007). The maximum permitted sulfur content of marine gas oil and distillate fuels under EU Directive 1999/32/EC is 0.2% and for marine gas oils used within UK waters, 0.1% (UK P&I Club, 2008a).

Bunkering involves the transfer of liquid hydrocarbons for propulsion or lubrication purposes and operations can include a pipeline connecting shore facilities, often a tank

Table 14.2: IMO requirements on bunker fuel sulfur content.

Date	Maximum percentage of sulfur
Globally	
2009	4.5
2012	3.5
2020–2025	0.5
In special emission control areas	
2009	1.5
2010	1.0
2015	0.1

Source: Adapted from IMO (2011).

farm, to ships berthed at a jetty; supply via a specialist bunker vessel or simple barge; fuel transfers using road tankers. Offshore marine bunkering requires specialist techniques to prevent pollution and avoid potential leaks of residue from bunker hoses when disconnecting from receiving vessels. Experienced human resources are essential (Chang & Chen, 2006). Marine oil spillages are well documented with tank barges generating more spills (Talley, Jin, & Kite-Powell, 2001). Bunkering operations must comply with MARPOL73/78 regulations and Safety of Life at Sea (SOLAS) Conventions (IMO, 2011) and codes regulating safety and environmental aspects of goods and ships guide marine fuel oil delivery. Conventions restrict and regulate discharges of oil and oily materials. Safe bunkering requires delivery barges to carry a Shipboard Oil Pollution Emergency Plan which conveys instructions from ship owner to master on how to act should a spill occur. Oil terminals must ensure that both direct and indirect fuel oil transfers are safe and supported by preventative measures, controls and systems to guide ship-shore transfers. All vessels carrying oil and fuel must comply with national and international rules and regulations as must port or terminal managers via risk assessment and analysis, a Safety Management System (SMS) and a Marine Terminal Operating Manual (Fisher & Lux 2004). Bunkering equipment is complex and guided by a system of survey, maintenance and certification. A holistic SMS highlights operating checks. ISM Codes (IMO, 2011) require every vessel to have safety procedures in place including equipment checks and clearly delineated roles for personnel. Oil-loss prevention measures include vessel SMS and implementation of a recognised oil transfer procedures. Procedures exhort terminal managers and masters of vessels and barges taking bunkers or supplying fuel jointly seek to eliminate human error and operational incidents. IMO and International Safety Guide for Oil Tankers and Terminals (ISGOTT) checklists span pre-transfer, bunkering and ship-shore operations (ICS, 2006). Procedures indicating the actions required are supplemented with crew training, locally accepted standards to guide fuel oil transfer procedures (e.g. ISO/FDIS 13739; ISO, 2009), checklists and adherence to predetermined routines. Vessel refuelling could produce spills which affect water and sediment quality, human and wildlife health, fisheries and recreational pursuits, and potentially food chains (EcoPorts, 2006). If oil spillages and leakages arise during bunkering operations, pollution harms the marine environment and is costly to clean up. Human error typically underpins most overflows and spillages (ICS, 2006) and to avoid significant claims, preparation for offshore bunkering is meticulous.

14.4. Results and Discussion

14.4.1. Strategic Inputs

Each prime strategic input (S1, S2...S7) comprises sub-components (e.g. i, ii, iii for S2) loosely mapped against SDM and ISO14001 (Table 14.3). The FHC mission

Table 14.3: Strategic level inputs.

Strategic level		Section of	
Input	**Port authority lists**	**ISO14001**	**SDM**
S1 Mission statement	Its environmental obligations	4.2	1A
S2 Physical conditions	Physical designations, e.g. (i) AONB (ii) SAC (iii) Heritage coast	1C	4.3.2
S3 Governance issues	Authorities it is answerable to (i) Locally (ii) Nationally (iii) Supranationally	1C	4.3.2
S4 Stakeholders	Groups interested in its operations (i) Marine agencies	4B	4.4.3
	(ii) Environmental interest groups, voluntary and statutory	1C	4.3.2
	(iii) Suppliers		
S5 Local data	Information available locally to (i) Baseline port operations (ii) Baseline resource monitoring	1D 1D	4.3.3 4.3.3
S6 Management system	How activities will be monitored via (i) An EMS (ii) Benchmarking (iii) Professional bodies	7A 8A, 8B 8A, 8B	4.5.1 4.5.4 4.5.4
S7 Resource assessment	How it will acquire and manage funding	1E	4.4.1

statement (S1) commits to working closely with environmental agencies, protecting and conserving the environment and adhering to national environmental legislation and internationally agreed conventions. It has an education and training dimension (Falmouth Port, 2009). Physical conditions (S2) list local designations. These eschew unsustainable developments (S2i, Cornwall-AONB, 2009), require avoidance of deterioration to habitats and disturbance to species (S2ii) and protect the coastline from undesirable development (S2iii). Establishing contacts with governance inputs oblige consultation and compliance locally (S3i). National government and statutory inputs (S3ii) engage the Environment Agency (UKEA) which seeks to protect and improve the environment, and via Water Framework Directives to prevent deterioration in, and to restore, water quality. Other inputs span the Department for Transport (DfT) and Department for Environment, Food and Rural Affairs (DEFRA) and Maritime Management Organisation which *inter alia* administers planning, licensing activities, marine nature conservation, public access to coastal areas and fisheries management. Bunkering operations are regulated supranationally (S3iii) via Codes of Practice to facilitate sustainability (ESPO, 2003); IMO and other conventions which guide transport, handling and storage of dangerous substances in ports (IMO 2011) and dumping at sea regulations (Paipai, 1999).

Engagement with stakeholder inputs includes agencies such as Cornwall Sea Fisheries charged with maintaining a well managed, sustainable and regulated fishery and flexible patrol service (S4i). Voluntary environmental interest groups (S4ii) include Friends of the Earth which aims to protect the rights of all people to live in a safe and healthy environment, and statutory groups. Suppliers and sub-contractors in building and maintenance works are screened (S4iii). Local data inputs of objectives and targets for a port EMS require mapping and monitoring of local management systems. Baseline operations are reviewed (S5i) alongside resource monitoring of databanks, information retrieval, surveys, recording systems and modelling software to predict oil spill movements (s5ii). Management systems require an EMS (S6i) to stow relevant legislation and data to drive continuous improvements in environmental quality and prevent pollution. Guidance is available (Saengsupavanich et al., 2009; ESPO, 2003). Local authorities (S6ii) detail EIAs required or environmental issues embedded in local policies, plans and programmes which must be complied with (Paipai, 1999). Membership (S6iii) of EcoPorts and BPA who collaborate and contribute to establish best practice can guide an EMS. Finally, resource assessment (S7) underpins the FHC mission of commercial viability, which requires the costing and funding of all activities. Financial resources accrue from harbour charges and other services provided or government funding such as Knowledge Transfer Partnerships with universities.

14.4.2.   *Tactical Level*

Table 14.4 describes tactical level service processes. To facilitate local familiarisation FHC arrange tours of relevant facilities (T1i) and research client organisations (T1ii). Establishing an internal stakeholder group (T1iii) embraces harbour authorities, bunker operator and pilotage and other services. Action T1iv requires systems to

Table 14.4: Service levels processes.

Service processes	Port authority plans	ISO14001 section	SDM section
T1 Local familiarisation	How to provide relevant information using		
	(i) Harbour tours	4B	4.4.3
	(ii) Researching client organisations	4A	4.4.3
	(iii) Establishing stakeholder groups	4B	4.4.3
	(iv) Local monitoring technologies	7B	4.5.1
T2 Operational conventions	What to comply with and how in local operations	1C	4.3.2
T3 Networking	Who to contact and how through	4B	4.4.3
	(i) Site visits to other ports		
	(ii) Developing relations with environmental agencies		
	(iii) Stakeholder analysis		
T4 Consultation	Who to consult and when including	4B	4.4.3
	(i) Experts		
	(ii) Professional bodies/trade associations		
	(iii) Stakeholders		
T5 Reviewing and monitoring	What data to gather, how, and how to analyse and store it including		
	(i) Incident records	7A,6	4.5.3,4.4.7
	(ii) Sampling operations	7B	4.5.2
	(iii) Monitoring incidence and impact	8B	4.6
	(iv) EMS and consumer satisfaction reporting	7B	4.5.1
T6 Hire expertise	Who to hire in and when including		
	(i) Environmental consultants	2A,2B	4.4.1
	(ii) Public relations companies	4B	4.4.3
	(iii) Staff training	3	4.4.2
	(iv) Client education and training	4B	4.4.3
T7 Reporting	How to store data on incidents/ operations	5D	4.4.5

record all bunkering operations and data to enable FHC to identify any changes, and the frequency of any environmental impacts. Buoys are acquired and set up to gather data to update tidal modelling and inform PISCES oil spill prediction software.

FHC requires procedures to guide those involved with supplying bunkers to ensure that operations minimise the risks of environmental damage (T2). These span MARPOL and SOLAS conventions and the design and construction of ships (IMO, 2011). EU Directive 2002/59/EC sets minimum standards for the safe transport of dangerous and polluting goods by sea, and port operations in Europe (ESPO, 2003). UK Merchant Shipping (Ship-to-Ship Transfer) Regulations 2008 govern transfers between ships, of cargo or bunker fuel involving hazardous substances in UK waters (MCA, 2008). Operating guidelines cover bunkering equipment and personnel (UK P&I Club, 2008b).

Tactical actions to establish networking instigate site visits and shared experiences with ports (T3i) that demonstrate best practice. To build relations with environmental groups and agencies (T3ii) requires regular meetings, email and telephone contact and stakeholder analysis (T3iii) to facilitate consultation (Falmouth Port, 2009). Actions to establish consultation engage experts from universities and Natural England (T4i) and initiate consultations (T4ii) with BPA to access advice on legislative and policy issues, exchange knowledge and develop best practice. When established, contacts in UKEA, DEFRA and other agencies email notifications or advertise meetings as environmental obligations arise. Action T4iii requires updated contacts lists, stakeholder analysis, identification of contacts and communication to identify their concerns.

Service processes to enable review and monitoring of the environmental impacts and assess scope for simplifying operations require a database detailing procedures, frequencies and their impacts (T5i). To assist national and local emergency authorities to enact oil spill contingency plans (ESPO, 2003) FHC undertakes proactive local oceanographic modelling of pollution incidents using GIS databases of hydrographic and tidal records. To update them requires tactical decisions on how and where to sample (T5ii). IMO's convention on Oil Pollution Preparedness, Response and Cooperation requires measures for dealing with oil pollution incidents. FHC cooperates with national and local authorities in preparing contingency plans, promoting awareness of existing contingency plans, communicating this knowledge internally and assisting coordination of contingency plans (ESPO, 2003). The UK Maritime Coastguard Agency maintains a national contingency plan for marine pollution from shipping and offshore installations (DfT, 2000). Under the PMSC risks must be identified and evaluated and suitable controls established to manage them, with clear linkages between risk controls, operating procedures, harbour by-laws and safety management (Risk Support, 2001). This standard offers a framework for preparing policies and plans (Paipai, 1999; Falmouth Port, 2009). Complex regulation requires actions to establish monitoring systems (T5iii) and report key indicators, consumer satisfaction and the impacts of mitigations and monitoring (T5iv).

Processes facilitate actions T6i and T6ii, perhaps to publicise particular activities or manage media engagement surrounding oil spills or pollution incidents. Tactical provision of environmental awareness training (T6iii) may encourage membership of trade associations including the BPA to facilitate conference attendance and port visits to share best practice. The FHC mission to provide 'education and training ... to ensure that everyone using our waterways does so with a respect for their impact on the environment' (Falmouth Port 2009), points towards processes to engage specialist training providers for users of bunkering facilities (T6iv). Procedures are required (T7) to archive records of bunkering operations which log changing port activities (Paipai, 1999). Records are available to authorities and stakeholders and inform the EMS and are updated as legislation changes.

14.4.3. Operational Level

Through well coordinated output processes (Table 14.5) FHC increasingly monitors how far consumers are satisfied with how it manages environmental assessments. Operational actions include monitoring programmes (O1i) to identify whether port users perform operations to standard. Environmental performance indicators are being defined to facilitate continuous updating and eventually, publication of an annual environmental report (ESPO, 2003). Action O1ii will document relevant issues and communications with environmental stakeholders. If shared electronically, it will assist staff to access information, raise awareness of legislation and obligations, and ensure compliance. Action O1iii will require a comprehensive baseline database which includes reports, documents and operator records.

Indicative action O2i raises FHC's professional profile and awareness of best practice and O2ii provides information sharing online before activities are assessed in compliance with Directive 2003/04EC, which requires port administrations to process and update environmental information pertaining to their activities and projects. Media contact (O2iii) broadcasts FHC's environmental credentials (ESPO, 2003) and updates for stakeholders (O2iv) enhance local engagement with for example local AONB Partners and visitors who pick up leaflets.

Updates to FHC's ECP (O3i) for public and commercial harbour users seek to ensure compliance with Water Framework, SAC and EU Habitat Directives. This action entices bunker operators to apply ISGOTT (ICS, 2006) and procedures should be incorporated in the ship's SMS to ensure that risks have been assessed and mitigation controls established. Oil spill contingency arrangements are required. Action O3ii requires networking with agencies such as DEFRA.

Action O4 requires FHC to explain how its evidence base is collated and monitoring procedures are established. Systems record (O4i) and assess (O4ii) performance. To retain clients and enhance customer relations, the system incorporates procedures to handle complaints, litigation, appeals against decisions and compensation issues.

To promote the ethos and practice of sustainability (O5), FHC conducts regular spot checks on operations to ensure compliance with relevant Codes. FHC underscores its own corporate environmental awareness (O6i) by aspiring to share knowledge of legislation and best practice with schools and community groups, perhaps via leaflets for marina users or instructions for ships requesting piloting services online. Given that human error causes most accidents, actions (O6ii) aim to share knowledge of legislation, good practice and mitigation procedures and ensure that personnel are qualified to conduct safe operations and prepared to tackle

Table 14.5: Output processes.

Output	Port authority will	ISO14001 section	SDM section
O1 Internal monitoring, reporting, archiving	Collect, record, present and store key data. Set up:		
	(i) Monitoring scheme	7A	4.5.1
	(ii) Environmental library	4A	4.4.3
	(iii) CSR reporting	4B	4.4.3
O2 External dissemination and communication	Share information with third parties via	4B	4.4.3
	(i) Trade associations and conferences		
	(ii) Stakeholder communications strategy		
	(iii) Press reporting		
	(iv) Newsletters		
O3 Recommendations	Inform and update users and authorities through		
	(i) Updated environmental codes of conduct	5B	4.4.6
	(ii) Inputs to policy making		
O4 Mitigations	Set up management procedures, manuals and systems to respond to issues of user compliance by		
	(i) Registering and recording complaints	5B	4.4.6
	(ii) Consumer satisfaction surveys	8B	4.6
O5 Sustainability	Promote and monitor sustainable operations	5A	4.3.4
O6 Awareness	Establish and promote best practice by		
	(i) Educating stakeholders	4B	4.4.3
	(ii) Establishing awareness and training materials	3	4.4.2

spillages. Training is time and cost-efficient in raising awareness, developing in-house capability and enhancing individual skill competences to ensure that policy objectives are implemented (ESPO, 2003).

5. Conclusions

The systems approach assists FHC to remain compliant with complex codes and regulations, and to pro-actively develop an evidence based approach to enhance the sustainability of routine maritime operations and developments in its bailiwick. By proactively encouraging professional engagement and collaboration with complementary initiatives from bodies including BPA, EcoPorts and ISO which engage extensively in benchmarking and sharing best practices, the systems approach complements the drive for continuous improvement. Further, because the approach is parsimonious (Table 14.6) direct implementation by port authorities, heightens local ownership of the evaluation process and organisational embedding of environmental awareness.

One spin-off of local engagement is increased stakeholder engagement which has stimulated numerous new contacts and offers of reciprocal information sharing. Environmental interest groups voluntarily contribute new monitoring capability. Proactive searches for additional funding attracted a Knowledge Transfer Partnership which funds a sustainable developments officer who relieves the Harbour Master from attending routine meetings and enhances the port authority's professional profile and capability to engage in technical developments, debate and policy making.

Explicit focus on developing new local data gathering, analysis and forecasting technologies including powerful PISCES oil spill modelling software, has significantly increased the capability of FHC to record, predict and mitigate the likely impacts of untoward events. Using the systems approach, explicit outputs relating to awareness, will enhance the link with employee and user training and community and stakeholder involvement, further reducing the risk of mishaps. Continuously enhanced outputs of data collection, monitoring, recording and consumer feedback raise FHC awareness of and capability to achieve its mission.

The systems approach is accessible to other port authorities. Few manage physical strategic inputs as sensitive as at Falmouth, and most will require fewer local data inputs. Many would benefit from tactical management of service processes, through networking and consultation which raises awareness of operational conventions and reduces costs of hiring in expertise. Local ownership of, and commitment to, the evaluation process is enhanced. Local adaptation of the taxonomy of inputs and outputs presented is likely as more ports embrace it. Authorities which currently rely on methodologies and tools driven by primarily physically based environmental monitoring and auditing systems will also benefit from complementary application of this mission-driven input–output process modelling technique which highlights the importance of stakeholder engagement and building social capital and awareness.

Table 14.6: Summary of the systems model.

Strategic level Input	Tactical level Service processes	Operational level Output
S1 Mission statement	T1 Local information (i) Harbour tour (ii) Research client (iii) Stakeholder group (iv) Local technology	O1 Internal reporting (i) Monitoring scheme (ii) Environmental library (iii) CSR reporting
S2 Physical conditions (i) AONB (ii) SAC (iii) Heritage coast	T2 Operational conventions	O2 External information body/conferences (i) Trade (ii) Body/conferences (iii) Stakeholder strategy (iv) Press reporting newsletters
S3 Governance issues (i) Issue (ii) Local (iii) National supranational	T3 Networking via (i) Port visits (ii) Agencies (iii) Stakeholders	O3 Recommendations on (i) Codes of conduct (iii) Policy making
S4 Stakeholders (i) Agencies (ii) Interest groups (iii) Suppliers	T4 Consult (i) Experts (ii) Professional body (iii) Stakeholders	O4 Mitigations (i) Register complaints (ii) Consumer surveys
S5 Local data: (i) Baseline operations (ii) Baseline resources	T5 Review, monitor (i) Incidents (ii) Operations (iii) Impacts (iv) EMS, consumers	O5 Promote Sustainability

Table 14.6: (*Continued*)

Strategic level Input	Tactical level Service processes	Operational level Output
S6 Management system (i) EMS (ii) Benchmarks (iii) Professional body	T6 Hire expertise (i) Consultants (ii) Public relations (iii) Staff training (iv) Client education	O6 Awareness (i) Educate stakeholders (ii) Training materials
S7 Assess resources	T7 Reporting	

Acknowledgements

Plymouth Business School teamed up with Falmouth Harbour Commissioners in a Knowledge Transfer Partnership (No. KTP007098). This Partnership received financial support from the Knowledge Transfer Partnerships programme. KTP aims to help businesses to improve their competitiveness and productivity through the better use of knowledge, technology and skills that reside within the UK Knowledge Base. KTP is funded by the Technology Strategy Board along with the other government funding organisations which included the National Environment Research Council, the Economic and Social Research Council and FHC. None of these bodies was involved in decisions relating to research design, data collection, data analysis, interpretation or dissemination.

References

Alizadeh, A. H., & Nomikos, N. K. (2004). The efficiency of the forward bunker market. *International Journal of Logistics: Research and Applications*, 7(3), 281–296.
Bellamy, J. A., Walker, D. H., McDonald, G. T., & Syme, G. J. (2001). A systems approach to the evaluation of natural resource management initiatives. *Journal of Environmental Management*, 63(4), 407–423.
BPA (2009). *Our goals*. London: British Port Association. Retrieved from http://www.bri tishports.org.uk/public/about_us/our_goal. Accessed on 4 August.
Buckley, W. (1968). *Modern systems research for the behavioral scientist*. Chicago: Aldine.
Cetin, C. K., & Cerit, A. G. (2010). Organisational effectiveness at seaports: A systems approach. *Maritime Policy and Management*, 37(3), 195–219.
Chang, Y. C., & Chen, C. C. (2006). Knowledge-based simulation of bunkering services in the port of Kaohsiung. *Civil Engineering and Environmental Systems*, 23(1), 21–34.
Churchman, C. W. (1979). *The systems approach* (2nd ed.). New York: Laurel.

Cornwall County Council (2005). *Cornwall and Scilly Urban Survey: Historic characterization.* Truro, UK: Historic Environment Service.

Cornwall-AONB. (2009). The Cornwall AONB Partnership, Truro, UK: Cornwall AONB. Retrieved from http://www.cornwall-aonb.gov.uk/partnership.html. Accessed 1 August.

Darbra, R., Pittam, N., Royston, K., Darbra, J., & Journee, H. (2009). Survey on environmental monitoring requirements of European ports. *Journal of Environmental Management, 90*(3), 1396–1403.

Darbra, R., Ronza, A., Casal, J., Stojanovic, T., & Wooldridge, C. (2004). The self diagnosis method: A new methodology to assess environmental management in sea ports. *Marine Pollution Bulletin, 48*(5–6), 420–428.

Darbra, R., Ronza, A., Stojanovic, T., Wooldridge, C., & Casal, J. (2005). A procedure for identifying significant environmental aspects in sea ports. *Marine Pollution Bulletin, 50*(8), 866–874.

DfT (2000). *Modern ports: A UK policy.* London: Department for Transport. Retrieved from http://www.dft.gov.uk/pgr/shippingports/ports/modern/modernportsaukpolicy?page = 1. Accessed on 23 May 2009.

DfT (2002). *A project appraisal framework for ports.* London: Department for Transport. Retrieved from http://www.dft.gov.uk/consultations/archive/2002/afp/. Accessed on 23 May 2009.

DfT (2006). *Focus on Ports, 2006 edition.* London: Department for Transport.

DfT (2009). *Maritime statistics 2008.* London: Department for Transport.

Dinwoodie, J., Tuck, S., Knowles, H., Benhin. J., & Sansom, M. (2011, in press). Sustainable development of maritime operations in ports. *Business Strategy and the Environment,* 10pp.

Dinwoodie, J., & Xu, J. (2008). Case studies in logistics: A review and tentative taxonomy. *International Journal of Logistics Research and Applications, 11*(5), 393–408.

EcoPorts (2006). *The top-10 port environmental issues.* Brussels: EcoPorts. Retrieved from http://www.ecoports.com/page.ocl?pageid=127. Accessed on 21 June 2009.

Edoho, F. M. (2008). Oil transnational corporations: Corporate social responsibility and environmental sustainability. *Corporate Social Responsibility and Environmental Management, 15*(4), 210–222.

ESPO. (2003). *ESPO environmental code of practice.* Brussels: European Sea Ports Organisation. Retrieved from http://www.espo.be/downloads/archive/85817e87-5a24-4c43-b570-146cb7f36b68.pdf. Accessed on 2 August 2009.

Falmouth Port. (2003). *The Falmouth and Truro ports handbook.* Falmouth, UK: Falmouth Port. Retrieved from http://www.falmouthport.co.uk/pdf/ports_handbook.pdf. Accessed on 20 May 2009.

Falmouth Port. (2007). *Falmouth Habour Commissioners' strategy.* Falmouth, UK: Falmouth Port. Retrieved from http://www.falmouthport.co.uk/pdf/strategy2007.pdf. Accessed on 20 May 2009.

Falmouth Port. (2009). *Falmouth Harbour Commissioners Environmental Policy.* Falmouth, UK: Falmouth Port. Retrieved from http://www.falmouthport.co.uk/pdf/FHC-environ mental-policy.pdf. Accessed on 20 May.

Fisher, C., & Lux, J. (2004). *Bunkers – an analysis of the practical, technical and legal issues* (English, 3rd ed.). London: Lloyds List Publications.

Fernandez, L. (2008). NAFTA and member country strategies for maritime trade and marine invasive species. *Journal of Environmental Management, 89*(4), 308–321.

FOS. (2009). Falmouth Oil Services Limited. Falmouth, UK. Retrieved from http://www.fosoil.com/. Accessed on 20 October.

Fox, W. M. (1974). The systems approach to organizational effectiveness. *Advanced Management Journal, 39*(2), 34–40.

Gilman, S. (2003). Sustainability and national policy in UK port development. *Maritime Policy and Management, 30*(4), 275–291.

Hannon, P. D., & Atherton, A. (1998). Small firm success and the art of orienteering: The value of plans, planning and strategic awareness in the competitive small firm. *Journal of Small Business and Enterprise Development, 5*(2), 102–119.

ICS. (2006). *ISGOTT: International Safety Guide for Oil Tankers and Terminals.* (5th ed.). International Chamber of Shipping, London; Oil Companies International Marine Forum, Bermuda; International Association of Ports and Harbors.

IEMA. (2010). *Introducing EMAS.* Lincoln: U.K. Institute of Environmental Management and Assessment. Retrieved from http://www.iema.net/ems/emas. Accessed on 3 September 2010.

IMO. (2011). "IMO", International Maritime Organisation. London. Retrieved from http://www.imo.org. Accessed on 3 April 2011.

ISO. (2009). *ISO/FDIS 13739, petroleum products: Procedures for transfer of bunkers to vessels.* Geneva: International Organisation for Standardisation. Retrieved from http://www.iso.org/iso/catalogue_detail.htm?csnumber = 43387. Accessed on 20 October 2009.

ISO14000. (2009). *ISO14000 ISO14001 environmental management.* Bootle, UK: ISO14000 Environmental Management Group. Retrieved from http://www.iso14000-iso14001-environmental-management.com/. Accessed on 12 June.

Kast, F. E., & Rosenzweig, J. E. (2005). General systems theory: Applications for organisation and management. *Academy of Management Journal, 15*(4), 447–465.

Korhonen, J. (2007). Environmental planning vs. systems analysis: Four prescriptive principles vs. four descriptive indicators. *Journal of Environmental Management, 82*(1), 51–59.

Lagoudis, I. N., Lalwani, C. S., & Naim, M. M. (2004). A generic systems model for ocean bulk shipping companies in the bulk sector. *Transportation Journal, 43*(1), 56–76.

MCA. (2008). *Guidance on the merchant shipping (ship-to-ship transfer) regulations 2008.* London: Maritime and Coastguard Agency. Retrieved from http://www.mcga.gov.uk/c4mca/080511_mgn_for_cons.pdf. Accessed on 5 August 2009.

Notteboom, T., & Rodrigue, J. (2005). Port regionalisation: Towards a new phase in development. *Maritime Policy and Management, 32*(3), 297–313.

Oxford Economics (2009). *The Economic Contribution of Ports to the UK Economy.* Oxford: Abbey House.

Paipai, E. (1999). *Guidelines for Port Environmental Management. Report SR 554,* HR Wallingford, Department of the Environment, Transport and the Regions, London.

Parnaby, J. (1979). Concept of manufacturing system. *International Journal of Production Research, 17*(2), 23–135.

Peris-Mora, E., Diez Orejas, J. M., Subirats, A., Ibanez, S., & Alvarez, P. (2005). Development of a system of indicators for sustainable port management. *Marine Pollution Bulletin, 50*(12), 1649–1660.

Pettit, S. (2008). United Kingdom ports policy: Changing government attitudes. *Marine Policy, 32*(4), 719–727.

Pidd, M. (2004). *Systems modelling: Theory and practice* (2nd ed.). London: Wiley.

Qin, X. S., Huang, G. H., & He, L. (2009). Simulation and optimization technologies for petroleum waste management and remediation process control. *Journal of Environmental Management, 90*(1), 54–76.

Risk Support. (2001). *Linking risk assessment of marine operations to safety management in ports*. London: Risk Support Limited. Retrieved from http://www.risk-support.co.uk/vmt_MTS2001.pdf. Accessed on 3 June 2009.

Royal Haskoning. (2009). *Green ports*. Peterborough, UK: Royal Haskoning. Retrieved from http://www.royalhaskoning.co.uk. Accessed on 5 February 2010.

Saengsupavanich, C., Coowanitwong, N., Gallardo, W., & Lertsuchatavanich, C. (2009). Environmental performance evaluation of an industrial port and estate: ISO14001, port state control-derived indicators. *Journal of Cleaner Production, 17*(2), 154–161.

Talley, W. K., Jin, D., & Kite-Powell, H. (2001). Vessel accident oil-spillage: Post US OPA-90. *Transportation Research Part D, 6*(6), 405–415.

UNESCAP. (2009). *Environmental impacts of port development*. Bangkok: United Nations Economic and Social Commission for Asia and the Pacific. Retrieved from http://www.unesca
p.org/ttdw/Publications/TFS_pubs/Pub_1234/pub_1234_ch2.pdf. Accessed on 19 June.

UK P&I Club. (2008a). *Sulphur content of gas oil – UK*. London: UK P&I Club. Retrieved from http://www.ukpandi.com/ukpandi/infopool.nsf/html/LPBulletin562. Accessed on 20 July 2009.

UK P&I Club. (2008b). *Preventing pollution during bunkering operations*. London: UK P&I Club. Retrieved from http://www.ukpandi.com/ukpandi/InfoPool.nsf/HTML/LPNews Head20081107. Accessed on 15 July 2009.

Verhoeven, P. (2010). A review of port authority functions: Towards a renaissance. *Maritime Policy and Management, 37*(3), 247–270.

Wang, C., & Corbett, J. J. (2007). The costs and benefits of reducing SO2 emissions from ships in the US West Coastal waters. *Transportation Research Part D, 12*(8), 577–588.

Weber, J. M., & Crew, R. E. (2000). Deterrence theory and marine oil spills: Do coast guard civil penalties deter pollution? *Journal of Environmental Management, 58*(3), 161–168.

World Port Source. (2005). *Port of Falmouth*. San Jose: World Port Source. Retrieved from http://www.worldportsource.com/ports/map.2866.1529.php. Accessed on 4 April 2011.

Yeo, G-T., Roe, M., & Dinwoodie, J. (2008). Evaluating the competitiveness of container ports in Korea and China. *Transportation Research A, 48*(6), 910–921.

Yeo, G-T., Song, D. W., Roe, M., & Dinwoodie, J. (2010). Weighting the competitiveness factors for container ports under conflicting interests. *Journal of the Operational Research Society, 61*, 1249–1257.

Concluding Remarks

Photis M. Panayides and Dong-Wook Song

Maritime logistics is a new concept in the field of shipping and transportation. Hence, a book on maritime logistics, despite being novel, has in its scope to provide a comprehensive description of all pertinent areas and to offer a platform upon which further studies can be based. Certainly the selection of works that makes up this book fulfils the scope and objectives of the volume. In particular, the 13 chapters cover a wide-ranging area of contemporary issues in maritime logistics that would be useful to practitioners, students and researchers.

In Chapter 2, Ng provides a comprehensive review of recent developments in liner shipping focusing, in particular, on the impact and implications for ports arising as a result of the business strategies of major liner shipping firms. Those strategies have been identified as the achievement of scale economies by seeking an increase in size through mergers, acquisitions and re-structurings; the achievement of competitiveness through differentiation, shipping network restructuring and the introduction of logistics-related services. In order for ports to deal with this new situation, they invested heavily in dedicated capital-intensive facilities and changed their management philosophy from acrimonious to co-operative particularly between regional and proximate ports. Port development and competition have evolved from technical efficiency-oriented to economic efficiency-oriented.

Ng in Chapter 3 reviews the impact of containerization on the various partners of the global supply chain as well as the challenges companies encounter and the solutions they use in dealing with empty container repositioning. Since its invention in the late 1950s containerization has become the main method for transporting cargo in the maritime logistics industry. However, globalization, the imbalanced flow of international trade and the mismatch in supply and demand have brought about the problem of empty container repositioning. Left on its own, empty containers would accumulate in the consumption markets while insufficient supply of them in the manufacturing countries would affect the efficiency of export. Ng recognizes that companies reduce the impact of empty container repositioning by improving on their liner network design and vessel fleet size planning at the strategic level and on their landside container dispatching and global empty container repositioning at the

Maritime Logistics: Contemporary Issues
Copyright © 2012 by Emerald Group Publishing Limited
All rights of reproduction in any form reserved
ISBN: 978-1-78052-340-8

operational level. They also use solutions that involve other parties, including collaborating with other supply chain partners, deploying innovative technology such as foldable containers, and investigating new markets for empty containers. Since so much is at stake and there is room to improve on the current practices, research on empty container repositioning is bound to grow in the years to come.

Congestion implies loss of time and money from the sub-optimal use of the assets, and therefore undermines the competitive position of ports and maritime logistics chains. Chapter 4 by Meersman et al. therefore looks at where port congestion occurs, both globally and in the port calling chain and analyses actual responses by various supply chain actors in its effort to shed some light on the potential future evolution and reaction patterns. More specifically, the chapter defines the congestion issue in transport economics, with special focus on seaport activity (including types of congestion, the corresponding money and time loss (at locks, berth etc.)). Observations are made as to how congestion developed lately and what are its causes are in a port congestion survey of European and American ports. Furthermore, a typology is made of reactions patterns by different actors and, a number of future scenarios are presented. With respect to the behaviour of the actors in this supply chain, it is clear that shipping companies opt for ports with sufficient available capacity. This avoids the risk of sub-optimal use of ships. Available capacity not only implies berths but also efficient terminal operations and good hinterland connections. It is up to all actors involved in terminal and hinterland operations to safeguard the provision of sufficient free capacity.

Park et al. in Chapter 5 describe a port choice model for transhipment cargo using system dynamics. The chapter identified factors that have been affecting the increase in transhipment cargoes of the port of Busan. In addition, it actually explored how those factors could be utilized more effectively to attract and increase transhipment cargoes. A port choice model was developed using the technique of system dynamics and two particular variables were identified as core factors: the so-called 'Mohring effect' and an total cost. It was recommended in particular that the port of Busan should develop incentive scheme so that feeder vessels can reduce their direct costs of call at the port.

Min in Chapter 6 raises the awareness for maritime security and assesses the impact of maritime security in the global supply chain operations by conceptualizing maritime security from the perspective of supply chain risk management. The analysis of real-world cases reveals that organizations with specific maritime and supply chain security measures are more likely to succeed in handling maritime and supply chain risks than those without them. Thus, risk preparedness is one of the first steps towards effective risk prevention and mitigation. The effectiveness of maritime security and the subsequent global supply chain planning often rests on the utilization of information technology such as radio frequency identification (RFID) and satellite communication that enables supply chain partners (e.g. shippers, carriers, port authorities) to share and then trace crucial order and shipment status information on a real-time basis. Based on the analysis, a total maritime security model is proposed. The aim of the model is to help carriers, shippers and port authorities to prepare for potential maritime risks and then mitigate those risks.

Furthermore, this chapter reports recent advances in maritime security measures from both practical and theoretical standpoints.

The importance of risk management in maritime logistics and supply chains as well as the inherent dangers and potential losses from failing to mitigate risks is illustrated by the treatment of the subject from Lam in Chapter 7. The chapter provides a critical analysis and classification of supply chain risks and disruptions and highlights the propagation effects thereof as well as discussing mitigation strategies. The author concludes that proper risk management needs to be embraced by the supply chain members and recognizes that at the moment there is very little or no such collaboration between the supply chain members in practice.

In Chapter 8 which is titled 'Information Technology in Maritime Logistics Management: A Case-Based Approach from CoA to SLA', Asbjørnslett et al. present a case-based road map for the use of transactional and analytical information and communication technology (ICT) in maritime logistics chains. The concept is based on a business case of changing the contractual regime between a shipping line (the logistics service provider) and a manufacturer (the logistics service client from a contract of affreightment (CoA) to a service level agreement (SLA). The authors recognize that addressing ICT in such a contractual framework brings ICT closer to the core business operation of shipping and maritime logistics, and could act both as a change agent and an enabler in the further development of maritime logistics solutions for shipping lines. The use of Web Services for information exchange purposes is suggested.

In Chapter 9, Vitsounis and Pallis analysed the ways that port actors operate within network configurations that emerge within port value chains. According to the authors, the value offered to the users of these chains is not determined only by the capabilities of each actor but from upstream and downstream counterparts as well. In order to increase this value, the actors involved in a chain choose either to remain fragmented or to take advantage of the network dynamics through the establishment of close relationships with other port stakeholders. The latter focus both on the selection of the right partners and the development of meaningful relationships between them that work towards value co-creation and, consequently, to augmented value proposition. Out of the three types of interdependencies identified in ports, pooled and reciprocal are the ones that favour the development of close relationships and as such the emergence of value co-creation schemes. On the contrary, the presence of serial interdependencies is not sufficient to motivate port stakeholders to pursue the co-creation of value.

Chapter 10 by Lagoudis provides an interesting and valuable contribution to container terminal industry studies. The study collates the work of 30 years (period 1980–2010) in an attempt to analyse the problems and methods used by the authors in this field of research. To facilitate the reader, studies have been grouped under five categories of addressed problems (Productivity and Competitiveness, Yard and Equipment Utilization, Equipment Scheduling, Berth Planning, Loading/Unloading) and four modelling methodologies (Mathematics and Operations Research, Management and Economics, Simulation, Stochastic Modelling). The analysis showed that most works focus on productivity and competitiveness issues followed by yard and equipment utilization and equipment scheduling. In reference to the methodologies used managerial and economic approaches lead followed by mathematics and operations research. In reference to future research, two fields have been identified where there is scope of significant contribution by the academic community: container terminal security and container terminal supply chain integration.

Pawlik et al. in Chapter 11 apply the concept of corporate social responsibility (CSR) to the container liner shipping industry. Through their analysis, the authors found that the leading liner shipping companies are tackling the major sustainability issues on an operative level. In addition, the majority of liner shipping companies have not integrated sustainability issues in the visionary and strategic decision-making processes. This is also a consequence of the high variety of CSR interpretations. Managers have problems to deviate concrete management actions. The authors conclude that the challenge for scientific research is to focus on this problem and to provide the liner service industry with industry-specific solutions for a comprehensive CSR.

In continuing with the concept of responsibility not just towards the community but also towards the environment, Lindstad et al. in Chapter 12 discuss issues pertinent to green maritime logistics and sustainability. They advocate and argue for the importance of green maritime logistics and offer a framework for measuring greenhouse gas emissions for transport systems. They go further to present a model for measuring seaborne transport and its greenhouse gas emissions, and to compare greenhouse gas emissions from different modes of transportation.

In Chapter 13, Goulielmos et al. examine the European Union's (EU) policies of 'Short Sea Shipping' (SSS), the 'motorways of the sea' and green ports, within short sea maritime logistics. The authors question the dominance of SSS over road. They argue that as road transport expands, hubs are expected to become larger and fewer with feeders. Road transport is not certain to follow SSS and its four motorways. According to the authors, this result was responsible for the relocation of industry from West to East and North-East inter-port competition.

Finally in Chapter 14, Dinwoodie et al. assess the environmental impact of maritime operations in ports. In a novel framing of environmental assessment, a business process modelling technique is deployed in a systems approach which highlights inputs, service processes and outputs. In an initial focus, primary processes at strategic level are defined which affect the environmental assessment of present and future operations and their potential impacts. Later, tactical service processes define the integrity of processes that guarantee service level and quality. Finally, outputs are defined by operational processes. The contribution of applying the systems approach to plan more sustainable maritime operations is assessed in a case study of Falmouth Harbour Commissioners (FHC). Following EU designation of a North Sea Sulphur Oxide Emissions Control Areas (SECA), Falmouth recently recorded a significant rise in the number of vessels calling, and volume of fuel sold as more passing vessels take on-board low-sulphur fuel. According to the authors, the systems approach which empowers FHC to mitigate potential risks and assess development proposals pro-actively is easily transferable to other ports.

A book on maritime logistics is certainly novel as the concepts concerned are new and unique. As such there is a variety of areas and applications that require further studies and empirical research. This is to some extent reflected in this volume both from the choice of what the authors decided to discuss but also from the content of these discussions. What is certain is the congruence in opinion as to the need for scientific research for an area that becomes essential in maritime transport (i.e. shipping and ports).